Spring Batch in Action

Spring Batch in Action

ARNAUD COGOLUEGNES
THIERRY TEMPLIER
GARY GREGORY
OLIVIER BAZOUD

MANNING
SHELTER ISLAND

Manning Publications Co.   Development editor: Cynthia Kane
20 Baldwin Road   Copyeditor: Linda Kern
PO Box 261   Proofreader: Katie Tennant
Shelter Island, NY 11964   Typesetter: Gordan Salinovic
                                        Cover designer: Marija Tudor

ISBN 9781935182955
Printed in the United States of America
1 2 3 4 5 6 7 8 9 10 – MAL – 16 15 14 13 12 11

brief contents

contents

foreword

The origin of Spring Batch as an open source project goes back to the time when I joined a relatively new and small company called Interface21.[1] Many existing clients, and one big partner (Accenture), had repeatedly run into problems because the open source community lacked such a framework. Every IT project that needed offline processing found that they had to reinvent the basic features of deployment, processing patterns, and reliability. Then, and to this day, these are the unavoidable but necessary features of many environments across a wide range of industries.

Who should read this book? For sure anyone who wants to learn how to use Spring Batch from the ground up. Some knowledge of the Spring Framework and familiarity with Spring programming models and common practices are more or less mandatory, but these are common skills and easily obtained elsewhere. Spring Batch isn't all that difficult to get started with once you have basic Spring knowledge. But the more you use a complex tool, the more you'll find that it pays to understand its inner workings, and even seasoned practitioners of Spring Batch applications will find much of the book rewarding reading.

The content of the book is laid out in a way that's very accessible for readers: get started in part 1; learn the basics with handy references for later in part 2; and then the rubber meets the road with more advanced topics in part 3. The highlights for me are the chapters on transactions and reliability in part 2 and the chapter on scalability

---

[1] Interface21 went on to rebrand itself as SpringSource (http://www.springsource.org) before becoming a division of VMware (http://www.vmware.com) in 2009.

and parallel processing in part 3. These are two topics that come up again and again with clients and on the online open community forum.

I'm very glad for two reasons that someone else decided to write this book. The first is selfish: it's a lot of work. The second is on behalf of the readers: when the author of a framework writes a handbook for users, the temptation is to reveal all the secrets and inner workings of the implementation, which isn't necessarily the best practical starting point for users. The authors of this book are well qualified and present Spring Batch from the point of view of an expert user, which is the optimum point of view for readers because the authors have come to this knowledge by solving the problems that readers also experience while learning to use the framework.

The authors of this book are good community citizens and can often be found educating or supporting other users and participating in discussions on the Spring Batch community forum[2] and issue tracker.[3] In fact, I warmly recommend these activities as learning tools and as companions to this book—there's no better way to learn than to get your hands dirty, and to share your questions, problems, and experiences with others.

DAVE SYER
SPRING BATCH LEAD

---

[2] http://forum.springsource.org/forumdisplay.php?41-Batch
[3] http://jira.springsource.org/browse/BATCH

preface

Gosh, batch processes are *hard* to write—especially when using a general language like Java. In spite of this, they're *exciting* to write, when you consider the large amount of data they process. Batch jobs run every night, making it easy for millions of people to do things like banking, online shopping, querying billing information, and so on. This ought to turn any (geeky) developer on.

That was the case with Thierry, who was the first to work on the proposal for a Spring Batch book with Manning. Arnaud joined soon afterwards. The funny thing is that we were still working on Manning's *Spring Dynamic Modules in Action* book at the time. Writing a book is a challenge, but you could consider writing two books at the same time a sign of madness. Gary joined after we wrote a couple of chapters. Although Gary didn't write any of the original material, he handled what is undoubtedly the more difficult task: editing and sometimes rewriting the source material of three French authors. He always put us back on the right track with the benefit of hindsight (which isn't an outstanding quality of hectic technical authors). Gary is French, but don't worry, he's also American and has been living in the U.S. for decades. The book doesn't contain any trace of our French accents! Olivier was the last to join the team. Fourteen chapters is a lot and another pair of hands was welcome.

We did our best to make this book as comprehensive and accessible as possible. We hope you'll benefit from our experience with Spring Batch and that our book will help you write fast, robust, and reliable batch jobs with this framework.

acknowledgments

We thank the team at Manning for their hard work during the process of writing this book. Michael Stephens first contacted us and helped us with the book proposal. Publisher Marjan Bace gave us the opportunity to write the book and provided us with valuable advice about its structure. Karen Tegtmeyer organized the reviews, which resulted in further improvements. Last, but not least, we thank our development editor, Cynthia Kane, who helped us polish our writing and sharpen the book's focus.

This book is about an open source project, so it would not exist were it not for the efforts of the people who spent their time creating and maintaining Spring Batch. Thanks to the Spring Batch team: Ben Hale, Lucas Ward, Robert Kasanicky, Thomas Risberg, Dan Garrette, Rob Harrop, and, of course, Dave Syer, the project lead, who kindly contributed the foreword to our book. An open source project is also a community project, so thanks to everyone who contributed to the project by answering questions on the forum or by participating in the bug-tracking process. This also helped us to learn more about how people use Spring Batch.

Special thanks to the reviewers who took the time to read the manuscript and make constructive remarks about its content. Their feedback was essential in keeping us on the right track: Cédric Exbrayat, John Ryan, David Sinclair, Deepak Vohra, Antti Koivisto, Doug Warren, John Guthrie, Clarence E. Scates, Rick Wagner, Willhelm Lehman, Ileana Lehman, Benjamin Muschko, Guillaume Perone, Micha Minicki, and Joshua A. White.

Our technical proofreader, Gordon Dickens, helped us produce a more accurate and polished book by carefully reviewing the manuscript one last time shortly before it went to press. Thank you for your contribution, Gordon.

ARNAUD COGOLUÈGNES

I would like to give many thanks to all the people around me for their patience and understanding while I was absorbed in this project. Thank you to my colleagues at Zenika, Carl Azoury and Pierre Queinnec, who supported me. Thanks to all the people who provided input on Spring Batch: Dave Syer, Joris Kuipers, the people on the Spring Batch forum, and everyone with whom I had the pleasure to train on this technology. Thanks to Leonard Cohen: I find your music perfect accompaniment to hours spent working on a book. In addition, thank you, Claire, for your patience putting up with all the long hours I spent on this book.

THIERRY TEMPLIER

I would like to thank my wife Séverine and our lovely little boy Maël for being by my side in life. I also want to thank all the people who made this project possible and who trusted me, especially my coauthors for their excellent work and advice and the Manning team for their confidence, support, and professionalism. Thanks finally to all people that help me move forward in life and be the best I can be.

GARY GREGORY

I'd like to thank my parents for getting me started on my journey, providing me with the opportunity for a great education, and giving me the freedom to choose my path. I'm eternally grateful to my wife Lori and my son Alexander for giving me the time to pursue a project like this one. Along the way, I've studied and worked with truly exceptional individuals too numerous to name. My father-in-law, Buddy Martin, deserves a special mention for providing wisdom and insights through great conversations and storytelling born of decades spent writing about sports (Go Gators!). I also found inspiration in the music of Wilco, Donald Fagen, Tom Waits, David Lindley, and Bach. Finally, I thank my coauthors and all of the people at Manning for their support, professionalism, and great feedback.

OLIVIER BAZOUD

Many thanks to Manning's publisher Marjan Bace and to my coauthors who encouraged me to write this book. Thanks to my mother, my father, and my sister for their love and support over the years. And I would like to thank my wonderful girlfriend Maria for her patience and for giving me a chance to participate in this great adventure.

about this book

Spring Batch is Java framework that makes it easy to write batch applications. Batch applications involve reliably and efficiently processing large volumes of data to and from various data sources (files, databases, and so on). Spring Batch is great at doing this and provides the necessary foundation to meet the stringent requirements of batch applications. Sir Isaac Newton said, "If I have seen further it is only by standing on the shoulders of giants." Spring Batch builds on the shoulders of one giant in particular: the Spring Framework. Spring is the framework of choice for a significant segment of the Enterprise Java development market. Spring Batch makes the Spring programming model—based on simplicity and efficiency—easier to apply for batch applications. Spring Batch leverages all the well-worn Spring techniques and components, like dependency injection, data access support, and transaction management.

Batch processing is a large topic and Spring Batch has a wide range of features. We don't claim this book to be exhaustive. Instead, we provide the reader with the most useful information, based on our own experience with real-world projects, feedback from Spring Batch users, and...our own mistakes! The excellent reference documentation[4] of the framework should be a useful complement to this book. We obviously focus on Spring Batch, but we also cover different, yet related, topics like schedulers. Batch jobs aren't islands, they're integrated in the middle of complex systems, and we cover this aspect too. That's why chapter 11 discusses how Spring Batch can cohabit with technologies like REST and Spring Integration. Again, we want to stick as close as possible to the reality of batch systems, and this is (one part of) our vision.

---

[4] http://static.springsource.org/spring-batch/reference/index.html

We use the latest release of the latest branch of the framework available at the time of this writing, Spring Batch 2.1.

Because this is an *In Action* book, we provide code and configuration examples throughout, both to illustrate the concepts and to provide a template for successful operation.

Who should read this book?

Our primary target audience for this book is Java developers and architects who want to write batch applications. Experience with Spring is a plus, but not a requirement. We strive to give the necessary pointers and reminders in dedicated sidebars. Read this book even if you don't know Spring—you can grab a copy of Manning's *Spring in Action, Third Edition,* by Craig Walls to discover this wonderful technology. For those familiar with Spring, basic knowledge of dependency injection, data access support, and transaction management is enough. With this Spring background and this book, you'll be Spring Batch-ing in a matter of minutes.

What if you don't know Java and want to write batch applications? Well, think about learning Java to make your batch writing life easier. Spring Batch is great for batch applications!

Roadmap

The book is divided into three parts. The first part introduces the challenges presented by batch applications and how to use Spring Batch to addresses them. The second part forms the core of the presentation of the Spring Batch feature set. It exhaustively covers all of the scenarios you'll meet writing real-life batch applications. The third and final part covers advanced topics, including monitoring, scaling, and testing. We also include appendixes covering the installation of a typical development environment for Spring Batch and the configuration of the Spring Batch Admin web-based administration console.

Chapter 1 discusses batch applications and gives an overview of Spring Batch features. It also introduces Spring Batch using a hands-on approach, based on a real-world use case. It's a great place to start if you want to discover how to implement common batch scenarios with Spring Batch.

Chapter 2 covers the way Spring Batch structures the world of batch jobs. We name and define each batch applications concept, using the domain language of batch applications. With a term for each concept forming the vocabulary of batch jobs, you'll be able to communicate clearly and easily with your team about your batch applications.

Chapter 3 covers the configuration of Spring Batch jobs. It explains in detail all the XML elements and annotations available to configure every aspect of your jobs.

Chapter 4 discusses launching batch jobs under different scenarios: from the command line, using a scheduler like cron, or from an HTTP request. It also covers how to stop a job properly.

Chapter 5 covers reading data efficiently from different sources, using Spring Batch components.

Chapter 6 is the mirror image of chapter 5 where we cover writing to various data targets. It lists all the available components to write to databases and files, send emails, and so on.

Chapter 7 discusses an optional step between reading and writing: processing. This is where you can embed business logic to transform or filter items.

Chapter 8 covers the Spring Batch built-in features that make jobs more robust: skipping incorrectly formatted lines from a flat file by using a couple of XML lines in your configuration, retrying operations transparently after a transient failure, and restarting a job exactly where it left off.

Chapter 9 discusses the tricky topic of transactions. It explains how Spring Batch handles transactions, the how, when, and why of tweaking transactions, and useful transaction management patterns for batch applications.

Chapter 10 covers the way Spring Batch handles the flow of steps inside a job: linear versus nonlinear flows, sharing data between steps of a job, and interacting with the execution context.

Chapter 11 explores how a Spring Batch job can end up being in the middle of a complex enterprise integration application. In this chapter, you'll see how Spring Batch, Spring Integration, and Spring REST cohabit happily to meet real-world enterprise integration scenarios.

Chapter 12 discusses the monitoring of Spring Batch jobs. Because Spring Batch maintains execution metadata, this chapter covers how—JMX, web application—to access this metadata to query the state of your jobs.

Chapter 13 tackles the complex topic of scaling. It covers the different strategies Spring Batch provides to parallelize the execution of your jobs on multiple threads or even multiple physical nodes.

Chapter 14 is about testing Spring Batch jobs. Unit testing isolated components and testing a whole job execution are covered.

Code convention and downloads

We've licensed the source code for the example applications in this book under the Apache Software Foundation License, version 2.0. This source code is available at http://code.google.com/p/springbatch-in-action/ and is freely available from Manning's website at www.manning.com/SpringBatchinAction.

Much of the source code shown in this book consists of fragments designed to illustrate the text. When a complete segment of code is presented, it appears as a numbered listing; code annotations accompany some of the listings where further explanations of the code are needed. When we present source code, we sometimes use a bold font to draw attention to specific elements.

In the text, we use Courier typeface to denote code (Java and XML) as well as Java methods, XML element names, and other source code identifiers:

- A reference to a method in the text will generally not include the signature. Note that there may be more than one form of the method call.
- A reference to an XML element in the text can include the braces but not the attributes or closing tag, for example, `<action>`.

Author Online

The purchase of *Spring Batch in Action* includes free access to a private web forum run by Manning Publications where you can make comments about the book, ask technical questions, and receive help from the authors and from other users. To access the forum and subscribe to it, point your web browser to www.manning.com/SpringBatchinAction. This page provides information on registering, getting on the forum, the kind of help available, and the rules of conduct on the forum.

Manning's commitment to our readers is to provide a venue where a meaningful dialogue between individual readers and between readers and the authors can take place. It's not a commitment to any specific amount of participation on the part of the authors, whose contribution to the Author Online forum remains voluntary (and unpaid). We suggest you try asking them some challenging questions lest their interest stray! The Author Online forum and the archives of previous discussions will be accessible from the publisher's website as long as the book is in print.

About the authors

ARNAUD COGOLUÈGNES is a software developer, Java EE architect, and author with deep expertise in middleware, software engineering, and Spring technologies. Arnaud spent a number of years developing complex business applications and integrating Java-based products. A SpringSource certified trainer, Arnaud has trained hundreds of people around the world on Spring technologies and the Java platform.

THIERRY TEMPLIER is a Java EE, Web2, and modeling architect and expert with more than 10 years of experience. He's a Spring addict and enthusiast and enjoys implementing any kind of applications and tools using it. He is also the coauthor of some French books on these subjects and *Spring Dynamic Modules in Action*. He recently joined Noelios Technologies, the company behind the Restlet framework, and lives in Brittany (France).

GARY GREGORY is the coauthor of *JUnit in Action, Second Edition*. He has more than 20 years of experience in building object-oriented systems, C/C++, Smalltalk, Java, and the whole soup of XML and database technologies. Gary has held positions at Ashton-Tate, ParcPlace-Digitalk, and several other software companies, including Seagull Software, where he currently develops application servers for legacy integration. He's an active member of the Apache Software Foundation and the Apache Commons Project Management Committee, and contributes regularly to various Apache Commons projects. Born and raised in Paris, France, Gary received a BA in Linguistics and Computer Science from the University of California at Los Angeles. He lives in Florida with his wife, their son, and assorted golf clubs. You can find him at http://www.garygregory.com.

OLIVIER BAZOUD is a software architect at Ekino, the IT branch of FullSIX Group. He's also a Spring technologies expert. With over 12 years of experience, he develops complex business applications and high-traffic websites based on Java and web technologies.

about the cover illustration

The figure on the cover of *Spring Batch in Action* is captioned "A Janisary in his Common Dress in 1700" and is taken from the four-volume *Collection of the Dresses of Different Nations* by Thomas Jefferys, published in London between 1757 and 1772. The collection, which includes beautifully hand-colored copperplate engravings of costumes from around the world, has influenced theatrical costume design ever since it was published.

The diversity of the drawings in the *Collection of the Dresses of Different Nations* speaks vividly of the richness of the costumes presented on the London stage over 200 years ago. The costumes, both historical and contemporaneous, offered a glimpse into the dress customs of people living in different times and in different countries, bringing them to life for London theater audiences.

Dress codes have changed in the last century and the diversity by region, so rich in the past, has faded away. It's now often hard to tell the inhabitant of one continent from another. Perhaps, trying to view it optimistically, we've traded a cultural and visual diversity for a more varied personal life—or a more varied and interesting intellectual and technical life.

We at Manning celebrate the inventiveness, the initiative, and the fun of the computer business with book covers based on the rich diversity of regional and historical costumes brought back to life by pictures from collections such as this one.

Part 1

Background

What is Spring Batch? What is it good for? Is it the right tool for you? You'll find the answers to these questions in the next two chapters. Of course, you won't be a Spring Batch expert by the end of this first part, but you'll have a good foundation and understanding of all the features in Spring Batch.

Chapter 1 provides an overview of batch applications and Spring Batch. To follow the In Action tradition, we also show you how to implement a real-world batch job with Spring Batch. This introduction not only covers how Spring Batch handles the classical read-process-write pattern for large amounts of data but also shows you the techniques used to make a job more robust, like skipping invalid lines in a flat file.

Chapter 2 clearly defines the domain language used in batch applications and explains how Spring Batch captures the essence of batch applications. What are a job, a step, and a job execution? Chapter 2 covers all of this and introduces how Spring Batch tracks the execution of jobs to enable monitoring and restart on failure.

Introducing Spring Batch

1

Batch applications are a challenge to write, and that's why Spring Batch was created: to make them easier to write but also faster, more robust, and reliable. What are batch applications? Batch applications process large amounts of data without human intervention. You'd opt to use batch applications to compute data for generating monthly financial statements, calculating statistics, and indexing files. You're about to discover more about batch applications in this chapter. You'll see why their requirements—large volumes of data, performance, and robustness—make them a challenge to implement correctly and efficiently. Once you understand the big picture, you'll be ready to meet Spring Batch and its main features: helping to efficiently process data with various types of technologies—databases, files, and queues. We also honor the *In Action* series by implementing a real-world Spring Batch job. By the end of this first chapter, you'll have an overview of what Spring Batch does, and you'll be ready to implement your first job with Spring Batch. Let's get started with batch applications!

1.1   *What are batch applications?*

The most common scenario for a batch application is exporting data to files from one system and processing them in another. Imagine you want to exchange data between two systems: you export data as files from system A and then import the data into a database on system B. Figure 1.1 illustrates this example.

Figure 1.1   A typical batch application: system A exports data to flat files, and system B uses a batch process to read the files into a database.

A batch application processes data automatically, so it must be robust and reliable because there is no human interaction to recover from an error. The greater the volume of data a batch application must process, the longer it takes to complete. This means you must also consider performance in your batch application because it's often restricted to execute within a specific time window. Based on this description, the requirements of a batch application are as follows:

- *Large data volume*—Batch applications must be able to handle large volumes of data to import, export, or compute.
- *Automation*—Batch applications must run without user interaction except for serious problem resolution.
- *Robustness*—Batch applications must handle invalid data without crashing or aborting prematurely.
- *Reliability*—Batch applications must keep track of what goes wrong and when (logging, notification).
- *Performance*—Batch applications must perform well to finish processing in a dedicated time window or to avoid disturbing any other applications running simultaneously.

How batch applications fit in today's software architectures

Performing computations and exchanging data between applications are good examples of batch applications. But are these types of processes relevant today? Computation-based processes are obviously relevant: every day, large and complex calculations take place to index billions of documents, using cutting-edge algorithms like MapReduce. For data exchange, message-based solutions are also popular, having the advantage over batch applications of being (close to) real time. Although messaging is a powerful design pattern, it imposes its own particular set of requirements in terms of application design and implementation.

> **(continued)**
> Clearly, messaging isn't a silver bullet, and you should apply it thoughtfully. Note that batch jobs and messaging aren't mutually exclusive solutions: you can use messaging to exchange data and still need batch applications to process the data with the same reliability and robustness requirements as the rest of your application stack. Even in our event- and notification-driven world, batch applications are still relevant!

How does Spring Batch fit in the landscape of batch applications? The next section introduces the Spring Batch framework and its main features. You'll see how Spring Batch helps meet the requirements of batch applications by providing ready-to-use components and processing large amounts of data in an efficient manner.

1.2   Meet Spring Batch

The goal of the Spring Batch project is to provide an open source batch-oriented framework that effectively addresses the most common needs of batch applications. The Spring Batch project was born in 2007 out of the collaboration of Accenture and SpringSource. Accenture brought its experience gained from years of working on proprietary batch frameworks and SpringSource brought its technical expertise and the proven Spring programming model. Table 1.1 lists the main features of Spring Batch.

Table 1.1   Main features of Spring Batch

Feature	Description
Spring Framework foundations	Benefits from enterprise support, dependency injection, and aspect-oriented programming
Batch-oriented processing	Enforces best practices when reading and writing data
Ready-to-use components	Provides components to address common batch scenarios (read and write data to and from databases and files)
Robustness and reliability	Allows for declarative skipping and retry; enables restart after failure

By using Spring Batch, you directly benefit from the best practices the framework enforces and implements. You also benefit from the many off-the-shelf components for the most popular formats and technologies used in the software industry. Table 1.2 lists the storage technologies that Spring Batch supports out of the box.

Table 1.2   Read-write technologies supported by Spring Batch

Data source type	Technology	Description
Database	JDBC	Leverages paging, cursors, and batch updates
Database	Hibernate	Leverages paging and cursors
Database	JPA (Java Persistence API)	Leverages paging

Table 1.2 Read-write technologies supported by Spring Batch *(continued)*

Data source type	Technology	Description
Database	iBATIS	Leverages paging
File	Flat file	Supports delimited and fixed-length flat files
File	XML	Uses StAX (Streaming API for XML) for parsing; builds on top of Spring OXM; supports JAXB (Java Architecture for XML Binding), XStream, and Castor

As you can see in table 1.2, Spring Batch supports many technologies out of the box, making the framework quite versatile. We study this support thoroughly in chapters 5 and 6.

Spring Batch isn't a scheduler!

Spring Batch drives batch jobs (we use the terms *job*, *batch*, and *process* interchangeably) but doesn't provide advanced support to launch them according to a schedule. Spring Batch leaves this task to dedicated schedulers like Quartz and cron. A scheduler triggers the launching of Spring Batch jobs by accessing the Spring Batch runtime (like Quartz because it's a Java solution) or by launching a dedicated JVM process (in the case of cron). Sometimes a scheduler launches batch jobs in sequence: first job A, and then job B if A succeeded, or job C if A failed. The scheduler can use the files generated by the jobs or exit codes to orchestrate the sequence. Spring Batch can also orchestrate such sequences itself: Spring Batch jobs are made of steps, and you can easily configure the sequence by using Spring Batch XML (covered in chapter 10). This is an area where Spring Batch and schedulers overlap.

How does Spring Batch meet the requirements of robustness and reliability of batch applications?

1.2.1 *Robustness and reliability*

Should a whole batch fail because of one badly formatted line? Not always. The decision to skip an incorrect line or an incorrect item is declarative in Spring Batch. It's all about configuration.

What happens if you restart a failed batch job? Should it start from the beginning—potentially processing items again and corrupting data—or should it be able to restart exactly where it left off? Spring Batch makes the latter easy: components can track everything they do, and the framework provides them with the execution data on restart. The components then know where they left off and can restart processing at the right place.

Spring Batch also addresses the robustness and reliability requirements. Chapter 2 provides an overview of restart, and chapter 8 covers robustness thoroughly.

Another requirement of batch applications is performance. How does Spring Batch meet the performance requirement?

1.2.2 Scaling strategies

Spring Batch processes items in chunks. We cover chunk processing later in this chapter, but here is the idea: a job reads and writes items in small chunks. Chunk processing allows streaming data instead of loading all the data in memory. By default, chunk processing is single threaded and usually performs well. But some batch jobs need to execute faster, so Spring Batch provides ways to make chunk processing multithreaded and to distribute processing on multiple physical nodes.

Chapter 13 thoroughly discusses the scaling strategies in Spring Batch. Let's take a look at one of these strategies: partitioning.

Partitioning splits a step into substeps, each of which handles a specific portion of the data. This implies that you know the structure of the input data and that you know in advance how to distribute data between substeps. Distribution can take place by ranges of primary key values for database records or by directories for files. The substeps can execute locally or remotely, and Spring Batch provides support for multithreaded substeps. Figure 1.2 illustrates partitioning based on filenames: A through D, E through H, and so on, up to Y through Z.

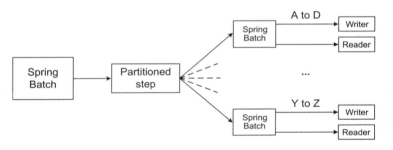

Figure 1.2 Scaling by partitioning: a single step partitions records and autonomous substeps handle processing.

Spring Batch and grid computing

When dealing with large amounts of data—petabytes (10^{15})—a popular solution to scaling is to divide the enormous amounts of computations into smaller chunks, compute them in parallel (usually on different nodes), and then gather the results. Some open source frameworks (Hadoop, GridGain, and Hazelcast, for example) have appeared in the last few years to deal with the burden of distributing units of work so that developers can focus on developing the computations themselves. How does Spring Batch compare to these grid-computing frameworks? Spring Batch is a lightweight solution: all it needs is the Java runtime installed, whereas grid-computing frameworks need a more advanced infrastructure. As an example, Hadoop usually works on top of its own distributed file system, HDFS (Hadoop Distributed File System). In terms of features, Spring Batch provides a lot of support to work with flat files, XML files, and relational databases.

(continued)

Grid-computing frameworks usually don't provide such high-level processing support.

Spring Batch and grid-computing frameworks aren't incompatible: at the time of this writing, projects integrating both technologies are appearing (Spring Hadoop, at https://github.com/SpringSource/spring-hadoop, is an example).

This ends our tour of the Spring Batch framework. You now have a good overview of the most important features of Spring Batch and the benefits it brings to your applications. Let's move on to the more practical part of this chapter with the implementation of a real-world batch job using Spring Batch.

1.3   *Introducing the case study*

This section introduces a real application that we use throughout this book to illustrate the use of Spring Batch: an online store application. This use case starts out small and simple but remains realistic in terms of technical requirements. It not only demonstrates Spring Batch features but also illustrates how this use case fits into the enterprise landscape.

By implementing this use case using Spring Batch, you gain a practical understanding of the framework: how it implements efficient reading and writing of large volumes of data, when to use built-in components, when to implement your own components, how to configure a batch job with the Spring lightweight container, and much more. By the end of this chapter, you'll have a good overview of how Spring Batch works, and you'll know exactly where to go in this book to find what you need for your batch applications.

1.3.1   *The online store application*

The ACME Corporation wants to expand its business by selling its products on the web. To do so, ACME chooses to build a dedicated online store application. ACME will use batch jobs to populate the online store database with the catalog from its internal proprietary system, as shown in figure 1.3. The system will process data every night to insert new products in the catalog or update existing products.

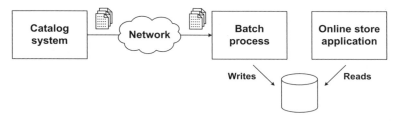

Figure 1.3   Thanks to this new application, anyone can buy ACME's products online. The system sends catalogs to a server where a batch process reads them and writes product records into the online store database.

That's it for the big picture, but you should understand why ACME decided to build an online store in the first place and populate it using batch processes.

1.3.2 *Why build an online store with batch jobs?*

Why did ACME choose to build an online, web-based application to sell its products? As we mentioned, this is the best way for ACME to expand its business and to serve more customers. Web applications are easy to deploy, easy to access, and can provide a great user experience. ACME plans to deploy the online store application to a local web hosting provider rather than hosting it on its own network. The first version of the online store will provide a simple but efficient UI; ACME focuses on the catalog and transactions first, before providing more features and a more elaborate UI.

Next, why did ACME choose to shuttle data from one system to the other instead of making its onsite catalog and the online store communicate directly? The software that powers the catalog has an API, so why not use it? The main reason is security: as illustrated in figure 1.4, ACME's own network hosts the catalog system, and the company doesn't want to expose the catalog system to the outside world directly, even via another application. This precaution is rather drastic, but that's how things are done at ACME.

Figure 1.4 Because ACME doesn't want its internal catalog system to be directly accessible from the outside world, it doesn't allow the two applications to communicate directly and exchange data.

Another reason for this architecture is that the catalog system's API and data format don't suit the needs of the online store application: ACME wants to show a summarized view of the catalog data to customers without overwhelming them with a complex catalog structure and supplying too many details. You could get this summarized catalog view by using the catalog system's API, but you'd need to make many calls, which would cause performance to suffer in the catalog system.

To summarize, a mismatch exists between the view of the data provided by the catalog system and the view of the data required by the online store application. Therefore, an application needs to process the data before exposing it to customers through the online store.

1.3.3 *Why use batch processes?*

The online store application scenario is a good example of two systems communicating to exchange data. ACME updates the catalog system throughout the day, adding new products and updating existing products. The online store application doesn't need to expose live data because buyers can live with day-old catalog information.

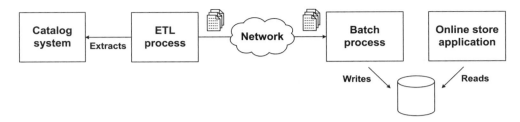

Figure 1.5   An extract, transform, and load (ETL) process extracts and transforms the catalog system data into a flat file, which ACME sends every night to a Spring Batch process. This Spring Batch process is in charge of reading the flat file and importing the data into the online store database.

Therefore, a nightly batch process updates the online store database, using flat files, as shown in figure 1.5.

> ### Extract, transform, and load (ETL)
>
> Briefly stated, ETL is a process in the database and data-warehousing world that performs the following steps:
>
> 1 Extracts data from an external data source
> 2 Transforms the extracted data to match a specific purpose
> 3 Loads the transformed data into a data target: a database or data warehouse
>
> Many products, both free and commercial, can help create ETL processes. This is a bigger topic than we can address here, but it isn't always as simple as these three steps. Writing an ETL process can present its own set of challenges involving parallel processing, rerunnability, and recoverability. The ETL community has developed its own set of best practices to meet these and other requirements.

In figure 1.5, an ETL process creates the flat file to populate the online store database. It extracts data from the catalog system and transforms it to produce the view expected by the online store application. For the purpose of our discussion, this ETL process is a black box: it could be implemented with an ETL tool (like Talend) or even with another Spring Batch job. We focus next on how the online store application reads and writes the catalog's product information.

1.3.4   *The import product use case*

The online store application sells products out of a catalog, making the product a main domain concept. The import product batch reads the product records from a flat file created by ACME and updates the online store application database accordingly. Figure 1.6 illustrates that reading and writing products is at the core of this batch job, but it contains other steps as well.

The read-write step forms the core of the batch job, but as figure 1.6 shows, this isn't the only step. This batch job consists of the following steps:

Figure 1.6 The Spring Batch job consists of the following steps: decompression and read-write.

1 *Decompression*—Decompresses the archive flat file received from the ACME network. The file is compressed to speed up transfer over the internet.

2 *Reading and writing*—The flat file is read line by line and then inserted into the database.

This batch process allows us to introduce the Spring Batch features displayed in table 1.3.

Table 1.3 Spring Batch features introduced by the import catalog job

Batch process step	Spring Batch feature
Decompression	Custom processing in a job (but not reading from a data store and writing to another)
Read-write	Reading a flat file Implementing a custom database writing component Skipping invalid records instead of failing the whole process
Configuration	Leveraging Spring's lightweight container and Spring Batch's namespace to wire up batch components Using the Spring Expression Language to make the configuration more flexible

Rather than describe each of Spring Batch's features in the order in which they appear as batch job steps, we start with the core of the process: reading and writing the products. Then we see how to decompress the incoming file before making the process more robust by validating the input parameters and choosing to skip invalid records to avoid the whole job failing on a single error.

1.4 Reading and writing the product data

Reading and writing the product catalog is at the core of the Spring Batch job. ACME provides the product catalog as a flat file, which the job needs to import into the online store database. Reading and writing is Spring Batch's sweet spot: for the import product job, you only have to configure one Spring Batch component to read the content of the flat file, implement a simple interface for the writing component, and create a configuration file to handle the batch execution flow. Table 1.3 lists the Spring Batch features introduced by the import catalog job. Let's start by using Spring Batch to implement the read-write use case.

1.4.1 Anatomy of the read-write step

Because read-write (and copy) scenarios are common in batch applications, Spring Batch provides specific support for this use case. Spring Batch includes many ready-to-use components to read from and write to data stores like files and databases. Spring

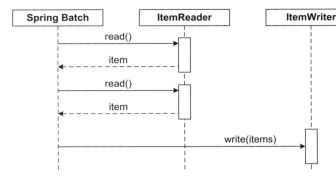

Figure 1.7   In read-write scenarios, Spring Batch uses *chunk processing*. Spring Batch reads items one by one from an `ItemReader`, collects the items in a chunk of a given size, and sends that chunk to an `ItemWriter`.

Batch also includes a batch-oriented algorithm to handle the execution flow, called *chunk processing*. Figure 1.7 illustrates the principle of chunk processing.

Spring Batch handles read-write scenarios by managing an `ItemReader` and an `ItemWriter`. Using chunk processing, Spring Batch collects items one at a time from the item reader into a configurable-sized chunk. Spring Batch then sends the chunk to the item writer and goes back to using the item reader to create another chunk, and so on, until the input is exhausted.

> **CHUNK PROCESSING**   Chunk processing is particularly well suited to handle large data operations because a job handles items in small chunks instead of processing them all at once. Practically speaking, a large file won't be loaded in memory; instead it's streamed, which is more efficient in terms of memory consumption. Chunk processing allows more flexibility to manage the data flow in a job. Spring Batch also handles transactions and errors around read and write operations.

Spring Batch provides an optional processing step in chunk processing: a job can process (transform) read items before sending them to the `ItemWriter`. The ability to process an item is useful when you don't want to write an item as is. The component that handles this transformation is an implementation of the `ItemProcessor` interface. Because item processing in Spring Batch is optional, the illustration of chunk processing shown in figure 1.7 is still valid. Figure 1.8 illustrates chunk processing combined with item processing.

What can you do in an `ItemProcessor`? You can perform any transformations you need on an item before Spring Batch sends it to the `ItemWriter`. This is where you implement the logic to transform the data from the input format into the format expected by the target system. Spring Batch also lets you validate and filter input items. If you return `null` from the `ItemProcessor` method `process`, processing for that item stops and Spring Batch won't insert the item in the database.

> **NOTE**   Our read-write use case doesn't have an item-processing step.

The following listing shows the definition of the chunk-processing interfaces `Item-Reader`, `ItemProcessor`, and `ItemWriter`.

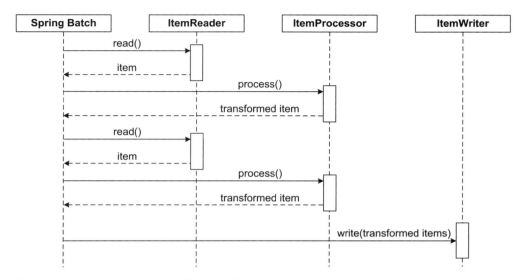

Figure 1.8 Chunk processing combined with item processing: an item processor can transform input items before calling the item writer.

Listing 1.1 Spring Batch interfaces for chunk processing

```
package org.springframework.batch.item;

public interface ItemReader<T> {

  T read() throws Exception, UnexpectedInputException,
                ParseException,
                NonTransientResourceException;

}
```
Reads item

```
package org.springframework.batch.item;

public interface ItemProcessor<I, O> {

  O process(I item) throws Exception;

}
```
Transforms item (optional)

```
package org.springframework.batch.item;

import java.util.List;

public interface ItemWriter<T> {

  void write(List<? extends T> items) throws Exception;

}
```
Writes a chunk of items

In chapters 5 and 6, we respectively cover all implementations of ItemReader and ItemWriter provided by Spring Batch. Chapter 7 covers the processing phase used to transform and filter items.

The next two subsections show how to configure the Spring Batch flat file ItemReader and how to write your own ItemWriter to handle writing products to the database.

1.4.2 *Reading a flat file*

Spring Batch provides the `FlatFileItemReader` class to read records from a flat file. To use a `FlatFileItemReader`, you need to configure some Spring beans and implement a component that creates domain objects from what the `FlatFileItemReader` reads; Spring Batch will handle the rest. You can kiss all your old boilerplate I/O code goodbye and focus on your data.

THE FLAT FILE FORMAT

The input flat file format consists of a header line and one line per product record. Here's an excerpt:

```
PRODUCT_ID,NAME,DESCRIPTION,PRICE
PR....210,BlackBerry 8100 Pearl,A cell phone,124.60
PR....211,Sony Ericsson W810i,Yet another cell phone!,139.45
PR....212,Samsung MM-A900M Ace,A cell phone,97.80
PR....213,Toshiba M285-E 14,A cell phone,166.20
PR....214,Nokia 2610 Phone,A cell phone,145.50
```

You may recognize this as the classic comma-separated value (CSV) format. There's nothing out of the ordinary in this flat file: for a given row, the format separates each column value from the next with a comma. Spring Batch maps each row in the flat file to a `Product` domain object.

THE PRODUCT DOMAIN CLASS

The `Product` class maps the different columns of the flat file. Note the instance variable declarations for product attributes like id, name, price, and so on, in this snippet; the getter and setter methods are excluded for brevity:

```java
package com.manning.sbia.ch01.domain;

import java.math.BigDecimal;

public class Product {

  private String id;
  private String name;
  private String description;
  private BigDecimal price;

  (...)

}
```

> **NOTE** We use a `BigDecimal` for the product price because the Java float and double primitive types aren't well suited for monetary calculations. For example, it's impossible to exactly represent 0.1.

Let's now use the `FlatFileItemReader` to create `Product` objects out of the flat file.

CREATING DOMAIN OBJECTS WITH A FLATFILEITEMREADER

The `FlatFileItemReader` class handles all the I/O for you: opening the file, streaming it by reading each line, and closing it. The `FlatFileItemReader` class delegates the mapping between an input line and a domain object to an implementation of the

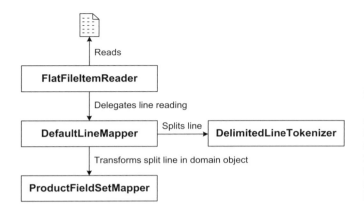

Figure 1.9 The `FlatFile-ItemReader` **reads the flat file and delegates the mapping** between a line and a domain object to a `LineMapper`. The `LineMapper` **implementation delegates the splitting of lines and the mapping between split lines and domain objects.**

`LineMapper` interface. Spring Batch provides a handy `LineMapper` implementation called `DefaultLineMapper`, which delegates the mapping to other strategy interfaces. Figure 1.9 shows all of this delegation work.

That's a lot of delegation, and it means you'll have more to configure, but such is the price of reusability and flexibility. You'll be able to configure and use built-in Spring Batch components or provide your own implementations for more specific tasks.

The `DefaultLineMapper` is a typical example; it needs

- *A LineTokenizer to split a line into fields.*
  You'll use a stock Spring Batch implementation for this.
- *A FieldSetMapper to transform the split line into a domain object.*
  You'll write your own implementation for this.

You'll soon see the whole Spring configuration in listing 1.2 (`LineTokenizer` is of particular interest), but next we focus on the `FieldSetMapper` implementation to create `Product` domain objects.

IMPLEMENTING A FIELDSETMAPPER FOR PRODUCT OBJECTS

You use a `FieldSetMapper` to convert the line split by the `LineTokenizer` into a domain object. The `FieldSetMapper` interface is straightforward:

```
public interface FieldSetMapper<T> {
  T mapFieldSet(FieldSet fieldSet) throws BindException;
}
```

The `FieldSet` parameter comes from the `LineTokenizer`. Think of it as an equivalent to the JDBC `ResultSet`: it retrieves field values and performs conversions between `String` objects and richer objects like `BigDecimal`. The following snippet shows the `ProductFieldSetMapper` implementation:

```
package com.manning.sbia.ch01.batch;

import org.springframework.batch.item.file.mapping.FieldSetMapper;
import org.springframework.batch.item.file.transform.FieldSet;
import org.springframework.validation.BindException;
```

```
import com.manning.sbia.ch01.domain.Product;

public class ProductFieldSetMapper implements FieldSetMapper<Product> {

  public Product mapFieldSet(FieldSet fieldSet) throws BindException {
    Product product = new Product();
    product.setId(fieldSet.readString("PRODUCT_ID"));
    product.setName(fieldSet.readString("NAME"));
    product.setDescription(fieldSet.readString("DESCRIPTION"));
    product.setPrice(fieldSet.readBigDecimal("PRICE"));
    return product;
  }
}
```

The `ProductFieldSetMapper` implementation isn't rocket science, and that's exactly the point: it focuses on retrieving the data from the flat file and converts values into `Product` domain objects. We leave Spring Batch to deal with all of the I/O plumbing and efficiently reading the flat file. Notice in the `mapFieldSet` method the `String` literals `PRODUCT_ID`, `NAME`, `DESCRIPTION`, and `PRICE`. Where do these references come from? They're part of the `LineTokenizer` configuration, so let's study the Spring configuration for `FlatFileItemReader`.

CONFIGURATION OF THE FLATFILEITEMREADER

The `FlatFileItemReader` can be configured like any Spring bean using an XML configuration file, as shown in the following listing.

Listing 1.2   Spring configuration of the `FlatFileItemReader`

```
<bean id="reader"
      class="org.springframework.batch.item.file.FlatFileItemReader">
  <property name="resource"
            value="file:./work/output/output.txt" />           ❶ Skips first
  <property name="linesToSkip" value="1" />                        line
  <property name="lineMapper">
    <bean
     class="org.springframework.batch.item.file.mapping.DefaultLineMapper">
      <property name="lineTokenizer">
        <bean class="org.springframework.batch.item.file.transform.
 DelimitedLineTokenizer">
          <property name="names" value="PRODUCT_ID,              Configures
 NAME,DESCRIPTION,PRICE" />                                     tokenization ❷
        </bean>
      </property>
      <property name="fieldSetMapper">
        <bean class="com.manning.sbia.ch01.batch.
 ProductFieldSetMapper" />
      </property>
    </bean>
  </property>
</bean>
```

In this example, the `resource` property defines the input file. Because the first line of the input file contains headers, you ask Spring Batch to skip this line by setting the property `linesToSkip` ❶ to 1. You use a `DelimitedLineTokenizer` ❷ to split each input line into fields; Spring Batch uses a comma as the default separator. Then you define the name of each field. These are the names used in the `ProductFieldSet-Mapper` class to retrieve values from the `FieldSet`. Finally, you inject an instance of `ProductFieldSetMapper` into the `DefaultLineMapper`.

That's it; your flat file reader is ready! Don't feel overwhelmed because flat file support in Spring Batch uses many components—that's what makes it powerful and flexible. Next up, to implement the database item writer, you need to do less configuration work but more Java coding. Let's dig in.

1.4.3 Implementing a database item writer

To update the database with product data, you have to implement your own `Item-Writer`. Each line of the flat file represents either a new product record or an existing one, so you must decide whether to send the database an `insert` or an `update` SQL statement. Nevertheless, the implementation of the `ProductJdbcItemWriter` is straightforward, as shown in the following listing.

Listing 1.3 Implementing the `ProductJdbcItemWriter`

```
package com.manning.sbia.ch01.batch;

import java.util.List;
import javax.sql.DataSource;
import org.springframework.batch.item.ItemWriter;
import org.springframework.jdbc.core.JdbcTemplate;
import com.manning.sbia.ch01.domain.Product;

public class ProductJdbcItemWriter implements ItemWriter<Product> {

  private static final String INSERT_PRODUCT = "insert into product "+
   "(id,name,description,price) values(?,?,?,?)";

  private static final String UPDATE_PRODUCT = "update product set "+
   "name=?, description=?, price=? where id=?";

  private JdbcTemplate jdbcTemplate;

  public ProductJdbcItemWriter(DataSource ds) {          ❶ Uses JDBC template
    this.jdbcTemplate = new JdbcTemplate(ds);                for data access
  }

  public void write(List<? extends Product> items) throws Exception {
    for (Product item : items) {
      int updated = jdbcTemplate.update(
        UPDATE_PRODUCT,
        item.getName(),item.getDescription(),          ❷ Tries to update
        item.getPrice(),item.getId()                        a product
      );
      if (updated == 0) {
        jdbcTemplate.update(
          INSERT_PRODUCT,
          item.getId(),item.getName(),                  ❸ Inserts new
          item.getDescription(),item.getPrice()              product
        );
```

```
        }
      }
    }
  }
}
```

The `ProductJdbcItemWriter` uses Spring's `JdbcTemplate` to interact with the database. Spring Batch creates the `JdbcTemplate` with a `DataSource` injected in the constructor ❶. In the `write` method, you iterate over a chunk of products and first try to update an existing record ❷. If the database tells you the `update` statement didn't update any record, you know this record doesn't exist, and you can insert it ❸.

That's it for the implementation! Notice how simple it was to implement this `ItemWriter` because Spring Batch handles getting records from the `ItemReader`, creating chunks, managing transactions, and so on. Next, let's configure the database item writer.

1.4.4   *Configuring a database item writer*

For the item writer to be configured as a Spring bean, it needs a `DataSource`, as shown in the following XML fragment:

```xml
<bean id="writer"
      class="com.manning.sbia.ch01.batch.ProductJdbcItemWriter">
  <constructor-arg ref="dataSource" />
</bean>
```

You'll configure the `DataSource` later, in a separate configuration file. You use a separate file because it decouples the application configuration—the item writer—from the infrastructure configuration—the `DataSource`. By doing so, you can use the same application configuration across different environments—production and testing, for example—and switch the infrastructure configuration file.

Now that you've created the two parts of the read-write step, you can assemble them in a Spring Batch job.

1.4.5   *Configuring the read-write step*

Configuring the read-write step is done through Spring. The step configuration can sit next to the declaration of the reader and writer beans, as shown in the following listing.

> **Listing 1.4   Spring configuration of the read-write step**

```xml
<beans xmlns="http://www.springframework.org/schema/beans"
    xmlns:xsi="http://www.w3.org/2001/XMLSchema-instance"
    xmlns:batch="http://www.springframework.org/schema/batch"
    xsi:schemaLocation="http://www.springframework.org/schema/beans
    http://www.springframework.org/schema/beans/spring-beans-3.0.xsd
    http://www.springframework.org/schema/batch
    http://www.springframework.org/schema/batch/spring-batch-2.1.xsd">

  <job id="importProducts"                                        ❶ Starts job
      xmlns="http://www.springframework.org/schema/batch">           configuration
    <step id="readWriteProducts">
```

```
      <tasklet>
        <chunk reader="reader" writer="writer"
              commit-interval="100" />
      </tasklet>
    </step>
  </job>

  <bean id="reader" (...)
  </bean>
  <bean id="writer" (...)
  </bean>

</beans>
```

❷ Configures chunk processing

❸ Sets commit interval

The configuration file starts with the usual declaration of the namespaces and associated prefixes: the Spring namespace and Spring Batch namespace with the batch prefix. The Spring namespace is declared as the default namespace, so you don't need to use a prefix to use its elements. Unfortunately, this is inconvenient for the overall configuration because you must use the batch prefix for the batch job elements. To make the configuration more readable, you can use a workaround in XML: when you start the job configuration XML element ❶, you specify a default XML namespace as an attribute of the job element. The scope of this new default namespace is the job element and its child elements.

The chunk element ❷ configures the chunk-processing step, in a step element, which is itself in a tasklet element. In the chunk element, you refer to the reader and writer beans with the reader and writer attributes. The values of these two attributes are the IDs previously defined in the reader and writer configuration. Finally, ❸ the commit-interval attribute is set to a chunk size of 100.

Choosing a chunk size and commit interval

First, the size of a chunk and the commit interval are the same thing! Second, there's no definitive value to choose. Our recommendation is a value between 10 and 200. Too small a chunk size creates too many transactions, which is costly and makes the job run slowly. Too large a chunk size makes transactional resources—like databases—run slowly too, because a database must be able to roll back operations. The best value for the commit interval depends on many factors: data, processing, nature of the resources, and so on. The commit interval is a parameter in Spring Batch, so don't hesitate to change it to find the most appropriate value for your jobs.

You're done with the copy portion of the batch process. Spring Batch performs a lot of the work for you: it reads the products from the flat file and imports them into the database. You didn't write any code for reading the data. For the write operation, you only created the logic to insert and update products in the database. Putting these components together is straightforward thanks to Spring's lightweight container and the Spring Batch XML vocabulary.

So far, you've implemented the box labeled "Reading and writing" from figure 1.6. As you've seen, Spring Batch provides a lot of help for this common use case. The framework is even richer and more flexible because a batch process can contain any type of write operation. You'll see an example of this next, when you decompress the input file for your job, as shown in figure 1.6 in the box labeled "Decompressing."

1.5   *Decompressing the input file with a tasklet*

Remember that the flat file is uploaded to the online store as a compressed archive. You need to decompress this file before starting to read and write products. Decompressing a file isn't a read-write step, but Spring Batch is flexible enough to implement such a task as part of a job. Before showing you how to decompress the input file, let's explain why you must compress the products flat file.

1.5.1   *Why compress the file?*

The flat file containing the product data is compressed so you can upload it faster from ACME's network to the provider that hosts the online store application. Textual data, as used in the flat file, can be highly compressed, with ratios of 10 to 1 commonly achieved. A 1-GB flat file can compress to 100 MB, which is a more reasonable size for file transfers over the internet.

Note that you could encrypt the file as well, ensuring that no one could read the product data if the file were intercepted during transfer. The encryption could be done before the compression or as part of it. In this case, assume that ACME and the hosting provider agreed on a secure transfer protocol, like Secure Copy (SCP is built on top of Secure Shell [SSH]).

Now that you know why you compress the file, let's see how to implement the decompression tasklet.

1.5.2   *Implementing the decompression tasklet*

Spring Batch provides an extension point to handle processing in a batch process step: the `Tasklet`. You implement a `Tasklet` that decompresses a ZIP archive into its source flat file. The following listing shows the implementation of the `Decompress-Tasklet` class.

Listing 1.5   Implementation of decompression tasklet

```
package com.manning.sbia.ch01.batch;

import java.io.BufferedInputStream;
import java.io.BufferedOutputStream;
import java.io.File;
import java.io.FileOutputStream;
import java.util.zip.ZipInputStream;
import org.apache.commons.io.FileUtils;
import org.apache.commons.io.IOUtils;
import org.springframework.batch.core.StepContribution;
import org.springframework.batch.core.scope.context.ChunkContext;
```

```
import org.springframework.batch.core.step.tasklet.Tasklet;
import org.springframework.batch.repeat.RepeatStatus;
import org.springframework.core.io.Resource;

public class DecompressTasklet implements Tasklet {

  private Resource inputResource;
  private String targetDirectory;
  private String targetFile;

  public RepeatStatus execute(StepContribution contribution,
      ChunkContext chunkContext) throws Exception {
    ZipInputStream zis = new ZipInputStream(
      new BufferedInputStream(
        inputResource.getInputStream()));

    File targetDirectoryAsFile = new File(
      targetDirectory);
    if(!targetDirectoryAsFile.exists()) {
      FileUtils.forceMkdir(targetDirectoryAsFile);
    }
    File target = new File(targetDirectory,targetFile);
    BufferedOutputStream dest = null;
    while(zis.getNextEntry() != null) {
      if(!target.exists()) {
        target.createNewFile();
      }
      FileOutputStream fos = new FileOutputStream(
        target
      );
      dest = new BufferedOutputStream(fos);
      IOUtils.copy(zis,dest);
      dest.flush();
      dest.close();
    }
    zis.close();
    if(!target.exists()) {
      throw new IllegalStateException(
        "Could not decompress anything from the archive!");
    }
    return RepeatStatus.FINISHED;
  }
  /* setters */
  (...)

}
```

① Implements Tasklet interface

② Declares Tasklet parameters

③ Opens archive

④ Creates target directory if absent

⑤ Decompresses archive

⑥ Tasklet finishes

The DecompressTasklet class implements the Tasklet interface **①**, which has only one method, called execute. The tasklet has three fields **②**, which represent the archive file, the name of the directory to which the file is decompressed, and the name of the output file. These fields are set when you configure the tasklet with Spring. In the execute method, you open a stream to the archive file **③**, create the target directory if it doesn't exist **④**, and use the Java API to decompress the ZIP archive **⑤**. Note that the FileUtils and IOUtils classes from the Apache Commons IO project are used to create the target directory and copy the ZIP entry content to the target file (Apache Commons IO provides handy utilities to deal with files and directories). At ➏, you return the FINISHED constant from the RepeatStatus enumeration to notify Spring Batch that the tasklet finished.

> ### Only a data file and no metadata file in the ZIP archive?
>
> It's common practice to have two files in a ZIP archive used for a batch job. One file contains the data to import, and the other contains information about the data to import (date, identifier, and so on). We wanted to keep things simple in our Spring Batch introduction, especially the tedious unzipping code, so our ZIP archive contains only a data file. Let's say the name of the unzipped file is made up of meaningful information such as the date and an identifier for the import.

Although the Tasklet interface is straightforward, its implementation includes a lot of code to deal with decompressing the file. Let's now see how to configure this tasklet with Spring.

1.5.3 Configuring the tasklet

The tasklet is configured as part of the job and consists of two changes in Spring: declare the tasklet as a Spring bean and inject it as a step in the job. To do this, you must modify the configuration you wrote for reading and writing products, as shown in the following listing.

Listing 1.6   Spring configuration of the decompress tasklet

```
<job id="importProducts"
     xmlns="http://www.springframework.org/schema/batch">
  <step id="decompress" next="readWriteProducts">              ➊ Sets tasklet
    <tasklet ref="decompressTasklet" />                             in job
  </step>
  <step id="readWriteProducts">
    <tasklet>
      <chunk reader="reader" writer="writer" commit-interval="100" />
    </tasklet>
  </step>
</job>

<bean id="decompressTasklet"
      class="com.manning.sbia.ch01.batch.
   ➥ DecompressTasklet">
  <property name="inputResource"
            value="file:./input/input.zip" />                 ➋ Declares
  <property name="targetDirectory"                                tasklet bean
            value="./work/output/" />
  <property name="targetFile"
            value="products.txt" />
</bean>
```

The configuration of a plain Tasklet is simpler than for a read-write step because you only need to point the Tasklet to the (decompression) bean ➊. Note that you control the job flow through the `next` attribute of the `step` element, which refers to the `read-WriteProducts` step by ID. Chapter 10 thoroughly covers how to control the flow of Spring Batch jobs and how to take different paths, depending on how a step ends, for example. The `tasklet` element ❶ refers to the `decompressTasklet` bean, declared at ❷. If you find that the `Tasklet` bean is configured too rigidly in the Spring file (because the values are hardcoded), don't worry: we'll show you later in this chapter how to make these settings more dynamic.

You now have all the parts of the job implemented and configured: you can decompress the input archive, read the products from the decompressed flat file, and write them to the database. You're now about to see how to launch the job inside an integration test.

1.6   *Testing the batch process*

Batch applications are like any other applications: you should test them using a framework like JUnit. Testing makes maintenance easier and detects regressions after refactoring. Let's test, then! This section covers how to write an integration test for a Spring Batch job. You'll also learn about the launching API in Spring Batch. But don't be too impatient—we need a couple of intermediary steps before writing the test: configuring a test infrastructure and showing you a trick to make the job configuration more flexible.

> **Spring Batch and test-driven development**
>
> Good news: Spring Batch and test-driven development are fully compatible! We introduce here some techniques to test a Spring Batch job, and chapter 14 is dedicated to testing. We don't show tests systematically in this book; otherwise, half of the book would contain testing code! We truly believe in test-driven development, so we test all the source code with automated tests. Download the source code, browse it, and read chapter 14 to discover more about testing techniques.

The next section is about setting up the test infrastructure: the ACME job needs a database to write to, and Spring Batch itself needs a couple of infrastructure components to launch jobs and maintain execution metadata. Let's see how to configure a lightweight test infrastructure to launch the test from an IDE.

1.6.1   *Setting up the test infrastructure*

Spring Batch needs infrastructure components configured in a Spring lightweight container. These infrastructure components act as a lightweight runtime environment to run the batch process. Setting up the batch infrastructure is a mandatory step for a batch application, which you need to do only once for all jobs living in the same Spring application context. The jobs will use the same infrastructure components to run and to store their state. These infrastructure components are the key to managing and monitoring jobs (chapter 12 covers how to monitor your Spring Batch jobs).

Spring Batch needs two infrastructure components:

- *Job repository*—To store the state of jobs (finished or currently running)
- *Job launcher*—To create the state of a job before launching it

For this test, you use the volatile job repository implementation. It's perfect for testing and prototyping because it stores execution metadata in memory. Chapter 2 covers how to set up a job repository that uses a database. The following listing shows how to configure the test infrastructure.

Listing 1.7   Spring configuration for the batch infrastructure

```xml
<?xml version="1.0" encoding="UTF-8"?>
<beans xmlns="http://www.springframework.org/schema/beans"
       xmlns:xsi="http://www.w3.org/2001/XMLSchema-instance"
       xmlns:jdbc="http://www.springframework.org/schema/jdbc"
       xsi:schemaLocation="http://www.springframework.org/schema/jdbc
       http://www.springframework.org/schema/jdbc/spring-jdbc-3.0.xsd
       http://www.springframework.org/schema/beans
       http://www.springframework.org/schema/beans/spring-beans-3.0.xsd">

  <jdbc:embedded-database id="dataSource" type="H2">        Declares and populates
    <jdbc:script location="/create-tables.sql"/>            data source
  </jdbc:embedded-database>

  <bean id="transactionManager"
        class="org.springframework.jdbc.datasource.        Declares transaction
  DataSourceTransactionManager">                            manager
    <property name="dataSource" ref="dataSource" />
  </bean>

  <bean id="jobRepository"
        class="org.springframework.batch.core.
  repository.support.MapJobRepositoryFactoryBean">          Declares job
    <property name="transactionManager"                     repository
             ref="transactionManager" />
  </bean>

  <bean id="jobLauncher"
        class="org.springframework.batch.core.launch.
  support.SimpleJobLauncher">                                Declares job
    <property name="jobRepository"                           launcher
             ref="jobRepository" />
  </bean>

  <bean class="org.springframework.jdbc.core.JdbcTemplate">
    <constructor-arg ref="dataSource" />
  </bean>

</beans>
```

This listing uses an open source in-memory database called H2; although it may look odd for an online application, it's easy to deploy and you won't have to install any database engine to work with the code samples in this chapter. And remember, this is the testing configuration; the application can use a full-blown, persistent database in production. For a more traditional relational database management system (RDBMS) setup, you could change the data source configuration to use a database like Postgre-SQL or Oracle. Listing 1.7 also runs a SQL script on the database to create the product table and configures a JdbcTemplate to check the state of the database during the test.

How does a job refer to the job repository?

You may have noticed that we say a job needs the job repository to run but we don't make any reference to the job repository bean in the job configuration. The XML step element can have its job-repository attribute refer to a job repository bean. This attribute isn't mandatory, because by default the job uses a jobRepository bean. As long as you declare a jobRepository bean of type JobRepository, you don't need to explicitly refer to it in your job configuration.

This leads us to the following best practice: when configuring a Spring Batch application, the infrastructure and job configuration should be in separate files.

> **SPLITTING INFRASTRUCTURE AND APPLICATION CONFIGURATION FILES** You should always split infrastructure and application configuration files (test-context.xml and import-products-job-context.xml in our example). This allows you to swap out the infrastructure for different environments (test, development, staging, production) and still reuse the application (job, in our case) configuration files.

In a split application configuration, the infrastructure configuration file defines the job repository and data source beans; the job configuration file defines the job and depends on the job repository and data source beans. For Spring to resolve the whole configuration properly, you must bootstrap the application context from both files.

You completed the infrastructure and job configuration in a flexible manner by splitting the configuration into an infrastructure file and a job file. Next, you make the configuration more flexible by leveraging the Spring Expression Language (SpEL) to avoid hardcoding certain settings in Spring configuration files.

1.6.2 Leveraging SpEL for configuration

Remember that part of your job configuration is hardcoded in the Spring configuration files, such as all file location settings (in bold):

```
<bean id="decompressTasklet"
      class="com.manning.sbia.ch01.batch.DecompressTasklet">
  <property name="inputResource" value="file:./input/input.zip" />
  <property name="targetDirectory" value="./work/output/" />
  <property name="targetFile" value="products.txt" />
</bean>
```

These settings aren't flexible because they can change between environments (testing and production, for example) and because rolling files might be used for the incoming archive (meaning the filename would depend on the date). An improvement is to turn these settings into parameters specified at launch time. When launching a Spring Batch job, you can provide parameters, as in the following:

```
jobLauncher.run(job, new JobParametersBuilder()
  .addString("parameter1", "value1")
  .addString("parameter2", "value2")
  .toJobParameters());
```

The good news is that you can refer to these parameters in your job configuration, which comes in handy for the DecompressTasklet and FlatFileItemReader beans, as shown in the following listing.

Listing 1.8   Referring to job parameters in the Spring configuration

```
<bean id="decompressTasklet"
      class="com.manning.sbia.ch01.batch.DecompressTasklet"          ❶ Uses step
      scope="step">                                                      scope
  <property name="inputResource"
    value="#{jobParameters['inputResource']}" />
  <property name="targetDirectory"                                   ❷ Refers to job
    value="#{jobParameters['targetDirectory']}" />                     parameters
  <property name="targetFile"
    value="#{jobParameters['targetFile']}" />
</bean>

<bean id="reader"
      class="org.springframework.batch.item.file.FlatFileItemReader"
      scope="step">                                                  ❶ Uses step
  <property name="resource"                                             scope
    value="file:#{jobParameters['targetDirectory']
  ➥ +jobParameters['targetFile']}" />
```

To be able to refer to job parameters, a bean must use the Spring Batch step scope ❶. The step scope means that Spring will create the bean only when the step asks for it and that values will be resolved then (this is the lazy instantiation pattern; the bean isn't created during the Spring application context's bootstrapping). To trigger the dynamic evaluation of a value, you must use the #{expression} syntax. The expression must be in SpEL, which is available as of Spring 3.0 (Spring Batch falls back to a less powerful language if you don't have Spring 3.0 on your class path). The job-Parameters variable behaves like a Map. That's how you refer to the inputResource, targetDirectory, and targetFile job parameters ❷. Note that you're not limited to plain references; you can also use more complex expressions; for example, notice how the target directory and file are concatenated for the resource property.

   You're done with the configuration: the job and infrastructure are ready, and part of the configuration can come from job parameters, which are set when you launch the job. It's time to write the test for your batch process.

1.6.3   *Writing the test for the job*

You use good old JUnit to write the test, with some help from the Spring testing support. The following listing shows the integration test for the job.

Listing 1.9 Integration test for the import product test

```
package com.manning.sbia.ch01.batch;

(...)

@RunWith(SpringJUnit4ClassRunner.class)
@ContextConfiguration(locations={
  "/import-products-job-context.xml",
  "/test-context.xml"
})
public class ImportProductsIntegrationTest {

  @Autowired
  private JobLauncher jobLauncher;

  @Autowired
  private Job job;

  @Autowired
  private JdbcTemplate jdbcTemplate;

  @Before
  public void setUp() throws Exception {
    jdbcTemplate.update("delete from product");        ❶ Cleans and
    jdbcTemplate.update("insert into product "+           populates
      "(id,name,description,price) values(?,?,?,?)",       database
      "PR....214","Nokia 2610 Phone","",102.23
    );
  }

  @Test
  public void importProducts() throws Exception {
    int initial = jdbcTemplate.queryForInt("select count(1) from product");
    jobLauncher.run(
      job, new JobParametersBuilder()
        .addString("inputResource",
          "classpath:/input/products.zip")
        .addString("targetDirectory",
          "./target/importproductsbatch/")    ❷ Launches job
        .addString("targetFile",                 with parameters
          "products.txt")
        .addLong("timestamp",
          System.currentTimeMillis())
        .toJobParameters()
    );
    int nbOfNewProducts = 7;
    Assert.assertEquals(
      initial+nbOfNewProducts,              ❸ Checks
      jdbcTemplate.queryForInt(                correct item
        "select count(1) from product")        insertion
    );
  }
}
```

The test uses the Spring TestContext Framework, which creates a Spring application context during the test and lets you inject some Spring beans into the test (with the @Autowired annotation). The @RunWith and @ContextConfiguration trigger the

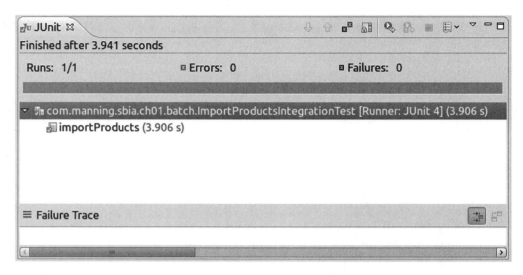

Figure 1.10   Launching the test in Eclipse. Despite all its features, Spring Batch remains lightweight, making jobs easy to test.

Spring TestContext Framework. Chapter 14 is all about testing, so give it a read if you want to learn more about this topic. At **❶**, you clean and populate the database. This creates a consistent database environment for each @Test method. At **❷**, you launch the job with its parameters and check at **❸** that the job correctly inserted the products from the test ZIP archive. The test ZIP archive doesn't have to contain thousands of records: it can be small so the test runs quickly.

You can now run the test with your favorite IDE (Eclipse, IDEA) or build tool (Maven, Ant). Figure 1.10 shows the result of the test execution in Eclipse.

That's it! You have a reliable integration test for your batch job. Wasn't it easy? Even if the job handles hundreds of thousands of records daily, you can test in an IDE in a couple of seconds.

> **NOTE**   A common requirement is launching jobs from the command line. Chapter 4 covers this topic.

The job works, great, but batch applications aren't common pieces of software: they must be bulletproof. What happens if the input file contains a badly formatted line? Could you live with your job crashing because of an extra comma? The next section covers how Spring Batch lets you skip incorrect lines instead of failing.

1.7   *Skipping incorrect lines instead of failing*

We listed the requirements for batch applications, including robustness. The import product job isn't robust yet: for example, it crashes abruptly if only a single line of the flat file is formatted incorrectly. The good news is that Spring Batch can help make the job more robust by changing the configuration or by implementing simple interfaces.

Spring Batch's features related to robustness are thoroughly covered in chapter 8. For now, we show you how to handle unexpected entries when you're reading data. By the end of this section, the import product job will be more robust and you'll have a better understanding of how Spring Batch can help improve robustness in general.

On a good day, the import product job will decompress the input archive, read each line of the extracted flat file, send data to the database, and then exit successfully. As you know, if something can go wrong, it will. For instance, if the FlatFileItemReader fails to read a single line of the flat file—because it's incorrectly formatted, for example—the job immediately stops. Perhaps this is acceptable behavior, but what if you can live with some invalid records? In this case, you could skip an invalid line and keep on chugging. Spring Batch allows you to choose declaratively a skip policy when something goes wrong. Let's apply a skip policy to your job's import step.

Suppose a line of the flat file hasn't been generated correctly, like the price (in bold) of the third product in the following snippet:

```
PRODUCT_ID,NAME,DESCRIPTION,PRICE
PR....210,BlackBerry 8100 Pearl,,124.60
PR....211,Sony Ericsson W810i,,139.45
PR....212,Samsung MM-A900M Ace,,97,80
PR....213,Toshiba M285-E 14,,166.20
```

The format of the price field of the third record is incorrect: is uses a comma instead of a period as the decimal separator. Note that the comma is the field separator Spring Batch uses to tokenize input lines: the framework would see five fields where it expects only four. The FlatFileItemReader throws a FlatFileParseException and, in the default configuration, Spring Batch immediately stops the process.

Assuming you can live with skipping some records instead of failing the whole job, you can change the job configuration to keep on reading when the reader throws a FlatFileParseException, as shown in the following listing.

Listing 1.10 Setting the skip policy when reading records from the flat file

```xml
<job id="importProducts"
     xmlns="http://www.springframework.org/schema/batch">
  <step id="decompress" next="readWriteProducts">
    <tasklet ref="decompressTasklet" />
  </step>
  <step id="readWriteProducts">
    <tasklet>
      <chunk reader="reader" writer="writer" commit-interval="100"
          skip-limit="5">
        <skippable-exception-classes>
          <include class="org.springframework.batch.
          item.file.FlatFileParseException" />
        </skippable-exception-classes>
      </chunk>
    </tasklet>
  </step>
</job>
```

❶ Fails job if Spring Batch skips five records

❷ Skips flat file parse exceptions

The skip policy is set in the chunk element. The skip-limit attribute ❶ is set to tell Spring Batch to stop the job when the number of skipped records in the step exceeds this limit. Your application can be tolerant, but not too tolerant! Then, the exception classes that trigger a skip are stated ❷. Chapter 8 details all the options of the skippable-exception-classes element. Here, we want to skip the offending line when the item reader throws a FlatFileParseException.

You can now launch the job with an input file containing incorrectly formatted lines, and you'll see that Spring Batch keeps on running the job as long as the number of skipped items doesn't exceed the skip limit. Assuming the ZIP archive contains incorrect lines, you can add a test method to your test, as shown in the following listing.

Listing 1.11   Testing the job correctly skips incorrect lines with a new test method

```
@RunWith(SpringJUnit4ClassRunner.class)
@ContextConfiguration(locations={"/import-products-job-context.xml","/test-
    context.xml"})
public class ImportProductsIntegrationTest {
  (...)
  @Test
  public void importProductsWithErrors() throws Exception {
    int initial = jdbcTemplate.queryForInt("select count(1) from product");

    jobLauncher.run(job, new JobParametersBuilder()
      .addString("inputResource",
        "classpath:/input/products_with_errors.zip")
      .addString("targetDirectory", "./target/importproductsbatch/")
      .addString("targetFile","products.txt")
      .addLong("timestamp", System.currentTimeMillis())
      .toJobParameters()
    );
    int nbOfNewProducts = 6;
    Assert.assertEquals(
      initial+nbOfNewProducts,
      jdbcTemplate.queryForInt("select count(1) from product")
    );
  }

}
```

Note that this code doesn't do any processing when something goes wrong, but you could choose to log that a line was incorrectly formatted. Spring Batch also provides hooks to handle errors (see chapter 8).

This completes the bullet-proofing of the product import job. The job executes quickly and efficiently, and it's more robust and reacts accordingly to unexpected events such as invalid input records.

That's it—you've implemented a full-blown job with Spring Batch! This shows how Spring Batch provides a powerful framework to create batch jobs and handles the heavy lifting like file I/O. Your main tasks were to write a couple of Java classes and do some XML configuration. That's the philosophy: focus on the business logic and Spring Batch handles the rest.

1.8 *Summary*

This chapter started with an overview of batch applications: handling large amounts of data automatically. The immediate requirements are performance, reliability, and robustness. Meeting these requirements is tricky, and this is where Spring Batch comes in, by processing data efficiently thanks to its chunk-oriented approach and providing ready-to-use components for the most popular technologies and formats.

After the introduction of batch applications and Spring Batch, the import product job gave you a good overview of what the framework can do. You discovered Spring Batch's sweet spot—chunk processing—by reading records from a flat file and writing them to a database. You used built-in components like the `FlatFileItemReader` class and implemented a database `ItemWriter` for business domain code. Remember that Spring Batch handles the plumbing and lets you focus on the business code. You also saw that Spring Batch isn't limited to chunk processing when you implemented a `Tasklet` to decompress a ZIP file.

Configuring the job ended up being quite simple thanks to the Spring lightweight container and Spring Batch XML. You even saw how to write an automated integration test. Finally, you learned how to make the job more robust by dealing with invalid data.

You're now ready to implement your first Spring Batch job. With this chapter under your belt, you can jump to any other chapter in this book when you need information to use a specific Spring Batch feature: reading and writing components, writing bulletproof jobs with skip and restart, or making your jobs scale. You can also continue on to chapter 2, where we present the Spring Batch vocabulary and the benefits it brings to your applications.

Spring Batch concepts

This chapter covers

- Defining the domain language
- Surveying infrastructure components
- Modeling jobs
- Understanding job execution

Chapter 1 introduced Spring Batch with some hands-on examples. You saw how to implement a batch process from soup to nuts: from business requirements to the batch implementation and finally to running the process. This introduction got you started with Spring Batch and gave you a good overview of the framework's features. It's time to strengthen this newly acquired knowledge by diving into batch applications concepts and their associated vocabulary, or *domain language*.

Batch applications are complex entities that refer to many components, so in this chapter we use the Spring Batch domain language to analyze, model, and define the components of batch applications. This vocabulary is a great communication tool for us in this book but also for you, your team, and your own batch applications. We first explore Spring Batch's services and built-in infrastructure components for batch applications: the job launcher and job repository. Then, we

32

dive into the heart of the batch process: the job. Finally, we study how to model a Spring Batch job and how the framework handles job execution.

By the end of this chapter, you'll know how Spring Batch models batch applications and what services the framework provides to implement and execute jobs. All these concepts lay the foundation for efficient configuration and runtime behavior as well as for features like job restart. These concepts form the starting point for you to unleash the power of Spring Batch.

2.1 The batch domain language

In chapter 1, we used many technical terms without proper definitions. We wrote this book with a gentle introduction and without overwhelming you with a large first helping of concepts and definitions. We introduced Spring Batch from a practical point of view. Now it's time to step back and take a more formal approach. Don't worry: we'll make this short and sweet.

In this section, we define the batch domain language: we pick apart the batch application ecosystem and define each of its elements. Naming can be hard, but we use some analysis already provided by the Spring Batch project itself. Let's start by looking at the benefits of using a domain language for our batch applications.

2.1.1 Why use a domain language?

Using well-defined terminology in your batch applications helps you model, enforce best practices, and communicate with others. If there's a word for something, it means the corresponding concept matters and is part of the world of batch applications. By analyzing your business requirements and all the elements of the batch ecosystem, you find matches, which help you design your batch applications.

In our introduction to chunk processing in chapter 1, we identified the main components of a typical batch process: the reader, the processor, and the writer. By using the chunk-processing pattern in your applications, you also structure your code with readers, processors, and writers. The good news about chunk processing is that it's a pattern well suited for batch applications, and it's a best practice in terms of memory consumption and performance.

Another benefit of using the domain language is that by following the model it promotes, you're more likely to enforce best practices. That doesn't mean you'll end up with perfect batch applications, but at least you should avoid the most common pitfalls and benefit from years of experience in batch processing.

At the very least, you'll have a common vocabulary to use with other people working on batch applications. This greatly improves communication and avoids confusion. You'll be able to switch projects or companies without having to learn a brand new vocabulary for the same concepts.

Now that you're aware of the benefits of using a domain language to work with batch applications, let's define some Spring Batch concepts.

2.1.2 *Main components of the domain language*

In this subsection, we focus on the core components of Spring Batch applications, and the next subsection covers external components that communicate with Spring Batch applications. Figure 2.1 shows the main Spring Batch components. The figure shows two kinds of Spring Batch components: infrastructure components and application components. The infrastructure components are the job repository and the job launcher. Spring Batch provides implementations for both—and you do need to configure these components—but there's little chance you'll have to create your own implementations.

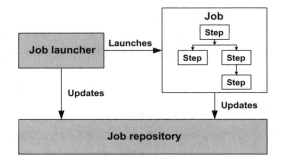

Figure 2.1   The main Spring Batch components. The framework provides a job repository to store job metadata and a job launcher to launch jobs, and the application developer configures and implements jobs. The infrastructure components—provided by Spring Batch—are in gray, and application components—implemented by the developer—are in white.

The application components in Spring Batch are the job and its constituent parts. From the previous chapter you know that Spring Batch provides components like item readers and item writers you only need to configure and that it's common to implement your own logic. Writing batch jobs with Spring Batch is a combination of Spring configuration and Java programming.

Figure 2.1 painted the big picture; table 2.1 gives a more comprehensive list of the components of a Spring Batch application and their interactions.

Table 2.1   The main components of a Spring Batch application

Component	Description
Job repository	An infrastructure component that persists job execution metadata
Job launcher	An infrastructure component that starts job executions
Job	An application component that represents a batch process
Step	A phase in a job; a job is a sequence of steps
Tasklet	A transactional, potentially repeatable process occurring in a step
Item	A record read from or written to a data source
Chunk	A list of items of a given size
Item reader	A component responsible for reading items from a data source
Item processor	A component responsible for processing (transforming, validating, or filtering) a read item before it's written
Item writer	A component responsible for writing a chunk to a data source

Going forward from this point, we use the terms listed in table 2.1. The remainder of this chapter describes the concepts behind these terms, but first we see how the components of a Spring Batch application interact with the outside world.

2.1.3 How Spring Batch interacts with the outside world

A batch application isn't an island: it needs to interact with the outside world just like any enterprise application. Figure 2.2 shows how a Spring Batch application interacts with the outside world.

A job starts in response to an event. You'll always use the `JobLauncher` interface and `JobParameters` class, but the event can come from anywhere: a system scheduler like cron that runs periodically, a script that launches a Spring Batch process, an HTTP request to a web controller that launches the job, and so on. Chapter 4 covers different scenarios to trigger the launch of your Spring Batch jobs.

Batch jobs are about processing data, and that's why figure 2.2 shows Spring Batch communicating with data sources. These data sources can be of any kind, the file system and a database being the most common, but a job can read and write messages to Java Message Service (JMS) queues as well.

> **NOTE** Jobs can communicate with data sources, but so does the job repository. In fact, the job repository stores job execution metadata in a database to provide Spring Batch reliable monitoring and restart features.

Note that figure 2.2 doesn't show whether Spring Batch needs to run in a specific container. Chapter 4 says more about this topic, but for now, you just need to know that Spring Batch can run anywhere the Spring Framework can run: in its own Java process, in a web container, in an application, or even in an Open Services Gateway initiative (OSGi) container. The container depends on your requirements, and Spring Batch is flexible in this regard.

Now that you know more about Spring Batch's core components and how they interact with each other and the outside world, let's focus on the framework's infrastructure components: the job launcher and the job repository.

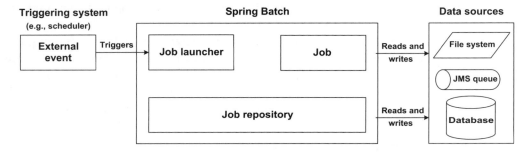

Figure 2.2 A Spring Batch application interacts with systems like schedulers and data sources (databases, files, or JMS queues).

2.2   *The Spring Batch infrastructure*

The Spring Batch infrastructure includes components that launch your batch jobs and store job execution metadata. As a batch application developer, you don't have to deal directly with these components, as they provide supporting roles to your applications, but you need to configure this infrastructure at least once in your Spring Batch application.

This section gives an overview of the job launcher, job repository, and their interactions, and then shows how to configure persistence of the job repository.

2.2.1   *Launching jobs and storing job metadata*

The Spring Batch infrastructure is complex, but you need to deal mainly with two components: the job launcher and the job repository. These concepts match two straightforward Java interfaces: `JobLauncher` and `JobRepository`.

THE JOB LAUNCHER

As figure 2.2 shows, the job launcher is the entry point to launch Spring Batch jobs: this is where the external world meets Spring Batch. The `JobLauncher` interface is simple:

```
package org.springframework.batch.core.launch;

(...)

public interface JobLauncher {

 public JobExecution run(Job job, JobParameters jobParameters)
    throws JobExecutionAlreadyRunningException,
        JobRestartException, JobInstanceAlreadyCompleteException,
        JobParametersInvalidException;

}
```

The `run` method accepts two parameters: `Job`, which is typically a Spring bean configured in Spring Batch XML, and `JobParameters`, which is usually created on the fly by the launching mechanism.

Who calls the job launcher? Your own Java program can use the job launcher to launch a job, but so can command-line programs or schedulers (like cron or the Java-based Quartz scheduler).

The job launcher encapsulates launching strategies such as executing a job synchronously or asynchronously. Spring Batch provides one implementation of the `JobLauncher` interface: `SimpleJobLauncher`. We look at configuring `SimpleJobLauncher` in chapter 3 and at fine-tuning in chapter 4. For now, it's sufficient to know that the `SimpleJobLauncher` class only launches a job—it doesn't create it but delegates this work to the job repository.

THE JOB REPOSITORY

The job repository maintains all metadata related to job executions. Here's the definition of the `JobRepository` interface:

```
package org.springframework.batch.core.repository;

(...)

public interface JobRepository {

  boolean isJobInstanceExists(String jobName, JobParameters jobParameters);

  JobExecution createJobExecution(
    String jobName, JobParameters jobParameters)
      throws JobExecutionAlreadyRunningException, JobRestartException,
           JobInstanceAlreadyCompleteException;

  void update(JobExecution jobExecution);

  void add(StepExecution stepExecution);

  void update(StepExecution stepExecution);

  void updateExecutionContext(StepExecution stepExecution);

  void updateExecutionContext(JobExecution jobExecution);

  StepExecution getLastStepExecution(JobInstance jobInstance,
    String stepName);

  int getStepExecutionCount(JobInstance jobInstance, String stepName);

  JobExecution getLastJobExecution(String jobName,
    JobParameters jobParameters);

}
```

The JobRepository interface provides all the services to manage the batch job lifecycle: creation, update, and so on. This explains the interactions in figure 2.2: the job launcher delegates job creation to the job repository, and a job calls the job repository during execution to store its current state. This is useful to monitor how your job executions proceed and to restart a job exactly where it failed. Note that the Spring Batch runtime handles all calls to the job repository, meaning that persistence of the job execution metadata is transparent to the application code.

What constitutes runtime metadata? It includes the list of executed steps; how many items Spring Batch read, wrote, or skipped; the duration of each step; and so forth. We won't list all metadata here; you'll learn more when we study the anatomy of a job in section 2.3.

Spring Batch provides two implementations of the JobRepository interface: one stores metadata in memory, which is useful for testing or when you don't want monitoring or restart capabilities; the other stores metadata in a relational database. Next, we see how to configure the Spring Batch infrastructure in a database.

2.2.2 *Configuring the Spring Batch infrastructure in a database*

Spring Batch provides a job repository implementation to store your job metadata in a database. This allows you to monitor the execution of your batch processes and their results (success or failure). Persistent metadata also makes it possible to restart a job exactly where it failed.

Configuring this persistent job repository helps illustrate the other concepts in this chapter, which are detailed in chapter 3.

Spring Batch delivers the following to support persistent job repositories:

- SQL scripts to create the necessary database tables for the most popular database engines
- A database implementation of JobRepository (SimpleJobRepository) that executes all necessary SQL statements to insert, update, and query the job repository tables

Let's now see how to configure the database job repository.

CREATING THE DATABASE TABLES FOR A JOB REPOSITORY

The SQL scripts to create the database tables are located in the core Spring Batch JAR file (for example, spring-batch-core-2.1.x.jar, depending on the minor version of the framework you're using) in the org.springframework.batch.core package. The SQL scripts use the following naming convention: schema-[database].sql for creating tables and schema-drop-[database].sql for dropping tables, where [database] is the name of a database engine. To initialize H2 for Spring Batch, we use the file schema-h2.sql.

> **Spring Batch database support**
>
> Spring Batch supports the following database engines: DB2, Derby, H2, HSQLDB, MySQL, Oracle, PostgreSQL, SQLServer, and Sybase.

All you have to do is create a database for Spring Batch and then execute the corresponding SQL script for your database engine.

CONFIGURING THE JOB REPOSITORY WITH SPRING

We already configured a job repository bean in chapter 1, but it was in an in-memory implementation (H2). The following listing shows how to configure a job repository in a database.

Listing 2.1   Configuration of a persistent job repository

```xml
<?xml version="1.0" encoding="UTF-8"?>
<beans xmlns="http://www.springframework.org/schema/beans"
  xmlns:xsi="http://www.w3.org/2001/XMLSchema-instance"
  xmlns:batch="http://www.springframework.org/schema/batch"
  xsi:schemaLocation="http://www.springframework.org/schema/beans
    http://www.springframework.org/schema/beans/spring-beans-3.0.xsd
    http://www.springframework.org/schema/batch
    http://www.springframework.org/schema/batch/spring-batch-2.1.xsd">

  <batch:job-repository id="jobRepository"
    data-source="dataSource"
    transaction-manager="transactionManager" />

  <bean id="jobLauncher"
    class="org.springframework.batch.core.launch.support.SimpleJobLauncher">
    <property name="jobRepository" ref="jobRepository" />
```

① Declares persistent job repository

```
    </bean>

    <bean id="dataSource"
        class="org.springframework.jdbc.datasource.
➡ SingleConnectionDataSource">
      <property name="driverClassName"
        value="org.h2.Driver" />
      <property name="url" value="
➡ jdbc:h2:mem:sbia_ch02;DB_CLOSE_DELAY=-1" />
      <property name="username" value="sa" />
      <property name="password" value="" />
      <property name="suppressClose" value="true" />
    </bean>

    <bean id="transactionManager" class="org.springframework.jdbc.datasource.
➡ DataSourceTransactionManager">
      <property name="dataSource" ref="dataSource" />
    </bean>

  </beans>
```

❷ **Declares data source**

The job-repository XML element in the batch namespace creates a persistent job repository ❶. To work properly, the persistent job repository needs a data source and a transaction manager. A data source implementation ❷ that holds a single JDBC connection and reuses it for each query is used because it's convenient and good enough for a single-threaded application (like a batch process). If you plan to use the data source in a concurrent application, then use a connection pool, like Apache Commons DBCP or c3p0. Using a persistent job repository doesn't change much in the Spring Batch infrastructure configuration: you use the same job launcher implementation as in the in-memory configuration.

Now that the persistent job repository is ready, let's take a closer look at it.

ACCESSING JOB METADATA

If you look at the job repository database, you see that the SQL script created six tables. If you want to see how Spring Batch populates these tables, launch the Launch-DatabaseAndConsole class and then the GeneratesJobMetaData class (in the source code from this book). The latter class launches a job several times to populate the batch metadata tables. (Don't worry if you see an exception in the console: we purposely fail one job execution.) We analyze the content of the job repository later in this chapter because it helps to explain how Spring Batch manages job execution, but if you're impatient to see the content of the batch tables, read the next note.

> **NOTE** The LaunchDatabaseAndConsole class provided with the source code of this book starts an in-memory H2 database and the HTTP-based H2 Console Server. You can access the Console Server at http://127.0.1.1:8082/ and provide the URL of the database: jdbc:h2:tcp://localhost/mem:sbia_ch02. The Console Server then provides the default username and password to log in. You can see that Spring Batch created all the necessary tables in the database (take a look at the root-database-context.xml file to discover how). Keep in mind that this is an in-memory database, so stopping the program will cause all data to be lost!

Figure 2.3 shows how you can use the Spring Batch Admin web application to view job executions. Spring Batch Admin accesses the job repository tables to provide this functionality.

What is Spring Batch Admin?

Spring Batch Admin is an open source project from SpringSource that provides a web-based UI for Spring Batch applications. We cover Spring Batch Admin in chapter 12, where we discuss Spring Batch application monitoring. Appendix B covers the installation of Spring Batch Admin. You'll also see more of Spring Batch Admin in this chapter when you use it to browse batch execution metadata.

We now have a persistent job repository, which we use to illustrate forthcoming runtime concepts. You have enough knowledge of the in-memory and persistent implementations of the job repository to compare them and see which best suits your needs.

CONSIDERATIONS ON JOB REPOSITORY IMPLEMENTATIONS

Spring Batch users sometimes see the persistent job repository as a constraint because it means creating dedicated Spring Batch tables in a database. They prefer to fall back on the in-memory job repository implementation, which is more flexible. These users don't always realize the consequences of using the in-memory implementation. Let's answer some frequently asked questions about the various job repository implementations.

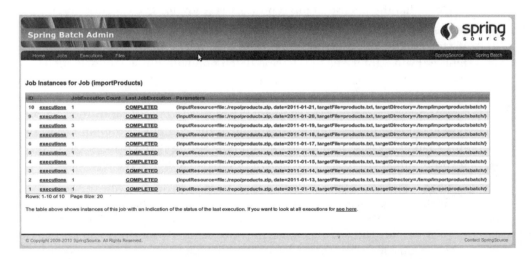

Figure 2.3 The Spring Batch Admin web application lists all job instances for a given job, in this case, import products. Spring Batch Admin uses job metadata stored in a database to monitor job executions.

- *Can I use the in-memory job repository in production?* You should avoid doing that; the in-memory job repository is meant for development and testing. Some people run the in-memory job repository successfully in production because it works correctly under specific conditions (it isn't designed for concurrent access, when multiple jobs can run at the same time). If you get errors with the in-memory job repository and if you really don't want to create batch tables in your database, use the *persistent* job repository with an *in-memory database* (like H2 or Derby).

- *What are the benefits of the persistent job repository?* The benefits are monitoring, restart, and clustering. You can browse the batch execution metadata to monitor your batch executions. When a job fails, the execution metadata is still available, and you can use it to restart the job where it left off. The persistent job repository, thanks to the isolation the database provides, prevents launching the exact same job from multiple nodes at the same time. Consider the persistent job repository as a safeguard against concurrency issues when creating batch entities in the database.

- *Does the persistent job repository add overhead?* Compared to the in-memory job repository, yes. Communicating with a potentially remote database is always more costly than speaking to local in-memory objects. But the overhead is usually small compared to the actual business processing. The benefits the persistent job repository brings to batch applications are worth the limited overhead!

- *Can I use a different database for the persistent job repository and my business data?* Yes, but be careful with transaction management. You can use the Java Transaction API (JTA) to make transactions span both databases: the batch tables and the business tables will always be synchronized, but you'll add overhead because managing multiple transactional resources is more expensive than managing just one. If transactions don't span the two databases, batch execution metadata and business data can get unsynchronized on failure. Data such as skipped items could then become inaccurate, or you could see problems on restart. To make your life easier (and your jobs faster and reliable), store the batch metadata in the same database as the business data.

This completes our coverage of the job repository. Let's dive into the structural and runtime aspects of the core Spring Batch concept: the job.

2.3 Anatomy of a job

The job is the central concept in a batch application: it's the batch process itself. A job has two aspects that we examine in this section: a static aspect used for job modeling and a dynamic aspect used for runtime job management. Spring Batch provides a well-defined model for jobs and includes tools—such as Spring Batch XML— to configure this model. Spring Batch also provides a strong runtime foundation to execute and dynamically manage jobs. This foundation provides a reliable way to control which instance of a job Spring Batch executes and the ability to restart a job where it failed. This section explains these two job aspects: static modeling and dynamic runtime.

2.3.1 *Modeling jobs with steps*

A Spring Batch job is a sequence of steps configured in Spring Batch XML. Let's delve into these concepts and see what they bring to your batch applications.

MODELING A JOB

Recall from chapter 1 that the import products job consists of two steps: decompress the incoming archive and import the records from the expanded file into the database. We could also add a cleanup step to delete the expanded file. Figure 2.4 depicts this job and its three successive steps.

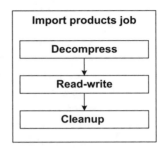

Decomposing a job into steps is cleaner from both a modeling and a pragmatic perspective because steps are easier to test and maintain than is one monolithic job. Jobs can also reuse steps; for example, you can reuse the decompress step from the import products job in any job that needs to decompress an archive—you only need to change the configuration.

Figure 2.4   A Spring Batch job is a sequence of steps, such as this import products job, which includes three steps: decompress, read-write, and cleanup.

Figure 2.4 shows a job built of three successive linear steps, but the sequence of steps doesn't have to be linear, as in figure 2.5, which shows a more advanced version of the import products job. This version generates and sends a report to an administrator if the read-write step skipped records.

To decide which path a job takes, Spring Batch allows for control flow decisions based on the status of the previous step (completed, failed) or based on custom logic

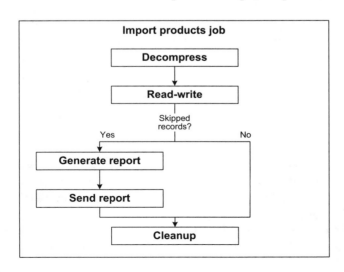

Figure 2.5   A Spring Batch job can be a nonlinear sequence of steps, like this version of the import products job, which sends a report if some records were skipped.

(by checking the content of a database table, for example). You can then create jobs with complex control flows that react appropriately to any kind of condition (missing files, skipped records, and so on). Control flow brings flexibility and robustness to your jobs because you can choose the level of control complexity that best suits any given job.

The unpleasant alternative would be to split a big, monolithic job into a set of smaller jobs and try to orchestrate them with a scheduler using exit codes, files, or some other means.

You also benefit from a clear separation of concerns between processing (implemented in steps) and execution flow, configured declaratively or implemented in dedicated decision components. You have less temptation to implement transition logic in steps and thus tightly couple steps with each other.

Let's see some job configuration examples.

CONFIGURING A JOB

Spring Batch provides an XML vocabulary to configure steps within a job. The following listing shows the code for the linear version of the import products job.

Listing 2.2 Configuring a job with linear flow

```
<job id="importProductsJob">
  <step id="decompress" next="readWrite">
    <tasklet ref="decompressTasklet" />
  </step>
  <step id="readWrite" next="clean">
    <tasklet>
      <chunk reader="reader" writer="writer"
        commit-interval="100" />
    </tasklet>
  </step>
  <step id="clean">
    <tasklet ref="cleanTasklet" />
  </step>
</job>
```

The next attribute of the step tag sets the execution flow, by pointing to the next step to execute. Tags like tasklet or chunk can refer to Spring beans with appropriate attributes.

When a job is made of a linear sequence of steps, using the next attribute of the step elements is enough to connect the job steps. The next listing shows the configuration for the nonlinear version of the import products job from figure 2.5.

Listing 2.3 Configuring a job with nonlinear flow

```
<job id="importProductsJob"
    xmlns="http://www.springframework.org/schema/batch">
  <step id="decompress" next="readWrite">
    <tasklet ref="decompressTasklet" />
  </step>
  <step id="readWrite" next="skippedDecision">          <--- Refers to flow decision logic
```

```
    <tasklet>
      <chunk reader="reader" writer="writer" commit-interval="100" />
    </tasklet>
  </step>
  <decision id="skippedDecision"                        Defines decision
          decider="skippedDecider">                     logic
    <next on="SKIPPED" to="generateReport"/>
    <next on="*" to="clean" />
  </decision>
  <step id="generateReport" next="sendReport">
    <tasklet ref="generateReportTasklet" />
  </step>
  <step id="sendReport" next="clean">
    <tasklet ref="sendReportTasklet" />
  </step>
  <step id="clean">
    <tasklet ref="cleanTasklet" />
  </step>
</job>

<bean id="skippedDecider"
      class="com.manning.sbia.ch02.structure.
   ➥ SkippedDecider" />
```

NOTE Chapter 10 covers the decider XML element, the corresponding JobExecutionDecider interface, and the job execution flow. We introduce these concepts here only to illustrate the structure of a Spring Batch job.

Notice from the previous XML fragment that Spring Batch XML is expressive enough to allow job configuration to be human readable. If your editor supports XML, you also benefit from code completion and code validation when editing your XML job configuration. An integrated development environment like the Eclipse-based Spring-Source Tool Suite also provides a graphical view of a job configuration, as shown in figure 2.6. To get this graph, open the corresponding XML file and select the Batch-Graph tab at the bottom of the editor.

NOTE The SpringSource Tool Suite is a free Eclipse-based product that provides tooling for Spring applications (code completion for Spring XML files, bean graphs, and much more). It also provides support for projects in the Spring portfolio like Spring Batch. Appendix A covers how to install and use the SpringSource Tool Suite for Spring Batch applications.

We won't go into further details here of configuration and execution flow, as chapters 3 and 10 respectively cover these topics thoroughly. Now that you know that a Spring Batch job is a sequence of steps and that you can control job flow, let's see what makes up a step.

PROCESSING WITH TASKLETSTEP

Spring Batch defines the Step interface to embody the concept of a step and provides implementations like FlowStep, JobStep, PartitionStep, and TaskletStep. The only implementation you care about as an application developer is TaskletStep, which delegates processing to a Tasklet object. As you discovered in chapter 1, the Tasklet

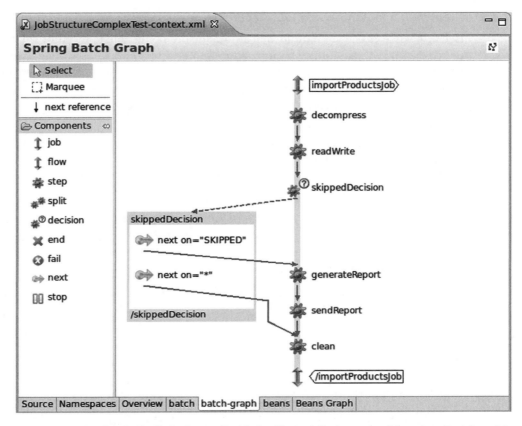

Figure 2.6 **A job flow in the SpringSource Tool Suite. The tool displays a graph based on the job model defined in Spring Batch XML.**

Java interface contains only one method, `execute`, to process some unit of work. Creating a step consists of either writing a `Tasklet` implementation or using one provided by Spring Batch.

You implement your own `Tasklet` when you need to perform processing, such as decompressing files, calling a stored procedure, or deleting temporary files at the end of a job.

If your step follows the classic read-process-write batch pattern, use the Spring Batch XML chunk element to configure it as a chunk-processing step. The chunk element allows your step to use chunks to efficiently read, process, and write data.

NOTE The Spring Batch chunk element is mapped to a `Tasklet` implemented by the `ChunkOrientedTasklet` class.

You now know that a job is a sequence of steps and that you can easily define this sequence in Spring Batch XML. You implement steps with `Tasklets`, which are either chunk oriented or completely customized. Let's move on to the runtime.

2.3.2 *Running job instances and job executions*

Because batch processes handle data automatically, being able to monitor what they're doing or what they've done is a must. When something goes wrong, you need to decide whether to restart a job from the beginning or from where it failed. To do this, you need to strictly define the identity of a job run and reliably store everything the job does during its run. This is a difficult task, but Spring Batch handles it all for you.

THE JOB, JOB INSTANCE, AND JOB EXECUTION

We defined a *job* as a batch process composed of a sequence of steps. Spring Batch also includes the concepts of *job instance* and *job execution*, both related to the way the framework handles jobs at runtime. Table 2.2 defines these concepts and provides examples.

Table 2.2 Definitions for job, job instance, and job execution

Term	Description	Example
Job	A batch process, or sequence of steps	The import products job
Job instance	A specific run of a job	The import products job run on June 27, 2010
Job execution	The execution of a job instance (with success or failure)	The first run of the import products job on June 27, 2010

Figure 2.7 illustrates the correspondence between a job, its instances, and their executions for two days of executions of the import products job.

Now that we've defined the relationship between job, job instance, and job execution, let's see how to define a job instance in Spring Batch.

DEFINING A JOB INSTANCE

In Spring Batch, a job instance consists of a job and job parameters. When we speak about the June 27, 2010, instance of our import products job, the date is the parameter that defines the job instance (along with the job itself). This is a simple yet powerful

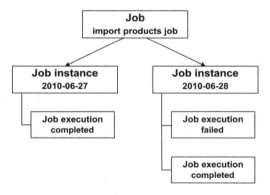

Figure 2.7 A job can have several job instances, which can have several job executions. The import products job executes daily, so it should have one instance per day and one or more corresponding executions, depending on success or failure.

way to define a job instance, because you have full control over the job parameters, as shown in the following snippet:

```
jobLauncher.run(job, new JobParametersBuilder()
  .addString("date", "2010-06-27")
  .toJobParameters()
);
```

As a Spring Batch developer, you must keep in mind how to uniquely define a job instance.

JOB INSTANCE A job instance consists of a job and job parameters. We define this contract with the following equation: `JobInstance = Job + Job-Parameters`.

The previous equation is important to remember. In our example, a job instance is temporal, as it refers to the day it was launched. But you're free to choose what parameters constitute your job instances thanks to job parameters: date, time, input files, or simple sequence counter.

What happens if you try to run the same job several times with the same parameters? It depends on the lifecycle of job instances and job executions.

THE LIFECYCLE OF A JOB INSTANCE AND JOB EXECUTION

Several rules apply to the lifecycle of a job instance and job execution:

- When you launch a job for the first time, Spring Batch creates the corresponding job instance and a first job execution.
- You can't launch the execution of a job instance if a previous execution of the same instance has already completed successfully.
- You can't launch multiple executions of the same instance at the same time.

We hope that by now all these concepts are clear. As an illustration, let's perform runs of the import products job and analyze the job metadata that Spring Batch stores in the database.

MULTIPLE RUNS OF THE IMPORT PRODUCTS JOB

The import products job introduced in chapter 1 is supposed to run once a day to import all the new and updated products from the catalog system. To see how Spring Batch updates the job metadata in the persistent job repository previously configured, make the following sequence of runs:

- Run the job for June 27, 2010. The run will succeed.
- Run the job a second time for June 27, 2010. Spring Batch shouldn't launch the job again because it's already completed for this date.
- Run the job for June 28, 2010, with a corrupted archive. The run will fail.
- Run the job for June 28, 2010, with a valid archive. The run will succeed.

Starting the database:

Step 1 Launch the `LaunchDatabaseAndConsole` program.

Running the job for June 27, 2010:

Step 1 Copy the products.zip file from the input directory into the root directory of the ch02 project.

Step 2 Run the `LaunchImportProductsJob` class: this launches the job for June 27, 2010.

Step 3 Run the `LaunchSpringBatchAdmin` program from the code samples to start an embedded web container with the Spring Batch Admin application running.

Step 4 View instances of the import products job at the following URL: http://
localhost:8080/springbatchadmin/jobs/importProducts. Figure 2.8 shows
the graphical interface with the job instances and the job repository created for this run.

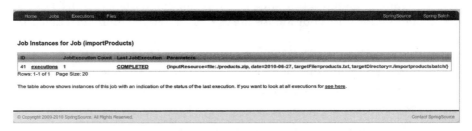

**Figure 2.8   After the run for June 27, 2010, Spring Batch created a job instance in the job
repository. The instance is marked as COMPLETED and is the first and only execution to complete
successfully.**

Step 3 Follow the links from the Job Instances view to get to the details of the corresponding execution, as shown in figure 2.9.

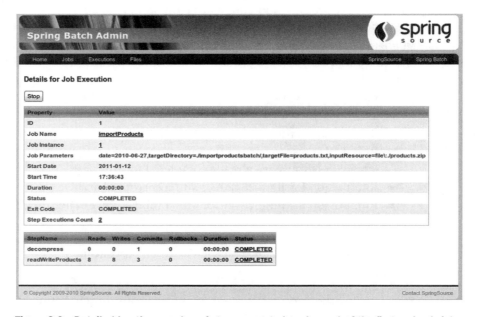

**Figure 2.9   Details (duration, number of steps executed, and so on) of the first and only job
execution for June 27, 2010. You can also learn about the job instance because the job
parameters appear in the table.**

NOTE You must check the job parameters to be sure of the execution
identity. For example, the date job parameter tells you that this is an
execution of the June 27, 2010, instance. The Start Date attribute indicates exactly when the job ran.

Running the job a second time for June 27, 2010:

Step 1 Run the `LaunchImportProductsJob` class. You get an exception because an execution already completed successfully, so you can't launch another execution of the same instance.

Running the job for June 28, 2010, with a corrupted archive:

Step 1 Delete the products.zip file and the importproductsbatch directory created to decompress the archive.

Step 2 Copy the products_corrupted.zip from the input directory into the root of the project and rename it products.zip.

Step 3 Simulate launching the job for June 28, 2010, by changing the job parameters in `LaunchImportProductsJob`; for example:

```
jobLauncher.run(job, new JobParametersBuilder()
  .addString("inputResource", "file:./products.zip")
  .addString("targetDirectory", "./importproductsbatch/")
  .addString("targetFile","products.txt")
  .addString("date", "2010-06-28")
  .toJobParameters()
);
```

Step 4 Run the `LaunchImportProductsJob` class. You get an exception saying that nothing can be extracted from the archive (the archive is corrupted).

Step 5 Go to http://localhost:8080/springbatchadmin/jobs/importProducts, and you'll see that the import products job has another instance, but this time the execution failed.

Running the job for June 28, 2010 with a valid archive:

Step 1 Replace the corrupted archive with the correct file (the same as for the first run).

Step 2 Launch the job again.

Step 3 Check in Spring Batch Admin that the instance for June 28, 2010, has completed. Figure 2.10 shows the two executions of the June 28, 2010, instance.

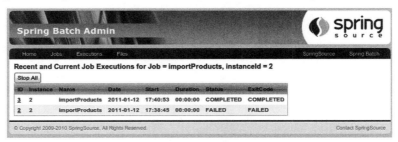

Figure 2.10 The two June 28, 2010, executions. The first failed because of a corrupted archive, but the second completed successfully, thereby completing the job instance.

NOTE To run the tests from scratch after you run the job several times, stop and restart the `LaunchDatabaseAndConsole` class.

You just put into practice the concepts of job instance and job execution. To do so, you used a persistent job repository, which allowed you to visualize job instances and executions. In this example, job metadata illustrated the concepts, but you can also use this metadata for monitoring a production system. The metadata is also essential to restart a failed job—a topic covered in depth in chapter 8.

2.1   *Summary*

This chapter is rich in Spring Batch concepts and terminology! Using a now well-defined vocabulary, you can paint a clear picture of your batch applications. You learned how the Spring Batch framework models these concepts, an important requirement to understanding how to implement batch solutions. You saw the static and dynamic aspects of jobs: static by modeling and configuring jobs with steps, dynamic through the job runtime handling of job instances and executions. Restarting failed jobs is an important requirement for some batch applications, and you saw how Spring Batch implements this feature by storing job execution metadata; you also saw the possibilities and limitations of this mechanism.

With this picture of the Spring Batch model in mind, let's move on to the next chapter and see how to configure our batch applications with the Spring lightweight container and Spring Batch XML.

Part 2

Core Spring Batch

Part 2 starts where part 1 left off. By now, you have a good understanding of what Spring Batch is capable of, so it's time to exhaustively cover the framework.

Chapter 3 is about configuration: how to configure jobs, steps in jobs, listeners, and infrastructure components like the job repository. You can use this chapter as a reference for the XML syntax and the annotations you can use to configure Spring Batch. You can also use this chapter to discover every single piece of Spring Batch configuration.

Chapter 4 covers how to launch batch jobs. There are myriads of ways to launch batch jobs, depending on your requirements and the systems you're working on. Chapter 4 shows how to launch Spring Batch jobs from the command line and from HTTP requests. It also shows you how to schedule the execution of jobs with the system scheduler cron and with a Java-based scheduler like Spring Scheduling. You'll also see how to stop jobs properly.

Do you remember chunk-oriented processing? This is the way Spring Batch efficiently handles the classical read-process-write pattern in batch applications. Chapters 5, 6, and 7 thoroughly cover each phase of chunk-oriented processing.

Chapter 5 is about reading. You'll learn how to configure ready-to-use components to read from different data sources: JDBC, JPA, and Hibernate; flat and XML files; and JMS queues.

Chapter 6 covers writing. Again, Spring Batch provides off-the-shelf components to write data to the most popular resources. Read this chapter to learn how to leverage batch updates to write to a database efficiently, send emails, and write to flat and XML files.

Chapter 7 covers the processing phase of a chunk-oriented step. This is where you can embed business logic to transform read items before they're written and where you can avoid sending an item to the writing phase through validation and filtering.

Chapters 8 and 9 are about making your jobs more robust and reliable. Chapter 8 covers Spring Batch built-in features for bulletproofing jobs, like skip, retry, and restart on failure. Chapter 9 provides an in-depth presentation of transaction management in Spring Batch, as well as some transaction patterns you'll definitely use in batch applications.

Batch configuration

This chapter covers

- Configuring batch processes using Spring Batch XML
- Configuring batch jobs and related entities
- Using advanced techniques to improve configuration

In chapter 2, we explored Spring Batch foundations, described all Spring Batch concepts and entities, and looked at their interactions. The chapter introduced configuring and implementing the structure of batch jobs and related entities with Spring Batch XML.

In this chapter, we continue the online store case study: reading products from files, processing products, and integrating products in the database. Configuring this process serves as the backdrop for describing all of Spring Batch's configuration capabilities.

After describing Spring Batch XML capabilities, we show how to configure batch jobs and related entities with this dedicated XML vocabulary. We also look at configuring a repository for batch execution metadata. In the last part of this chapter, we focus on advanced configuration topics and describe how to make configuration easier.

53

How should you read this chapter? You can use it as a reference for configuring Spring Batch jobs and either skip it or come back to it for a specific configuration need. Or, you can read it in its entirety to get an overview of nearly all the features available in Spring Batch. We say an "overview" because when you learn about configuring a skipping policy, for example, you won't learn all the subtleties of this topic. That's why you'll find information in dedicated sections in other chapters to drill down into difficult topics.

3.1 The Spring Batch XML vocabulary

Like all projects in the Spring portfolio and the Spring framework itself, Spring Batch provides a dedicated XML vocabulary and namespace to configure its entities. This feature leverages the Spring XML schema–based configuration introduced in Spring 2 and simplifies bean configuration, enabling configurations to operate at a high level by hiding complexity when configuring entities and related Spring-based mechanisms.

In this section, we describe how to use Spring Batch XML and the facilities it offers for batch configuration. Without this vocabulary, we'd need intimate knowledge of Spring Batch internals and entities that make up the batch infrastructure, which can be tedious and complex to configure.

3.1.1 Using the Spring Batch XML namespace

Like most components in the Spring portfolio, Spring Batch configuration is based on a dedicated Spring XML vocabulary and namespace. By hiding internal Spring Batch implementation details, this vocabulary provides a simple way to configure core components like jobs and steps as well as the job repository used for job metadata (all described in chapter 2). The vocabulary also provides simple ways to define and customize batch behaviors.

Before we get into the XML vocabulary and component capabilities, you need to know how use Spring Batch XML in Spring configuration files. In the following listing, the `batch` namespace prefix is declared and used in child XML elements mixed with other namespace prefixes, such as the Spring namespace mapped to the default XML namespace.

Listing 3.1   Spring Batch XML namespace and prefix

```
<?xml version="1.0" encoding="UTF-8"?>
<beans xmlns="http://www.springframework.org/schema/beans"
  xmlns:xsi="http://www.w3.org/2001/XMLSchema-instance"
  xmlns:batch="http://www.springframework.org/schema/batch"
  xsi:schemaLocation="http://www.springframework.org/schema/beans
    http://www.springframework.org/schema/beans/spring-beans.xsd
    http://www.springframework.org/schema/batch
    http://www.springframework.org/schema/batch/spring-batch.xsd">

  <batch:job id="importProductsJob">
    (...)
  </batch:job>

</beans>
```

Spring Batch uses the Spring standard mechanism to configure a custom XML namespace: the Spring Batch XML vocabulary is implemented in Spring Batch jars, automatically discovered, and handled by Spring. In listing 3.1, because Spring XML Beans uses the default namespace, each Spring Batch XML element is qualified with the batch namespace prefix.

Note that a namespace prefix can be whatever you want; in our examples, we use the batch and beans prefixes by convention.

Spring XML schema–based configuration

As of version 2.0, Spring uses an XML schema–based configuration system. XML schemas replace the previous Document Type Definition (DTD)-driven configuration system that mainly used two tags: bean for declaring a bean and property for injecting dependencies (with our apologies to Spring for this quick-and-dirty summary). While this approach works for creating beans and injecting dependencies, it's insufficient to define complex tasks. The DTD bean and property mechanism can't hide complex bean creation, which is a shortcoming in configuring advanced features like aspect-oriented programming (AOP) and security. Before version 2.0, XML configuration was non-intuitive and verbose.

Spring 2.0 introduced a new, extensible, schema-based XML configuration system. On the XML side, XML schemas describe the syntax, and on the Java side, corresponding namespace handlers encapsulate the bean creation logic. The Spring framework provides namespaces for its modules (AOP, transaction, Java Message Service [JMS], and so on), and other Spring-based projects can benefit from the namespace extension mechanism to provide their own namespaces. Each Spring portfolio project comes with one or more dedicated vocabularies and namespaces to provide the most natural and appropriate way to configure objects using module-specific tags.

Listing 3.2 declares the Spring Batch namespace as the default namespace in the root XML element. In this case, the elements without a prefix correspond to Spring Batch elements. Using this configuration style, you don't need to repeat using the Spring Batch namespace prefix for each Spring Batch XML element.

Listing 3.2 Using the Spring Batch namespace as the default namespace

```xml
<?xml version="1.0" encoding="UTF-8"?>
<beans:beans
  xmlns="http://www.springframework.org/schema/batch"
  xmlns:xsi="http://www.w3.org/2001/XMLSchema-instance"
  xmlns:beans="http://www.springframework.org/schema/beans"
  xsi:schemaLocation="http://www.springframework.org/schema/batch
    http://www.springframework.org/schema/batch/spring-batch.xsd
    http://www.springframework.org/schema/beans
    http://www.springframework.org/schema/beans/spring-beans.xsd">

  <job id="importProductsJob">
```

```
    (...)
  </job>

</beans:beans>
```

With a configuration defined using Spring Batch XML, you can now leverage all the facilities it provides. In the next section, we focus on Spring Batch XML features and describe how to configure and use those capabilities.

3.1.2 Spring Batch XML features

Spring Batch XML is the central feature in Spring Batch configurations. You use this XML vocabulary to configure all batch entities described in chapter 2. Table 3.1 lists and describes the main tags in Spring Batch XML.

Table 3.1 Main tags in Spring Batch XML

Tag name	Description
job	Configures a batch job
step	Configures a batch step
tasklet	Configures a tasklet in a step
chunk	Configures a chunk in a step
job-repository	Configures a job repository for metadata

Spring Batch XML configures the structure of batches, but specific entities need to be configured using Spring features. Spring Batch XML provides the ability to interact easily with standard Spring XML. You can configure other entities like item readers and writers as simple beans and then reference them from entities configured with Spring Batch XML. Figure 3.1 describes the possible interactions between the Spring Batch namespace and the Spring default namespace.

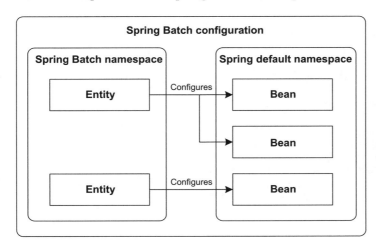

Figure 3.1 Interactions between Spring Batch and Spring XML vocabularies. The batch vocabulary defines the structure of batches. Some batch entities, such as a job, can refer to Spring beans defined with the beans vocabulary, such as item readers and writers.

Now that you've seen the capabilities provided for Spring Batch configuration, it's time to dive into details. In our case study, these capabilities let you configure a batch job and its steps.

3.2 Configuring jobs and steps

As described in chapter 2, the central entities in Spring Batch are jobs and steps, which describe the details of batch processing. The use case entails defining what the batch must do and how to organize its processing. For our examples, we use the online store case study. After defining the job, we progressively extend it by adding internal processing.

We focus here on how to configure the core entities of batch processes; we also examine their relationships at the configuration level. Let's first look at the big picture.

3.2.1 Job entities hierarchy

Spring Batch XML makes the configuration of jobs and related entities easier. You don't need to configure Spring beans corresponding to internal Spring Batch objects; instead you can work at a higher level of abstraction, specific to Spring Batch. Spring Batch XML configures batch components such as job, step, tasklet, and chunk, as well as their relationships. Together, all these elements make up batch processes. Figure 3.2 depicts this hierarchy.

Within Spring Batch XML, this hierarchy corresponds to nested XML elements with the ability to specify parameters at each level, as shown in the following listing. For example, a job defined with the job element can contain one or more steps, which you define with step elements within the job element. Similar types of configurations can be used for steps, tasklets, and chunks.

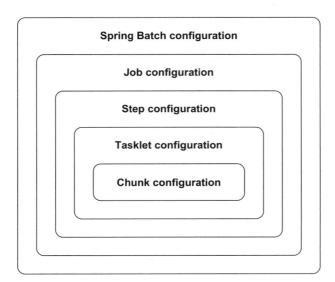

Figure 3.2 The entity configuration hierarchy for batch processing. The Spring configuration contains the job configuration, which contains the step configuration, which contains the tasklet configuration, which contains the chunk configuration.

Listing 3.3   Nested configuration of a job

```
<batch:job id="importProductsJob">
  (...)
  <batch:step id="readWriteStep">
    <batch:tasklet transaction-manager="transactionManager">
      <batch:chunk
              reader="productItemReader"
              processor="productItemProcessor"
              writer="productItemWriter"
              commit-interval="100"/>
    </batch:tasklet>
  </batch:step>
</batch:job>
```

For our case study, these nested elements are used to define each job, particularly the reading, processing, and writing logic.

Now that we've described high-level configuration concepts for Spring Batch entities, let's examine configuration details using Spring Batch XML.

3.2.2   Configuring jobs

When implementing a batch application with Spring Batch, the top-level entity is the job, and it's the first entity you configure when defining a batch process. In the context of our case study, the job is a processing flow that imports and handles products for the web store. (The job concept is described in chapter 2, section 2.3.)

To configure a job, you use the Spring Batch XML `job` element and the attributes listed in Table 3.2.

Table 3.2   Job attributes

Job attribute name	Description
`id`	Identifies the job.
`restartable`	Specifies whether Spring Batch can restart the job. The default is `true`.
`incrementer`	Refers to an entity used to set job parameter values. This entity is required when trying to launch a batch job through the `startNextInstance` method of the `JobOperator` interface.
`abstract`	Specifies whether the job definition is abstract. If `true`, this job is a parent job configuration for other jobs. It doesn't correspond to a concrete job configuration.
`parent`	Defines the parent of this job.
`job-repository`	Specifies the job repository bean used for the job. Defaults to a `jobRepository` bean if none specified.

The attributes `parent` and `abstract` deal with configuration inheritance in Spring Batch; for details, see section 3.4.4. Let's focus here on the `restartable`, `incrementer`, and `job-repository` attributes.

The `restartable` attribute specifies whether Spring Batch can restart a job. If `false`, Spring Batch can't start the job more than once; if you try, Spring Batch throws the exception `JobRestartException`. The following snippet describes how to configure this behavior for a job:

```
<batch:job id="importProductsJob" restartable="false">
    (...)
</batch:job>
```

The `job-repository` attribute is a bean identifier that specifies which job repository to use for the job. Section 3.3 describes this task.

The `incrementer` attribute provides a convenient way to create new job parameter values. Note that the `JobLauncher` doesn't need this feature because you must provide all parameter values explicitly. When the `startNextInstance` method of the `JobOperator` class launches a job, though, the method needs to determine new parameter values and use an instance of the `JobParametersIncrementer` interface:

```
public interface JobParametersIncrementer {
  JobParameters getNext(JobParameters parameters);
}
```

The `getNext` method can use the parameters from the previous job instance to create new values.

You specify an `incrementer` object in the job configuration using the `incrementer` attribute of the `job` element, for example:

```
<batch:job id="importProductsJob" incrementer="customIncrementer">
    (...)
</batch:job>

<bean id="customIncrementer" class="com.manning.sbia
               ➥.configuration.job.CustomIncrementer"/>
```

Chapter 4, section 4.5.1, describes the use of the `JobOperator` class in more detail.

Besides these attributes, the `job` element supports nested elements to configure listeners and validators. We describe listeners in section 3.4.3.

You can configure Spring Batch to validate job parameters and check that all required parameters are present before starting a job. To validate job parameters, you implement the `JobParametersValidator` interface:

```
public interface JobParametersValidator {
  void validate(JobParameters parameters)
    throws JobParametersInvalidException;
}
```

The `validate` method throws a `JobParametersInvalidException` if a parameter is invalid. Spring Batch provides a default implementation of this interface with the `DefaultJobParametersValidator` class that suits most use cases. This class allows you to specify which parameters are required and which are optional. The following listing describes how to configure and use this class in a job.

Listing 3.4   Configuring a job parameter validator

```
<batch:job id="importProductsJob">
  (...)
  <batch:validator ref="validator"/>
</batch:job>

<bean id="validator" class="org.springframework.batch
                      ➥ .core.job.DefaultJobParametersValidator">
  <property name="requiredKeys">
    <set>
      <value>date</value>
    </set>
  </property>
  <property name="optionalKeys">
    <set>
      <value>productId</value>
    </set>
  </property>
</bean>
```

The validator element's ref attribute references the validator bean. This configuration uses a bean of type DefaultJobParametersValidator to specify the required and optional parameter keys. The requiredKeys and optionalKeys properties of the validator class are used to set these values.

Now let's look at configuring job steps to define exactly what processing takes place in that job.

3.2.3   *Configuring steps*

Here, we go down a level in the job configuration and describe what makes up a job: steps. Don't hesitate to refer back to figure 3.2 to view the relationships between all the batch entities. A step is a phase in a job; chapter 2, section 2.3.1, describes these concepts. Steps define the sequence of actions a job will take, one at a time. In the online store use case, you receive products in a compressed file; the job decompresses the file before importing and saving the products in the database, as illustrated in figure 3.3.

You configure a job step using the step element and the attributes listed in table 3.3.

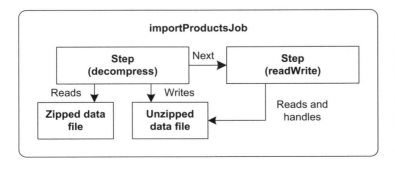

Figure 3.3   **The steps of the import products job:** decompress **and** readWrite. **The** decompress **step first reads a zip file and decompresses it to another file. The** readWrite **step reads the decompressed file.**

Table 3.3 Step attributes

Step attribute name	Description
next	The next step to execute in a sequence of steps.
parent	The parent of the step configuration.
abstract	Specifies whether the step definition is abstract. If `true`, this step is a parent step configuration for other steps. It doesn't correspond to a concrete step configuration.

The attributes `parent` and `abstract` deal with configuration inheritance in Spring Batch; for details, see section 3.4.4.

Configuring a step is simple because a step is a container for a tasklet, executed at a specific point in the flow of a batch process. For our use case, you define what steps take place and in what order. Product files come in as compressed data files to optimize file uploads. A first step decompresses the data file, and a second step processes the data. The following fragment describes how to configure this flow:

```
<job id="importProductsJob">
  <step id="decompress" next="readWrite">
    (...)
  </step>
  <step id="readWrite">
    (...)
  </step>
</job>
```

You always define the `step` element as a child element of the `job` element. Spring Batch uses the `id` attribute to identify objects in a configuration. This aspect is particularly important to use steps in a flow. The `next` attribute of the `step` element is set to define which step to execute next. In the preceding fragment, the step identified as `decompress` is executed before the step identified as `readWrite`.

Now that we've described the job and step elements, let's continue our tour of Spring Batch core objects with tasklets and chunks, which define what happens in a step.

3.2.4 Configuring tasklets and chunks

The tasklet and chunk are `step` elements used to specify processing. Chapter 2, section 2.3.1, describes these concepts. To import products, you successively configure how to import product data, how to process products, and where to put products in the database, as illustrated in figure 3.4.

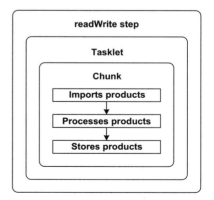

Figure 3.4 The import product tasklet configuration and chunk configuration define three steps: import, process, and store products.

TASKLET

A tasklet corresponds to a transactional, potentially repeatable process occurring in a step. You can write your own tasklet class by implementing the `Tasklet` interface or use the tasklet implementations provided by Spring Batch. Implementing your own tasklets is useful for specific tasks, such as decompressing an archive or cleaning a directory. Spring Batch provides more generic tasklet implementations, such as to call system commands or to do chunk-oriented processing.

To configure a tasklet, you define a `tasklet` element within a `step` element. Table 3.4 lists the attributes of the `tasklet` element.

Table 3.4   Tasklet attributes

Tasklet attribute name	Description
ref	A Spring bean identifier whose class implements the `Tasklet` interface. You must use this attribute when implementing a custom tasklet.
transaction-manager	The Spring transaction manager to use for tasklet transactions. By default, a tasklet is transactional, and the default value of the attribute is `transactionManager`.
start-limit	The number of times Spring Batch can restart a tasklet for a retry.
allow-start-if-complete	Specifies whether Spring Batch can restart a tasklet even if it completed for a retry.

Listing 3.5 shows how to use the last three attributes of the `tasklet` element, whatever the tasklet type. Because you want to write the products from the compressed import file to a database, you must specify a transaction manager to handle transactions associated with inserting products in the database. This listing also specifies additional parameters to define restart behavior.

Listing 3.5   Configuring tasklet attributes

```
<batch:job id="importProductsJob">
  (...)
  <batch:step id="readWriteStep">
    <batch:tasklet
            transaction-manager="transactionManager"
            start-limit="3"
            allow-start-if-complete="true">
      (...)
    </batch:tasklet>
  </batch:step>
</batch:job>

<bean id="transactionManager" class="(...)">
  (...)
</bean>
```

The `transaction-manager` attribute contains the bean identifier corresponding to the Spring transaction manager to use during the tasklet's processing. The bean must implement the Spring `PlatformTransactionManager` interface. The attributes `start-limit` and `allow-start-if-complete` specify that Spring Batch can restart the tasklet three times in the context of a retry even if the tasklet has completed. We describe in section 3.2.5 how to control rollback for a step.

In the case of a custom tasklet, you can reference the Spring bean implementing the `Tasklet` interface with the `ref` attribute. Spring Batch delegates processing to this class when executing the step. In our use case, decompressing import files doesn't correspond to processing that Spring Batch natively supports, so you need a custom tasklet to implement decompression. The following snippet describes how to configure this tasklet:

```
<job id="importProductsJob">
  <step id="decompress" next="readWrite">
    <tasklet ref="decompressTasklet" />
  </step>
</job>
```

Listing 1.5 in chapter 1 shows the code for the `DecompressTasklet` tasklet and listing 1.6 shows its configuration.

Spring Batch also supports using chunks in tasklets. The `chunk` child element of the `tasklet` element configures chunk processing. Note that you don't need to use the `ref` attribute of the `tasklet` element. On the Java side, the `ChunkOrientedTasklet` class implements chunk processing.

Configuring a tasklet can be simple, but to implement chunk processing, the configuration gets more complex because more objects are involved.

CHUNK-ORIENTED TASKLET

Spring Batch provides a tasklet class to process data in chunks: the `ChunkOrientedTasklet`. You typically use chunk-oriented tasklets for read-write processing. In chunk processing, Spring Batch reads data chunks from a source and transforms, validates, and then writes data chunks to a destination. In the online store case study, this corresponds to importing products into the database.

To configure chunk objects, you use an additional level of configuration using the `chunk` element with the attributes listed in table 3.5.

Table 3.5 Chunk attributes

Chunk attribute name	Description
reader	Bean identifier used to read data from a chunk. The bean must implement the Spring Batch `ItemReader` interface.
processor	Bean identifier used to process data from a chunk. The bean must implement the Spring Batch `ItemProcessor` interface.
writer	Bean identifier used to write data from a chunk. The bean must implement the Spring Batch `ItemWriter` interface.

Table 3.5   Chunk attributes *(continued)*

Chunk attribute name	Description
commit-interval	Number of items to process before issuing a commit. When the number of items read reaches the commit interval number, the entire corresponding chunk is written out through the item writer and the transaction is committed.
skip-limit	Maximum number of skips during processing of the step. If processing reaches the skip limit, the next exception thrown on item processing (read, process, or write) causes the step to fail.
skip-policy	Skip policy bean that implements the `SkipPolicy` interface.
retry-policy	Retry policy bean that implements the `RetryPolicy` interface.
retry-limit	Maximum number of retries.
cache-capacity	Cache capacity of the retry policy.
reader-transactional-queue	When reading an item from a JMS queue, whether reading is transactional.
processor-transactional	Whether the processor used includes transactional processing.
chunk-completion-policy	Completion policy bean for the chunk that implements the `CompletionPolicy` interface.

The first four attributes (`reader`, `processor`, `writer`, `commit-interval`) in table 3.5 are the most commonly used in chunk configuration. These attributes define which entities are involved in processing chunks and the number of items to process before committing.

Listing 3.6   Using tasklet configuration attributes

```
<batch:job id="importProductsJob">
  (...)
  <batch:step id="readWrite">
    <batch:tasklet>
      <batch:chunk
            reader="productItemReader"
            processor="productItemProcessor"
            writer="productItemWriter"
            commit-interval="100"/>
    </batch:tasklet>
  </batch:step>
</batch:job>

<bean id="productItemReader" class="(...)">
  (...)
</bean>

<bean id="productItemProcessor" class="(...)">
  (...)
</bean>
```

❶ Specifies entities used by the chunk

❷ Specifies commit interval

```
<bean id="productItemWriter" class="(...)">
  (...)
</bean>
```

The attributes `reader`, `processor`, and `writer` ❶ correspond to Spring bean identifiers defined in the configuration. For more information on these topics, see chapter 5 for configuring item readers; chapter 6 for configuring item writers; and chapter 7 for configuring item processors. The `commit-interval` attribute ❷ defines that Spring Batch will execute a database commit after processing each 100 elements.

Other attributes deal with configuring the skip limit, retry limit, and completion policy aspects of a chunk. The following listing shows how to use these attributes.

Listing 3.7 Configuring chunk retry, skip, and completion

```
<batch:job id="importProductsJob">
  (...)
  <batch:step id="readWrite">
    <batch:tasklet>
      <batch:chunk
              (...)
              skip-limit="20"
              retry-limit="3"
              cache-capacity="100"
              chunk-completion-policy="timeoutCompletionPolicy"/>
    </batch:tasklet>
  </batch:step>
</batch:job>

<bean id="timeoutCompletionPolicy"
      class="org.springframework.batch.repeat
                      ➥ .policy.TimeoutTerminationPolicy">
  <constructor-arg value="60"/>

</bean>
```

In listing 3.7, the `skip-limit` attribute configures the maximum number of items that Spring Batch can skip. The `retry-limit` attribute sets the maximum number of retries. The `cache-capacity` attribute sets the cache capacity for retries, meaning the maximum number of items that can fail without being skipped or recovered. If the number is exceeded, an exception is thrown. The `chunk-completion-policy` attribute configures the completion policy to define a chunk-processing timeout.

We've described rather briefly how to configure skip, retry, and completion in steps. We look at this topic in more detail in chapter 8, where we aim for batch robustness and define error handlers.

The last attributes correspond to more advanced configurations regarding transactions. We describe these in section 3.2.5.

Most of the attributes described in table 3.5 have equivalent child elements to allow embedding beans in the chunk configuration. These beans are anonymous and specially defined for the chunk. Table 3.6 describes `chunk` children elements usable in this context.

Table 3.6   Chunk child elements

Chunk child element	Description
reader	Corresponds to the `reader` attribute
processor	Corresponds to the `processor` attribute
writer	Corresponds to the `writer` attribute
skip-policy	Corresponds to the `skip-policy` attribute
retry-policy	Corresponds to the `retry-policy` attribute

The following listing describes how to rewrite listing 3.6 using child elements instead of attributes for the reader, processor, and writer.

Listing 3.8   Using child elements in the tasklet configuration

```
<batch:job id="importProductsJob">
  (...)
  <batch:step id="readWrite">
    <batch:tasklet>
      <batch:chunk commit-interval="100">
        <batch:reader>                          ◁───┐
          <bean class="(...)">                       │
            (...)                                     │
          </bean>                                     │
        </batch:reader>                               │  Uses child
        <batch:processor>               ◁─────────────│  element
          <bean class="(...)">                        │  instead of
            (...)                                      │  attribute
          </bean>                                      │
        </batch:processor>                             │
        <batch:writer>                  ◁──────────────┘
          <bean class="(...)">
            (...)
          </bean>
        </batch:writer>
      </batch:chunk>
    </batch:tasklet>
  </batch:step>
</batch:job>
```

You can configure other objects with child elements in chunks. Table 3.7 lists these additional elements.

Table 3.7   Additional chunk child elements

Chunk child element name	Description
retry-listeners	See section 3.4.3.
skippable-exception-classes	A list of exceptions triggering skips.

Table 3.7 Additional chunk child elements *(continued)*

Chunk child element name	Description
`retryable-exception-classes`	A list of exceptions triggering retries.
`streams`	Each stream element involved in the step. By default, objects referenced using a `reader`, `processor`, and `writer` are automatically registered. You don't need to specify them again here.

The `chunk` element can configure which exceptions trigger skips and retries using, respectively, the elements `skippable-exception-classes` and `retryable-exception-classes`. The following listing shows these elements specifying which exceptions will trigger an event (`include` child element) and which ones won't (`exclude` child element).

Listing 3.9 Configuring skippable exceptions

```
<batch:job id="importProductsJob">
  (...)
  <batch:step id="readWrite">
    <batch:tasklet>
      <batch:chunk commit-interval="100"
                   skip-limit="10">
        <skippable-exception-classes>
          <include class="org.springframework.batch
                    ➥ .item.file.FlatFileParseException"/>
          <exclude class="java.io.FileNotFoundException"/>
        </skippable-exception-classes>
      </batch:chunk>
    </batch:tasklet>
  </batch:step>
</batch:job>
```

You can use the same mechanism for the `retryable-exception-classes` element as used for the `skippable-exception-classes` element to configure retries. The following fragment configures retries when `DeadlockLoserDataAccessExceptions` are caught:

```
<batch:chunk commit-interval="100" retry-limit="3">
  <retryable-exception-classes>
    <include
        class="org.springframework.dao.DeadlockLoserDataAccessException"/>
  </retryable-exception-classes>
</batch:chunk>
```

The last item in table 3.7 deals with streams. We provide a short description of the feature and show how to configure it. Chapter 8 provides more details on this topic. Streams provide the ability to save state between executions for step restarts. The step needs to know which instance is a stream (by implementing the `ItemStream` interface). Spring Batch automatically registers as streams everything specified in the

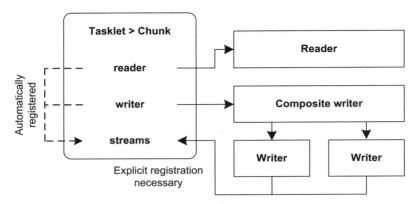

Figure 3.5   Registration of entities as streams. Spring Batch automatically registers readers, processors, and writers if they implement the `ItemStream` interface. Explicit registration is necessary if Spring Batch doesn't know about the streams to register, such as the writers in the figure used through a composite writer.

reader, processor, and writer attributes. Note that it's not the case when the step doesn't directly reference entities. That's why these entities must be explicitly registered as streams, as illustrated in figure 3.5.

Let's look at an example. If you use a composite item writer that isn't a stream and that internally uses stream writers, the step doesn't have references to those writers. In this case, you must define explicitly the writers as streams for the step in order to avoid problems on restarts when errors occur. The following listing describes how to configure this aspect using the streams child element of the chunk element.

Listing 3.10   Configuring streams in a chunk

```
<batch:job id="importProductsJob">
  (...)
  <batch:step id="readWrite">
    <batch:tasklet>
      <batch:chunk reader="productItemReader" writer="compositeWriter"/>
        <streams>
          <stream ref="productItemWriter1"/>          ❶ References writers
          <stream ref="productItemWriter2"/>               as stream
        </streams>
    </batch:tasklet>
  </batch:step>
</batch:job>

<bean id="compositeWriter"
      class="org.springframework.batch.item.support.CompositeItemWriter">
  <property name="delegates">
    <list>
      <ref bean="productItemWriter1"/>                 ❷ References writers in
      <ref bean="productItemWriter2"/>                      composite writer
    </list>
  </property>
</bean>
```

In listing 3.10, you must register as streams ❶ the item writers ❷ involved in the composite item writer for the step using the streams element as a child of the chunk element. The streams element then defines one or more stream elements—in this example, two stream elements ❶.

In this section, we described how to configure a batch job with Spring Batch. We detailed the configuration of each related core object. We saw that transactions guarantee batch robustness and are involved at several levels in the configuration. Because this is an important issue, we gather all configuration aspects related to transactions in the next section.

3.2.5 *Configuring transactions*

Transactions in Spring Batch are an important topic: transactions contribute to the robustness of batch processes and work in combination with chunk processing. You configure transactions at different levels because transactions involve several types of objects. In the online store use case, you validate a set of products during processing.

The first thing to configure is the Spring transaction manager because Spring Batch is based on the Spring framework and uses Spring's transaction support. Spring provides built-in transaction managers for common persistent technologies and frameworks. For JDBC, you use the DataSourceTransactionManager class as configured in the following snippet:

```
<bean id="transactionManager">
  class="org.springframework.jdbc.datasource.DataSourceTransactionManager">
  <property name="dataSource" ref="batchDataSource"/>
</bean>
```

Every Spring transaction manager must be configured using the factory provided by the framework to create connections and sessions. In the case of JDBC, the factory is an instance of the DataSource interface.

Once you configure the transaction manager, other configuration elements can refer to it from different levels in the batch configuration, such as from the tasklet level. The next snippet configures the transaction manager using the transaction-manager attribute:

```
<batch:job id="importProductsJob">
  (...)
  <batch:step id="readWrite">
    <batch:tasklet transaction-manager="transactionManager" (...)>
      (...)
    </batch:tasklet>
  </batch:step>
</batch:job>
```

Section 3.3 explains that you must also use a transaction manager to configure entities to interact with a persistent job repository.

Now that you know which Spring transaction manager to use, you can define how transactions are handled during processing. As described in chapter 1, section 1.4.1,

The Spring transaction manager

The Spring framework provides generic transactional support. Spring bases this support on the `PlatformTransactionManager` interface that provides a contract to handle transaction demarcations: beginning and ending transactions with a commit or rollback. Spring provides implementations for a large range of persistent technologies and frameworks like JDBC, Java Persistence API (JPA), and so on. For JDBC, the implementing class is `DataSourceTransactionManager`, and for JPA it's `JpaTransactionManager`.

Spring builds on this interface to implement standard transactional behavior and allows configuring transactions with Spring beans using AOP or annotations. This generic support doesn't need to know which persistence technology is used and is completely independent of it.

Spring Batch uses chunk processing to handle items. That's why Spring Batch provides a commit interval tied to the chunk size. The `commit-interval` attribute configures this setting at the chunk level and ensures that Spring Batch executes a commit after processing a given number of items. The following example sets the commit interval to 100 items:

```
<batch:tasklet>
  <batch:chunk (...) commit-interval="100"/>       <─── Sets commit interval
</batch:tasklet>
```

Transactions have several attributes defining transactional behaviour, isolation, and timeout. These attributes specify how transactions behave and can affect performance. Because Spring Batch is based on Spring transactional support, configuring these attributes is generic and applies to all persistent technologies supported by the Spring framework. Spring Batch provides the `transaction-attributes` element in the `tasklet` element for this purpose, as described in following snippet:

```
<batch:tasklet>
  <batch:chunk reader="productItemReader"
        writer="productItemReader"
        commit-interval="100"/>
    <batch:transaction-attributes isolation="DEFAULT"       ❶ Configures
                      propagation="REQUIRED"                   transaction
                      timeout="30"/>                           attributes
  </batch:chunk>
</batch:tasklet>
```

Transactional attributes are configured using the `transaction-attributes` element ❶ and its attributes. The `isolation` attribute specifies the isolation level used for the database and what is visible from outside transactions. The READ_COMMITTED level prevents dirty reads (reading data written by a noncommitted transaction); READ_UNCOMMITTED specifies that dirty reads, nonrepeatable reads, and phantom reads can occur, meaning that all intermediate states of transactions are visible for other transactions;

REPEATABLE_READ prevents dirty reads and nonrepeatable reads, but phantom reads can still occur because intermediate data can disappear between two reads; and SERIALIZABLE prevents dirty reads, nonrepeatable reads, and phantom reads, meaning that a transaction is completely isolated and no intermediate states can be seen. Choosing the DEFAULT value leaves the choice of the isolation level to the database, which is a good choice in almost all cases.

The propagation attribute specifies the transactional behavior to use. Choosing REQUIRED implies that processing will use the current transaction if it exists and create a new one if it doesn't. The Spring class TransactionDefinition declares all valid values for these two attributes. Finally, the timeout attribute defines the timeout in seconds for the transaction. If the timeout attribute is absent, the default timeout of the underlying system is used.

> **Rollback and commit conventions in Spring and Java Enterprise Edition**
>
> Java defines two types of exceptions: checked and unchecked. A checked exception extends the Exception class, and a method must explicitly handle it in a try-catch block or declare it in its signature's throws clause. An unchecked exception extends the RuntimeException class, and a method doesn't need to catch or declare it. You commonly see checked exceptions used as business exceptions (recoverable) and unchecked exceptions as lower-level exceptions (unrecoverable by the business logic).
>
> By default, in Java EE and Spring, commit and rollback are automatically triggered by exceptions. If Spring catches a checked exception, a commit is executed. If Spring catches an unchecked exception, a rollback is executed. You can configure Spring's transactional support to customize this behavior by setting which exceptions trigger commits and rollbacks.

The Spring framework follows the conventions outlined in the sidebar "Rollback and commit conventions in Spring and Java Enterprise Edition." In addition, Spring Batch lets you configure specific exception classes that don't trigger rollbacks when thrown. You configure this feature in a tasklet using the no-rollback-exception-classes element, as described in the following snippet:

```
<batch:tasklet>
  (...)
  <batch:no-rollback-exception-classes>
    <batch:include
     class="org.springframework.batch.item.validator.ValidationException"/>
  </batch:no-rollback-exception-classes>
</batch:tasklet>
```

In this snippet, Spring issues a commit even if the unchecked Spring Batch exception ValidationException is thrown during batch processing.

Spring Batch also provides parameters for special cases. The first case is readers built on a transactional resource like a JMS queue. For JMS, a step doesn't need to buffer data because JMS already provides this feature. For this type of resource, you need to specify the `reader-transactional-queue` attribute on the corresponding chunk, as shown in the following listing.

Listing 3.11   Configuring a transactional JMS item reader

```
<batch:tasklet>
  <batch:chunk reader="productItemReader"
               reader-transactional-queue="true" (...)/>
</batch:tasklet>

<bean id="productItemReader"
      class="org.springframework.batch.item.jms.JmsItemReader">
  <property name="itemType"
            value="com.manning.sbia.reader.jms.ProductBean"/>
  <property name="jmsTemplate" ref="jmsTemplate"/>
  <property name="receiveTimeout" value="350"/>
</bean>
```

As described throughout this section, configuring batch processes can involve many concepts and objects. Spring Batch eases the configuration of core entities like job, step, tasklet, and chunk. Spring Batch also lets you configure transaction behavior and define your own error handling. The next section covers configuring the Spring Batch job repository to store batch execution data.

3.3   *Configuring the job repository*

Along with the batch feature, the job repository is a key feature of the Spring Batch infrastructure because it provides information about batch processing. Chapter 2, section 2.2, describes the job repository: it saves information about the details of job executions. In this section, we focus on configuring the job repository in Spring Batch XML. The job repository is part of the more general topic concerning batch process monitoring. Chapter 12 is dedicated to this topic.

3.3.1   *Choosing a job repository*

Spring Batch provides the `JobRepository` interface for the batch infrastructure and job repository to interact with each other. Chapter 2, section 2.2.1, shows this interface. The interface provides all the methods required to interact with the repository. We describe the job repository in detail in chapter 12.

For the `JobRepository` interface, Spring Batch provides only one implementation: the `SimpleJobRepository` class. Spring Batch bases this class on a set of Data Access Objects (DAOs) used for dedicated interactions and data management. Spring Batch provides two kinds of DAOs at this level:

- In-memory with no persistence
- Persistent with metadata using JDBC

You can use the in-memory DAO for tests, but you shouldn't use it in production environments. In fact, batch data is lost between job executions. You should prefer the persistent DAO when you want to have robust batch processing with checks on startup. Because the persistent DAO uses a database, you need additional information in the job configuration. Database access configuration includes data source and transactional behavior.

3.3.2 Specifying job repository parameters

In this section, we configure the in-memory and persistent job repositories.

CONFIGURING AN IN-MEMORY JOB REPOSITORY

The first kind of job repository is the in-memory repository. Spring Batch provides the `MapJobRepositoryFactoryBean` class to make its configuration easier. The persistent repository uses a Spring bean for configuration and requires a transaction manager. Spring Batch provides the `ResourcelessTransactionManager` class as a NOOP (NO OPeration) implementation of the `PlatformTransactionManager` interface.

The following listing describes how to use the Spring Batch `MapJobRepository-FactoryBean` and `ResourcelessTransactionManager` classes to configure an in-memory job repository.

Listing 3.12 Configuring an in-memory job repository

```
<bean id="jobRepository"
      class="org.springframework.batch.core.repository
                         .support.MapJobRepositoryFactoryBean"
  <property name="transactionManager-ref" ref="transactionManager"/>
</bean>

<bean id="transactionManager"
      class="org.springframework.batch.support
                         .transaction.ResourcelessTransactionManager"/>
<batch:job id="importInvoicesJob"
           job-repository="jobRepository">
  (...)
</batch:job>
```

The in-memory job repository is first defined using the `MapJobRepositoryFactory` class provided by Spring Batch. The `transactionManager-ref` attribute is specified to reference a configured transaction manager. This particular transaction manager is a `ResourcelessTransactionManager` because the job repository is in-memory. Finally, the job repository is referenced from the job using the `job-repository` attribute of the `job` element. The value of this attribute is the identifier of the job repository bean.

CONFIGURING A PERSISTENT JOB REPOSITORY

Configuring a persistent job repository isn't too complicated, thanks to Spring Batch XML, which hides all the bean configuration details that would otherwise be required with Spring XML. Our configuration uses the `job-repository` element and specifies the attributes listed in table 3.8.

The following listing shows how to use the `job-repository` element and its attributes to configure a persistent job repository for a relational database.

Table 3.8 `job-repository` **attributes**

Repository attribute name	Description
`data-source`	Bean identifier for the repository data source used to access the database. This attribute is mandatory, and its default value is `dataSource`.
`transaction-manager`	Bean identifier for the Spring transaction manager used to handle transactions for the job repository. This attribute is mandatory, and its default value is `transactionManager`.
`isolation-level-for-create`	Isolation level used to create job executions. This attribute is mandatory, and its default value is `SERIALIZABLE`, which prevents accidental concurrent creation of the same job instance multiple times (`REPEATABLE_READ` would work as well).
`max-varchar-length`	Maximum length for VARCHAR columns in the database.
`table-prefix`	Table prefix used by the job repository in the database. This prefix allows identifying the tables used by the job repository from the tables used by the batch. The default value is `BATCH_`.
`lob-handler`	Handler for large object (LOB)-type columns. Use this attribute only with Oracle or if Spring Batch doesn't detect the database type. This attribute is optional.

Listing 3.13 Configuring a persistent job repository

```
<bean id="dataSource"
      class="org.apache.commons.dbcp.BasicDataSource"
      destroy-method="close">
  <property name="driverClassName" value="${batch.jdbc.driver}" />
  <property name="url" value="${batch.jdbc.url}" />                      Configures data     ❶
  <property name="username" value="${batch.jdbc.user}" />               source and
  <property name="password" value="${batch.jdbc.password}" />           transaction
</bean>                                                                   manager

<bean id="transactionManager" lazy-init="true"
      class="org.springframework.jdbc.datasource
                      ➥ .DataSourceTransactionManager">
  <property name="dataSource" ref="dataSource" />
</bean>                                                    ❷ Configures persistent
                                                             job repository
<batch:job-repository id="jobRepository"
            data-source="dataSource"
            transaction-manager="transactionManager"
            isolation-level-for-create="SERIALIZABLE"
            table-prefix="BATCH_"
/>
<batch:job id="importInvoicesJob"                          ❸ Links job
           job-repository="jobRepository">                    repository in job
  (...)
</batch:job>
```

The configuration in listing 3.13 uses a data source named `dataSource` and the Apache DBCP library for connection pooling ❶. The listing also configures a transaction manager named `transactionManager` as a Spring `DataSourceTransactionManager` ❶, which uses JDBC for database access.

The `job-repository` element can then configure the persistent job repository ❷. This element references the data source and transaction manager previously configured. It also uses additional parameters to force the use of the `SERIAL-IZABLE` isolation level when creating new job executions and to identify Spring Batch tables with the `BATCH_` prefix. This job repository is then referenced from the job configuration ❸.

How does the job repository act as a synchronizer?

What happens if you launch the same Spring Batch job from different physical nodes? There's a small risk that you create the same job instance twice. This is bad for the batch metadata: Spring Batch would have a hard time restarting a failed execution of the instance—which instance should it choose? That's where the job repository and the `isolation-level-for-create` attribute of the `job-repository` element come in. The job repository maintains batch metadata such as job instances and executions. When creating these entities, the job repository also acts as a centralized safeguard: it prevents the creation of identical job instances when jobs launch concurrently. The job repository relies on the transactional capabilities of the underlying database to achieve this synchronization. With an aggressive value for the `iso-lation-level-for-create` attribute—`SERIALIZABLE` is the default—you can avoid concurrency issues when creating entities like job instances. Thanks to this safeguard, you can distribute Spring Batch on multiple nodes and be sure not to start the same instance twice due to a race condition.

3.4 Advanced configuration topics

The job repository is an important part of the Spring Batch infrastructure because it records batch-processing information to track which jobs succeed and fail. Although Spring Batch provides an in-memory job repository, you should use it only for tests. Use the persistent job repository in production. In chapter 12, we monitor batch applications using the job repository. This section focuses on advanced Spring Batch configurations that leverage the Spring Expression Language (SpEL), modularize configurations with inheritance, and use listeners. Our goal is to simplify batch-processing configuration. Let's begin with the Spring Batch step scope feature.

3.4.1 Using step scope

Spring Batch provides a special bean scope class—`StepScope`—implemented as a custom Spring bean scope. The goal of the step scope is to link beans with steps within batches. This mechanism allows instantiation of beans configured in Spring only when steps begin and allows you to specify configuration and parameters for a step.

If you use Spring Batch XML, the step scope is automatically registered for the current Spring container and is usable without additional configuration. If you don't use

What is a bean scope?

Starting in version 2, Spring supports custom bean scopes. A bean scope specifies how to create instances of the class for a given bean definition. Spring provides scopes like `singleton`, `prototype`, `request`, and `session` but also allows custom scopes to be plugged in. You must register a custom scope in the container using the `CustomScopeConfigurer` Spring class.

A custom scope implementation handles how an instance is served in a given Spring container. For example, with the `singleton` scope, the same instance is always provided by Spring. With the `prototype` scope, Spring always creates a new instance.

The `scope` attribute of the `bean` element defines the bean scope; for example:

```
<bean id="myBean" class="(...)" scope="prototype">
```

Spring Batch XML, you must define the step scope with its `StepScope` class, as described in the following snippet:

```
<bean class="org.springframework.batch.core.scope.StepScope"/>
```

Developers using custom Spring scopes may be surprised by this configuration. In fact, the `StepScope` class implements the Spring `BeanFactoryPostProcessor` interface, which automatically applies the step scope to beans.

The step scope is particularly useful and convenient when combined with SpEL to implement late binding of properties. Let's describe this feature next.

3.4.2 *Leveraging SpEL*

To configure Spring Batch entities, SpEL offers interesting possibilities. It handles cases when values can't be known during development and configuration because they depend on the runtime execution context.

Spring Expression Language (SpEL)

Spring version 3 introduced the Spring Expression Language to facilitate configuration. SpEL was created to provide a single language for use across the whole Spring portfolio, but it's not directly tied to Spring and can be used independently. SpEL supports a large set of expression types, such as literal, class, property access, collection, assignment, and method invocation.

The power of this language is in its ability to use expressions to reference bean properties present in a particular context. You can view this feature as a more advanced and generic Spring `PropertyPlaceholderConfigurer`. SpEL can resolve expressions not only in a properties file but also in beans managed in Spring application contexts.

Spring Batch leverages SpEL to access entities associated with jobs and steps and to provide *late binding* in configurations. The typical use case of late binding is to use batch parameters specified at launch time in the batch configuration. The values are unknown at development time when configuring batch processes. Spring evaluates these values at runtime during the batch process execution.

Table 3.9 describes all entities available from the step scope.

Table 3.9   Entities available from the step scope

Entity name	Description
jobParameters	Parameters specified for the job
jobExecutionContext	Execution context of the current job
stepExecutionContext	Execution context of the current step

With this approach, it's now possible to specify property values filled in at launch time, as shown in the following listing.

Listing 3.14   Configuring batch parameters with SpEL

```
<bean id="decompressTasklet"
      class="com.manning.sbia.ch01.batch.DecompressTasklet"
      scope="step">
  <property name="inputResource"
            value="#{jobParameters['inputResource']}" />
  <property name="targetDirectory"
            value="#{jobParameters['targetDirectory']}" />
  <property name="targetFile"
            value="#{jobParameters['targetFile']}" />
</bean>
```

You configure the decompressTasklet bean using the Spring Batch step scope. Specifying this scope allows you to use SpEL's late binding feature for job parameters within values of bean properties. The jobParameters object acts as a map for a set of parameters and elements and is accessed using notation delimited by #{ and }. You also use this format in the example with the objects jobExecutionContext and stepExecutionContext.

In the context of the case study, this mechanism makes it possible to specify at batch startup the file to use to import product data. You don't need to hardcode the filename in the batch configuration, as illustrated in figure 3.6.

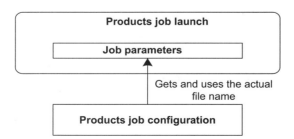

Figure 3.6   Using the filename to import from the job configuration

3.4.3 *Using listeners to provide additional processing*

Spring Batch provides the ability to specify and use listeners at the job and step levels within batches. This feature is particularly useful and powerful because Spring Batch can notify each level of batch processing, where you can plug in additional processing. For example, in the online store case study, you can add a listener that Spring Batch calls when a batch fails, or you can use a listener to record which products Spring Batch skips because of errors, as shown in figure 3.7.

We provide concrete examples of this feature in chapter 8. Table 3.10 describes the listener types provided by Spring Batch.

Table 3.10 Listener types

Listener type	Description
Job listener	Listens to processing at the job level
Step listeners	Listens to processing at the step level
Item listeners	Listens to item repeat or retry

JOB LISTENERS

The job listener intercepts job execution and supports the before and after job execution events. These events add processing before a job and after a job according to the completion type of a batch process. They're particularly useful to notify external systems of batch failures. Such listeners are implementations of the `JobExecutionListener` interface:

```
public interface JobExecutionListener {
  void beforeJob(JobExecution jobExecution);
  void afterJob(JobExecution jobExecution);
}
```

You configure a listener in a job configuration with the `listeners` element as a child of the `job` element. The `listeners` element can configure several listeners by referencing Spring beans. The following snippet describes how to register the `ImportProductsJobListener` class as a listener for the `importProductsJob` job:

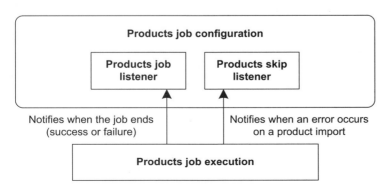

Figure 3.7 Notifications of lifecycle events and errors during job execution

```
<batch:job id="importProductsJob">
  <batch:listeners>
    <batch:listener ref="importProductsJobListener"/>
  </batch:listeners>
</batch:job>

<bean id="importProductsJobListener" class="ImportProductsJobListener"/>
```

The `ImportProductsJobListener` class receives notifications when Spring Batch starts and stops a job regardless of whether the job succeeds or fails. A `JobExecution` instance provides information regarding job execution status with `BatchStatus` constants. The following listing shows the `ImportProductsJobListener` class.

Listing 3.15 Listening to job execution with a listener

```
public class ImportProductsJobListener
                        implements JobExecutionListener {
  public void beforeJob(JobExecution jobExecution) {
    // Called when job starts
  }

  public void afterJob(JobExecution jobExecution) {
    if (jobExecution.getStatus()==BatchStatus.COMPLETED) {
      // Called when job ends successfully
    } else if (jobExecution.getStatus()==BatchStatus.FAILED) {
      // Called when job ends in failure
    }
  }
}
```

The listener class must implement the `JobExecutionListener` interface and define the `beforeJob` method that Spring Batch calls before the job starts and the `afterJob` method called after the job ends.

Spring Batch can also use annotated classes as listeners. In this case, you don't implement the `JobExecutionListener` interface. To specify which methods do the listening, you use the `BeforeJob` and `AfterJob` annotations. The following listing shows the annotated class (`AnnotatedImportProductsJobListener`) corresponding to the standard listener class (`ImportProductsJobListener`).

Listing 3.16 Listening to job execution with annotations

```
public class AnnotatedImportProductsJobListener {
  @BeforeJob
  public void executeBeforeJob(JobExecution jobExecution) {
    //Notifying when job starts
  }

  @AfterJob
  public void executeAfterJob(JobExecution jobExecution) {
    if (jobExecution.getStatus()==BatchStatus.COMPLETED) {
      //Notifying when job successfully ends
    } else if (jobExecution.getStatus()==BatchStatus.FAILED) {
      //Notifying when job ends with failure
```

```
        }
    }
}
```

This listener class is a plain old Java object (POJO) and defines which methods to execute before the job starts with the `BeforeJob` annotation and after the job ends with the `AfterJob` annotation.

STEP LISTENERS

Steps also have a matching set of listeners to track processing during step execution. You use step listeners to track item processing and to define error-handling logic. All step listeners extend the `StepListener` marker interface. `StepListener` acts as a parent to all step domain listeners. Table 3.11 describes the step listeners provided by Spring Batch.

Table 3.11   Step listeners provided by Spring Batch

Listener interface	Description
ChunkListener	Called before and after chunk execution
ItemProcessListener	Called before and after an `ItemProcessor` gets an item and when that processor throws an exception
ItemReadListener	Called before and after an item is read and when an exception occurs reading an item
ItemWriteListener	Called before and after an item is written and when an exception occurs writing an item
SkipListener	Called when a skip occurs while reading, processing, or writing an item
StepExecutionListener	Called before and after a step

The `StepExecutionListener` and `ChunkListener` interfaces relate to lifecycle. They're respectively associated to the step and chunk and provide methods for before and after events. The `StepExecutionListener` interface uses a `StepExecution` parameter for each listener method to access current step execution data. The `afterStep` method triggered after step completion must return the status of the current step with an `ExistStatus` instance. The following snippet describes the `StepExecution-Listener` interface:

```
public interface StepExecutionListener extends StepListener {
    void beforeStep(StepExecution stepExecution);
    ExitStatus afterStep(StepExecution stepExecution);
}
```

The `ChunkListener` interface provides methods called before and after the current chunk. These methods have no parameter and return void, as described in the following snippet:

```
public interface ChunkListener extends StepListener {
  void beforeChunk();
  void afterChunk();
}
```

The item listener interfaces (read, process, and write) listed in table 3.11 each deal with a single item and support Java 5 generics to specify item types. Each interface provides three methods triggered before, after, and on error. Each interface accepts as a parameter a single item from a list of handled entities for before and after methods. For error-handling methods, Spring Batch passes the thrown exception as a parameter.

For item processing, these methods are beforeProcess, afterProcess, and onProcessError. The following snippet lists the ItemProcessListener interface:

```
public interface ItemProcessListener<T, S> extends StepListener {
  void beforeProcess(T item);
  void afterProcess(T item, S result);
  void onProcessError(T item, Exception e);
}
```

For the ItemReadListener interface, these methods are beforeRead, afterRead, and onReadError, as shown in the following snippet:

```
public interface ItemReadListener<T> extends StepListener {
  void beforeRead();
  void afterRead(T item);
  void onReadError(Exception ex);
}
```

For the ItemWriteListener interface, these methods are beforeWrite, afterWrite, and onWriteError, as shown in the following snippet:

```
public interface ItemWriteListener<S> extends StepListener {
  void beforeWrite(List<? extends S> items);
  void afterWrite(List<? extends S> items);
  void onWriteError(Exception exception, List<? extends S> items);
}
```

The last kind of interface in table 3.11 listens for skip events. Spring Batch calls the SkipListener interface when processing skips an item. The interface provides three methods corresponding to when the skip occurs: onSkipInRead during reading, onSkipInProcess during processing, and onSkipInWrite during writing. The following snippet lists the SkipListener interface:

```
public interface SkipListener<T,S> extends StepListener {
  void onSkipInRead(Throwable t);
  void onSkipInProcess(T item, Throwable t);
  void onSkipInWrite(S item, Throwable t);
}
```

You can also define listeners for all these events as annotated POJOs. Spring Batch leaves the choice up to you. Spring Batch provides annotations corresponding to each method defined by the interfaces in table 3.11. For example, for the ExecutionListener interface, the BeforeStep annotation corresponds to the beforeStep method and the AfterStep annotation to the afterStep method. Configuring listeners using annotations follows the same rules as the interface-based configurations described in the next section. The following listing shows how to implement an annotation-based listener for step execution.

Listing 3.17   Implementing an annotation-based step listener

```
public class ImportProductsExecutionListener {
  @BeforeStep
  public void handlingBeforeStep(StepExecution stepExecution) {
    (...)
  }

  @AfterStep
  public ExitStatus afterStep(StepExecution stepExecution) {
    (...)
    return ExitStatus.FINISHED;
  }
}
```

As is done for a job, configuring a step listener is done using a listeners element as a child of the tasklet element. You can configure all kinds of step listeners at this level in the same manner. For example:

```
<batch:job id="importProductsJob">
  <batch:step id="decompress" next="readWrite">
    <batch:tasklet ref="decompressTasklet">
      <batch:listeners>
        <batch:listener ref="stepListener"/>
      </batch:listeners>
    </batch:tasklet>
  </batch:step>
</ batch:job>
```

Note that you can also specify several listeners at the same time.

REPEAT AND RETRY LISTENERS

Another type of listener provided by Spring Batch deals with robustness and provides notification when repeats and retries occur. These listeners support the methods listed in table 3.12 and allow processing during repeat or retry.

Table 3.12   Methods for retry and repeat listeners

Method	Description
after (repeat listener only)	Called after each try or repeat
before (repeat listener only)	Called before each try or repeat
close	Called after the last try or repeat on an item, whether successful or not in the case of a retry

Table 3.12   Methods for retry and repeat listeners *(continued)*

Method	Description
onError	Called after every unsuccessful attempt at a retry or every repeat failure with a thrown exception
open	Called before the first try or repeat on an item

The following snippet lists the `RepeatListener` interface called when repeating an item:

```
public interface RepeatListener {
  void before(RepeatContext context);
  void after(RepeatContext context, RepeatStatus result);
  void open(RepeatContext context);
  void onError(RepeatContext context, Throwable e);
  void close(RepeatContext context);
}
```

The following snippet lists the content of the `RetryListener` interface called when retrying an item:

```
public interface RetryListener {
  <T> void open(RetryContext context, RetryCallback<T> callback);
  <T> void onError(RetryContext context,
          RetryCallback<T> callback, Throwable e);
  <T> void close(RetryContext context,
          RetryCallback<T> callback, Throwable e);
}
```

Such listeners must be configured like step listeners using the `listeners` child element of the `tasklet` element, as described at the end of the previous section.

The next and last feature in our advanced configuration discussion is the Spring Batch inheritance feature used to modularize entity configurations.

3.4.4   *Configuration inheritance*

As emphasized in section 3.2.2, Spring Batch XML provides facilities to ease configuration of batch jobs. While this XML vocabulary improves Spring Batch configuration, duplication can remain, and that's why the vocabulary supports configuration inheritance like Spring XML.

This feature is particularly useful when configuring similar jobs and steps. Rather than duplicating XML fragments, Spring Batch allows you to define abstract entities to modularize configuration data. In the online store case study, you define several jobs with their own steps. As a best practice, you want to apply default values of the batch processes. To implement this, you define abstract jobs and steps. The default configuration parameters then apply to all child jobs and steps. Modifying one parameter affects all children automatically, as shown in figure 3.8.

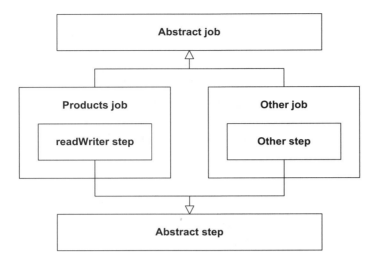

Figure 3.8   Using configuration inheritance lets jobs inherit from an abstract job and steps inherit from an abstract step.

Configuration inheritance in Spring

Configuration inheritance is a built-in feature of the default Spring XML vocabulary since version 2.0. Its aim is to allow modularizing configuration and to prevent configuration duplication. It targets the same issue that Spring XML addresses: making configuration less complex.

Spring allows defining abstract bean definitions that don't correspond to instances. Such bean definitions are useful to modularize common bean properties and avoid duplication in Spring configurations. Spring provides the `abstract` and `parent` attributes on the `bean` element. A bean with the attribute `abstract` set to `true` defines a virtual bean, and using the `parent` attribute allows linking two beans in a parent-child relationship.

Inheriting from a parent bean means the child bean can use all attributes and properties from the parent bean. You can also use overriding from a child bean.

The following fragment describes how to use the `abstract` and `parent` attributes:

```
<bean id="parentBean" abstract="true">
  <property name="propertyOne" value="(...)"/>
</bean>
<bean id="childBean" parent="parentBean">
  <property name="propertyOne" value="(...)"/>
  <property name="propertyTwo" value="(...)"/>
</bean>
```

You can use Spring Batch configuration inheritance at both the job and step levels. Spring Batch also supports configuration merging. Table 3.13 describes the `abstract` and `parent` configuration inheritance attributes.

As we've seen, configuration inheritance in Spring Batch is inspired by Spring and is based on the `abstract` and `parent` attributes. Configuration inheritance allows you

Table 3.13 Configuration inheritance attributes

Attribute	Description
abstract	When `true`, specifies that the job or step element isn't a concrete element but an abstract one used only for configuration. Abstract configuration entities aren't instantiated.
parent	The parent element used to configure a given element. The child element has all properties of its parent and can override them.

to define abstract batch entities that aren't instantiated but are present in the configuration only to modularize other configuration elements.

Let's look at an example that uses steps. A common use case is to define a parent step that modularizes common and default step parameters. The following listing shows how to use configuration inheritance to configure step elements.

Listing 3.18 Listing 3.18 Using configuration inheritance for steps

```
<step id="parentStep">
  <tasklet allow-start-if-complete="true">
    <chunk commit-interval="100"/>
  </tasklet>
</step>

<step id="productStep" parent="parentStep">
  <tasklet start-limit="5">
    <chunk reader="productItemReader"
           writer="productItemWriter"
           processor="productItemProcessor"
           commit-interval="15"/>
  </tasklet>
</step>
```

The parent step named parentStep includes a tasklet element, which also includes a chunk element. Each element includes several attributes for its configuration, allow-start-if-complete for tasklet and commit-interval for chunk. You name the second step productStep and reference the previous step as its parent. The productStep step has the same element hierarchy as its parent, which includes all elements and attributes. In some cases, a parent defines attributes but children don't, so Spring Batch adds the attributes to the child configurations. In other cases, attributes are present in both parent and child steps, and the values of child elements override the values of parent elements.

An interesting feature of Spring Batch related to configuration inheritance is the ability to merge lists. By default, Spring Batch doesn't enable this feature; lists in the child element override lists in the parent element. You can change this behavior by setting the merge attribute to true. The following listing combines the list of listeners present in a parent job with the list in the child job.

Listing 3.19   Merging two lists with configuration inheritance

```
<job id="parentJob" abstract="true">
  <listeners>
    <listener ref="globalListener"/>
  <listeners>
</job>

<job id="importProductsJob" parent="parentJob">
  (...)
  <listeners merge="true">                      ❶ Enables
    <listener ref="specificListener"/>            merging
  <listeners>
</job>
```

We specify the merge attribute ❶ for the listeners element in the configuration of the child job. In this case, Spring Batch merges the listeners of the parent and child jobs, and the resulting list contains listeners named globalListener and specificListener.

With configuration inheritance in Spring Batch, we close our advanced configuration section. These features allow easier and more concise configurations of Spring Batch jobs.

3.5   *Summary*

Spring Batch provides facilities to ease configuration of batch processes. These facilities are based on Spring Batch XML—an XML vocabulary dedicated to the batch domain—which leverages Spring XML. This vocabulary can configure all batch entities described in chapter 2, such as jobs, tasklets, and chunks. Spring Batch supports entity hierarchies in its XML configuration and closely interacts with Spring XML to use Spring beans.

XML configuration of batch processes is built in and allows plug-in strategies to handle errors and transactions. All these features contribute to making batches more robust by providing support for commit intervals, skip handling, and retry, among other tasks. We focus on batch robustness in chapter 8.

Spring Batch provides support to configure access to the job repository used to store job execution data. This feature relates to the more general topic of batch monitoring, and chapter 12 addresses it in detail.

Spring Batch XML also includes advanced features that make configuration flexible and convenient. Features include the step scope and the ability to interact with the batch execution context using SpEL late binding of parameter values at runtime. You can implement job, step, and chunk listeners with interfaces or by using annotations on POJOs. Finally, we saw that Spring Batch provides modularization at the configuration level with the ability to use inheritance to eliminate configuration duplication.

Chapter 4 focuses on execution and describes the different ways to launch batch processes in real systems.

Running batch jobs

If you've been reading this book from page one, you know the basics of Spring Batch, and you know about jobs, steps, and chunks. You must be eager to get your jobs up and running. Launching a Spring Batch job is easy because the framework provides a Java-based API for this purpose. However, how you call this API is another matter and depends on your system. Perhaps you'll use something simple like the cron scheduler to launch a Java program. Alternatively, you may want to trigger your jobs manually from a web application. Either way, we have you covered because this chapter discusses both scenarios.

This chapter covers many launching scenarios, so you may not want to read it from beginning to end, especially if you're in a hurry. You may read this chapter à la carte: think about your scenario and read only what you need. Nevertheless, you should read section 4.1 covering the concepts of launching Spring Batch jobs, and especially section 4.1.3 that guides you through the chapter to pick up the launching solution that best suits your needs.

4.1   *Launching concepts*

It's time to launch your Spring Batch job! You're about to see that launching a Spring Batch job is quite simple thanks to the Spring Batch launcher API. But how you end up launching your batch jobs depends on many parameters, so we provide you with basic concepts and some guidelines. By the end of this section, you'll know where to look in this chapter to set up a launching environment for your jobs.

4.1.1   *Introducing the Spring Batch launcher API*

The heart of the Spring Batch launcher API is the JobLauncher interface. Here's a shortened version of this interface (we removed the exceptions for brevity):

```
public interface JobLauncher {
  public JobExecution run(Job job, JobParameters jobParameters) throws (…);
}
```

The JobLauncher and the Job you pass to the run method are Spring beans. The call site typically builds the JobParameters argument on the fly. The following snippet shows how to use the job launcher to start a job execution with two parameters:

```
ApplicationContext context = (...)
JobLauncher jobLauncher = context.getBean(JobLauncher.class);
Job job = context.getBean(Job.class);
jobLauncher.run(
  job,
  new JobParametersBuilder()
    .addString("inputFile", "file:./products.txt")
    .addDate("date", new Date())
    .toJobParameters()
);
```

Note the use of a JobParametersBuilder to create a JobParameters instance. The JobParametersBuilder class provides a fluent-style API to construct job parameters. A job parameter consists of a key and a value. Spring Batch supports four types for job parameters: string, long, double, and date.

> **JOB PARAMETERS AND JOB INSTANCE**   Remember that job parameters define the *instance* of a job and that a job instance can have one or more corresponding *executions*. You can view an execution as an attempt to run a batch process. If the notions of job, job instance, and job execution aren't clear to you, please refer to chapter 2, which covers these concepts.

Spring Batch provides an implementation of JobLauncher, whose only mandatory dependency is a job repository. The following snippet shows how to declare a job launcher with a persistent job repository:

```
<batch:job-repository id="jobRepository" />

<bean id="jobLauncher" class="org.springframework.
  ➥ batch.core.launch.support.SimpleJobLauncher">
  <property name="jobRepository" ref="jobRepository" />
</bean>
```

That's it; you know everything about the Spring Batch launcher API! Okay, not everything—we didn't describe the JobExecution object returned by the run method. As you can guess, this object represents the execution coming out of the run method. The JobExecution interface provides the API to query the status of an execution: if it's running, if it has finished, or if it has failed. Because batch processes are often quite long to execute, Spring Batch offers both synchronous and asynchronous ways to launch jobs.

4.1.2 Synchronous vs. asynchronous launches

By default, the JobLauncher run method is synchronous: the caller waits until the job execution ends (successfully or not). Figure 4.1 illustrates a synchronous launch.

Synchronous launching is good in some cases: if you write a Java main program that a system scheduler like cron launches periodically, you want to exit the program only when the execution ends. But imagine that an HTTP request triggers the launching of a job. Writing a web controller that uses the job launcher to start Spring Batch jobs on HTTP requests is a handy way to integrate with external triggering systems. What happens if the launch is synchronous? The batch process executes in the calling thread, monopolizing web container resources. Submit many batch processes in this way and they'll use up all the threads of the web container, making it unable to process any other requests.

The solution is to make the job launcher asynchronous. Figure 4.2 shows how launching behaves when the job launcher is asynchronous.

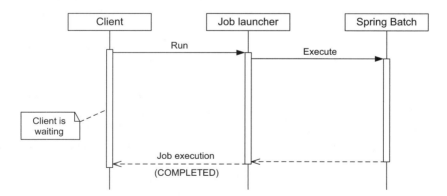

Figure 4.1 **The job launcher is synchronous by default. The client waits until the job execution ends (successfully or not) before the job launcher returns the corresponding job execution object. Synchronous execution can be problematic, for example, when the client is a controller from a web application.**

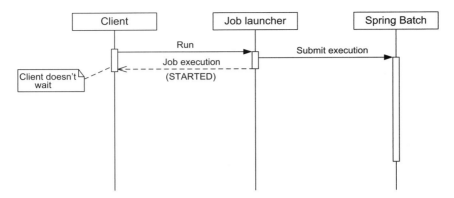

Figure 4.2   The job launcher can use a task executor to launch job executions asynchronously. The task executor handles the threading strategy, and the client has immediate access to the job execution object.

To make the job launcher asynchronous, just provide it with an appropriate `Task-Executor`, as shown in the following snippet:

```
<task:executor id="executor" pool-size="10" />

<bean id="jobLauncher" class="org.springframework.
  batch.core.launch.support.SimpleJobLauncher">
  <property name="jobRepository" ref="jobRepository" />
  <property name="taskExecutor" ref="executor" />
</bean>
```

In this example, we use a task executor with a thread pool of size 10. The executor reuses threads from its pool to launch job executions asynchronously. Note the use of the `executor` XML element from the `task` namespace. This is a shortcut provided in Spring 3.0, but you can also define a task executor like any other bean (by using an implementation like `ThreadPoolTaskExecutor`).

It's now time to guide you through the launching solutions that this chapter covers.

4.1.3   *Overview of launching solutions*

This chapter covers many solutions to launch your Spring Batch jobs, and you're unlikely to use them all in one project. Many factors can lead you to choose a specific launching solution: launching frequency, number of jobs to launch, nature of the triggering event, type of job, duration of the job execution, and so on. Let's explore some cases and present some guidelines.

LAUNCHING FROM THE COMMAND LINE

A straightforward way to launch a Spring Batch job is to use the command line, which spawns a new Java Virtual Machine (JVM) process for the execution, as figure 4.3 illustrates.

The triggering event can be a system scheduler like cron or even a human operator who knows when to launch the job. If you're interested in launching jobs this way,

Figure 4.3   You can launch a Spring Batch job as a plain JVM process. The triggering system can be a scheduler or a human operator. This solution is simple but implies initializing the batch environment for each run.

read section 4.2 on command-line launching. You'll see that Spring Batch provides a generic command-line launcher that you can use to launch any job from the command line. If you choose the scheduler option, you should also look at section 4.3.1, which covers cron.

EMBEDDING SPRING BATCH AND A SCHEDULER IN A CONTAINER

Spawning a JVM process for each execution can be costly, especially if it opens new connections to a database or creates object-relational mapping contexts. Such initializations are resource intensive, and you probably don't want the associated costs if your jobs run every minute. Another option is to embed Spring Batch into a container such that your Spring Batch environment is ready to run at any time and there's no need to set up Spring Batch for each job execution. You can also choose to embed a Java-based scheduler to start your jobs. Figure 4.4 illustrates this solution.

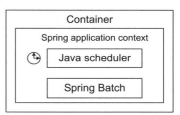

Figure 4.4   You can embed Spring Batch in a container along with a Java scheduler. A web container is a good candidate because Spring integrates easily in web applications.

A web container is a popular way to embed a Spring Batch environment. Remember that Spring Batch runs everywhere the Spring Framework runs. If you want to learn how to deploy Spring Batch in a web application, read section 4.4.1. Java-based schedulers also run in Spring, so read section 4.3.2 to learn about Spring scheduling support.

EMBEDDING SPRING BATCH AND TRIGGERING JOBS BY AN EXTERNAL EVENT

You can also have a mix of solutions: use cron because it's a popular solution in your company and embed Spring Batch in a web application because it avoids costly recurring initializations. The challenge here is to give cron access to the Spring Batch environment. Figure 4.5 illustrates this deployment.

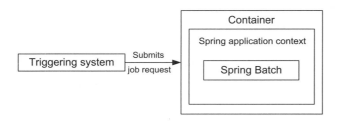

Figure 4.5   An external system submits a job request to the container where the Spring Batch environment is deployed. An example is a cron scheduler submitting an HTTP request to a web controller. The web controller would use the job launcher API to start the job execution.

To see how the Spring Batch job launcher works with HTTP, please see section 4.4.2, which covers Spring MVC (Model-View-Controller).

The list of launching solutions this chapter covers is by no means exhaustive. The Spring Batch launcher API is simple to use, so you can imagine building other types of solutions—for example, event-driven with JMS or remote with Java Management Extension (JMX). And don't forget to read section 4.5 on stopping job executions when you're done launching all these jobs!

4.2   *Launching from the command line*

Using the command line is perhaps the most common way to launch a batch process. Triggering the process can be done manually (by a human), but most of the time you'll be using a system scheduler (cron on UNIX systems, for example) to trigger the launch. Why? Because batch processes are launched at specific times (at night, on the last Sunday of the month, and so on). We cover schedulers later; in this section, we focus on how to launch a batch process through the command line.

Because Spring Batch is a Java-based framework, launching a Spring Batch process means spawning a new JVM process for a class and using the Spring Batch launcher API in that class's `main` method.

The Spring Batch launcher API is straightforward; the `JobLauncher` has one method—`run`—that takes a `Job` and a `JobParameters` argument, so writing a `main` method to launch a job is quick and easy. We won't bother writing such a class because Spring Batch already provides one: the `CommandLineJobRunner`!

4.2.1   *Using Spring Batch's command-line job runner*

Spring Batch provides the `CommandLineJobRunner` class to launch jobs. This launcher should remove any need for custom command-line launchers because of its flexibility. Table 4.1 lists the `CommandLineJobRunner` settings.

Table 4.1   Settings for the generic command-line launcher

Setting	Description
Spring configuration file	The file used to start the Spring application context; the file configures the Spring Batch infrastructure, jobs, and necessary components (data source, readers, writers, and so forth)
Job	The name of the job to execute (refers to a Spring bean name)
Job parameters	The job parameters to pass to the job launcher
Exit code mapping	A strategy to map the executed job exit status to a system exit status

To cover the different uses of the `CommandLineJobRunner`, imagine you have an `importProductsJob` job defined in an import-products-job.xml file located at the root of the classpath.

How to launch the command-line job runner as a Java process

The `CommandLineJobRunner` is a simple Java class with a `main` method. The first step to use it is to package everything in a Java Archive (JAR) file: all application classes—the launcher class itself but also custom item readers, writers, processors, data access objects, and so on—as well as resources, like the import-products-job.xml file. We can do all of this with a tool like Maven to end up with an import-products.jar file. The second step is to create a neat layout on the file system such that the JVM can locate all the necessary Java classes and resources on the classpath. What should be on the classpath? The import-products.jar file, of course, but also all the dependencies of your batch: Spring Batch, the corresponding dependencies from the Spring Framework, and any other dependencies for your application (XML, persistence, and database connection pooling libraries, for example). We assume a `lib` directory contains all of these JAR files. We refer to this directory with the `classpath` argument of the `java` program.

But how to gather these JAR files? The easiest way is to use a dependency manager, like Maven. If you're using Maven, the `mvn package` command packages your project as a JAR file in the `target` directory of your project. To get all the dependencies, launch the `mvn dependency:copy-dependencies` command. This command copies all the dependencies you need in the `target/dependency` directory. You can then gather all your JAR files in a common directory (the snippets of this chapter use a `lib` directory) to launch the job from the command line.

LAUNCHING WITHOUT JOB PARAMETERS

The simplest use of the `CommandLineJobRunner` is to launch a job that doesn't require any parameters. You launch the `importProductsJob` job this way:

```
java -classpath "./lib/*"
    ➥ org.springframework.batch.core.launch.support.CommandLineJobRunner
    ➥ import-products-job.xml importProductsJob
```

The first parameter to the `CommandLineJobRunner` is the location of the Spring configuration file, and the second parameter is the name of the `Job` (the name of the corresponding Spring bean).

> **NOTE** The `CommandLineJobRunner` uses a `ClassPathXmlApplicationContext`, which means it locates the configuration file on the classpath by default. You can use Spring's resource abstraction prefixes to override this default—for example, file:./import-products-job.xml, if your configuration file is on the file system in the current directory.

There's little chance that your jobs won't need any job parameters, especially if the job instance identity is relevant (to benefit from Spring Batch's restart features, for instance), so let's see how to specify job parameters to the command line job runner.

LAUNCHING WITH JOB PARAMETERS

Recall that the import products job needs two parameters: the location of the input file and the current date. The following snippet shows how to specify those parameters from the command line:

```
java -classpath "./lib/*"
  ➥ org.springframework.batch.core.launch.support.CommandLineJobRunner
  ➥ import-products-job.xml importProductsJob
  ➥ inputFile=file:./products.txt date=2010/12/08
```

The syntax is simple: you specify job parameters after the name of the job, using the name=value syntax. Remember that a job parameter can have a data type in Spring Batch. The way parameters are defined in the previous snippet creates String–typed parameters. What if the parameter type is relevant? Spring Batch offers a way to specify the type of a parameter by using the syntax name(type)=value, where type can be a string, date, long, or double (string is the default). Let's now launch our job by passing in the date parameter as a real Date object:

```
java -classpath "./lib/*"
  ➥ org.springframework.batch.core.launch.support.CommandLineJobRunner
  ➥ import-products-job.xml importProductsJob
  ➥ inputFile=file:./products.txt date(date)=2010/12/08
```

Note the format of the date: yyyy/mm/dd. Table 4.2 lists the different types of job parameters along with examples.

Table 4.2 Job parameters types for CommandLineJobRunner

Type	Java type	Example
String	java.lang.String	inputFile(string)=products.txt
Date	java.util.Date	date(date)=2010/12/08
Long	Long	timeout(long)=1000
Double	Double	delta(double)=20.1

This completes our tour of the CommandLineJobRunner class. This command-line launcher is handy because it allows you to specify a Spring configuration file, the name of the job you want to start, and job parameters (with some advanced type conversion).

Let's now see an advanced feature of the runner that you use when you need to set the system exit code returned by the launcher. Use this feature if you want to run a series of jobs and choose precisely which job should follow a previous job.

HANDLING EXIT CODES

The CommandLineJobRunner lets you set the exit code to return when the job execution ends. The triggering system (a system scheduler, for example) can use this exit code to decide what to do next (see the sidebar on the use of exit codes). For example, after the execution of job A, you want to run either job B or job C. The scheduler decides on the basis of the exit code returned by job A.

If you use the `CommandLineJobRunner` but don't care about exit codes, because you don't execute sequences of jobs or you organize all the sequencing of your batch processes as Spring Batch steps, you can skip this subsection. But if your batch system relies on exit codes to organize the sequencing of your jobs, you'll learn here how Spring Batch lets you easily choose which exit code to return from a job execution.

What's the deal with exit codes?

A system process always returns an integer exit code when it terminates. As previously mentioned, system schedulers commonly trigger batch processes launched from the command line, and these schedulers can be interested in the exit code of the batch process. Why? To determine the course of action. An exit code of 0 could mean that everything went okay, 1 could mean that a fatal error occurred, and 2 could mean that the job must be restarted. That's why the Spring Batch command-line launcher provides advanced support to map job exit statuses (string) with system exit codes (integer).

The `CommandLineJobRunner` uses an *exit code mapper* to map a job's exit status (a string) with a system exit code (an integer). Figure 4.6 illustrates this mapping.

Figure 4.6   The command-line job runner uses an exit code mapper to translate the string exit status of a Spring Batch job into an integer system exit code. The triggering system—a system scheduler here—can then use this system exit code to decide what to do next.

What is the exit code for a Spring Batch job? A job's exit code is a property of the job's exit status, which is itself part of the job execution returned by the job launcher. Spring Batch provides an `ExitStatus` class, which includes an exit code typed as a `String`. Don't confuse `BatchStatus` (an enumeration) and `ExitStatus` (a simple string)! These are different concepts, even if, in most cases, the exit status is directly determined from the batch status. Chapter 10 provides in-depth coverage of the batch status and exit status. For now, just remember that, by default, Spring Batch gets the exit status from the batch status (either COMPLETED or FAILED) and that you can override this default behavior if you want to return a specific exit status.

Table 4.3 explains the `CommandLineJobRunner` default behavior for exit code mappings (the `SimpleJvmExitCodeMapper` class implements this behavior).

System exit code	Job's exit status
0	The job completed successfully (COMPLETED).
1	The job failed (FAILED).
2	Used for errors from the command-line job runner—for example, the runner couldn't find the job in the Spring application context.

Table 4.3 Default exit code mappings

You can override the defaults listed in table 4.3 if they don't suit your needs. How do you do that? Write an implementation of the ExitCodeMapper interface and declare a Spring bean of the corresponding type in the job's Spring application context. There's nothing more to do, because the CommandLineJobRunner automatically uses the ExitCodeMapper.

Let's look at an example to illustrate overriding the default exit code mapper. Remember, the goal is to use the exit code returned by a job to decide what to do next. Imagine that this job (call it job A) deals with importing items from a file into a database. The system scheduler you're using runs job A and behaves as follows depending on the exit code returned by job A:

- 0—Starts job B (job A completed)
- 1—Does nothing (job A failed)
- 2—Does nothing (job A exited with an unknown job exit status)
- 3—Starts job C (job A completed but skipped some items during processing)

Your job as the developer of job A is to return the correct exit code such that the system scheduler uses it to decide what to do next. To do so, you write an implementation of ExitCodeMapper to handle the exit code strategy and install it in job A. The following listing shows the implementation of an ExitCodeMapper that honors this contract.

Listing 4.1 Writing an `ExitCodeMapper` to map job and system exit codes

```
package com.manning.sbia.ch04;

import org.springframework.batch.core.ExitStatus;
import org.springframework.batch.core.launch.support.ExitCodeMapper;

public class SkippedAwareExitCodeMapper implements ExitCodeMapper {

  @Override
  public int intValue(String exitCode) {
    if(ExitStatus.COMPLETED.getExitCode().equals(exitCode)) {
      return 0;
    } else if(ExitStatus.FAILED.getExitCode().equals(exitCode)) {
      return 1;
    } else if("COMPLETED WITH SKIPS".equals(exitCode)) {
      return 3;
    } else {
      return 2;
    }
  }

}
```

Note that the exitCode argument of the intValue method comes from the ExitStatus object of the job, which has a getExitCode() method. Implementing an exit code mapper is straightforward: you get a String and return a matching integer. But how can the job's exit code (the String argument of the exitCode method) get values like COMPLETED WITH SKIPS? This isn't magic: you set the value at the step level (chapter 10 teaches you how to do that). Let's assume here that you configured your job correctly to receive the appropriate exit status if the job skipped some items.

Now that the exit code mapper is implemented, you must declare it in the Spring configuration, as shown in the following snippet:

```
<bean class="com.manning.sbia.ch04.SkippedAwareExitCodeMapper" />

<job id="importProductsJob"
    xmlns="http://www.springframework.org/schema/batch">
  (...)
</job>
(...)
```

That's it; you map exactly what Spring Batch exit code maps to what system exit code! All you do is declare an exit code mapper bean alongside your job configuration, and the `CommandLineJobRunner` detects and uses the mapper automatically.

You now know how to launch Spring Batch jobs from the command line. When using the command line to launch a batch job, you need someone or something to trigger this command line. There are many ways to trigger batch jobs, and job schedulers are great tools to trigger jobs at specific times or periodically. This is the topic of our next section.

4.3 Job schedulers

A job scheduler is a program in charge of periodically launching other programs, in our case, batch processes. Imagine that you have a time frame between 2 a.m. and 4 a.m. to re-index your product catalog (because there are few users connected to the online application at that time) or that you want to scan a directory every minute between 6 a.m. and 8 p.m. for new files to import. How would you do that? You can implement a solution yourself using a programming language like Java, but this is time consuming and error prone, and system utilities probably aren't the focus of your business. Alternatively, job schedulers are perfect for this work: triggering a program at a specific time, periodically or not.

> **WARNING** Don't confuse job scheduling with process scheduling, which is about assigning processes to CPUs at the operating system level.

Our goal here is to use several job schedulers to launch Spring Batch jobs. We don't cover these job schedulers just for fun. We picked popular, mainstream, and free job schedulers to provide you with guidelines for choosing one over another, depending on the context of your applications. Before we dive into the descriptions of each solution, table 4.4 lists the job schedulers we cover and their main characteristics.

The descriptions in table 4.4 might already have helped you make up your mind: if your application doesn't run on a UNIX-like system, you won't be using cron! Note that you can use cron expressions outside of cron: Spring supports cron expressions.

Table 4.4   Overview of the job schedulers covered in this section

Job scheduler	Description
Cron	A job scheduler available on UNIX-like systems; uses cron expressions to periodically launch commands or shell scripts
Spring scheduler	The Spring framework scheduler; configurable with XML or annotations, it supports cron expressions; available in Spring 3.0 and later

4.3.1   *Using cron*

The cron program is the de facto job scheduler on UNIX-like systems. The name *cron* comes from the Greek *chronos* (time). Cron enables launching commands or shell scripts periodically, using *cron expressions*. Configuring cron is simple: you set up commands to launch and when to launch them in the *crontab* file.

CONFIGURING CRON WITH CRONTAB

The systemwide crontab file is stored in the /etc/ directory. Figure 4.7 shows the structure of a line of the crontab file.

The command can be anything; in our case, it can be something we covered in section 4.2. The following snippet shows an entry to launch a job with Spring Batch's command-line job launcher with the acogoluegnes user:

```
0 4 * * ?     acogoluegnes     java -classpath "/usr/local/bin/sb/lib/*"
   ➥ org.springframework.batch.core.launch.support.CommandLineJobRunner
   ➥ import-products-job.xml importProductsJob
   ➥ inputFile=file:/home/sb/import/products.txt date=2010/12/08
```

From the preceding snippet, you should recognize the structure of a cron entry (cron expression, user, and command). The command is long: it must set the classpath, the Java class to launch, the Spring configuration file to use, the name of the job to launch, and the job parameters. You can use any command in a crontab entry: Spring Batch's command-line launcher or any other command to launch a job process. Next is choosing when to trigger the command, which is where you use a cron expression.

If you're new to cron, the start of the entry in the previous snippet must be puzzling: this is a cron expression, which says to launch the job every day at 4 a.m. Cron expressions are to scheduling what regular expressions are to string matching. Depending on your background with regular expressions, this assertion can be appealing or scary!

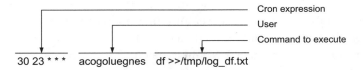

Figure 4.7   An entry in the crontab file has three parts: (1) the cron expression, which schedules the job execution; (2) the user who runs the command; and (3) the command to execute. Some cron implementations don't have the user option.

NOTE Cron expressions are beyond the scope of this book. If you want a good introduction to cron expressions, take a look at this web page: www.quartz-scheduler.org/docs/tutorials/crontrigger.html.

Now that you know how to trigger Spring Batch jobs periodically with cron, let's see some recommendations about the use of cron.

CRON FOR MY SPRING BATCH JOBS?

Is cron suited to launch your Spring Batch job? Remember, cron is a system scheduler: it spawns a new JVM process for each Spring Batch command-line launcher. Imagine that you need to launch a job every night. Cron triggers the command-line launcher, which creates a Spring application context before launching the job itself. Everything is fine. But imagine now that you need to launch another job that scans a directory for new files to import. You set up cron to trigger this job every minute. If bootstrapping the Spring application context is CPU intensive—because it initializes a Hibernate `SessionFactory` or a Java Persistence API context, for example—the job execution will perhaps be faster than the creation of the Spring application context! In this second case, you prefer to have your Spring application context already running and then simply launch the job from the existing `JobLauncher`. You can't easily achieve this from the command line (hence with cron), but a Java scheduler like the Spring scheduler will do the trick.

4.3.2 *Using the Spring scheduler*

Let's now look at the second scheduling option from table 4.4: the Spring scheduler. Do you want to schedule a job with a simple-to-deploy and yet powerful solution? Good news: Spring includes such a feature. As of version 3.0, the Spring Framework offers a declarative way to schedule jobs without requiring extra dependencies for your Spring Batch jobs, because Spring Batch sits on top of Spring.

Spring's lightweight scheduling provides features like cron expressions, customization of threading policy, and declarative configuration with XML or annotations. For XML configuration, Spring provides the task XML vocabulary (under the namespace www.springframework.org/schema/task), which comes in handy to configure and schedule tasks. The Spring scheduler needs a running Spring application context to work, so you typically embed it in a web application, but you can use any other managed environment, like an Open Services Gateway initiative (OSGi) container. We cover how to embed Spring Batch in a web application in section 4.4.1.

NOTE The cron system scheduler doesn't support seconds in cron expression, but Spring's scheduler does.

Follow these steps to use the Spring scheduler:

- *Set up the scheduler.* This is where you decide whether or not to use a thread pool. This setup is optional, and Spring uses a single-threaded scheduler by default.
- *Set up the Java methods to launch periodically.* You can use XML or annotations on the target methods. In our case, those methods use the Spring Batch API to launch jobs.

The next sections cover these steps, but let's first see what kind of scheduling configuration Spring supports.

SCHEDULING OPTIONS

Your scheduling requirements can be as simple as "every minute" or as complex as "the last weekday of the month at 23:00." Section 4.3.1 shows that cron expressions meet both requirements, but do you really need to unleash the big guns for "every minute"? Could you use something simple for simple requirements and fall back to cron expressions only when necessary? Spring allows you to do that by supporting cron expressions—with its own engine—but also lets you trigger a job at a fixed rate without resorting to cron expressions. Table 4.5 lists the scheduling options that Spring offers.

Table 4.5   Spring scheduling options

Scheduling option	XML attribute	Annotation attribute	Description
Fixed rate	`fixed-rate`	`fixedRate`	Launches periodically, using the *start* time of the previous task to measure the interval
Fixed delay	`fixed-delay`	`fixedDelay`	Launches periodically, using the *completion* time of the previous task to measure the interval
Cron	`cron`	`cron`	Launches using a cron expression

The fixed-rate and fixed-delay options are the simple options, depending on whether you want to launch job executions independently (fixed rate) or depending on the completion time of the previous execution (fixed delay). For more complex cases, use cron expressions. The next sections show you the use of the fixed-rate option with both XML and annotations; remember that you can use the attributes in table 4.5 for fixed rate or cron.

SCHEDULER SETUP

Spring uses a dedicated bean to schedule jobs. You can declare this bean using the `task` namespace prefix:

```
<task:scheduler id="scheduler" />
```

> **NOTE**   Remember that declaring a scheduler is optional. Spring uses the default single-threaded scheduler as soon as you declare scheduled tasks.

Even though Spring uses reasonable defaults, declaring a scheduler explicitly is good practice because it reminds you that an infrastructure bean takes care of the actual scheduling. It also serves as a reminder that you can tweak this scheduler to use a thread pool:

```
<task:scheduler id="scheduler" pool-size="10" />
```

Multiple threads are useful when you need to schedule multiple jobs and their launch times overlap. You don't want some jobs to wait because the single thread of your scheduler is busy launching another job.

Now that the scheduler's ready, let's schedule a job using XML.

SCHEDULING WITH XML

Imagine you have the following Java code that launches your Spring Batch job, and you want Spring to execute this code periodically:

```
package com.manning.sbia.ch04;

import java.util.Date;
import org.springframework.batch.core.Job;
import org.springframework.batch.core.JobParameters;
import org.springframework.batch.core.JobParametersBuilder;
import org.springframework.batch.core.launch.JobLauncher;

public class SpringSchedulingLauncher {

  private Job job;

  private JobLauncher jobLauncher;

  public void launch() throws Exception {          Launches
    JobParameters jobParams = createJobParameters();   job
    jobLauncher.run(job, jobParams);
  }

  private JobParameters createJobParameters() {    Creates job
    (...)                                          parameters
  }
  (...)
}
```

This snippet elides setter methods for brevity. It also elides the creation of job parameters, as job parameters are job specific. Most of the time, you'll be using a timestamp or a sequence to change the job identity for each run. Finally, exception handling is up to you: here, the `launch` method just propagates any exception that the job launcher throws. You could also catch the exception and log it.

You now need to tell Spring to call this code periodically. Fortunately, you inherit from all of Spring's configuration features: dependency injection and the `task` namespace to configure the scheduling. The following listing shows a scheduling configuration using XML.

Listing 4.2 Scheduling with Spring and XML

```
<bean id="springSchedulingLauncher"
      class="com.manning.sbia.ch04.SpringSchedulingLauncher">
  <property name="job" ref="job" />
  <property name="jobLauncher" ref="jobLauncher" />
</bean>

<task:scheduler id="scheduler" />

<task:scheduled-tasks scheduler="scheduler">
```

```
<task:scheduled ref="springSchedulingLauncher"
                method="launch"
                fixed-rate="1000" />
</task:scheduled-tasks>
```

You first declare the bean that launches the Spring Batch job. The `task:scheduled-tasks` element contains the tasks to schedule. For each task you schedule, you use the `task:scheduled` element and refer to the bean and the method to call, using the `ref` and `method` attributes, respectively. This listing uses a fixed rate, but remember that you can also schedule with a fixed delay or a cron expression.

An XML configuration has many advantages: it doesn't affect your Java code—making it easier to reuse—and it's flexible because you can externalize part of your configuration in a property file, using a Spring property placeholder. This allows switching the scheduling configuration between the development and production environments, for example. The XML configuration is external to your code: when you look at your Java code, you have no idea a scheduler launches it periodically. If you change the name of the Java method to launch periodically, you need to reflect this change in the XML configuration. If you want the scheduling configuration to be closer to your code than in a separate XML file, then annotations are the way to go.

SCHEDULING WITH ANNOTATIONS

Spring lets you schedule your jobs by annotating Java methods. The following snippet shows how to schedule a job with the Spring `@Scheduled` annotation:

```java
package com.manning.sbia.ch04;

import java.util.Date;
import org.springframework.batch.core.Job;
import org.springframework.batch.core.JobParameters;
import org.springframework.batch.core.JobParametersBuilder;
import org.springframework.batch.core.launch.JobLauncher;
import org.springframework.scheduling.annotation.Scheduled;

public class SpringSchedulingAnnotatedLauncher {

  private Job job;

  private JobLauncher jobLauncher;

  @Scheduled(fixedRate=1000)                          │ Schedules job
  public void launch() throws Exception {           ◁─┘ with fixed rate
    JobParameters jobParams = createJobParameters();
    jobLauncher.run(job, jobParams);
  }
  private JobParameters createJobParameters() {
    (...)
  }
  (...)
}
```

NOTE   Don't forget: you can use the `fixedDelay` or `cron` annotation attributes instead of `fixedRate`.

When using the @Scheduled annotation, the Java class does part of the configuration itself. The XML configuration is shorter, but you need to tell Spring to look for @Scheduled annotations with the task:annotation-driven element, as shown in the following snippet:

```
<bean id="springSchedulingAnnotatedLauncher"
      class="com.manning.sbia.ch04.SpringSchedulingAnnotatedLauncher">
  <property name="job" ref="job" />
  <property name="jobLauncher" ref="jobLauncher" />
</bean>

<task:scheduler id="scheduler" />

<task:annotation-driven scheduler="scheduler" />
```

Detects @Scheduled annotations

Using the @Scheduled annotation is straightforward: you activate its support with the task:annotation-driven element, and you add new tasks directly in Java without going back to the XML configuration. The annotation solution is less flexible, though: the scheduling configuration is hardcoded and it works only on that code (you can't annotate code you don't control).

What about Quartz?

Quartz is a Java-based job scheduler that you can integrate in any Java environment (standalone or Java Enterprise Edition). We chose not to cover Quartz here because you can do pretty much the same thing with the built-in scheduling support in Spring. Spring provides some support to integrate with Quartz. You can refer to Spring reference documentation for more information.

This ends the coverage of schedulers used to launch Spring Batch jobs. You can use a system scheduler like cron to launch Spring Batch jobs, which spawns a plain Java process for each job. But cron isn't suited for all cases, especially if bootstrapping the Spring application context is resource intensive and the job is triggered every second, for example. In such cases, use a Java-based scheduler, like Spring scheduler.

Remember, when using a Java scheduler, you already have a Spring Batch environment ready; you don't need to spawn a new JVM process for every job (as you do with cron, for example). You now have everything ready, assuming you found a container to run your application. A popular way to embed a Spring Batch environment and a scheduler is to use a web application. This is the second scenario presented in section 4.1.3. In the next section, we see how to embed Spring Batch in a web application.

4.4   *Launching from a web application*

Spring Batch is a lightweight framework that can live in a simple Spring application context. Here, we look at configuring a Spring Batch environment in a web application. This makes Spring Batch available at any time; there's no need to spawn a dedicated Java process to launch a job. We can also embed a Java scheduler in the same web application context and become independent of any system schedulers. Figure 4.8 illustrates that a Spring application context can be contained in a web application. Note that the job beans can also use any available services, like data sources, data access objects, and business services.

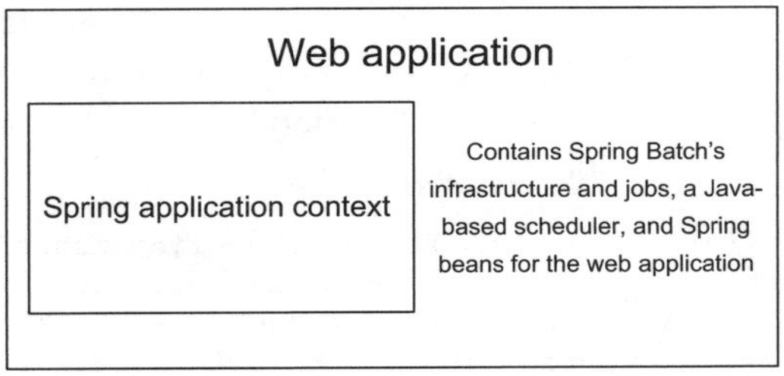

Hosting Spring Batch in a web application is convenient, but what about pushing this architecture further and triggering jobs through HTTP requests? This is useful when an external system triggers jobs and that system cannot easily communi-

Figure 4.8   A web application can contain a Spring application context. This Spring application context can host Spring Batch's infrastructure (job launcher, job repository) and jobs. The context can also host a Java-based scheduler (like Spring scheduler or Quartz) and any Spring beans related to the web application (data access objects, business services).

cate with the Spring Batch environment. But before we study how to use HTTP to trigger jobs, let's see how to configure Spring Batch in a web application.

4.4.1   Embedding Spring Batch in a web application

The Spring Framework provides a servlet listener class, the `ContextLoaderListener`, that manages the application context's lifecycle according to the web application lifecycle. The application context is called the *root* application context of the web application. You configure the servlet listener in the web.xml file of the web application, as shown in the following listing.

> **Listing 4.3   Configuring Spring in a web application**

```
<?xml version="1.0" encoding="UTF-8"?>
<web-app xmlns="http://java.sun.com/xml/ns/javaee"
    xmlns:xsi="http://www.w3.org/2001/XMLSchema-instance"
    xsi:schemaLocation="http://java.sun.com/xml/ns/javaee
    http://java.sun.com/xml/ns/javaee/web-app_2_5.xsd"
    version="2.5">
  <display-name>Spring Batch in a web application</display-name>

  <listener>
    <listener-class>
    org.springframework.web.context.ContextLoaderListener
    </listener-class>
  </listener>

</web-app>
```

By default, the `ContextLoaderListener` class uses an applicationContext.xml file in the WEB-INF directory of the web application to create the application context. This file should contain the configuration of the Spring Batch infrastructure, the jobs, the scheduler (if any), and application services. A best practice is to split up this configuration into multiple files. This avoids having a large and monolithic configuration file and encourages reuse of configuration files. Should you redefine all your jobs for integration testing? No, so define the jobs in a dedicated file and import this file from a master Spring file. The following snippet shows how the default applicationContext.xml imports other files to create a more maintainable and reusable configuration:

```
<?xml version="1.0" encoding="UTF-8"?>
<beans xmlns="http://www.springframework.org/schema/beans"
  xmlns:xsi="http://www.w3.org/2001/XMLSchema-instance"
  xsi:schemaLocation="http://www.springframework.org/schema/beans
  http://www.springframework.org/schema/beans/spring-beans-3.0.xsd">

  <import resource="batch-infrastructure.xml"/>
  <import resource="batch-jobs.xml"/>
  <import resource="scheduling.xml"/>

</beans>
```

If you follow the configuration of the previous snippet, the structure of the web application on disk should be as follows:

```
web application root directory/
  WEB-INF/
    applicationContext.xml
    batch-infrastructure.xml
    batch-jobs.xml
    scheduling.xml
    web.xml
```

What's next? If you use the Spring scheduler to start your jobs, the scheduling.xml file contains the corresponding configuration, and you're done! You can deploy the web application in your favorite web container, and the embedded Java scheduler will trigger jobs according to the configuration. Figure 4.9 shows this configuration.

In many cases, this configuration is fine. In others, the triggering event doesn't come from an embedded scheduler but from an external system. Next, we use HTTP to let this external system get access to our Spring Batch environment.

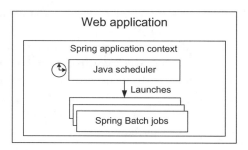

Figure 4.9 Once Spring Batch is in a web application, you can use an embedded Java scheduler such as Spring scheduler to launch jobs periodically.

4.4.2 Launching a job with an HTTP request

Imagine that you deployed your Spring Batch environment in a web application, but a system scheduler is in charge of triggering your Spring Batch jobs. A system scheduler like cron is easy to configure, and that might be what your administration team prefers to use. But how can cron get access to Spring Batch, which is now in a web application? You can use a command that performs an HTTP request and schedule that

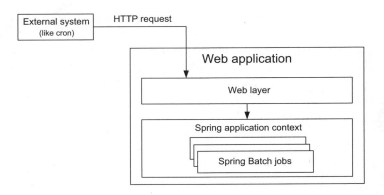

Figure 4.10 Once Spring Batch is in a web application, you can add a web layer to launch Spring Batch jobs on incoming HTTP requests. This solution is convenient when the triggering system is external to Spring Batch (like cron).

command in the crontab! Here's how to perform an HTTP request with a command-line tool like wget:

```
wget "http://localhost:8080/sbia/joblauncher?job=importProductsJob&
➥ date=20101218"
```

Figure 4.10 illustrates launching a Spring Batch job with an HTTP request.

To implement this architecture, you need a web controller that analyzes the HTTP parameters and triggers the corresponding job with its parameters. We use Spring MVC to do that, but we could have used any other web framework. We chose Spring MVC because it's part of the Spring Framework, so it's free to our Spring Batch application.

IMPLEMENTING A SPRING MVC CONTROLLER TO LAUNCH JOBS

Spring MVC is part of the Spring Framework and provides a simple yet powerful way to write web applications or Representational State Transfer (REST) web services. In Spring MVC, controllers are plain Java classes with some annotations. The following listing shows the job launcher controller.

Listing 4.4 A Spring MVC controller job launcher

```java
package com.manning.sbia.ch04.web;

import java.util.Enumeration;
import javax.servlet.http.HttpServletRequest;
import org.springframework.batch.core.JobParametersBuilder;
import org.springframework.batch.core.configuration.JobRegistry;
import org.springframework.batch.core.launch.JobLauncher;
import org.springframework.http.HttpStatus;
import org.springframework.stereotype.Controller;
import org.springframework.web.bind.annotation.RequestMapping;
import org.springframework.web.bind.annotation.RequestMethod;
import org.springframework.web.bind.annotation.RequestParam;
import org.springframework.web.bind.annotation.ResponseStatus;

@Controller
public class JobLauncherController {

  private static final String JOB_PARAM = "job";

  private JobLauncher jobLauncher;
```

```
    private JobRegistry jobRegistry;

    public JobLauncherController(JobLauncher jobLauncher,
        JobRegistry jobRegistry) {
      super();
      this.jobLauncher = jobLauncher;                        Gets job name   ❶
      this.jobRegistry = jobRegistry;                          from HTTP
    }                                                          parameter

    @RequestMapping(value="joblauncher",method=RequestMethod.GET)
    @ResponseStatus(HttpStatus.ACCEPTED)
    public void launch(@RequestParam String job,
        HttpServletRequest request) throws Exception {
      JobParametersBuilder builder = extractParameters(      ❷  Converts HTTP
        request                                                  parameters to
      );                                                         job parameters
      jobLauncher.run(
        jobRegistry.getJob(request.getParameter(JOB_PARAM)),  ❸  Launches
        builder.toJobParameters()                                 job
      );
    }

    private JobParametersBuilder extractParameters(
          HttpServletRequest request) {
      JobParametersBuilder builder = new JobParametersBuilder();
      Enumeration<String> paramNames = request.getParameterNames();
      while(paramNames.hasMoreElements()) {
        String paramName = paramNames.nextElement();
        if(!JOB_PARAM.equals(paramName)) {
          builder.addString(paramName,request.getParameter(paramName));
        }
      }
      return builder;
    }

}
```

The @RequestMapping annotation tells Spring MVC which URL and which HTTP operation to bind to the launch method. With the @RequestParam annotation on the job parameter ❶, you tell Spring MVC to pass the value of the job HTTP parameter to the method. As you probably guessed, this parameter is the name of the job you want to launch. At ❷, you extract HTTP parameters and convert them to job parameters. At ❸, you use the job launcher to launch the job. You use the @ResponseStatus annotation to return an empty HTTP response, with a 202 (ACCEPTED) status code.

> **NOTE** When using an HTTP request to start jobs, you should consider making the Spring Batch job launcher asynchronous; otherwise, the job execution will monopolize the web container's thread.

The launching request URL path should follow this syntax:

```
/launcher?job=importProductsJob&param1=value1&param2=value2
```

Finally, you may have noticed the jobRegistry property in the web controller in listing 4.4. The JobRegistry is a Spring Batch interface used to look up Job beans configured in the Spring application context. This is exactly what the launching controller does: from the job name passed in the request, it retrieves the corresponding Job bean. You need to declare the job registry in the Spring application context, typically where you declare the Spring Batch infrastructure. Following the structure previously listed, you add the following code in the /WEB-INF/batch-infrastructure.xml file to declare the job registry:

```
<bean id="jobRegistry"
      class="org.springframework.batch.core.configuration.support.
  ➥ MapJobRegistry" />
<bean class="org.springframework.batch.core.configuration.support.
  ➥ JobRegistryBeanPostProcessor">
  <property name="jobRegistry" ref="jobRegistry" />
</bean>
```

Now the controller is ready—let's configure Spring MVC!

CONFIGURING SPRING MVC

At the heart of Spring MVC is a servlet class, DispatcherServlet, which you declare in the web.xml file of your web application, as shown in the following listing.

> **Listing 4.5   Declaring Spring MVC's servlet in web.xml**

```
<?xml version="1.0" encoding="UTF-8"?>
<web-app xmlns="http://java.sun.com/xml/ns/javaee"
  xmlns:xsi="http://www.w3.org/2001/XMLSchema-instance"
  xsi:schemaLocation="http://java.sun.com/xml/ns/javaee
    http://java.sun.com/xml/ns/javaee/web-app_2_5.xsd"
  version="2.5">
  <display-name>Spring Batch in a web application</display-name>

  <listener>
    <listener-class>
    org.springframework.web.context.ContextLoaderListener
    </listener-class>
  </listener>

  <servlet>
    <servlet-name>sbia</servlet-name>
    <servlet-class>
    org.springframework.web.servlet.DispatcherServlet      ◁── Declares Spring
    </servlet-class>                                            MVC servlet
  </servlet>

  <servlet-mapping>
    <servlet-name>sbia</servlet-name>                       ◁── Maps servlet
    <url-pattern>/*</url-pattern>                               to URLs
  </servlet-mapping>
</web-app>
```

A Spring MVC servlet creates its own Spring application context. By default, its configuration file is [servlet-name]-servlet.xml. In this case, you create an sbia-servlet.xml file in the WEB-INF directory of the web application. You must declare the web controller in this file, as shown in the following snippet:

```
<?xml version="1.0" encoding="UTF-8"?>
<beans xmlns="http://www.springframework.org/schema/beans"
    xmlns:xsi="http://www.w3.org/2001/XMLSchema-instance"
    xsi:schemaLocation="http://www.springframework.org/schema/beans
    http://www.springframework.org/schema/beans/spring-beans-3.0.xsd">

  <bean class="com.manning.sbia.ch04.web.
➥ JobLauncherController">
    <constructor-arg ref="jobLauncher" />
    <constructor-arg ref="jobRegistry" />
  </bean>

</beans>
```

Declares job launcher web controller

In this configuration, you declare the controller and inject some dependencies, but where do these dependencies come from? From the root application context configured with the Context-LoaderListener. The Spring application context of the Spring MVC servlet can see the beans from the root application context because they share a parent-child relationship, as figure 4.11 shows.

You can now launch your Spring Batch jobs with a simple HTTP request! You should use this launching mechanism when an external system triggers your jobs and that system doesn't have direct access to your Spring Batch environment. Otherwise, you can just

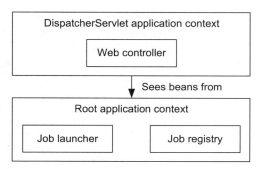

Figure 4.11 The web controller is defined in the servlet's application context. The root application context defines the job registry and the job launcher. Because the two application contexts share a parent-child relationship, you can inject beans from the root application context into the web controller.

deploy your Spring Batch environment in a web application and use an embedded Java-based scheduler to trigger your jobs. Remember, you can use Spring Batch wherever you can use the Spring Framework, and web applications are no exception.

We covered a lot of information on triggering and launching Spring Batch jobs. By now, you should know which solution to adopt for your batch system. Next, we learn how to stop all of these jobs.

4.5   Stopping jobs gracefully

We started many jobs in this chapter, but how do we stop them? Stopping a job is unfortunate because it means that something went wrong. If everything is okay, a job execution ends by itself without any external intervention. When it comes to stopping job executions, we distinguish two points of view. The first is the operator's point of view. The operator monitors batch processes but doesn't know much about Spring Batch. When something goes wrong, the operator receives an alert and stops a job execution, by using a JMX console, for example.

The second is the developer's point of view. The developer writes Spring Batch jobs and knows that under certain circumstances, a job should be stopped. What are these certain circumstances? They are any business decision that should prevent the job from going any further: for example, the job shouldn't import more than 1000 products a day, so the code should count the imported items and stop the execution just after the 1000th item.

Spring Batch provides techniques to stop a job for both the operator and the developer.

4.5.1   *Stopping a job for the operator*

Imagine that the import job has been running for two hours when you receive the following phone call: "The import file contains bad data—there's no use letting the import run!" Obviously, you want the import to stop as soon as possible to avoid wasting system resources on your server. Spring Batch provides the JobOperator interface to perform such an operation. The following snippet shows how to stop a job execution through a JobOperator:

```
Set<Long> runningExecs = jobOperator.getRunningExecutions("importJob");
Long executionId = runningExecs.iterator().next();
boolean stopMessageSent = jobOperator.stop(executionId);
```

> **NOTE**   Chapter 12 covers the JobOperator thoroughly. We focus here on the way to use JobOperator for stopping job executions.

The steps are simple: the job operator returns the identifiers of the running job executions for a given job name. You then ask the job operator to send a stop message to an execution using an execution ID. We discuss the notion of sending a stop message in the section, "Understanding the stop message."

INVOKING THE JOB OPERATOR

The next question is, how do you invoke this code? The most common way is to expose the job operator to JMX and call its method from a JMX console, as figure 4.12 illustrates using JConsole.

Another way to call job operator methods is to provide a user interface in your application that lets an administrator stop any job execution. You can create this user interface yourself, or you can use Spring Batch Admin, the web administration application introduced in chapter 2.

> **NOTE**   Chapter 12 covers how to expose a Spring bean to JMX as well as how to monitor Spring Batch with the Spring Batch Admin application.

Now that you know how to use the job operator, let's see how to configure it.

CONFIGURING THE JOB OPERATOR

The job operator isn't automatically available; you need to declare it in your Spring configuration. The following listing shows the Spring configuration required to declare the job operator.

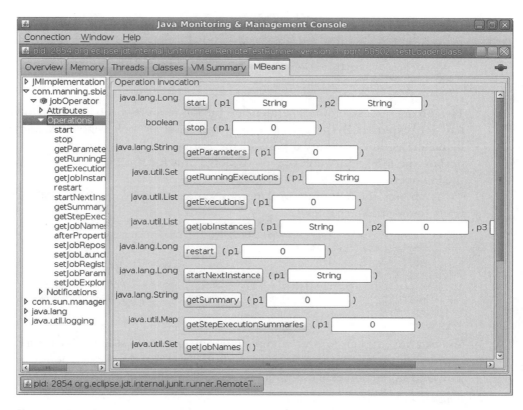

Figure 4.12 You can expose the job operator bean to JMX and then call its methods remotely from a JMX client like JConsole. An operator can learn about the Spring Batch runtime and stop or restart jobs.

Listing 4.6 Configuring the job operator in Spring

```
<bean id="jobOperator" class="org.springframework.
  ➥ batch.core.launch.support.SimpleJobOperator">
  <property name="jobRepository" ref="jobRepository"/>
  <property name="jobLauncher" ref="jobLauncher" />
  <property name="jobRegistry" ref="jobRegistry" />
  <property name="jobExplorer" ref="jobExplorer" />
</bean>
```
                                                      **Declares job
                                                      operator bean**

```
<batch:job-repository id="jobRepository" data-source="dataSource" />

<bean id="jobLauncher" class="org.springframework.batch.core.launch.
  ➥ support.SimpleJobLauncher">
  <property name="jobRepository" ref="jobRepository" />
</bean>

<bean class="org.springframework.batch.core.configuration.
  ➥ support.JobRegistryBeanPostProcessor">
  <property name="jobRegistry" ref="jobRegistry" />
</bean>
```

```
<bean id="jobRegistry"class="org.springframework.batch.core.
➥ configuration.support.MapJobRegistry" />

<bean id="jobExplorer" class="org.springframework.batch.core.explore.
➥ support.JobExplorerFactoryBean">
  <property name="dataSource" ref="dataSource" />
</bean>
```

The job operator has four dependencies: the job repository, job launcher, job registry, and job explorer. By now, you're used to seeing the job repository and the job launcher, as they're essential parts of the Spring Batch infrastructure. You need to declare the job registry and the job explorer only for specific tasks, and configuring the job operator is one.

As a bonus, the following configuration exposes the job operator to JMX. This saves you a round trip to chapter 12.

```
<bean class="org.springframework.jmx.export.MBeanExporter">
  <property name="beans">
    <map>
      <entry key="com.manning.sbia:name=jobOperator"
             value-ref="jobOperator" />
    </map>
  </property>
</bean>
```

You can now explain to your administration team how to stop a job execution. But a member of the administration team might tell you that a job execution doesn't stop. The next subsection explains what happens when you request to stop a job execution.

UNDERSTANDING THE STOP MESSAGE

When we showed the job operator in action, you may have found this line intriguing:

```
boolean stopMessageSent = jobOperator.stop(executionId);
```

The job operator returns a Boolean when you request to stop a job execution. This Boolean value tells you whether the stop message was sent successfully. A stop *message*? When you call the `stop` method on a job operator, there's no guarantee that the execution immediately stops after the call. Why? In Java, you can't stop code from executing immediately.

When does job execution stop after you request it? Let's imagine some business code is executing when you send the stop message. There are two possibilities:

1. The business code takes into account that the thread can be interrupted by checking `Thread.currentThread().isInterrupted()`. If the code detects the thread interruption, it can choose to end processing by throwing an exception or returning immediately. This means that the execution will stop almost immediately.

2. The business code doesn't deal with thread interruption. As soon as the business code finishes and Spring Batch gets control again, the framework stops the job execution. This means that the execution will stop only after the code finishes. If the code is in the middle of a long processing sequence, the execution can take a long time to stop.

Stopping in the middle of a chunk-oriented step shouldn't be a problem: Spring Batch drives all the processing in this case, so the execution should stop quickly (unless some custom reader, processor, or writer takes a long time to execute). But if you write a custom tasklet whose processing is long, you should consider checking for thread interruption.

Understanding the stop message is a first step toward the developer's point of view, so let's now see how to stop a job execution from application code.

4.5.2 Stopping a job for the application developer

We saw that an administrator can use the job operator to stop a job execution, but sometimes stopping the execution from within the job itself is necessary. Imagine you're indexing your product catalog with a Spring Batch job. The online store application can work with some unindexed products, but the job execution shouldn't overlap with periods of high activity, so it shouldn't run after 8 a.m. You can check the time in various places in the job and decide to stop the execution after 8 a.m.

The first way to stop execution is to throw an exception. This works all the time, unless you configured the job to skip some exceptions in a chunk-oriented step!

The second and preferred way to stop execution is to set a stop flag in the step execution object. To set this stop flag, call the method `StepExecution.setTerminate-Only()`, which is equivalent to sending a stop message. As soon as Spring Batch gets control of the processing, it stops the job execution. The next topic to cover is how to get access to the `StepExecution` object from a job. Getting access to the `StepExecution` depends on whether you're working directly with a tasklet or in a chunk-oriented step. Let's study both cases now.

STOPPING FROM A TASKLET

A tasklet has direct access to the `StepExecution` through the step context, itself in the chunk context. The following listing shows a tasklet that processes items, checks a stop condition, and sets the stop flag accordingly. The stop condition could be any business decision, such as the time restriction mentioned previously.

Listing 4.7 Setting the stop flag from a tasklet

```
package com.manning.sbia.ch04.stop;

import org.springframework.batch.core.StepContribution;
import org.springframework.batch.core.scope.context.ChunkContext;
import org.springframework.batch.core.step.tasklet.Tasklet;
import org.springframework.batch.repeat.RepeatStatus;

public class ProcessItemsTasklet implements Tasklet {

  @Override
  public RepeatStatus execute(StepContribution contribution,
      ChunkContext chunkContext) throws Exception {
    if(shouldStop()) {
      chunkContext.getStepContext()
        .getStepExecution().setTerminateOnly();          Sets stop flag
```

```
  }
  processItem();
  if(moreItemsToProcess()) {
    return RepeatStatus.CONTINUABLE;
  } else {
    return RepeatStatus.FINISHED;
  }
}

(...)

}
```

Setting the stop flag in a tasklet is straightforward; let's now see how to do this in a chunk-oriented step.

STOPPING FROM A CHUNK-ORIENTED STEP

Remember how a chunk-oriented step works: Spring Batch drives the flow and lets you plug in your business logic or reuse off-the-shelf components to read, process, or write items. If you look at the `ItemReader`, `ItemProcessor`, and `ItemWriter` interfaces, you won't see a `StepExecution`. You access the `StepExecution` to stop the execution using *listeners*.

> **NOTE** Not dealing with stopping a job in item readers, processors, and writers is a good thing. These components should focus on their processing to enforce separation of concerns.

Chapter 3 covers the configuration of listeners, but we give you enough background here to use them for stopping jobs. The idea of a listener is to react to the lifecycle events of a step. You register a listener on a step by using annotations or implementing interfaces, and Spring Batch calls corresponding methods throughout the lifecycle of that step. What lifecycle events can you listen for? A lot of them: step start; after each read, processed, or written item; step end, and so on. The following listing shows a listener that keeps a reference to the `StepExecution` and checks a stopping condition after each read item. This listener uses annotations.

Listing 4.8   An annotated listener to stop a job execution

```
package com.manning.sbia.ch04.stop;

import org.springframework.batch.core.StepExecution;
import org.springframework.batch.core.annotation.AfterRead;
import org.springframework.batch.core.annotation.BeforeStep;

public class StopListener {

  private StepExecution stepExecution;

  @BeforeStep
  public void beforeStep(
      StepExecution stepExecution) {            Registers step
    this.stepExecution = stepExecution;         execution
  }
```

```
@AfterRead
public void afterRead() {
  if(stopConditionsMet()) {                          Sets stop flag
    stepExecution.setTerminateOnly();                if necessary
  }
}
}
(...)
}
```

The real work is to implement the stopping condition, which is a business decision (the body of the stopConditionsMet method in our example). The following listing shows how to register the listener on the chunk-oriented step.

Listing 4.9 Registering the stop listener on the step

```
<bean id="stopListener" class="com.manning.sbia.ch04.stop.StopListener" />

<batch:job id="importProductsJob">
  <batch:step id="importProductsStep">
    <batch:tasklet>
      <batch:chunk reader="reader" writer="writer" commit-interval="100"/>
      <batch:listeners>
        <batch:listener ref="stopListener" />           Registers
      </batch:listeners>                                 listener
    </batch:tasklet>
  </batch:step>
</batch:job>
```

Note how the listener mechanism makes the stopping decision a crosscutting concern: no component in the step—only the dedicated listener—knows about stopping.

Combining scheduling and stopping jobs

Scheduling isn't only for starting jobs; you can also schedule stopping your jobs. If a job runs at night but must stop at 6 a.m., you can schedule a task to send a stop signal. By doing so, you won't embed the stop logic in your job.

This concludes the coverage of stopping a Spring Batch job. You saw how to stop a job execution from the operator's point of view. You configure a job operator bean that you can expose to JMX and call the appropriate sequence of methods to stop a specific job execution. Don't forget that stopping an execution is only a request message: your code must be aware of this message if you want the execution to stop quickly. As soon as Spring Batch gets control of the processing, it does its best to stop the execution gracefully. Finally, remember that you can choose to stop the execution from within your business code.

4.6   *Summary*

Launching Spring Batch jobs is easy, and we covered the most common scenarios you're likely to encounter in batch systems. With Spring Batch, you can stick to the popular cron-plus-command-line scenario by using either your own Java program or Spring Batch's generic command-line runner. You can also choose to embed Spring Batch in a web application combined with a Java scheduler. Spring provides lightweight support for scheduling.

We provided you with the following guidelines:

- The generic command-line launcher-plus-cron solution is good for jobs that don't run with a high frequency. For example, you shouldn't use this solution when the batch environment initialization is costly and the batch job runs every 30 seconds.
- If you want your batch environment ready all the time, embed your Spring Batch environment in a web application.
- Once your batch environment is in a web application, also embed a Java scheduler to start your jobs. If the triggering event comes from an external system that doesn't have direct access to Spring Batch, use an HTTP request to trigger the execution.
- Imagine any launching system that suits your needs—the Spring Batch launching API is in Java, so you're limited only by the Java language and your imagination!
- Stopping a job execution uses a stop message. You should take this message into account in your code, but you can also count on Spring Batch to stop gracefully when it retakes control of the flow.

It's now time to go back to the heart of Spring Batch: chunk-oriented processing. The next three chapters cover the three corresponding phases of chunk processing: reading, writing, and processing.

Reading data

In the previous two chapters, we concentrated on configuring and launching batch jobs. It's now time to dig into the features at the heart of batch processes. As described in chapter 2, Spring Batch provides types for batch processes based on the concepts of *job* and *step*. A job uses a tasklet to implement chunk processing. Chunk-oriented processing allows jobs to implement efficiently the most common batch processing tasks: reading, processing, and writing.

We focus here on the first step of this process, reading. We describe general concepts and types implemented by Spring Batch. These built-in types are the foundation used to support the most common use cases. Spring Batch can use different data sources as input to batch processes. Data sources correspond to flat files, XML, and JavaScript Serialized Object Notation (JSON). Spring Batch also supports other types of data sources, such as Java Message Service (JMS), in the message-oriented middleware world.

In some cases, the Spring Batch built-in implementations aren't enough, and it's necessary to create custom implementations. Because Spring Batch is open source, implementing and extending core types for reading is easily achievable.

Another thing to keep in mind is that reading data is part of the general processing performed by the chunk tasklet. Spring Batch guarantees robustness when executing such processing. That's why built-in implementations implicitly provide integration with the execution context to store current state. The stored data is particularly useful to handle errors and restart batch processes. We concentrate here on the data-reading capabilities of Spring Batch and leave chapter 8 to cover in detail these other aspects.

We use our case study to describe concrete use cases taken from the real world. We explain how to import product data from different kinds of input, with different formats, and how to create data objects.

5.1   *Data reading concepts*

In this section, we introduce key concepts and types related to reading data in Spring Batch. These concepts are the foundation for the Spring Batch reading feature. This feature and its related types operate within the chunk tasklet, as illustrated in figure 5.1.

This chapter focuses on the first part of chunk processing. At this level, the first key type is the `ItemReader` interface that provides a contract for reading data. This interface supports generics and contains a `read` method that returns the next element read:

```
public interface ItemReader<T> {
  T read() throws Exception, UnexpectedInputException,
              ParseException, NonTransientResourceException;
}
```

If you've toured the Spring Batch documentation, you've noticed that readers implement another key interface: `ItemStream`. The `ItemStream` interface is important because it allows interaction with the execution context of the batch process to store and restore state. It's also useful when errors occur. In this chapter, we concentrate on the `ItemReader`, and we discuss state management in chapter 8. At this point, it's only necessary to know that readers can save state to properly handle errors and restart.

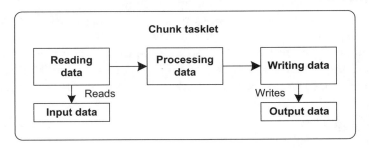

Figure 5.1   A chunk tasklet reads, processes, and writes data.

The following snippet describes the content of the `ItemStream` interface. The `open` and `close` methods open and close the stream. The `update` method allows updating the state of the batch process:

```
public interface ItemStream {
  void open(ExecutionContext executionContext)
                  throws ItemStreamException;
  void update(ExecutionContext executionContext)
                  throws ItemStreamException;
  void close() throws ItemStreamException;
}
```

You can create your own implementations of the `ItemReader` and `ItemStream` interfaces, but Spring Batch provides implementations for common data sources to batch processes. Throughout this chapter, we use our case study as the background story and describe how to import product data into the online store using different data sources.

5.2   *Reading flat files*

The first data source we describe to input data in batch processes is files. A *file* contains a set of data to integrate into an information system. Each type of file has its own syntax and data structure. Each structure in the file identifies a different data element. To configure a file type in Spring Batch, we must define its format.

Figure 5.2 illustrates the batch process inputs in our case study. Look at each box in figure 5.2 and see how Spring Batch handles that format.

Flat files are pure data files and contain little or no metadata information. Some flat file formats, such as comma-separate value (CSV), may contain one header line as the first line that names columns. In general, though, the file provider defines the file format. This information can consist of field lengths or correspond to a separator splitting data fields. Configuring Spring Batch to handle flat files corresponds to defining the file format to map file records to data objects.

The item reader for flat files is responsible for identifying records in the file and then creating data objects from these records, as shown in figure 5.3.

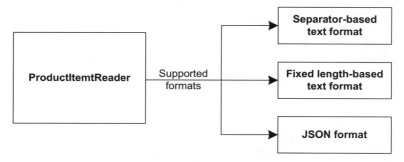

Figure 5.2   The supported file formats in the case study are separator-based text, fixed length-based text, and JSON.

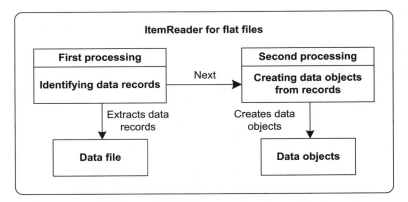

Figure 5.3 `ItemReader` **processing for flat files. The item reader first identifies records, and then creates data objects.**

The `ItemReader` implementation for flat files is the `FlatFileItemReader` class. Several other types work in conjunction with the `FlatFileItemReader` to identify data fields from file lines and to create data objects, as pictured in figure 5.4.

Three interfaces work closely with the `FlatFileItemReader` class. The `Record-SeparatorPolicy` interface identifies data records in a file. The `LineMapper` interface is responsible for extracting data from lines. The `LineCallbackHandler` interface handles data lines in special cases.

The `DefaultLineMapper` class is the default and most commonly used implementation of the `LineMapper` interface. Two additional interfaces related to the `DefaultLine-Mapper` class come into play. The `DefaultLineMapper` class holds a `LineTokenizer` responsible for splitting data lines into tokens and a `FieldSetMapper` to create data objects from tokens.

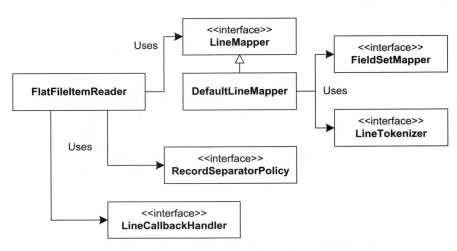

Figure 5.4   Classes and interfaces involved in reading and parsing flat files

Table 5.1 summarizes the interfaces from figure 5.4.

Table 5.1 Interfaces for flat file processing with the `FlatFileItemReader` class

Entity	Description
`LineMapper`	Maps a data line to a data object
`FieldSetMapper`	Creates a data object from tokens; invoked by the `DefaultLine-Mapper` class, the default implementation of the `LineMapper` interface
`LineTokenizer`	Splits a data line into tokens; invoked by the `DefaultLineMapper` class, the default implementation of the `LineMapper` interface
`RecordSeparatorPolicy`	Identifies beginning and end of data records
`LineCallbackHandler`	Provides data lines in special cases; the common usage is for lines skipped by the `FlatFileItemReader` class during processing

These interfaces are all involved when configuring the `FlatFileItemReader` class for a file format. You'll use these interfaces and their corresponding implementations to handle various file formats in this chapter.

This section on flat files introduced all concepts and types related to the item reader for flat files to import data files as objects. In the next section, we describe the general configuration of a `FlatFileItemReader` bean in Spring Batch as well as implementations for record-separator policies and line mappers. We then explain how to handle delimited, fixed-length, and JSON file formats and describe advanced concepts to support records split over several lines and heterogonous records.

5.2.1 *Configuring the FlatFileItemReader class*

The `FlatFileItemReader` class is configured as a Spring bean and accepts the properties described in table 5.2.

Table 5.2 `FlatFileItemReader` properties

Property	Type	Description
`bufferedReaderFactory`	`BufferedReaderFactory`	Creates `BufferReader` instances for the input file. The default factory (`DefaultBufferedReader-Factory`) provides a suitable instance for text files. Specifying another factory is useful for binary files.
`comments`	`String[]`	Specifies comment prefixes in the input file. When a line begins with one of these prefixes, Spring Batch ignores that line.

Table 5.2 `FlatFileItemReader` properties *(continued)*

Property	Type	Description
encoding	String	The input file's encoding. The default value is the class's `DEFAULT_CHARSET` constant.
lineMapper	LineMapper<T>	Creates objects from file data records.
linesToSkip	int	The number of lines to skip at the beginning of the file. This feature is particularly useful to handle file headers. If the `skippedLinesCallback` property is present, the item reader provides each line to the callback.
recordSeparatorPolicy	RecordSeparatorPolicy	How the input file delimits records. The provided class can detect single or multiline records.
resource	Resource	The input resource. You can use standard Spring facilities to locate the resource.
skippedLinesCallback	LineCallbackHandler	The callback for lines skipped in the input file. Used jointly with the `linesToSkip` property.
strict	boolean	Whether item reader throws an exception if the resource doesn't exist. The default value is `true`.

The following listing describes how to configure an instance of the `FlatFileItem-Reader` class in Spring Batch using the properties `linesToSkip`, `recordSeparatorPolicy`, and `lineMapper`. You use this type of configuration for the online store use case with flat files.

Listing 5.1 Configuring a `FlatFileItemReader`

```
<bean id="productItemReader"
      class="org.springframework.batch.item.file.FlatFileItemReader">
  <property name="resource" value="datafile.txt"/>
  <property name="linesToSkip" value="1"/>
  <property name="recordSeparatorPolicy"
            ref="productRecordSeparatorPolicy"/>
  <property name="lineMapper" ref="productLineMapper"/>
</bean>

<bean id="productRecordSeparatorPolicy" class="(...)">
  (...)
</bean>
```

```
<bean id="productLineMapper" class="(...)">
  (...)
</bean>
```

Specifying the value 1 for the linesToSkip property means that the reader doesn't consider the first line as a data line and that the line will be skipped. In the context of the use case, this line corresponds to the file header describing the record fields. The recordSeparatorPolicy property determines how to delimit product records in the file. Finally, the code specifies how to create a product object from a data record using the lineMapper property. To lighten the listing, we elided the beans corresponding to the two last entities but we detail them next.

The first type, the RecordSeparatorPolicy interface, delimits data records with the following methods:

```
public interface RecordSeparatorPolicy {
  boolean isEndOfRecord(String line);
  String postProcess(String record);
  String preProcess(String record);
}
```

The RecordSeparatorPolicy interface detects the end of a record and can preprocess and postprocess lines. Implementations can support continuation markers and unbalanced quotes at line ends. The FlatFileItemReader class uses a RecordSeparatorPolicy to build data records when parsing the data file. Spring Batch provides several implementations of this interface, described in table 5.3.

Table 5.3 `RecordSeparatorPolicy` built-in implementations

Implementation	Description
SimpleRecordSeparatorPolicy	Separates input as one record per line; the simplest implementation and root class for all other implementations.
DefaultRecordSeparatorPolicy	Supports unbalanced quotes at line end and a continuation string.
JsonRecordSeparatorPolicy	Uses JSON as the record format and can detect JSON objects over multiple lines, based on numbers of tokens delimited by characters { and }.
SuffixRecordSeparatorPolicy	Expects a specific string at line end to mark the end of a record. By default, this string is a semicolon.

Configuring record separation policy classes can be simple because their default constructors cover the most common cases. The following XML fragment is an example:

```
<bean id="productRecordSeparatorPolicy"
      class="org.springframework.batch.item.file
                          .separator.DefaultRecordSeparatorPolicy">
```

Another important interface present as a property of the FlatFileItemReader class is the LineMapper interface. The LineMapper interface provides data objects from

---

JavaScript Object Notation (JSON)

JSON is an open and lightweight text-based standard designed for human-readable data interchange. It provides a way to structure text data using braces and brackets. This technology is similar to XML but requires about 30% fewer characters.

The JSON format is commonly associated with JavaScript because the language uses it to perform I/O for data structures and objects. The JSON format is language independent, but you usually see it used in Asynchronous JavaScript + XML (AJAX)-styled web applications.

---

record lines without knowing how Spring Batch obtained the lines. The LineMapper interface contains one method called mapLine:

```
public interface LineMapper<T> {
  T mapLine(String line, int lineNumber) throws Exception;
}
```

Spring Batch provides several implementations of this interface for different use cases and file formats, as described in table 5.4.

Table 5.4 LineMapper built-in implementations

Class	Description
DefaultLineMapper	The default implementation tokenizes lines and maps items to objects.
JsonLineMapper	Supports the JSON format for records and extracts data to a map for each record. This implementation is based on the jackson-mapper-asl.jar file that can be reached at the website http://jackson .codehaus.org/.
PassThroughLineMapper	Provides the original record string instead of a mapped object.
PatternMatchingCompositeLineMapper	Parses heterogeneous record lines. For each line type, a line tokenizer and a field-set mapper must be configured.

We describe in detail the DefaultLineMapper, JsonLineMapper, and PatternMatchingCompositeLineMapper implementations in the next sections. First, we take a quick look at the PassThroughLineMapper class.

The PassThroughLineMapper class performs no parsing or data extraction. It's simple to configure because it doesn't define properties. The configuration of this class is shown in the following XML fragment:

```
<bean id="lineMapper" class="org.springframework.batch.item
                    ➥ .file.mapping.PassThroughLineMapper"/>
```

The `DefaultLineMapper` class is the most commonly used implementation because it handles files with implicit structures using separators or fixed-length fields. In our use case, we accept several data formats for incoming data. We describe next how to configure Spring Batch to handle data structures based on separators and fixed-length fields.

5.2.2 *Introducing the DefaultLineMapper class*

The most commonly used implementation of the `LineMapper` interface is the `DefaultLineMapper` class. It implements line processing in two phases:

- Parses a line to extract fields using an implementation of the `LineTokenizer` interface
- Creates data objects from fields using an implementation of the `FieldSet-Mapper` interface

Figure 5.5 illustrates how the `LineTokenizer` and `FieldSetMapper` interfaces described in the preceding list interact within the `DefaultLineMapper`.

The `lineTokenizer` and `fieldSetMapper` properties configure the `DefaultLine-Mapper` class's `LineTokenizer` and `FieldSetMapper`. For example:

```
<bean id="productLineMapper"
    class="org.springframework.batch.item.file.mapping.DefaultLineMapper">
  <property name="lineTokenizer" ref="productLineTokenizer"/>
  <property name="fieldSetMapper" ref="productFieldSetMapper"/>
</bean>

<bean id="productLineTokenizer" class="(...)"> (...) </bean>
<bean id="productFieldSetMapper" class="(...)"> (...) </bean>
```

This example uses bean references (using the `ref` attribute), but you could also use an inner bean. The `lineTokenizer` property is set to an instance of `LineTokenizer`. The `fieldSetMapper` property is set to an instance of `FieldSetMapper`.

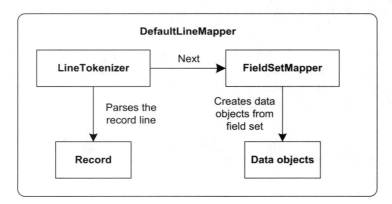

Figure 5.5 **Interactions between `LineTokenizer` and `FieldSetMapper` in a `DefaultLineMapper`. The `LineTokenizer` parses record lines, and the `FieldSetMapper` creates objects from field sets.**

5.2.3   *Using the DefaultLineMapper class*

It's now time to use `DefaultLineMapper` in our case study. The `FieldSetMapper` implementation remains the same; it creates objects from a `FieldSet`. The `LineTokenizer` implementation depends on the record format and provides the contract to create a field set from lines in a data file, as defined here:

```
public interface LineTokenizer {
  FieldSet tokenize(String line);
}
```

A `FieldSet` is returned by the `tokenize` method, which parses the record. A `FieldSet` contains all extracted record fields and offers several methods to manage them. Table 5.5 lists the Spring Batch implementations of the `LineTokenizer` interface for different ways to delimit fields in data lines.

Table 5.5   `LineTokenizer` built-in implementations

Implementation	Description
DelimitedLineTokenizer	Uses a delimiter to split a data line into fields. Defaults correspond to comma-separated values.
FixedLengthTokenizer	Uses field lengths to split a data line into fields.

5.2.4   *Extracting character-separated fields*

Let's take concrete examples from our case study. The first example contains product records that use the comma character to separate fields, as shown in the following example:

```
PR....210,BlackBerry 8100 Pearl,,124.60
PR....211,Sony Ericsson W810i,,139.45
PR....212,Samsung MM-A900M Ace,,97.80
PR....213,Toshiba M285-E 14,,166.20
PR....214,Nokia 2610 Phone,,145.50
PR....215,CN Clogs Beach/Garden Clog,,190.70
PR....216,AT&T 8525 PDA,,289.20
```

For this example, configuring a `LineTokenizer` consists of defining a `Delimited-LineTokenizer` with the names and delimiter properties. The `names` property defines the names of the fields, and the `delimiter` property defines the field delimiter; for example:

```
<bean id=" productLineTokenizer"
      class="org.springframework.batch.item.file
                 ➥ .transform.DelimitedLineTokenizer">
  <property name="delimiter" value=","/>
  <property name="names"
            value="id,name,description,price"/>
</bean>
```

The delimiter property specifies the character used to separate fields in a data file—in this case, the comma: ",". The names property defines the field names as an ordered list separated by commas: "id,name,description,price". When the tokenizer extracts a field from the data line, the corresponding name is associated with it so it's possible to get the field value by name.

EXTRACTING FIXED-LENGTH FIELDS

Another supported data structure in the case study is fixed-length fields. Note that such a data structure is potentially larger because all fields must have the same length. Here's an example of this structure:

```
PR....210BlackBerry 8100 Pearl              124.60
PR....211Sony Ericsson W810i                139.45
PR....212Samsung MM-A900M Ace                97.80
PR....213Toshiba M285-E 14                  166.20
PR....214Nokia 2610 Phone                   145.50
PR....215CN Clogs Beach/Garden Clog         190.70
PR....216AT&T 8525 PDA                       289.20
```

For this example, table 5.6 describes the lengths of each field. This format doesn't use a separator character.

Field name	Length in characters
id	9
name	26
description	15
price	6

Table 5.6 Fixed record field names and lengths

To configure the LineTokenizer for this type of example, you define a FixedLength-Tokenizer with names and columns properties. The properties respectively define the names of fields and the column ranges used to identify them:

```
<bean id=" productLineTokenizer"
     class="org.springframework.batch.item.file
                    ➥ .transform.FixedLengthTokenizer">
  <property name="columns" value="1-9,10-35,36-50,51-56"/>
  <property name="names"
          value="id,name,description,price"/>
</bean>
```

The columns property configures column ranges for each field. This property accepts a list of Range instances, but you can also configure it using a comma-separated string of ranges. You can see that this property numbers from 1 and not 0 because Spring's RangeArrayPropertyEditor class is internally used to configure the specified value into the value to set. The names property sets field names, as with the DelimitedLine-Tokenizer class.

> **Spring built-in `PropertyEditor` support**
>
> Spring provides support to configure properties as strings. The `PropertyEditor` interface describes how to convert strings to beans, and vice versa. For nonstring type properties, Spring automatically tries to convert to the appropriate type using the registered property editors. They come from the JavaBean specification and can be seen as a to/from string conversion service.
>
> This support is extensible: you can register your own property editors to convert strings to custom objects with the `CustomEditorConfigurer` class. Spring Batch uses this mechanism to register its own property editors to make some types easier to configure. For example, the `Range` class is configured with the `RangeArrayPropertyEditor` class.

5.2.5 *Creating objects from fields*

Now that you've configured extracting fields from data lines, it's time to specify how to create data objects from these fields. This process isn't specific to a particular `LineMapper` but relates to the field set structure.

The `FieldSetMapper` interface defines this process and uses generics to type implementations to application-specific types. Spring Batch defines the `FieldSetMapper` interface as

```
public interface FieldSetMapper<T> {
  T mapFieldSet(FieldSet fieldSet) throws BindException;
}
```

The `mapFieldSet` method implements the mapping where a `LineTokenizer` implementation has created the `FieldSet` instance. Table 5.7 lists the Spring Batch implementations of this interface for different ways to handle fields and create data objects.

Table 5.7 `FieldSetMapper` built-in implementations

Class	Description
BeanWrapperFieldSetMapper	Uses field names to set data in properties of data beans.
PassThroughFieldSetMapper	Provides the `FieldSet` without doing any mappings to objects. Useful if you need to work directly with the field set.

Before using a `FieldSetMapper`, you must implement the bean to receive the data. In the case study, as you import product data, the bean is a plain old Java object (POJO) that contains the id, `name`, `description`, and `price` properties, as shown in the following listing.

Listing 5.2 The `Product` bean

```
public class Product {
  private String id;
  private String name;
```

```
    private String description;
    price float price;

    public String getId() { return id; }
        public void setId(String id) { this.id = id; }
    (...)
    public float getPrice() { return price; }
    public void setPrice(float price) { this. price = price; }
}
```

To map the `FieldSet` instance to the `Product` data bean, you implement a `FieldSet-Mapper` to populate `Product` instances from a `FieldSet` instance. The following listing shows the `FieldSetMapper` implementation that creates `Product` instances.

Listing 5.3 Custom `FieldSetMapper` for creating `Product` objects

```
public class ProductFieldSetMapper implements FieldSetMapper<Product> {
  public Product mapFieldSet(FieldSet fieldSet) {
    Product product = new Product();
    product.setId(fieldSet.readString("id"));
    product.setName(fieldSet.readString("name"));
    product.setDescription(fieldSet.readString("description"));
    product.setPrice(fieldSet.readFloat("price"));
    return product;
  }
}
```

In the `mapFieldSet` method implementation, an uninitialized instance of a `Product` is first created. The `mapFieldSet` method then uses the `FieldSet` instance and its various read methods. The `FieldSet` class provides multiple read methods, one for each primitive Java type, plus `String`, `Date`, and `BigDecimal`. Each read method takes a field name or field index as a parameter; some methods also provide an argument for a default value.

You configure `ProductFieldSetMapper` as follows:

```
<bean id="productFieldSetMapper"
      class="com.manning.sbia.reading.ProductFieldSetMapper"/>
```

As described in table 5.7, Spring Batch provides a bean-based implementation of the `FieldSetMapper` interface: the `BeanWrapperFieldSetMapper` class. This class makes working with field sets easier because you don't have to write a custom `FieldSetMapper`.

You specify a data template for the bean using the `prototypeBeanName` property, where the value is the bean name for this template. You must configure the corresponding bean with the prototype scope. When a `Product` is instantiated, its properties are set using field set data. The bean property names and field names must match exactly for the mapping to take place. The following XML fragment shows this configuration:

```
<bean id="productFieldSetMapper"
      class="org.springframework.batch.item.file
                          ➡ .mapping.BeanWrapperFieldSetMapper">
  <property name="prototypeBeanName" value="product"/>
</bean>
```

```
<bean id="product"
      class="com.manning.sbia.reading.Product"
      scope="prototype"/>
```

After defining a bean of type `BeanWrapperFieldSetMapper`, you set its `prototype-BeanName` property to the identifier of the bean used to create data instances. For our case study, the bean type is `Product`.

Another interesting data format that Spring Batch supports is JSON. We introduced this format in tables 5.3 and 5.4 with dedicated Spring Batch types. In the next section, we describe how to implement and configure processing to support JSON-formatted data in our case study.

5.2.6 *Reading JSON*

Spring Batch provides support for JSON with a `LineMapper` implementation called `JsonLineMapper`. The following listing shows the JSON content of a data file corresponding to the data presented in the previous section. This is the last format for flat files in our case study.

Listing 5.4 Product data file using JSON

```
{ "id": "PR....210",
  "name": "BlackBerry 8100 Pearl",
  "description": "",
  "price": 124.60 }
{ "id": "PR....211",
  "name": "Sony Ericsson W810i",
  "description": "",
  "price": 139.45 }
{ "id": "PR....212",
  "name": "Samsung MM-A900M Ace",
  "description": "",
  "price": 97.80 }
(...)
```

Configuring the `JsonLineMapper` class is simple because line parsing is built into the class, and each `FieldSet` maps to a `java.util.Map`. No additional types are required to configure the class, as shown in the following XML fragment:

```
<bean id="productsLineMapper"
      class="org.springframework.batch.item.file.mapping.JsonLineMapper"/>
```

Using a `JsonLineMapper`, you get a list of `Map` instances containing all data from the JSON structure. If you were to convert this processing to code, you'd have a listing similar to the following.

Listing 5.5 JSON data processing as Java code

```
List<Map<String,Object>> products = new ArrayList<Map<String,Object>>();

Map<String,Object> product210 = new HashMap<String,Object>();
product210.put("id", "PR....210");
```

```
product210.put("name", "BlackBerry 8100 Pearl");
product210.put("description", "");
product210.put("price", 124.60);
products.add(product210);

Map<String,Object> product211 = new HashMap<String,Object>();
product211.put("id", "PR....211");
product211.put("name", "Sony Ericsson W810i");
product211.put("description", "");
product211.put("price", 139.45);
products.add(product211);

Map<String,Object> product212 = new HashMap<String,Object>();
product212.put("id", "PR....212");
product212.put("name", "Samsung MM-A900M Ace");
product212.put("description", "");
product212.put("price", 97.80);
products.add(product212);
```

Using the `JsonLineMapper` class is convenient to get data as `Map` objects, but it's perhaps not exactly what you need. At this point in the case study, you want to support several input data formats homogenously. For every type of format, data must come through as `Product` instances.

For this reason, your work isn't finished. You need to create an additional class implementing the `LineMapper` interface to wrap a `JsonLineMapper`. The purpose of this class, called `WrappedJsonLineMapper`, is to delegate processing to the target `Json-LineMapper` instance and then to create `Product` instances from `Map` objects. The following listing shows the `JsonLineMapperWrapper` class.

Listing 5.6 A `JsonLineMapper` wrapper to create data objects

```
public class JsonLineMapperWrapper implements LineMapper<Product> {
  private JsonLineMapper delegate;

  public Product mapLine(String line, int lineNumber) {        ❶ Delegates to target
    Map<String,Object> productAsMap                               JsonLineMapper
                  = delegate.mapLine(line, lineNumber);

    Product product = new Product();
    product.setId((String)productAsMap.get("id"));
    product.setName(                                             ❷ Populates
            (String)productAsMap.get("name"));                      product
    product.setDescription(                                         from map
            (String)productAsMap.get("description"));
    product.setPrice(
            new Float((Double)productAsMap.get("price")));

    return product;
  }
}
```

The `WrappedJsonLineMapper` class is a wrapper for a target `JsonLineMapper` instance defined with the `delegate` property. This makes it possible to delegate processing ❶ within the `mapLine` method and to get the corresponding result as a `Map`. The `mapLine` method then converts the `Map` to a `Product` object ❷.

We've described all the supported formats for flat files in Spring Batch. Before moving on to XML data input support in Spring Batch, we explain how to handle records spread over multiple lines and how to support several record types within the same data file.

5.2.7 *Multiline records*

The RecordSeparatorPolicy interface identifies record boundaries using its isEndOfRecord method. For files using only one line per record, unbalanced quotes, or continuation markers exceptions, you can use the default implementation of this interface, the DefaultRecordSeparatorPolicy class.

When an input source spreads records over several lines, a custom implementation is required to specify the conditions that delimit records. Imagine that each product record extends over two lines. The first line provides general data such as product identifier and name, and the second line includes additional information like the description and price. Here's an example of this format:

```
PR....210,BlackBerry 8100 Pearl,
,124.60
PR....211,Sony Ericsson W810i,
,139.45
PR....212,Samsung MM-A900M Ace,
,97.80
PR....213,Toshiba M285-E 14,
,166.20
(...)
```

In this case, the implementation of the isEndOfRecord method needs to detect if the line starts with a product identifier. If true, this *isn't* the end of the record. The following listing implements this format and assumes that no unbalanced quotes and continuation markers are present.

Listing 5.7 Reading multiline records with a custom RecordSeparatorPolicy

```
public class TwoLineProductRecordSeparatorPolicy
                        implements RecordSeparatorPolicy {

  public String postProcess(String record) {
    return record;
  }

  public String preProcess(String line) {
    return line;
  }

  private int getCommaCount(String s) {
    String tmp = s;
    int index = -1;
    int count = 0;
    while ((index=tmp.indexOf(","))!=-1) {
      tmp = tmp.substring(index+1);
      count++;
```

```
    }
    return count;
  }
  public boolean isEndOfRecord(String line) {
    return getCommaCount(line)==3;
  }
}
```

① **Checks comma count**

To determine if the current line is the end of the product record, you check if the string contains three commas **①** because a valid product must have four properties separated by commas (if a valid product required five properties, getCommaCount would be set to check for four commas). The remaining task is to set the implementation on the FlatFileItemReader bean using its recordSeparatorPolicy property, as described in listing 5.2.

To close the topic of reading from flat files, the following section describes heterogonous record handling within the same file.

5.2.8 *Reading heterogonous records*

Records present in flat files may not always be uniform. Each record still corresponds to one line, including support for unbalanced quotes and a continuation character, but can correspond to different data records. In our case study, this corresponds to having several product types with different data in the same file. The following file example contains mobile phone records as before and new book records:

```
PRM....210,BlackBerry 8100 Pearl,,BlackBerry,124.60
PRM....211,Sony Ericsson W810i,,Sony Ericson,139.45
PRB....734,Spring Batch in action,,Manning,34.95
PRM....212,Samsung MM-A900M Ace,,Samsung,97.80
PRB....735,Spring Roo in action,,Manning,34.95
PRM....213,Toshiba M285-E 14,,Toshiba,166.20
PRB....736,Spring in action,,Manning,44.95
PRM....214,Nokia 2610 Phone,,Nokia,145.50
```

In this data file example, lines beginning with PRM correspond to mobile phones (product-mobile), and lines beginning with PRB to books (product-book). In this case, you use polymorphism to create a basic product class and subclasses for specific types of products, mobile phones and books, as illustrated in figure 5.6.

Because the data file mixes different types of products, you must define rules to detect the product type for a given line. The prefix of the product identifier is used here: an identifier beginning with PRM is a mobile phone, and one with PRB is a book. To associate a line mapper for each line type, you use a LineMapper implementation called PatternMatchingCompositeLineMapper.

The PatternMatchingCompositeLineMapper class detects different records, parses them, and extracts data objects. The following listing describes how to configure the class as a bean to handle a multiproduct data file.

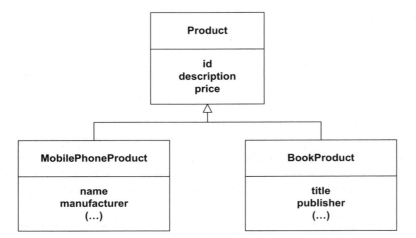

**Figure 5.6   Inheritance relationships between different kinds of products. The
MobilePhoneProduct and BookProduct classes inherit from the Product class.**

Listing 5.8   Configuring a composite `LineMapper`

```
<bean id="productLineMapper"                              Sets line tokenizers   ❶
      class="org.springframework.batch.item.file
                    .mapping.PatternMatchingCompositeLineMapper">
  <property name="tokenizers">
    <map>
      <entry key="PRM*" value-ref="mobileProductLineTokenizer"/>
      <entry key="PRB*" value-ref="bookProductLineTokenizer"/>
    </map>                                               ❷  Sets field set
  </property>                                                mappers
  <property name="fieldSetMappers">
    <map>
      <entry key="PRM*" value-ref="mobileProductFieldSetMapper"/>
      <entry key="PRB*" value-ref="bookProductFieldSetMapper"/>
    </map>
  </property>
</bean>

<bean id="mobileProductLineTokenizer" class="(...)"> (...) </bean>
<bean id="mobileProductFieldSetMapper" class="(...)"> (...) </bean>

<bean id="bookProductLineTokenizer" class="(...)"> (...) </bean>
<bean id="bookProductFieldSetMapper" class="(...)"> (...) </bean>
```

The first property, tokenizers ❶, registers all LineTokenizers in a map. The map
keys contain patterns that select a tokenizer for a given line. The wildcard "*" can be
used as a map key. The fieldSetMappers property ❷ configures field set mappers.

This section ends our description of flat file support in Spring Batch. This support
is powerful, flexible, and can handle varied data formats. To complete our presentation of using files as input, we look at XML. The main difference between XML and flat
files is that Java provides support for XML, which Spring Batch can use.

5.3   *Reading XML files*

As opposed to flat files, the Java runtime provides supports for XML. Java can process XML input using different techniques, including using a Streaming API for XML (StAX) parser. StAX is a standard XML-processing API that streams XML data to your application. StAX is particularly suitable to batch processing because streaming is a principal Spring Batch feature used to provide the best possible performance and memory consumption profile.

> **Batch performance and XML**
>
> Not all XML parsing approaches are suitable for obtaining the best performance for batch processes. For example, DOM (Document Object Model) loads all content in memory, and SAX (Simple API for XML) implements event-driven parsing. These two approaches aren't suitable and efficient in the context of batch processing because they don't support streaming.

Using XML alone in Java applications (and object-oriented applications) has limitations because of a mismatch between the XML and object-oriented models. To address this limitation and provide efficient conversion between XML and objects, the Spring framework includes the Object/XML Mapping framework (aka OXM or O/X Mapper). Spring OXM provides generic components called *marshaller* and *unmarshaller* to convert, respectively, objects to XML, and vice versa, as shown in figure 5.7.

In addition to the `Marshaller` and `Unmarshaller` interfaces, Spring OXM supports the object-to-XML mapping libraries listed in table 5.8.

Before diving into Spring Batch support for XML files, let's describe the XML vocabulary used for products in our case study. The following listing shows the contents of the file after conversion, as described in the section 5.2.3. This file format is the last supported import format in our case study.

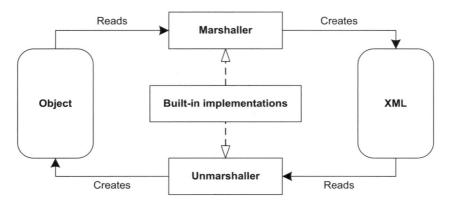

Figure 5.7   Spring OXM components

Library	Spring OXM `Marshaller` class
JAXB 1 and 2	`Jaxb1Marshaller` and `Jaxb2Marshaller`
Castor XML	`CastorMarshaller`
XMLBeans	`XmlBeansMarshaller`
JiBX	`JibxMarshaller`
XStream	`XStreamMarshaller`

Table 5.8   Built-in Spring OXM marshallers

Listing 5.9   XML product data converted from JSON

```
<products>
  <product>
    <id>PR....210</id>
    <name>BlackBerry 8100 Pearl</name>
    <description/>
    <price>124.60</price>
  </product>
  <product>
    <id>PR....211</id>
    <name>Sony Ericsson W810i</name>
    <description/>
    <price>139.45</price>
  </product>
  (...)
</products>
```

① product element

Each product corresponds to a `product` XML element ① under the root `products` element. Every product has four XML children elements for identifier, name, description, and price.

The `StaxEventItemReader` class implements the Spring Batch `ItemReader` interface using StAX to read XML documents. Because of its reliance on Spring OXM, it's independent of a parser implementation. Table 5.9 lists the `StaxEventItemReader` properties.

Table 5.9   `StaxEventItemReader` properties

Property	Description
`fragmentRootElementName`	The XML element name to import for each object.
`maxItemCount`	The maximum number of items to retrieve. The default value is `Integer.MAX_VALUE`.
`resource`	The resource to use as input. Because the property is of type `Resource`, you can use Spring to load the resource. See table 5.10.
`strict`	Whether the item reader throws an exception if the resource doesn't exist. The default is `false`.
`unmarshaller`	The Spring OXM `Unmarshaller` implementation used to convert XML to objects.

The key properties of the `StaxEventItemReader` class are `fragmentRootElementName`, used to identify the XML element to import, and `unmarshaller` to define XML-to-object conversions.

Table 5.10 lists most common built-in implementations of the `Resource` interface.

Table 5.10   Spring `Resource` implementations

Class	Description
UrlResource	Gets `java.net.URL` resources
ClassPathResource	Gets `classpath` resources
FileSystemResource	Gets `java.io.File` resources
ServletContextResource	Gets `ServletContext` resources from a web application
InputStreamResource	Gets `java.io.InputStream` resources
ByteArrayResource	Gets `byte[]` resources

The following listing describes how to configure a `StaxEventItemReader` bean to import product data from an XML file.

Listing 5.10   Configuring a `StaxEventItemReader`

```
<bean id="productItemReader"
      class="org.springframework.batch.item.xml.StaxEventItemReader">
  <property name="resource" value="datafile.xml"/>
  <property name="fragmentRootElementName" value="product"/>
  <property name="unmarshaller" ref="productMarshaller"/>
</bean>

<bean id="productMarshaller"
      class="org.springframework.oxm.castor.CastorMarshaller">
  <property name="mappingLocation"
        value="classpath:/com/manning/sbia/reading/xml/mapping.xml"/>
</bean>
```

You configure the `StaxEventItemReader` class by setting the value of the `fragmentRootElementName` property to `product`, which is the XML element name for a product. The `unmarshaller` property points to the bean definition used to convert XML to objects. You define this bean with the ID `productMarshaller`. This marshaller uses Castor through the Spring OXM class `CastorMarshaller`, which implements both the `Marshaller` and `Unmarshaller` interfaces.

Before tackling databases as input sources, we describe how to handle a file set with item readers. This approach is particularly useful for handling files in a directory. In our case study, this corresponds to product data files sent using FTP or Secure Copy (SCP) to an input directory.

5.4   *Reading file sets*

Input can enter an application as a set of
files, not only as a single file or resource. For
example, files can periodically arrive via FTP
or SCP in a dedicated input directory. In this
case, the application doesn't know in
advance the exact filename, but the names
will follow a pattern that you can express as
a regular expression. Figure 5.8 shows this
architecture with Spring Batch. A dedicated
multiresource reader accepts several
resources as input and delegates processing
to individual resource readers.

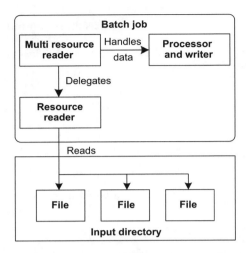

The `MultiResourceReader` class is the
resource reader used for this input scenario.
It handles multiple resources (`Resource[]`)
and a delegate, `ResourceAwareItemReader-`
`ItemStream`. The `MultiResourceReader`
handles one resource at a time, sequentially,
by iterating over all configured resources,
and delegates processing to a resource-aware
item reader.

**Figure 5.8   How Spring Batch reads data from
multiple files. A multiresource reader delegates
to a resource reader that reads files from an
input directory.**

This class is powerful because it leverages Spring resource support to easily configure multiple resources with simple patterns from different sources such as the file system or class path. A `MultiResourceReader` has two properties:

- `resources` configures resources with a list or patterns.
- `delegate` specifies the target `ResourceAwareItemReaderItemStream` to delegate processing for each resource.

The following XML fragment configures a `MultiResourceItemReader` to handle several files with an item reader. A file expression defines which files the reader uses as
input:

```
<bean id="multiResourceReader"
      class="org.springframework.batch.item.file.MultiResourceItemReader">
  <property name="resources" value="file:/var/data/input/file-*.txt"/>
  <property name="delegate" ref="flatFileItemReader"/>
</bean>

<bean id="flatFileItemReader"
      class="org.springframework.batch.item.file.FlatFileItemReader">
  (...)
</bean>
```

The `resources` property configures the resource reader with files that match the pattern /var/data/input/file-*.txt. The `delegate` property references the identifier of

the item reader used to process data. This item reader is configured as a bean in the Spring configuration and must be designed to handle resources. In Spring Batch, these item readers implement the `ResourceAwareItemReaderItemStream` interface.

> **Going beyond the multiresource item reader with partitioning**
> When using the `MultiResourceItemReader`, Spring Batch reads files one after the other. The processing is, by default, single threaded. If you face performance issues when dealing with multiple input files, Spring Batch has built-in support to parallelize processing. Spring Batch can process each file on its own thread and calls this technique *partitioning*. Chapter 13 covers scaling strategies like partitioning.

Spring Batch provides broad, flexible, and extensible support for flat files and XML. You can configure Spring Batch with the most common data file formats and integrate custom types. Next, we look at another input source for batch processes, relational databases.

5.5 Reading from relational databases

Another standard data input source is the relational database. In this case, data to import come from database tables. Spring Batch provides two approaches for batch processing to stream data from databases: JDBC and Object-Relational Mapping (ORM). We first see how Spring Batch leverages JDBC to read data from relational databases.

5.5.1 Using JDBC item readers

JDBC is the Java platform component providing the interface to relational databases in Java. JDBC is a Java technology that makes it possible to interact with relational databases using the SQL language for both querying and updating data. JDBC, in principle at least, keeps things simple and independent from databases' implementations. JDBC provides an abstraction over the specifics of different databases by using the concept of a *driver*, which is responsible for implementing communication with a specific database, as shown in figure 5.9. But it doesn't provide a complete solution to handle the specifics of each SQL dialect. The client application must deal with these issues. Spring uses JDBC but hides the JDBC plumbing and error-prone code and leaves the application to contain business-specific code.

Spring Batch bases its database support on the Spring JDBC layer and hides its use by managing request calls and transactions. In a batch job, you need to configure how to set request parameters and handle results. Spring Batch also bases its database support on the Spring `RowMapper` interface and JDBC `PreparedStatement` interface. In the next sections, we look at different reading techniques based on JDBC and supported by Spring Batch.

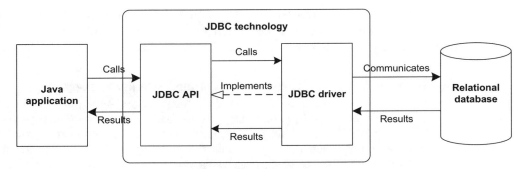

Figure 5.9   High-level JDBC architecture. An application uses the vendor-neutral JDBC API. A database-specific JDBC driver implements communication with the database system.

READING WITH DATABASE CURSORS AND JDBC RESULT SETS

In this approach, Spring Batch leaves the responsibility of reading data to the JDBC ResultSet interface. This interface is the object representation of a database cursor, which allows browsing result data of a SELECT statement. In this case, the result set integrates mechanisms to stream data. With this approach, Spring Batch executes only one request and retrieves result data progressively using JDBC with data batches, as shown in figure 5.10. Spring Batch relies on JDBC configuration and optimizations to perform efficiently.

The Spring Batch JdbcCursorItemReader class implements this technique and has the properties listed in table 5.11.

The minimal set of properties to use a JdbcCursorItemReader is dataSource, sql, and rowMapper. The properties specify the data source to access the database (data-Source), the SQL SELECT statement to execute to get data (sql), and the class to map

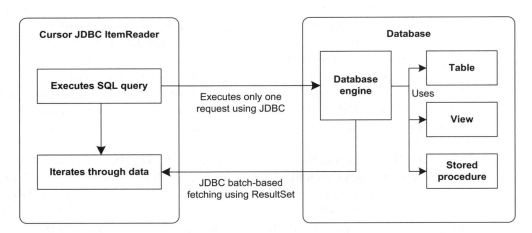

Figure 5.10   Getting input data from a JDBC ResultSet corresponding to result of a SQL request within the JdbcCursorItemReader class

Table 5.11 `JdbcCursorItemReader` properties

Property	Description
`dataSource`	The data source used to access the database.
`driverSupportsAbsolute`	Whether the JDBC driver supports using absolute row positioning on `ResultSet` using the `absolute` method. The default value is `false`.
`fetchSize`	The number of rows to fetch to transparently retrieve data by group. The default value is `-1`.
`ignoreWarnings`	Whether Spring Batch ignores SQL warnings. If `true`, Spring Batch logs warnings. If `false`, it throws exceptions when detecting warnings. The default value is `true`.
`maxRows`	The maximum number of rows that can be retrieved from SQL `SELECT` statements. The default value is `-1`.
`preparedStatementSetter`	The `PreparedStatementSetter` instance to set parameters for SQL statements.
`queryTimeout`	The maximum amount of time to wait for a response. If the timeout is exceeded, a `SQLException` is thrown. The default value is `-1`.
`rowMapper`	The `RowMapper` instance to build objects from `ResultSet` objects.
`sql`	The SQL `SELECT` to execute to get data.
`useSharedExtendedConnection`	Whether the connection is shared by the cursor and all other processing, therefore sharing the same transaction. If `false`, the cursor operates on its own connection and won't participate in any transactions started for the rest of the step processing. The default value is `false`.
`verifyCursorPosition`	Verifies the cursor position after processing the current row with `RowMapper` or `RowCallbackHandler`. The default value is `true`.

data into objects (`rowMapper`). If a statement has parameters, use the `preparedStatementSetter` property to set SQL statement parameters. In our use case, the SQL `SELECT` returns all the products to import from the `product` table and uses the `ProductRowMapper` class to convert data in the `ResultSet` to instances of the `Product` class. The following listing describes how to configure the `JdbcCursorItemReader` for this case.

Listing 5.11 Configuring a `JdbcCursorItemReader`

```
<bean id="productItemReader"
      class="org.springframework.batch.item.database.JdbcCursorItemReader">
  <property name="dataSource" ref="dataSource"/>
```

```
    <property name="sql"
              value="select id, name, description, price from product"/>
    <property name="rowMapper"
              ref="productRowMapper"/>
</bean>

<bean id="productRowMapper"
      class="com.manning.sbia.reading.jdbc.ProductRowMapper"/>
```

You set the SQL SELECT statement to get product data from the product table using the sql property of a JdbcCursorItemReader instance. Next, you set the RowMapper implementation for the product mapper to a bean reference. Finally, you declare the product row mapper to use the ProductRowMapper class.

The following listing defines a RowMapper implementation called ProductRow-Mapper, which is used in all our JDBC examples.

Listing 5.12   RowMapper implementation for Product

```
public class ProductRowMapper implements RowMapper<Product> {
    public Product mapRow(ResultSet rs, int rowNum)            ❶ Maps result set
        throws SQLException {                                     to domain object
        Product product = new Product();
        product.setId(rs.getString("id"));
        product.setName(rs.getString("name"));
        product.setDescription(rs.getString("description"));
        product.setPrice(rs.getFloat("price"));
        return product;
    }
}
```

The mapRow method ❶ is a factory method that creates Product instances based on a given JDBC ResultSet and row number.

You use the preparedStatementSetter property if the SQL statement includes parameters. The property value is a class that works directly on the Prepared-Statement instance managed internally by Spring to set the parameters. The following listing describes how to configure this feature in a JdbcCursorItemReader instance. In this listing, you get the subset of products for the names that start with "Samsung."

Listing 5.13   Setting SQL statement parameters in a JdbcCursorItemReader

```
<bean id="productItemReader"
      class="org.springframework.batch.item.database.JdbcCursorItemReader">
    <property name="dataSource" ref="datasource"/>
    <property name="sql"
              value="select id, name, description, price from product
                         where name like ?"/>
    <property name="preparedStatementSetter"
              ref="samsungStatementSetter"/>
    <property name="rowMapper" ref="productRowMapper"/>
</bean>

<bean id="samsungStatementSetter"
      class=" com.manning.sbia.reading.jdbc.SamsungStatementSetter"/>
```

You set the property prepared StatementSetter to reference the bean samsungStatementSetter. Then, you define the bean samsungStatementSetter as a SamsungStatementSetter that implements the PreparedStatementSetter interface. The SamsungStatementSetter class is

```
public class SamsungStatementSetter implements PreparedStatementSetter {
  void setValues(PreparedStatement ps) throws SQLException {
    ps.setString(1, "Samsung%");
  }
}
```

The JdbcCursorItemReader class provides advanced configuration for tuning batch processes. You can specify the maximum number of rows to retrieve through the maxRows property. The fetchSize property allows a reader to transparently retrieve data in fixed-sized groups. The following XML fragment describes how to configure these two properties:

```
<bean id="productItemReader"
      class="org.springframework.batch.item.database.JdbcCursorItemReader">
  <property name="dataSource" ref="datasource"/>
  <property name="sql"
            value="select id, name, description, price from product"/>
  <property name="rowMapper" ref="productRowMapper"/>
  <property name="maxRows" value="3000"/>
  <property name="fetchSize" value="100"/>
</bean>
```

In this example, you set the maximum number of rows to read to 3000 rows and the fetch group size to 100.

You don't always define SQL statements (here, a SELECT) outside the database in a configuration file; instead, a stored procedure can define the SQL to execute. This feature is supported by JDBC and Spring, and Spring Batch provides an Item-Reader implementation for stored procedures using the cursor-based approach. This item reader class is called StoredProcedureItemReader and accepts the properties listed in table 5.12 in addition to the properties for JdbcCursorItemReader listed in table 5.11.

Table 5.12 StoredProcedureItemReader **properties**

Property	Description
function	Whether the stored procedure is a function. A function returns a value; a stored procedure doesn't.
parameters	Parameter types for the stored procedure.
procedureName	Name of the stored procedure.
refCursorPosition	When results of the stored procedure are returned using a ref cursor in an out parameter, this value specifies the position of this parameter in the parameter list. This index is 0-based, and its default value is 0.

Using the `StoredProcedureItemReader` class is similar to using the `JdbcCursorItem-Reader` class. For common cases, replace the `sql` property with `procedureName`. In our case study, we have a stored procedure called sp_product that returns a product result set. The following XML fragment configures a `StoredProcedureItemReader`:

```
<bean id="reader"
 class="org.springframework.batch.item.database.StoredProcedureItemReader">
  <property name="dataSource" ref="dataSource"/>
  <property name="procedureName" value="sp_product"/>        ◁─┐ Sets stored
  <property name="rowMapper" ref="productRowMapper"/>           │ procedure name
</bean>
```

By default, the `procedureName` property configures a stored procedure that returns a `ResultSet` instance.

Databases also provide another way to obtain results, reflected in Spring Batch with the `function` and `refCursorPosition` properties of the `StoredProcedureItem-Reader` class. When the SQL code executed in the database is a stored function call, the `function` property must be set to `true`. If a ref cursor in an out parameter returns data, then the `cursorRefPosition` property must be set to the position of the cursor in the output parameter list, as described in the following XML fragment:

```
<bean id="reader"
 class="org.springframework.batch.item.database.StoredProcedureItemReader">
  <property name="dataSource" ref="dataSource"/>
  <property name="procedureName" value="sp_product"/>        ❶ Sets out
  <property name="parameters">                               ◁─┘ parameters
    <list>
      <bean class="org.springframework.jdbc.core.SqlOutParameter">
        <constructor-arg index="0" value="products"/>
        <constructor-arg index="1">
          <util:constant static-field="oracle.jdbc.OracleTypes.CURSOR"/>
        </constructor-arg>
      </bean>
    </list>
  </property>                                                 ❷ Sets cursor
  <property name="cursorRefPosition" value="1"/>             ◁─┘ ref position
  <property name="rowMapper" ref="productRowMapper"/>
</bean>
```

In this example, you define parameters for a stored procedure. The procedure has one output parameter that corresponds to a cursor ❶. Because only one parameter is involved, the cursor ref position is 1 and is set in the `StoredProcedureItemReader` using the `cursorRefPosition` property ❷.

The Spring Batch cursor-based technique relies on JDBC and leverages streaming results using JDBC's own `ResultSet`. This mechanism allows retrieving data in batches and is useful with large data sets, as is often the case in batch processing. Spring Batch also allows you to control data set retrieval using data pages, which we see next.

USING PAGING TO MANAGE JDBC DATA RETRIEVAL

Instead of leaving JDBC to manage the data retrieval, Spring Batch allows you to handle this process using paging. In this case, retrieving data consists in successively executing

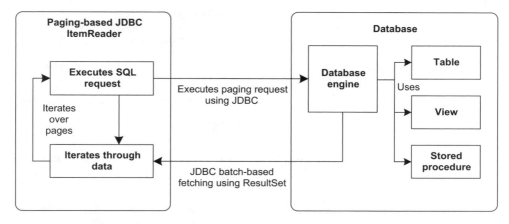

Figure 5.11   Using JDBC batch-based fetching to provide input data to an `ItemReader` by pages with fixed size

several requests with criteria. Spring Batch dynamically builds requests to execute based on a sort key to delimit data for a page. To retrieve each page, Spring Batch executes one request to retrieve the corresponding data. Figure 5.11 shows JDBC paging with an item reader.

Choosing between cursor-based and page-based item readers

Why does Spring Batch provide two ways to read from a database? The reason is that there's no one-size-fits-all solution. Cursor-based readers issue one query to the database and stream the data to avoid consuming too much memory. Cursor-based readers rely on the cursor implementation of the database and of the JDBC driver. Depending on your database engine and on the driver, cursor-based readers can work well . . . or not. Page-based readers work well with an appropriate page size (see the sidebar on page size). The trick is to find the best page size for your use case. With Spring Batch, switching from cursor- to page-based item readers is a matter of configuration and doesn't affect your application code. Don't hesitate to test both!

The `JdbcPagingItemReader` class is the new component we present here to implement JDBC paging with Spring Batch. The `JdbcPagingItemReader` class defines the properties listed in table 5.13.

Table 5.13   `JdbcPagingItemReader` properties

Property	Description
dataSource	Data source used to access the database
fetchSize	Number of rows to fetch to retrieve data in groups
parameterValues	Parameter values for the query

Table 5.13   `JdbcPagingItemReader` properties *(continued)*

Property	Description
queryProvider	PagingQueryProvider responsible for creating SQL requests used to retrieve data for pages
rowMapper	RowMapper instance used to build data object from the returned result set
pageSize	Number of rows per page

The following listing describes how to configure a JdbcPagingItemReader to retrieve product data using paging.

Listing 5.14   Configuring a `JdbcPagingItemReader`

```
<bean id="productItemReader"
      class="org.springframework.batch.item.database.JdbcPagingItemReader">
  <property name="dataSource" ref="dataSource"/>
  <property name="queryProvider" ref="productQueryProvider"/>
  <property name="pageSize" value="1500"/>
  <property name="rowMapper" ref="productRowMapper"/>
</bean>

<bean id="productRowMapper" class=" (...) "/>
<bean id="productQueryProvider" class=" (...) "/>
```

The queryProvider property configures an instance of PagingQueryProvider responsible for creating SQL queries to retrieve paged data. The generated SQL query limits the number of retrieved rows to the page size specified by the pageSize property. Finally, you set the RowMapper that creates business domain objects from ResultSet objects. For this example, the product RowMapper from listing 5.12 is reused.

Choosing a page size

There's no definitive value for the page-size setting. Let's venture a hint though: the size of a page should be around 1,000 items—this is a rule of thumb. The page size is usually higher than the commit interval (whose reasonable values range from 10 to 200 items). Remember, the point of paging is to avoid consuming too much memory, so large pages aren't good. Small pages aren't good either. If you read 1 million items in pages of 10 items (a small page size), you'll send 100,000 queries to the database. The good news is that the page size is a parameter in Spring Batch, so you can test multiple values and see which works best for your job.

Spring Batch provides a dedicated factory class called SqlPagingQueryProvider-FactoryBean used to configure a SQL paging query provider.

Table 5.14 lists the SqlPagingQueryProviderFactoryBean properties.

In our use case, we always need to have a SQL query returning products for cursor-based data retrieval. This query uses the product table and returns the id, name,

> ## The Spring `FactoryBean` classes
> When using a constructor (with the `new` keyword) to create beans doesn't fit your needs, use a Spring `FactoryBean`. A `FactoryBean` provides a level of indirection from the target bean by acting as a factory. After the Spring `BeanFactory` (be careful, the names are similar) initializes the factory bean, the target bean instances are obtained through the `getObject` method.

Table 5.14 `SqlPagingQueryProviderFactoryBean` properties

Property	Description
ascending	Whether sorting is ascending (or descending). The default value is `true` (ascending).
databaseType	The underlying database type. If you omit this property, the value is determined directly using the database through the specified data source.
dataSource	The data source to obtain connections to the database. Note that it's unnecessary to specify this field if the database type is set.
fromClause	The `FROM` clause of the SQL statement.
selectClause	The `SELECT` clause of the SQL statement.
sortKey	The sort column to identify data pages.
whereClause	Specifies the `WHERE` clause of the SQL statement.

description, and price columns. The following XML fragment describes how to configure this query for page-based data retrieval using the `SqlPagingQueryProvider-FactoryBean` class:

```
<bean id=" productQueryProvider"
      class="org.springframework.batch.item.database
                            ➥ .support.SqlPagingQueryProviderFactoryBean">
  <property name="dataSource" ref="dataSource"/>
  <property name="selectClause"
           value="select id, name, description, price"/>
  <property name="fromClause" value="from product"/>
  <property name="sortKey" value="id"/>
</bean>
```

After configuring the `SqlPagingQueryProviderFactoryBean` as a bean in the Spring configuration, you specify the SQL `SELECT` and `FROM` clauses followed by the sort key set to the `id` column. With this configuration, the `SqlPagingQueryProviderFactory-Bean` configures and returns the appropriate class according to the database type in use. For example, for PostgreSQL, the `PostgresPagingQueryProvider` class is instantiated, configured, and returned. The returned class is then responsible for generating SQL paging queries. The query pattern is as follows: the first query is simple, using configured `SELECT`, `FROM`, and `WHERE` clauses with a hint limit for the number of returned rows:

```
SELECT id, name, description, price FROM product LIMIT 1500
```

For the next pages, queries include additional clauses to specify the beginning of the page using the specified sort key:

```
SELECT id, name, description, price FROM product where id>? LIMIT 1500
```

As we've seen in this section, Spring Batch provides sophisticated integration with JDBC to support batch processes. As for nonbatch Java applications, we must explicitly define SQL queries to execute.

ORM tools provide interesting solutions to address this issue but don't account for batch processes in their design. Next, we see the solutions Spring Batch provides for using ORM with batch applications.

5.5.2   *Using ORM item readers*

In traditional Java and Java EE applications, ORM is commonly used to interact with relational databases. The goal of ORM is to handle the mismatch between the relational database model and the object-oriented model. ORM tools efficiently manage conversions between these models. ORM tools also remove the need to explicitly specify SQL statements by automatically generating SQL on your behalf.

Is ORM the right tool for batch applications?

ORM works great for online applications but can be difficult to deal with in batch applications. It's not that ORM is a bad match for batch applications, but the high-level features ORM tools provide—such as lazy loading—don't always work well in batch scenarios. In Spring Batch, reading takes place in a separate transaction from processing and writing (this is a constraint of cursor- and page-based readers). This works well in normal cases, but when Murphy's law kicks in, the combination of a failure, the separate transaction, and lazy loading is explosive. Failure scenarios are numerous and tricky to solve. A solution is to apply the driving query pattern: the reader reads only item identifiers (using JDBC cursors or paging), and the processor uses the ORM tool to load the corresponding objects. In this case, a second-level cache can help performance. The goal is to have the ORM tool use the same transaction as the writer. Chapter 7 covers the driving query pattern.

As it does for JDBC, Spring provides supports for ORM. We don't describe here how Spring provides this support because Spring Batch does a good job of hiding it. Next, we focus on solutions (which are similar to JDBC) that Spring Batch provides to use ORM with batch processes efficiently.

READING WITH ORM CURSORS

Reading with ORM cursors implies that code responsible for managing domain classes doesn't use a first-level cache. Only Hibernate supports this feature through an interface called `StatelessSession` that provides the same methods as the classic `Session` but without caching and checking dirty state.

You first define a model class mapping to a relational database entity. For the online store case study, you define a `Product` class to map the `product` database table using Hibernate annotations, as shown in the following listing.

Listing 5.15 ORM mapping class

```
@Entity("product")
public class Product {
  @Id("id")
  private String id;
  @Column("label")
  private String label;
  @Column("description")
  private String description;
  @Column("price")
  private float price;
  (...)
}
```

The `Entity` annotation on the `Product` class specifies that the class maps to the product table. The `Id` and `Column` annotations map class properties to table columns using the name in the annotation values.

Using ORM cursors is similar to JDBC, shown in figure 5.10. The only difference is that ORM is an additional layer on top of JDBC. For ORM, Spring Batch only supports Hibernate through the `HibernateCursorItemReader` class, which accepts the properties listed in table 5.15.

The following listing shows how to configure a `HibernateCursorItemReader` bean for our case study to retrieve products from the `product` table.

Table 5.15 `HibernateCursorItemReader` properties

Property	Description
fetchSize	Number of rows to fetch transparently when retrieving data in groups.
maxItemCount	Maximum number of items to retrieve. The default value is `Integer.MAX_VALUE`.
parameterValues	Statement parameter values.
queryProvider	`HibernateQueryProvider` for creating Hibernate Query Language (HQL) queries to retrieve data pages.
queryString	The HQL query to retrieve entities.
sessionFactory	Hibernate `SessionFactory` for interacting with the database through Hibernate.
useStatelessSession	Whether the Hibernate session must be stateless. The default value is `true`.

Listing 5.16   Configuring a `HibernateCursorItemReader`

```
<bean id="productItemReader"
 class="org.springframework.batch.item.database.HibernateCursorItemReader">
  <property name="sessionFactory" ref="sessionFactory"/>
  <property name="queryString" value="from Product"/>
</bean>

<bean id="sessionFactory"
      class="org.springframework.orm.hibernate3.LocalSessionFactoryBean">
  <property name="dataSource" ref="dataSource"/>

  <property name="configurationClass"
          value="org.hibernate.cfg.AnnotationConfiguration"/>
  <property name="configLocation"
      value="classpath:/com/manning/sbia/reading/dao/hibernate.cfg.xml"/>
  <property name="hibernateProperties">
    <value>
      hibernate.dialect=org.hibernate.dialect.HSQLDialect
      hibernate.show_sql=true
    </value>
  </property>
</bean>
```

After configuring the `SessionFactory` using facilities provided by Spring Hibernate, this entity is configured with a `HibernateCursorItemReader` bean using the `session-Factory` property. The `queryString` property sets the query to retrieve products.

The following XML fragment describes the content of `hibernate.cfg.xml`, which specifies that Hibernate must manage the `Product` class:

```
<!DOCTYPE hibernate-configuration PUBLIC
    "-//Hibernate/Hibernate Configuration DTD 3.0//EN"
    "http://hibernate.sourceforge.net/hibernate-configuration-3.0.dtd">

<hibernate-configuration>                                    Defines Product as
  <session-factory>                                             managed class
    <mapping class="com.manning.sbmia.reading.model.Product"/>   <─┐
  </session-factory>                                               ┘
</hibernate-configuration>
```

As emphasized at the beginning of this section, only Hibernate supports this approach. For other ORM providers, Spring Batch provides a paging mechanism similar to the one described for JDBC.

USING PAGING TO MANAGE ORM DATA RETRIEVAL

ORM frameworks don't usually support the approach described in the previous section regarding Hibernate. For example, the Java Persistence API (JPA) technology doesn't provide cacheless support. In this case, paging is the natural solution because ORM caches only a page of objects in memory.

As with JDBC, ORM paging retrieves data in batches. Spring Batch performs data retrieval by successively executing several queries, as shown in figure 5.11. The only difference is that ORM is an additional layer on top of JDBC. For Hibernate, Spring Batch provides the `HibernatePagingItemReader` and `JpaPagingReader` classes for

> **Java Persistence API**
>
> The Java EE 5 specification includes ORM support defined as the JPA in Java Specification Request 220: Enterprise JavaBeans 3. Its aim is to provide a standardized layer so that ORM tools are implementations of this specification. The specification describes how to map managed entities to database tables and an API to interact with databases. New features are the ability to use this technology outside an Enterprise JavaBeans (EJB) container and to use local transactions instead of global transactions with JTA.
>
> The main JPA implementations are Hibernate JPA, Apache OpenJPA, and EclipseLink JPA (based on TopLink).

JPA. Properties are almost the same as those described in table 5.15 with the addition of the `pageSize` property to specify the number of items per data page. Note that for the `JpaPagingReader` class, the `useStateless` property doesn't apply and the `query-Provider` property is of type `JpaQueryProvider`.

The following XML fragment describes how to configure a `HibernatePagingItem-Reader` bean to retrieve products from the `product` table:

```
<bean id="productItemReader"
 class="org.springframework.batch.item.database.HibernatePagingItemReader">
  <property name="sessionFactory" ref="sessionFactory"/>
  <property name="queryString" value="from Product"/>
</bean>

<bean id="sessionFactory" class="(...)"> (...) </bean>
```

As you can see, configuring paging is similar to configuring cursors, and properties are generally the same; here you set the factory for the ORM and the query.

This section closes the description of relational databases as input sources using JDBC directly and through ORM with cursors and paging. Spring Batch integrates mechanisms to guarantee performance and memory consumption when using ORM for batch processes. In the next section, we focus on other input sources for importing data.

5.6 *Using other input sources*

Files and databases are the main data sources used as input for batch processes, but they aren't the only ones. You may want to reuse services provided by existing applications or integrate with an information system with asynchronous and event-driven features. Spring Batch provides implementations of the `ItemReader` interface for such cases, which this section examines.

5.6.1 *Services as input*

Reusability of existing services is a key concept of modern applications. This avoids reinventing the wheel, provides robustness, and saves time. Batch processes can integrate in existing systems that already provide entities to read data. These sources can

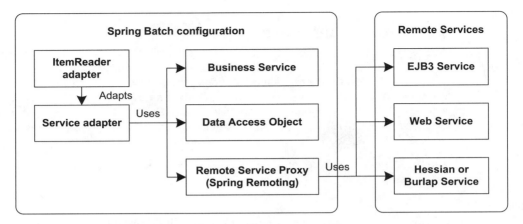

Figure 5.12   Reusing methods of existing entities and services to get data to provide as input for batch processes

be POJOs that implement business services; data access objects; or more complex entities managed by a container, such as EJB3 or by services accessible with lightweight protocols provided by Caucho, such as Hessian and Burlap. Figure 5.12 describes different patterns for batch processes to read data from existing entities.

To implement these patterns, Spring Batch provides the `ItemReaderAdapter` class, which makes it possible to see an existing entity as an `ItemReader`. The `ItemReaderAdapter` class holds the bean and method to delegate data retrieval. The only constraints at this level are that the delegated method must not have parameters and that it returns the same type as the `read` method of the `ItemReader` interface.

For this reason, it isn't possible to use the target service directly, and you must implement an adapter class for the service. The `ItemReader` adapter retrieves elements one by one, which isn't the case for services because they usually return a set of elements. The following listing shows the `ProductServiceAdapter` class, which implements this technique.

Listing 5.17   Service adapter for the `ProductService` service

```
public class ProductServiceAdapter implements InitializingBean {
  private ProductService productService;
  private List<Product> products;

  public void afterPropertiesSet() throws Exception {
    this.products = productService.getProducts();        ❶ Initializes products
  }                                                           from service

  public Product nextProduct() {
    if (products.size()>0) {
      return products.remove(0);                         ❷ Gets products
    } else {                                                one by one
      return null;
    }
  }
}
```

```
public void setProductService(ProductService productService) {
    this.productService = productService;
  }
}
```

The `ProductServiceAdapter` class initializes the product list at startup using the `afterPropertiesSet` method ❶ from the Spring `InitializingBean` callback interface. Products are then retrieved one by one with the `getProduct` method ❷ using the product list initially loaded.

The next listing shows how to configure this mechanism for a POJO configured in Spring to reuse the `ProductService` entity managing products.

Listing 5.18 Configuring the `ProductService` as an `ItemReader`

```
<bean id="productItemReader"
      class="org.springframework.batch.item.adapter.ItemReaderAdapter">
  <property name="targetObject"
            ref="productServiceAdapter"/>                    ◁──┐   Sets
  <property name="targetMethod" value="nextProduct"/>   ◁──┐   │   product
</bean>                                                     │   │   service
                               Sets target method ❷ ──────┘   ❶  object
<bean id="productServiceAdapter"
      class="com.manning.sbia.reading.service.ProductServiceAdapter">
  <property name="productService" ref="productService"/>
</bean>

<bean id="productService"
      class="com.manning.sbia.reading.service.ProductServiceImpl">
  (...)
</bean>
```

Having configured the `ProductService` as a bean in the Spring configuration, you can reference it as the target object for the `ItemReader` adapter through the `targetObject` property ❶. The `ItemReaderAdapter` delegates import processing to the `productService` bean. You then specify which method to use to get product data with the `targetMethod` property ❷. In this case, the method is `getProducts`.

You adapted listing 5.18 to remotely access an EJB3 rather than a POJO using the http://www.springframework.org/schema/jee Spring XML namespace and `jee` namespace prefix. This vocabulary provides facilities for Java EE–related configuration for JNDI and EJB. The `remote-slsb` XML element configures a remote EJB3 proxy as a bean, which transparently provides a delegated business implementation. For our case study, the EJB3 corresponds to a remote service that manages products. The following snippet shows how to use a remote EJB3 with an `ItemReader` adapter:

```
<bean id="productItemReader"
      class="org.springframework.batch.item.adapter.ItemReaderAdapter">
  <property name="targetObject" ref="productService"/>
  <property name="targetMethod" value="nextProduct"/>
</bean>

<jee:remote-slsb id="productService"
                 jndi-name="ejb/remoteProductService">
```

For a remote EJB3 service, the configuration of the `ItemReader` adapter remains the same. For the `productService` bean, the configuration changes and the `remote-slsb` element's `jndi-name` property is set to the name in the JNDI entry for the EJB3 session.

Be aware that the target entity is entirely responsible for importing data in this case, and there's no possible interaction with the Spring Batch execution context. In fact, existing entities aren't linked to Spring Batch mechanisms and objects. The consequence is that state can't be stored. You also need to check that the use of the target entity in a batch process performs efficiently.

Before describing advanced issues regarding importing data with Spring Batch, we see how to implement and configure importing data using message-oriented middleware (MOM) and JMS.

5.6.2 *Reading from JMS*

The JMS API is to MOM what JDBC is to databases. JMS defines a vendor-neutral API and wrapper classes for MOM vendors to implement. MOM systems guarantee message delivery to applications and integrate fault tolerance, load scaling, and loosely coupled distributed communication and transaction support. JMS uses communication channels named *destinations* (like a *queue* or *topic*) to implement asynchronous communication.

The JMS specification tackles application messaging by providing a generic framework to send and receive messages synchronously and asynchronously. JMS provides a standard abstraction level for MOM providers to implement. In the context of batch processes, this makes it possible to handle incoming data automatically.

> **If JMS is event driven, why use it in batch applications?**
> One benefit of JMS is notification of new messages queued on destinations. Java objects wait to be called by containers like Spring's `MessageListenerContainers`. These Java objects are message-driven objects. Sometimes, you don't want to process messages as soon as they arrive because their processing is costly and you want to postpone this processing to reduce load on the server (which is busy doing something else at the moment). A batch job can consume JMS messages while *throttling* processing. You can choose to trigger the job when appropriate (every 10 minutes or at night, for example). The message-driven and batch approaches can work together: you can enable JMS listeners when your servers aren't too busy and disable them when there's too much load. You're also free to launch a dequeuing batch job whenever you want. This approach helps optimize usage of your hardware resources.

Spring Batch bases its JMS support on Spring's JMS support. The Spring Batch class `JmsItemReader` implements the `ItemReader` interface and internally uses the Spring `JmsTemplate` class. The `JmsItemReader` class reads data directly from a JMS destination (queue or topic). In the case study, the import job receives products as payload from JMS messages read from a JMS queue. The following listing shows how to configure reading from a JMS destination using a `JmsItemReader`.

Listing 5.19 Configuring a `JmsItemReader` class

```
<bean id="productItemReader"
      class="org.springframework.batch.item.jms.JmsItemReader">
  <property name="itemType"
            value="com.manning.sbia.reading.Product"/>           ❶ Defines
  <property name="jmsTemplate" ref="jmsTemplate"/>        ◁─┐      item type
</bean>                                                    Sets JMS
                                                        ❷ template
<bean id="jmsTemplate" class="org.springframework.jms.core.JmsTemplate">
  <property name="connectionFactory" bean="jmsFactory"/>
  <property name="defaultDestination" ref="productDestination"/>
  <property name="receiveTimeout" value="500"/>
  <property name="sessionTransacted" value="true" />
</bean>

<bean id="jmsFactory" class="(...)"> (...) </bean>
<bean id="productDestination" class="(...)"> (...) </bean>
```

You first define the data object type contained in JMS messages ❶. For our case study, this type is `Product`. You then configure how to interact with the JMS provider through Spring's JMS support and its `JmsTemplate` class. To configure a `JmsTemplate`, you specify the JMS connection factory and destination. This template must then be set in the item reader using the `jmsTemplate` property ❷.

> **JMS and transactions**
>
> JMS provides transactional features for consuming messages. Chapter 9 includes guidelines to properly deal with JMS transactions.

In this chapter, we described all built-in capabilities of Spring Batch used to import data from different input sources. Spring Batch supports several file formats, relational databases, MOM, and reusing existing services. In some cases, the `ItemReader` implementations provided by Spring Batch aren't enough, and you must implement custom readers, which we discuss next.

5.7   *Implementing custom readers*

If Spring Batch `ItemReader` implementations don't suit your needs, you can provide your own implementations. We don't describe interacting with the execution context here because it's covered in chapter 8.

Imagine that you want to handle all files present in a directory at batch startup. The list of files in the directory is loaded when the item reader is instantiated. For each read, you return the first list element after removing it from the list. The following listing shows the implementation of the `ListDirectoryItemReader` class.

Listing 5.20 Custom `ItemReader` implementation

```
public class ListDirectoryItemReader
        implements ItemReader<File> {
  private List<File> files;
```

```
public ListDirectoryItemReader(File directory) {
  if (directory==null) {
    throw new IllegalArgumentException("The directory can be null.");
  }
  if (!directory.isDirectory()) {
    throw new IllegalArgumentException(
                      "The specified file must be a directory.");
  }
  files = Arrays.asList(directory.listFiles());
}

public File read() throws Exception, UnexpectedInputException,
                    ParseException, NonTransientResourceException {
  if (!files.isEmpty()) {
    return files.remove(0);
  }
  return null;
}
}
```

As a custom item reader, this class implements the `ItemReader` interface. Because the `ItemReader` interface supports generics, you specify the associated type for the class (`File`). In the constructor, you initialize the list of files in the given directory. Implementing the `ItemReader` interface requires defining the `read` method. Spring Batch calls this method until it returns `null`, indicating that the method returned all files in the list, one at a time.

When you create a custom reader in Spring Batch, you implement the `ItemReader` interface. The `read` method performs all read processing, which returns elements one by one.

5.8 Summary

Reading data from batch processes is the first step of a chunk-based tasklet. Spring Batch provides support for this step with the generic `ItemReader` and `ItemStream` interfaces. Spring Batch implements these interfaces for common technologies used in batch processes to import data. Using our case study as an example, we described how to read data from various types of flat files and XML files. We also described how to get data from a database, how to integrate with existing services, and how to interact with a MOM like JMS.

We briefly mentioned that reading is involved in the complete batch process execution. This aspect is fundamental to restart batch processes and avoid reading data again when things go wrong later in processing and writing. We didn't go into details about reading, but we deal with this issue in chapter 8.

In chapter 6, we describe the other side of reading data—writing data—where Spring Batch supports the same technologies we saw in this chapter.

Writing data 6

In chapter 5, we learned how to read data with Spring Batch. In this chapter, we focus on another core feature of the batch process: writing.

Reading input items takes place at the beginning of a chunk-oriented step and writing items takes place at the end. In Spring Batch, a writer is responsible for data persistence.

We start by looking at data-writing concepts. We use our case study to illustrate how to write data into flat files, XML files, and relational databases using both JDBC and ORM (Object Relational Mapping). Spring Batch provides various implementations out of the box for these targets, but it may be necessary to create your own writer implementations, which we demonstrate. If you already have legacy services that produce or save data, Spring Batch can delegate to and reuse these services.

157

We also learn how to write to a Java Message Service (JMS) queue and send emails. Finally, we discuss some advanced writing techniques.

6.1   *Data-writing concepts*

Here we look at core concepts of writing with Spring Batch, particularly writing in a chunk-oriented tasklet. Figure 6.1 shows what we already know from chapter 5, but we focus now on writing data.

In a chunk-oriented tasklet, an `ItemReader` reads input data, an `ItemProcessor` (optionally) processes it, and an `ItemWriter` writes it. Spring Batch provides the plumbing to aggregate reading and passing the data to the writer. The interface `ItemWriter` represents the writer, which is the counterpart to the `ItemReader` interface. The following snippet lists the `ItemWriter` interface:

```
public interface ItemWriter<T> {
  void write(List<? extends T> items) throws Exception;
}
```

The `ItemWriter` interface defines a single method called `write`, which saves output data. Most writers have the ability to write a set of items all at once, which is why the writer takes a list of items as a parameter. After writing items, the writer can flush before the process continues. For files, writers flush the underlying stream to guarantee that it passes all bytes to the operating system. It's the same with Hibernate: the `HibernateItemWriter` flushes the Hibernate session after saving or updating objects at the end of a chunk, by default. It's the responsibility of each writer implementation to deal with flushing if applicable. After all items are processed, Spring Batch commits the current transaction. With built-in JDBC writers, Spring Batch uses batch updates to send all SQL statements in one operation to get the best performance. The following snippet shows you how to configure the number of items to write for a transaction; Spring Batch commits the transaction for each chunk:

```
<tasklet>
  <chunk reader="itemReader" writer="itemWriter" commit-interval="100"/>
</tasklet>
```

The `commit-interval` attribute on the chunk element defines the chunk size. Spring Batch is smart enough to avoid loading all data in memory. It treats items in chunks to lower memory consumption.

As you'll see later, you can also create your own `ItemWriter` implementations. Now that the concepts are clear, let's start writing.

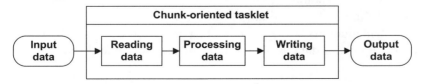

Figure 6.1   A chunk-oriented tasklet implements the chunk-oriented processing pattern in Spring Batch. This chapter focuses on the writing phase.

> **What are batch updates?**
>
> Batch updates are good: they make insert and update statements execute efficiently. Instead of sending SQL statements one after another—and making a round-trip to the database each time—batch updates send SQL statements in groups. The database can even perform optimizations of its own. By providing a list of items to the item writer, Spring Batch facilitates batch updates, but that's not enough: you need to send the batch updates correctly. How do you do that? The Spring Framework provides everything you need: look at the `batchUpdate` method in the `JdbcTemplate` and the `Batch-SqlUpdate` class.

6.2   *Writing files*

Spring Batch provides item writers that write files in various formats: delimited text, fixed-field widths, and XML. We discuss these formats using our case study as an example. Figure 6.2 displays these formats.

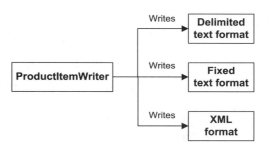

In our application, an item reader first reads `Products` from a flat file. We can then use different writers to produce output files in different formats. Spring Batch supports flat files and XML files. Let's start with flat files.

Figure 6.2   Spring Batch supports writing to multiple file formats thanks to the various item writer implementations it provides.

6.2.1   *Writing flat files*

The flat file format is one of the earliest formats used to store information. A flat file is a plain text file that holds records, usually one per line. Fields compose a record, and a separator, usually a comma or tab character, may delimit each field. Alternatively, each field can be of a predetermined fixed length, where spaces pad values to get each field to its desired length. Additionally, a flat file may include an optional header and footer line, which can define additional metadata or add comments.

The following snippet shows a comma-delimited flat file for two product records with fields for ID, name, description, and price:

```
PR....210,BlackBerry 8100 Pearl,RIM phone,124.60
PR....211,Sony Ericsson W810i,Sony phone,139.45
```

In the next fixed-length flat file example, each field has a fixed length with no separator; it also has footer and header lines. The field lengths are 9 characters for the ID, 26 for the name, 15 for the description, and 6 for the price.

```
My header
PR....210BlackBerry 8100 Pearl     RIM phone      124.60
PR....211Sony Ericsson W810i       Sony phone     139.45
My footer
```

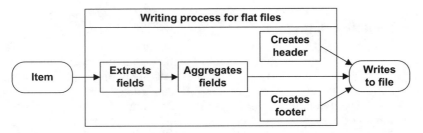

Figure 6.3   Spring Batch extracts and aggregates fields for each item when writing to a flat file. The framework also handles writing a header and footer to the file (both are optional).

Spring Batch writes a flat file in the following steps:

1 Writes the header (optional)
2 Extracts fields for each item and aggregates them to produce a line
3 Writes the footer (optional)

Figure 6.3 shows the process of writing a flat file.

We use the FlatFileItemWriter class to write flat files. The FlatFileItemWriter implements the ItemWriter interface and additional interfaces to do its job. Figure 6.4 shows the interfaces and classes involved to support the features in figure 6.3.

A FlatFileItemWriter implements the ItemStream interface and follows the stream lifecycle. When Spring Batch calls the open stream method, the FlatFileItemWriter writes the header through a FlatFileHeaderCallback. When Spring Batch calls the close stream method, the FlatFileItemWriter writes the footer through a FlatFile-FooterCallback. Both the header and footer are optional in flat files.

A FlatFileItemWriter uses a LineAggregator to transform each item into a String. The most basic implementation of the LineAggregator interface is the PassThroughLineAggregator class, which calls toString() on each item object. If you use domain-specific classes, you may need to convert each object into a more complex

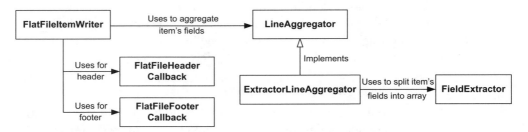

Figure 6.4   The interfaces and classes involved in writing items to a flat file with the FlatFileItemReader. The FlatFileItemWriter also provides optional callbacks for the header and the footer of a flat file. The LineAggregator transforms an item into a string. The ExtractorLineAggregator implementation uses a FieldExtractor to "split" an item into an array of objects and calls business logic to render the array as a string.

`String`. For this case, Spring Batch defines an abstract class called `ExtractorLine-Aggregator`, where subclasses extract fields from a given item into an array using a `FieldExtractor` and then aggregate them for the given file format.

Table 6.1 describes the classes and interfaces from figure 6.4.

Table 6.1   Interfaces and classes used with a `FlatFileItemWriter`

Type	Description
`LineAggregator`	Creates a `String` representation of an object
`ExtractorLineAggregator`	Implements `LineAggregator` to extract field data from a domain object
`FieldExtractor`	Creates an array containing item parts
`FlatFileHeaderCallback`	Callback interface to write a header
`FlatFileFooterCallback`	Callback interface to write a footer

These interfaces and classes all play a part in writing flat files, whatever the format. But how does Spring Batch know how and what to write in a flat file? We start to answer this question next, with the configuration of a `FlatFileItemWriter`.

CONFIGURING A FLATFILEITEMWRITER

The `FlatFileItemWriter` class is the starting point for writing flat files. You define a `FlatFileItemWriter` as a bean in an XML Spring context. Table 6.2 describes the `FlatFileItemWriter` properties.

Table 6.2   `FlatFileItemWriter` properties

Property	Type	Description
`appendAllowed`	`boolean`	Whether to append to the target file if it exists; default is `false`
`encoding`	`String`	Character encoding for writing to a file; defaults to `UTF-8`
`footerCallback`	`FlatFileFooterCallback`	Callback class used to write a footer
`headerCallback`	`FlatFileHeaderCallback`	Callback class used to write a header
`lineAggregator`	`LineAggregator<T>`	Convert an item into a line; required property
`lineSeparator`	`String`	Line separator; defaults to the system property `line.separator`
`resource`	`Resource`	Location of resource to write
`saveState`	`boolean`	Whether to save the state in the execution context; defaults to `true`

Table 6.2 `FlatFileItemWriter` properties *(continued)*

Property	Type	Description
shouldDeleteIfEmpty	boolean	Whether to delete the target file if the writer doesn't write any lines; defaults to `false`
shoudDeleteIfExists	boolean	Whether to delete the target file if it already exists; default is `true`
transactional	boolean	Whether an active transaction delays writing to the file buffer; default is `true`

The following listing shows a minimal `FlatFileItemWriter` configuration with `line-Aggregator` and `resource` properties.

Listing 6.1   A minimal `FlatFileItemWriter` configuration

```
<bean id="productItemWriter"
    class="org.springframework.batch.item.file.FlatFileItemWriter">
  <property name="resource"
    value="file:target/outputs/passthrough.txt"/>
  <property name="lineAggregator">
    <bean
      class="org.springframework.batch.item.file.transform.
➥ PassThroughLineAggregator" />
  </property>
</bean>
```

The `resource` property contains a URL pointing to the file to write. The `FlatFile-ItemWriter` class inherits the `setResource` method from its superclass, `Resource-AwareItemWriterItemStream`, which implements the `ItemStream` and `ItemWriter` interfaces. The `FlatFileItemWriter` class also has a required property named `Line-Aggregator`. The purpose of the `LineAggregator` interface is to create the `String` representation of an item.

Spring Batch provides the `LineAggregator` implementations listed in table 6.3.

Table 6.3   Spring Batch `LineAggregator` implementations

Class	Description
PassThroughLineAggregator	A simple implementation that calls `toString()`.
ExtractorLineAggregator	An abstract implementation that uses a `FieldExtractor` to extracts item fields as an array. Subclasses decide how to aggregate the array elements.
DelimitedLineAggregator	An `ExtractorLineAggregator` subclass that produces a delimited string. The default delimiter is the comma character.
FormatterLineAggregator	An `ExtractorLineAggregator` subclass that formats each element with a `java.util.Formatter`.

In more advanced use cases, the `FlatFileItemWriter` class uses an `ExtractorLine-Aggregator` and a `FieldExtractor` to format data and write the file.

INTRODUCING THE LINEAGGREGATOR INTERFACE

We introduced the `LineAggregator` interface in the previous section, but here we look at it in more detail:

```
public interface LineAggregator<T> {
  String aggregate(T item);
}
```

The interface is simple and focuses on converting an object to a `String`. The `PassThroughLineAggregator` implementation calls `toString()` on each item. The `ExtractorLineAggregator` implementation is more interesting because it serves as a base class for more elaborate aggregation algorithms. The `aggregate` method extracts fields from the given item using a `FieldExtractor` and then aggregates them into a `String`. The `FieldExtractor`'s only job is to convert an object into an array of its parts. Finally, the `FlatFileItemWriter` writes the `String` to a file. Let's see how a `FieldExtractor` works. To see an illustration of these objects, see figure 6.4.

INTRODUCING THE FIELDEXTRACTOR CLASS

An `ExtractorLineAggregator` uses a `FieldExtractor` to create an array of item values that an item writer writes to a file. Implementers of the `FieldExtractor` interface extract the bean information you want to write to a file:

```
public interface FieldExtractor<T> {
  Object[] extract(T item);
}
```

Listing 6.2 writes to a delimited file to demonstrate the use of a `FieldExtractor`, but don't worry about the details; we get to that in the next section. The `PassThrough-FieldExtractor` class implements the `FieldExtractor` interface to return an array of fields as close as possible to the input item. The extractor returns the input if it's a `FieldSet`, the result of `toArray()` on a `Collection`, or the result (as an array) of `values()` on a `Map`, and wraps other types of objects in a one-element array.

Listing 6.2 A delimited pass-through field extractor

```
<bean id="productItemWriter"
      class="org.springframework.batch.item.file.FlatFileItemWriter">
  <property name="resource"
    value="file:target/outputs/delimited-passthroughextractor.txt"/>
  <property name="lineAggregator">
     <bean
       class="org.springframework.batch.item.file.transform.
➥ DelimitedLineAggregator">
        <property name="fieldExtractor">
          <bean
            class="org.springframework.batch.item.file.transform.
➥ PassThroughFieldExtractor" />
        </property>
```

```
    </bean>
  </property>
</bean>
```

This listing configures a flat file item writer with a `LineAggregator`, which contains a `PassThroughFieldExtractor`. All classes in this example are stock Spring Batch.

The following snippet shows the result of running this example:

```
Product [id=PR....210, name=BlackBerry 8100 Pearl]
Product [id=PR....211, name=Sony Ericsson W810i]
Product [id=PR....212, name=Samsung MM-A900M Ace]
Product [id=PR....213, name=Toshiba M285-E 14]
```

The output file contains one line per product and is the result of calling `toString()` on each `Product` object. It's not sexy, but it's efficient, even if you don't have access to all the object properties or if you can't control the column order or formatting.

For more control over the output, you can select which properties to write with the `BeanWrapperFieldExtractor` class. This extractor takes an array of property names, reflectively calls the getters on a source item object, and returns an array of values. The following listing configures a `BeanWrapperFieldExtractor` for our use case.

Listing 6.3   Configuring a `BeanWrapperFieldExtractor`

```xml
<bean
  id="productItemWriter"
  class="org.springframework.batch.item.file.FlatFileItemWriter">
  <property name="resource" value="file:target/outputs/delimited-
    beanwrapperhextractor.txt"/>
  <property name="lineAggregator">
    <bean class="org.springframework.batch.item.file.transform.
  ➥ DelimitedLineAggregator">
      <property name="fieldExtractor">
        <bean class="org.springframework.batch.item.file.transform.
  ➥ BeanWrapperFieldExtractor">
          <property name="names"
          ➥ value="id,price,name" />
        </bean>
      </property>
    </bean>
  </property>
</bean>
```

You configure a `BeanWrapperFieldExtractor` with the list of property names that you want to output. For each product, the field extractor calls the getter (via reflection) of each property in the list and creates a new value array. A `DelimitedLineAggregator` aggregates this array, which we see in the next section.

The following snippet shows that you control the properties and their order:

```
PR....210,124.60,BlackBerry 8100 Pearl
PR....211,139.45,Sony Ericsson W810i
PR....212,97.80,Samsung MM-A900M Ace
PR....213,166.20,Toshiba M285-E 14
```

Next, you get even more control over the output by adding computed fields.

WRITING COMPUTED FIELDS

To add computed fields to the output, you create a `FieldExtractor` implementation named `ProductFieldExtractor` to add and compute additional fields. Here, you add `BEGIN` and `END` at the beginning and the end of each array and compute a tax field. Because you configure the `ProductFieldExtractor` in a Spring context, you can also inject/wire existing beans to create other `FieldExtractors`. The following listing implements the `ProductFieldExtractor`.

Listing 6.4 Computing fields in a `FieldExtractor`

```
public class ProductFieldExtractor implements FieldExtractor<Product> {
  public Object[] extract(Product item) {
    return new Object [] {
      "BEGIN",
      item.getId(),
      item.getPrice(),
      item.getPrice().multiply(new BigDecimal("0.15")),
      item.getName(),
      "END"};
  }
}
```

The next listing configures the `ProductFieldExtractor` as a property of the item writer's `LineAggregator`.

Listing 6.5 Configuring a `FieldExtractor`

```
<bean id="productItemWriter"
     class="org.springframework.batch.item.file.FlatFileItemWriter">
  <property name="resource" value="file:target/outputs/delimited-
     productextractor.txt"/>
  <property name="lineAggregator">
    <bean class="org.springframework.batch.item.file.transform.
  ➥ DelimitedLineAggregator">
      <property name="fieldExtractor">
        <bean class="com.manning.sbia.ch06.file
  ➥.ProductFieldExtractor" />                    <-- Sets ProductFieldExtractor
      </property>
    </bean>
  </property>
</bean>
```

The following snippet shows the result of using the product field extractor:

```
BEGIN,PR....210,124.60,18.6900,BlackBerry 8100 Pearl,END
BEGIN,PR....211,139.45,20.9175,Sony Ericsson W810i,END
BEGIN,PR....212,97.80,14.6700,Samsung MM-A900M Ace,END
BEGIN,PR....213,166.20,24.9300,Toshiba M285-E 14,END
```

Remember to use a `FieldExtractor` to control exactly what you want to write to a file. The following sections explore how to write delimited and fixed-length fields and how to add headers and footers.

WRITING DELIMITED FILES

The `DelimitedLineAggregator` class implements the `LineAggregator` interface to create delimited files. A character, typically a comma or a tab, separates each field value from the next. The `DelimitedLineAggregator` class is responsible for transforming an item into a `String`. The following listing configures a `DelimitedLineAggregator` bean in a Spring context. Note that the default delimiter is a comma.

Listing 6.6   Configuring writing to a delimited file

```
<bean id="productItemWriter"
  class="org.springframework.batch.item.file.FlatFileItemWriter">
  (...)
  <property name="lineAggregator">
  <bean class="org.springframework.batch.item.file.transform.
  ➥ DelimitedLineAggregator">
    <property name="delimiter" value="|">
    <property name="fieldExtractor">
    (...)
    </property>
  </bean>
 </property>
</bean>
```

You set a `DelimitedLineAggregator` as the `LineAggregator` to indicate that you want a delimited file as the output format. You also set the `delimiter` attribute to separate each field with the given string, which by default is the comma character.

The following snippet shows the result of running this example:

```
PR....210|124.60|BlackBerry 8100 Pearl
PR....211|139.45|Sony Ericsson W810i
PR....212|97.80|Samsung MM-A900M Ace
PR....213|166.20|Toshiba M285-E 14
```

Now that you know how to use Spring Batch to write a delimited file, let's see how to write a fixed-width file.

WRITING FIXED-WIDTH FILES

In a fixed-width file, fixed-length fields make up each record. Spaces may pad each field value to get to the desired field length. The `FormatterLineAggregator` class implements the `LineAggregator` interface to format fields and uses the format syntax of the `java.util.Formatter` class. The `Formatter` class, inspired by C's `printf` function, allows developers to specify text representations of data for strings, numbers, dates, and time. This formatter is used by `PrintStream`'s `printf(String format, Object ... args)`, and `String.format(String format, Object ... args)`. The first parameter is the format string, and the other values are data to format with `java.util.Locale` support.

In brief, a `FormatterLineAggregator` produces `Strings` by aggregating fields with a `Formatter`. The following listing configures a `FormatterLineAggregator` in a Spring context.

Listing 6.7 Configuring a `FormatterLineAggregator`

```
<bean id="productItemWriter"
      class="org.springframework.batch.item.file.FlatFileItemWriter">
  <property name="resource"
    value="file:target/outputs/fixedwidth-beanwrapperextractor.txt"/>
  <property name="lineAggregator">
    <bean class="org.springframework.batch.item.file.transform.
➡ FormatterLineAggregator">
      <property name="fieldExtractor">
        <bean class="org.springframework.batch.item.file.transform.
➡ BeanWrapperFieldExtractor">
          <property name="names" value="id,price,name" />
        </bean>
      </property>
      <property name="format" value="%-9s%6.2f%-30s" />
    </bean>
  </property>
</bean>
```

You configure a `FormatterLineAggregator` with a `fieldExtractor` to build arrays of fields from items. You use a `BeanWrapperFieldExtractor` to extract the id, price, and name fields from `Product` objects. To format these fields, you set the format property to `%-9s%6.2f%-30s`. The format string looks complicated, so let's take a closer look:

- id output is 9 characters and padded to the left
- price output is 6 characters as a float with 2 precision characters
- name output is 30 characters and padded to the left

Figure 6.5 shows the mapping between bean property, format expression, and output line.

The following snippet shows the result of running this example:

```
PR....210124.60BlackBerry 8100 Pearl
PR....211139.45Sony Ericsson W810i
PR....212 97.80Samsung MM-A900M Ace
PR....213166.20Toshiba M285-E 14
```

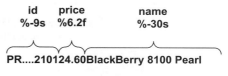

Figure 6.5 Mapping between bean property, format expression, and output line

The Javadoc for the `Formatter` class tells us that the general form of a format string is `%[argument_index$][flags][width][.precision]conversion`. Let's pick this one apart too:

- The optional `argument_index` field is a decimal integer indicating the position of the argument in the argument list.
- The optional `flags` field is a set of characters that modify the output format. The set of valid flags depends on the conversion. For example, the dash (-) flag creates left-justified output.
- The optional `width` field is a nonnegative decimal integer indicating the minimum number of characters to write.

- The optional `precision` field is a nonnegative decimal integer normally used to restrict the number of characters.
- The required `conversion` field is a character indicating how to format the argument. The set of valid conversions for a given argument depends on the argument's data type.

Table 6.4 shows the different `conversion` values.

Table 6.4 Formatter conversions

Character	Description
b	Converts a `boolean` to the `String` `true` or `false`
h	A hexadecimal hash code string, the result of `Integer.toHexString(arg.hashCode())`
s	The result of `arg.toString()` or, if `arg` implements `Formattable`, `arg.formatTo()`
c	A Unicode character
d	A decimal integer
c	An octal integer
x	A hexadecimal integer
e	A decimal integer in scientific notation
f	A decimal number
g	A decimal integer in scientific notation or decimal format, depending on the precision and the value after rounding
a	A hexadecimal floating-point number with a significant and an exponent
t	Prefix for date and time conversion characters
%	The % character
n	The platform line separator

Table 6.5 lists examples of using a `Formatter` through `System.printf()`.

Table 6.5 Examples of using a `Formatter` through `System.printf()`

Code	Output
`System.printf("Spring Batch in Action has %d co-authors", 4)`	`Spring Batch in Action has 4 co-authors`
`System.printf("Chapter %d is \"%s\"", 6, "Writing data")`	`Chapter 6 is "Writing data"`

Table 6.5 Examples of using a Formatter through System.printf() (continued)

Code	Output
System.printf("Chapter %d is \"%15s\"", 6, "Writing data")	Chapter 6 is " Writing data"
System.printf("Chapter %d is \"%-15s\"", 6, "Writing data");	Chapter 6 is "Writing data "
System.printf("MEAP + Ebook only: \$%f", 44.99)	MEAP + Ebook only: $44.990000
System.printf("MEAP + Ebook only: \$%5.2f", 44.99)	MEAP + Ebook only: $44.99
System.printf("MEAP + Ebook only: \$%6.2f", 44.99)	MEAP + Ebook only: $ 44.99
System.printf("%s !", "MEAP is available");	MEAP is available !
System.printf("%20s !", "MEAP is available")	MEAP is available !
System.printf("%-20s !", "MEAP is available");	MEAP is available !

Spring Batch lets you easily create files with fixed-length columns by using the java.util.Formatter class. You only need to think about the format pattern.

Next, let's see how to deal with heterogeneous items before moving on to adding headers and footers.

MATCHING CLASSES TO LINEAGGREGATORS

In chapter 5, you saw how to read a flat file containing a mix of different product types. Here, you learn how to do the same thing for writing. First, you write a flat file with a LineAggregator based on the product type. Figure 6.6 shows the product hierarchy.

When the import job reads a product file, you create a MobilePhoneProduct or a BookProduct depending on the prefix of the product ID. If a product ID begins with PRM, you create a MobilePhoneProduct; if it begins with PRB, you create a BookProduct.

To write products to a file, the writer receives these same two types of

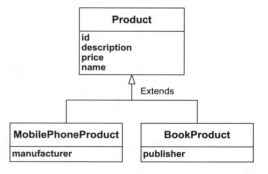

Figure 6.6 The domain model of the batch application uses several classes. The flat file item writer can use a custom LineAggregator to delegate aggregation to dedicated LineAggregators (one for each product subclass).

products. A `FlatFileItemWriter` uses a `LineAggregator` to get a `String` representation of each item. The following listing shows the `ProductsLineAggregator` class, which chooses the right `LineAggregator` depending on the `Class` of the `Product`.

Listing 6.8   Choosing a `LineAggregator`

```
public class ProductsLineAggregator implements LineAggregator<Product> {
    private Map<Class<LineAggregator<Product>>,
              LineAggregator<Object>> aggregators;

  @Override
  public String aggregate(Product product) {
    return aggregators.get(product.getClass()).aggregate(product);
  }

  public void setAggregators(Map<Class<LineAggregator<Product>>,
                            LineAggregator<Object>> aggregators) {
    this.aggregators = aggregators;
  }
}
```

To configure multiple `LineAggregators`, you inject a `Map` whose key is the `Product`'s `Class` and the value an instance of `LineAggregator`. The aggregate method uses this `Map` to find the right `LineAggregator` and then calls its aggregate method. The following listing shows how to configure multiple `LineAggregators` with a `Map`.

Listing 6.9   Configuring multiple `LineAggregators` with a Map

```
<bean id="productItemWriter"
    class="org.springframework.batch.item.file.FlatFileItemWriter">
  <property name="resource"
            value="file:target/outputs/fixedwidth-lineaggregator.txt" />
  <property name="lineAggregator">
    <bean class="com.manning.sbia.ch06.file.          ❶ Sets product
      ProductsLineAggregator">                             aggregator
      <property name="aggregators">
        <map>
          <entry key="com.manning.sbia.ch06.BookProduct"
              value-ref="bookProductLineAggregator" />   ❷ Sets aggregator
          <entry key="com.manning.sbia.ch06.                map
      MobilePhoneProduct"
      value-ref="mobileProductLineAggregator" />
        </map>
      </property>
    </bean>
  </property>
</bean>

<bean id="bookProductLineAggregator"
    class="org.springframework.batch.item.file.transform.   ❸ Sets book line
      FormatterLineAggregator">                                  aggregator
  <property name="fieldExtractor">
    <bean class="org.springframework.batch.item.file.transform.
      BeanWrapperFieldExtractor">
```

```
        <property name="names" value="id,price,name,publisher" />
      </bean>
  </property>
  <property name="format" value="%-9s%6.2f%-30s%-12s" />
</bean>

<bean id="mobileProductLineAggregator"
      class="org.springframework.batch.item.file.transform.
  ➥ FormatterLineAggregator">
  <property name="fieldExtractor">
  <bean class="org.springframework.batch.item.file.transform.
  ➥ BeanWrapperFieldExtractor">
    <property name="names" value="id,price,name,manufacturer" />
  </bean>
  </property>
  <property name="format" value="%-9s%6.2f%-30s%-12s" />
</bean>
```

❹ Sets mobile line aggregator

You start by configuring a `FlatFileItemWriter` with the `ProductLineAggregator` as its line aggregator ❶. You inject your `ProductLineAggregator` with a `Map` of Line-Aggregators ❷. The `Map` keys are `Product` subclass names, and the values are Line-Aggregator references to bean configurations of `bookProductLineAggregator` ❸ and `mobileProductLineAggregator` ❹.

The following snippet shows the result of running this example:

```
PRM....210124.60BlackBerry 8100 Pearl        BlackBerry
PRM....211139.45Sony Ericsson W810i          Sony Ericson
PRB....734 34.95Spring Batch in action       Manning
PRB....736 44.95Spring in action             Manning
PRM....214145.50Nokia 2610 Phone             Nokia
```

Depending of the type of `Product`, the last column is either a publisher or manufacturer, each using a dedicated formatter.

You can see how Spring Batch gives you the ability to customize a writer's output. Another common feature is to add a footer and a header to a flat file, which is what you do in the next section.

ADDING A FOOTER AND A HEADER

A header is a text record that Spring Batch inserts before item processing. A footer is a text record added at the end of the file after item processing. Spring Batch provides the single method interfaces `FlatFileHeaderCallback` and `FlatFileFooterCall-back` to implement these features, shown in the following listing. In this example, you write a simple description in the header, and you write the item count and the `Step` execution time in the footer.

Listing 6.10   Implementing a flat file footer and header

```
public class ProductHeaderCallback implements FlatFileHeaderCallback {

  @Override
  public void writeHeader(Writer writer) throws IOException {
    writer.write(
      "# Generated by FlatFileHeaderCallback");
```

❶ Writes header

```
    }
  }
public class ProductFooterCallback
            extends StepExecutionListenerSupport
            implements FlatFileFooterCallback {
  private StepExecution stepExecution;

  @Override
  public void writeFooter(Writer writer) throws IOException {
    writer.write("# Write count: "
      + stepExecution.getWriteCount());
    writer.write(
      System.getProperty("line.separator"));
    long delta = stepExecution.getEndTime().getTime()
      - stepExecution.getStartTime().getTime();
    writer.write("# Done in: " + delta + " ms");
  }

  @Override
  public void beforeStep(StepExecution stepExecution) {
      this.stepExecution = stepExecution;
  }
}
```

❷ Writes footer

Spring Batch passes a `Writer` to the `writeHeader` method ❶ to output the header, in this case, a simple description. The `ProductFooterCallback` class extends `StepExecutionListenerSupport` to get access to the item count and start and end times from the `writeFooter` method ❷.

In the next listing, you configure the header and footer of a `FlatFileItemWriter`.

Listing 6.11 Configuring header and footer callbacks for a flat file

```
<bean id="headerCallback" class="com.manning.sbia.
    ➥ ch06.file.ProductHeaderCallback" />
<bean id="footerCallback" class="com.manning.sbia.
    ➥ ch06.file.ProductFooterCallback" />

<job id="writeProductsJob" xmlns="http://www.springframework.org/schema/
    batch">
  <step id="readWrite">
    <tasklet>
      <chunk reader="productItemReader"
             writer="productItemWriter"
             commit-interval="100" />
      <listeners>
        <listener ref="footerCallback" />
      </listeners>
    </tasklet>
  </step>
</job>

<bean id="productItemWriter"
    class="org.springframework.batch.item.file.FlatFileItemWriter">
  <property name="resource"
```

❶ Creates header and footer callbacks

❷ Registers listener

```
                    value="file:target/outputs/fixedwidth-headerfooter.txt" />
  <property name="headerCallback"          ❸  Sets header
            ref="headerCallback" />            callback
  <property name="footerCallback"              ❹  Sets footer
            ref="footerCallback" />                callback
  <property name="lineAggregator">
    <bean class="org.springframework.batch.item.file.transform.
➥ FormatterLineAggregator">
      <property name="fieldExtractor">
        <bean class="org.springframework.batch.item.file.transform.
➥ BeanWrapperFieldExtractor">
          <property name="names" value="id,price,name" />
        </bean>
      </property>
      <property name="format" value="%-9s%6.2f%-30s" />
    </bean>
  </property>
</bean>
```

To configure your footer and header, you create header and footer callback beans ❶. The important point here is to configure the footer as a step listener ❷, which implements StepExecutionListenerSupport in order to access the StepExecution. You set the footer ❸ and the header ❹ as properties of the FlatFileItemWriter.

The following snippet shows the result of running this example:

```
# Generated by FlatFileHeaderCallback
PR....210124.60BlackBerry 8100 Pearl
PR....211139.45Sony Ericsson W810i
 (...)
PR....217 13.70Canon Digital Rebel XT 8MP
# Write count: 8
# Done in: 12 ms
```

The first line is the header, which tells who generated the file. The last two lines make up the footer, which includes the number of items written and how long the operation took.

This section ends our discussion on writing flat files. We saw Spring Batch write different types of flat file formats: delimited and fixed width. Next, we work with a different type of file, XML.

6.2.2 *Writing XML files*

Spring Batch includes an implementation of ItemWriter for XML files called Stax-EventItemWriter. This writer uses a marshaller to write XML files. A Marshaller is a generic interface provided by the Spring Object/XML Mapping[1] module to convert objects to XML, and vice versa. Spring OXM supports Java Architecture for XML Binding (JAXB) 1.0 and 2.0, Castor XML, XMLBeans, JiBX, and XStream.

The following listing shows the XML output for our case study.

---

[1] Spring OXM: http://static.springsource.org/spring/docs/3.0.x/spring-framework-reference/html/oxm.html

Listing 6.12   Example of XML file output

```
<?xml version="1.0" encoding="UTF-8"?>
<products>
  <header>(...)</header>
  <product>
    <id>PR....210</id>
    <name>BlackBerry 8100 Pearl</name>
    <description></description>
    <price>124.60</price>
  </product>
  <product>
  (...)
  </product>
  (...)
  <footer>(...)</footer>
</products>
```

This XML document has a root element named `products` followed by a `header` child element. A sequence of `product` elements defines each product. After all the products, the document has a footer and ends by closing the root element.

The `StaxEventItemWriter` class implements the `ItemWriter` interface. This writer uses a `Marshaller` to convert each item to XML and then writes them to an XML file using StAX (Streaming API for XML). In this example, you use the `XStreamMarshaller` class because it's simple to configure. Table 6.6 lists the `StaxEventItemWriter` properties.

Table 6.6   `StaxEventItemWriter` properties

Property	Type	Description
encoding	String	Encoding for writing the file; defaults to UTF-8
footerCallback	StaxWriterCallback	Callback class used to write the footer
headerCallback	StaxWriterCallback	Callback class used to write the header
marshaller	Marshaller	Spring OXM marshaller used to convert objects to XML
overwriteOutput	boolean	Whether to overwrite the output file; defaults to `true`
resource	Resource	Output resource
rootElementAttributes	Map<String,String>	Adds root element attributes; if a key name begins with `xmlns`, it's an XML namespace declaration
rootTagName	String	Tag name of root element; defaults to `root`
saveState	Boolean	Whether to save state in the execution context; defaults to `true`

Table 6.6 `StaxEventItemWriter` **properties** *(continued)*

Property	Type	Description
transactional	Boolean	Whether to delay writing to the buffer if a transaction is active; default value is `true`
version	String	XML version; default value is `1.0`

You now know all you need to implement this use case. You've already chosen a Mar-shaller class, and you know how to set the root tag element with the `rootTagName` property.

To write the header and footer, you implement the `StaxWriterCallback` interface and its `write` method. For the header element, you want to create an attribute called `generated`, as illustrated by the following snippet:

```
(...)
<header generated="Jan 27, 2011 5:30:16 PM"></header>
(...)
```

Because you're now in the StAX world, you create an `XMLEvent` object using the `XMLEventFactory` class. The following listing shows the `ProductHeaderStaxCallback` implementation.

Listing 6.13 Implementing an XML header callback

```java
public class ProductHeaderStaxCallback implements StaxWriterCallback {
    @Override
    public void write(XMLEventWriter writer) throws IOException {
        try {
            XMLEventFactory eventFactory = XMLEventFactory.newInstance();
            XMLEvent event = eventFactory.createStartElement("", "", "header");
            writer.add(event);
            event = eventFactory.createAttribute(
                    "generated",
                    DateFormat.getInstance().format(new Date()));
            writer.add(event);
            event = eventFactory.createEndElement("", "", "header");
            writer.add(event);
        } catch (XMLStreamException e) {
        }
    }
}
```

The `write` method starts by creating an instance of `XMLEventFactory` to help you cre-ate an element and an attribute with the current date.

The footer is like the header, and you implement the same interface. Here, you want to create an element named `writeCount`. The following listing shows the `ProductFooterStaxCallback` class that implements `StaxWriterCallback` and extends `StepExecutionListenerSupport` to access the `StepExecution`.

Listing 6.14   Implementing an XML footer callback

```
public class ProductFooterStaxCallback
            extends StepExecutionListenerSupport
            implements StaxWriterCallback {
  private StepExecution stepExecution;

  @Override
  public void write(XMLEventWriter writer) throws IOException {
    try {
      XMLEventFactory eventFactory = XMLEventFactory.newInstance();
      XMLEvent event = eventFactory.createStartElement("", "", "footer");
      writer.add(event);
      event = eventFactory.createStartElement("", "", "writeCount");
      writer.add(event);
      event = eventFactory.createCharacters(
        String.valueOf(stepExecution.getWriteCount())     ❶ Creates writeCount
      );                                                       element
      writer.add(event);
      event = eventFactory.createEndElement("", "", "writeCount");
      writer.add(event);
      event = eventFactory.createEndElement("", "", "footer");
      writer.add(event);
    } catch (XMLStreamException e) {
    }
  }

  @Override
  public void beforeStep(StepExecution
                  stepExecution) {              ❷ Injects
    this.stepExecution = stepExecution;            stepExecution
  }
}
```

With the `XMLEventFactory` class, you create an XML character for the `writeCount` element ❶. Spring Batch injects the `StepExecution` ❷ to give you access to the write-Count value.

This configuration is almost complete; your last task is to configure a `StaxEventItemWriter` to write the XML file, as shown in the following listing.

Listing 6.15   Configuring a `StaxEventItemWriter`

```
<job id="writeProductsJob" xmlns="http://www.springframework.org/schema/
    batch">
  <step id="readWrite">
    <tasklet>
      <chunk reader="productItemReader"
          writer="productItemWriter"
          commit-interval="100" />
        <listeners>
          <listener ref="footerCallback"/>
        </listeners>
    </tasklet>
  </step>
</job>
```

```
<bean id="productItemWriter"
      class="org.springframework.batch.item.xml.StaxEventItemWriter">
  <property name="resource"
            value="file:target/outputs/
  ➥ products-headerfooter.xml" />
  <property name="marshaller" ref="productMarshaller" />
  <property name="rootTagName" value="products" />
  <property name="overwriteOutput" value="true" />
  <property name="headerCallback"
            ref="headerCallback" />
  <property name="footerCallback"
            ref="footerCallback" />
</bean>

<bean id="productMarshaller" class="org.
  ➥ springframework.oxm.xstream.XStreamMarshaller">
  <property name="aliases">
    <map>
      <entry key="product" value="com.manning.sbia.
  ➥ ch06.Product" />
    </map>
  </property>
</bean>

<bean id="headerCallback"
      class="com.manning.sbia.ch06.file.ProductHeaderStaxCallback" />
<bean id="footerCallback"
      class="com.manning.sbia.ch06.file.ProductFooterStaxCallback" />
```

❶ Sets resource

❷ Sets marshaller

This Spring context contains a job definition with a special listener, the footer call-back, which Spring Batch injects with a StepExecution. You configure a StaxEvent-ItemWriter with an output resource ❶ and footer and header callbacks. Finally, you define an XStream Marshaller ❷ with an alias map to serialize Product objects to XML product elements.

The following listing shows the XML output of this StaxEventItemWriter example.

Listing 6.16 StaxEventItemWriter output

```
<?xml version="1.0" encoding="UTF-8"?>
<products>
  <header generated="Jan 28, 2011 5:30:16 PM"></header>
  <product>
    <id>PR....210</id>
    <name>BlackBerry 8100 Pearl</name>
    <description></description>
    <price>124.60</price>
  </product>
  <product>
  (...)
  </product>
  <footer>
    <writeCount>8</writeCount>
  </footer>
</products>
```

This XML products document contains elements for a footer, a header, and for each product.

In the next section, you discover how to "roll over" XML files depending on the number of items you want in a file, creating a set of files instead of a single file.

6.2.3   Writing file sets

Spring Batch provides a mechanism to write file sets instead of a single file (see figure 6.7). It's useful if you want to create files with a maximum number of items.

The `MultiResourceItemWriter` class is an `ItemWriter` implementation for multiple output files. The following listing shows how to configure this writer.

Listing 6.17   Configuring multiple output files

```
<job id="writeProductsJob" xmlns="http://www.springframework.org/schema/
    batch">
  <step id="readWrite">
    <tasklet>
      <chunk reader="productItemReader"
             writer="productItemWriter"
             commit-interval="100" />                 ❶ Sets commit
    </tasklet>                                              interval
  </step>
</job>

<bean id="productItemWriter"
      class="org.springframework.batch.item.file.MultiResourceItemWriter"
      scope="step">
  <property name="resource"
            value="file:target/outputs/products-multi.xml" />
  <property name="itemCountLimitPerResource"
            value="10000" />                           ❷ Sets max item
                                                           count per resource
  <property name="delegate" ref="delegateWriter" />
</bean>                                                     Configures
<bean id="delegateWriter" class="org.springframework.               writer
  ➥ batch.item.xml.StaxEventItemWriter">
(...)
</bean>
```

We set the commit interval to 100 ❶ (the commit interval can impact the number of items in a file; more on this later!). If you have 40,100 products and an `itemCountLimitPerResource` of 10,000 ❷, the `MultiResourceItemWriter` will create five files, the

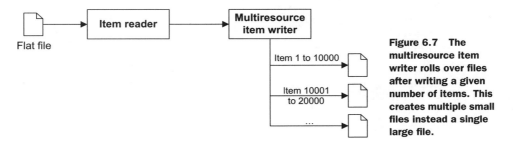

Figure 6.7   The multiresource item writer rolls over files after writing a given number of items. This creates multiple small files instead a single large file.

first four with 10,000 records, and the last with 100. The `MultiResourceItemWriter` also sets the resource for the writer. In this case, the writer is a `StaxEventItemWriter`, working with the file writer. By default, a multiresource writer suffixes the output filenames with an index. For example:

```
products-multi.xml.1
products-multi.xml.2
products-multi.xml.3
```

You can create your own suffix policy by implementing the `ResourceSuffixCreator` interface:

```
public interface ResourceSuffixCreator {
  String getSuffix(int index);
}
```

Be aware that the `MultiResourceItemWriter` creates a new resource after the commit interval if it reaches the count specified in the `itemCountLimitPerResource` property. Otherwise, the `MultiResourceItemWriter` creates a new resource the next time around.

> **NOTE** The `MultiResourceItemWriter` works also for flat files, not only for XML files. It can roll over any writer that implements ResourceAwareItem-WriterItemStream.

This section ends our discussion on writing flat files and XML files. We saw how to write delimited and fixed-width flat files. We also discussed how to write XML files using the Spring OXM `Marshaller` interface. The next section focuses on how to write items into a relational database.

6.3 Writing to databases

In the Java world, you access relational databases with JDBC or an ORM tool. Spring Batch provides writers for both. Our use case for this section is to write `Product` objects into a relational database. We first look at the JDBC item writer.

6.3.1 Writing with JDBC

The `JdbcBatchItemWriter` class is an implementation of the `ItemWriter` interface for JDBC that sits on top of the Spring JDBC layer, which itself hides the complexities of using the JDBC API directly. The `JdbcBatchItemWriter` class uses JDBC's batch features to execute a group of SQL statements all at once for an item set, as illustrated in figure 6.8.

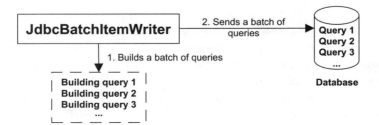

Figure 6.8 Sending a batch of SQL statements to a relational database is more efficient than sending one query at a time.

The SQL batch size is equal to the commit interval configured in the chunk-oriented tasklet. Sending SQL statements to a database in a SQL batch is faster than sending them one at a time. Table 6.7 lists the properties of the JdbcBatchItem-Writer class.

Table 6.7   JdbcBatchItemWriter properties

Property	Type	Description
assertUpdates	boolean	Whether to throw an exception if at least one item doesn't update or delete a row; defaults to true
itemPreparedState-mentSetter	ItemPreparedStatement-Setter<T>	SQL statement parameter values from ? positional parameter markers
itemSqlParameter-SourceProvider	ItemSqlParameterSource-Provider<T>	SQL statement parameter values from named parameters
sql	String	SQL statement to execute

The main JdbcBatchItemWriter properties are sql and your choice of itemPrepared-StatementSetter or itemSqlParameterSourceProvider. The ItemPreparedState-mentSetter class executes SQL with ? parameter markers. The ItemSqlParameter-SourceProvider class executes SQL statements with named parameters.

The following listing configures a JdbcBatchItemWriter to use a SQL statement with named parameters.

Listing 6.18   Configuring a JdbcBatchItemWriter with named parameters

```
<bean id="productItemWriter"
    class="org.springframework.batch.item.database.
➥ JdbcBatchItemWriter">
 <property name="assertUpdates" value="true" />
 <property name="itemSqlParameterSourceProvider">
   <bean class="org.springframework.batch.item.database.
➥ BeanPropertyItemSqlParameterSourceProvider" />
 </property>
 <property name="sql"
   value="INSERT INTO PRODUCT (ID, NAME, PRICE)
         VALUES(:id, :name, :price)" />
 <property name="dataSource" ref="dataSource" />
</bean>
```

You configure the JdbcBatchItemWriter with assertUpdates set to true, such that if a statement execution doesn't update a row, Spring Batch throws an EmptyResult-DataAccessException. The key point in a JdbcBatchItemWriter configuration is to set itemSqlParameterSourceProvider to a BeanPropertySqlParameterSource to bind item properties to SQL parameter names from JavaBeans properties. At runtime, the SQL parameter name called name (defined with :name in the SQL statement) is set to the `Product` name property. This is the best and fastest way to insert data in a relational database.

Another way to execute a SQL statement in Spring Batch is to use a `JdbcBatch-ItemWriter` with an `ItemPreparedStatementSetter`. The `ItemPreparedStatement-Setter` interface lets you implement how a JDBC `PreparedStatement` matches your bean to tables and columns.

The following listing shows you how to implement an `ItemPreparedStatement-Setter`.

Listing 6.19 Implementing an `ItemPreparedStatementSetter`

```
public class ProductItemPreparedStatementSetter
      implements ItemPreparedStatementSetter<Product> {
  @Override
  public void setValues(Product item,
                  PreparedStatement ps) throws SQLException {
    ps.setString(1, item.getId());
    ps.setString(2, item.getName());                 ❶ Sets SQL
    ps.setBigDecimal(3, item.getPrice());               parameter string
  }
}
```

In this listing, you set a value for each SQL parameter ❶ from bean properties. Here, you use the JDBC API directly to set each SQL statement parameter. JDBC provides different methods for different data types and can perform some conversions between data types on your behalf.

Finally, you configure a `JdbcBatchItemWriter` with SQL ? positional parameter markers, as in the following listing.

Listing 6.20 Configuring a SQL statement with ? parameter markers

```
<bean id="productItemWriter" class="org.springframework.batch.item.
  ➥ database.JdbcBatchItemWriter">
  <property name="assertUpdates" value="true" />
  <property name="itemPreparedStatementSetter">
    <bean class="com.manning.sbia.ch06.database.
  ➥ ProductItemPreparedStatementSetter" />
  </property>
  <property name="sql"
    value="INSERT INTO PRODUCT (ID, NAME, PRICE)
  ➥ VALUES(?, ?, ?)" />
  <property name="dataSource" ref="dataSource" />
</bean>
```

You set your `ItemPreparedStatementSetter` implementation, which binds SQL parameters with your custom code. Note that this statement uses ? positional parameter markers instead of named parameters.

You can configure a `JdbcBatchItemWriter` in two ways: with named and positional parameters, depending on your beans and database tables. The next section explores ORM tools, another way to interact with a relational database.

6.3.2   *Writing with ORM*

ORM provides a data persistence bridge between an object-oriented system and a database. ORM manages data I/O between objects and a database, and in Spring Batch, hides the data access layer, in this case, the JDBC layer. Spring Batch supports several ORMs with `ItemWriter` implementations: Hibernate, the Java Persistence API (JPA), and iBATIS.

In our case study, you use Hibernate to persist the `Product` objects to a table in the database. You first annotate the `Product` domain class with database mapping annotations, as described in the following listing.

Listing 6.21   Annotating a domain class for ORM

```
@Entity("product")
public class Product {
  @Id("id")
  private String id;
  @Column("label")
  private String label;
  @Column("description")
  private String description;
  @Column("price")
  private float price;
  (...)
}
```

The `Entity` annotation on the `Product` class specifies that the class maps to the product table in the database. The `Id` and `Column` annotations map instance variables to table columns using the database column name in the annotation values.

You must configure a `HibernateItemWriter` with a `HibernateTemplate` or a `SessionFactory`, as shown the following fragment:

```
<bean id="productItemWriter"
      class="org.springframework.batch.item.database.HibernateItemWriter">
  <property name="hibernateTemplate" ref="hibernateTemplate" />
</bean>
```

The following Spring Batch code fragment shows the core of the `HibernateItemWriter` class, which uses a Spring `HibernateTemplate`.

Listing 6.22   `HibernateItemWriter` implementation

```
(...)
protected void doWrite(HibernateOperations hibernateTemplate,
                       List<? extends T> items) {
  if (!items.isEmpty()) {
  for (T item : items) {
    if (!hibernateTemplate.contains(item)) {
      hibernateTemplate.saveOrUpdate(item);
    }
  }
}
}
```

```
@Override
public final void write(List<? extends T> items) {
  doWrite(hibernateTemplate, items);
  hibernateTemplate.flush();
}
(...)
```

In this implementation, Spring Batch checks if each item is a Hibernate entity and calls saveOrUpdate. The writer flushes the Hibernate session to synchronize the object model with the database.

If a Hibernate entity calls saveOrUpdate and isn't already in the session, Hibernate executes a SQL SELECT to find the object in the database. If Hibernate finds the object, it executes a SQL UPDATE; if not, it executes a SQL INSERT.

Hibernate uses fetch strategies to determine how and when to retrieve objects. It uses fetch modes to fetch associations with an outer join, a SELECT or sub-SELECT, and for lazy or eager loading. This may create overhead compared to JDBC where you can control SQL statements directly.

Spring Batch also provides a JPA writer named JpaItemWriter that takes an EntityManagerFactory as a parameter, as described in the following configuration fragment:

```
<bean id="productItemWriter"
      class="org.springframework.batch.item.database.JpaItemWriter">
  <property name="entityManagerFactory" ref="entityManagerFactory" />
</bean>
```

You also need to configure the entity managed by JPA in META-INF/persistence.xml:

```
<persistence-unit name="product" transaction-type="RESOURCE_LOCAL">
  <class>com.manning.sbia.ch06.Product</class>
  <exclude-unlisted-classes>true</exclude-unlisted-classes>
</persistence-unit>
```

Spring Batch provides another ItemWriter based on iBATIS, the IbatisBatchItem-Writer.

This section covered database item writers. We saw the Spring Batch implementations for JDBC, the JdbcBatchItemWriter, and one ORM implementation, the HibernateItemWriter. In the next sections, we focus on other targets like JMS and email senders.

6.4   Adapting existing services for reuse

Spring Batch supports other writers for other targets such as existing business services and JMS and email senders. To avoid reinventing the wheel, it's a good idea to reuse existing business services. After discussing reuse, we see how to send an item in a JMS message and via email.

If you want to reuse existing services to implement an ItemWriter, Spring Batch provides helper classes.

The first helper class is the `ItemWriterAdapter` class used to delegate writing to another service. Let's say you have an existing `ProductService` bean, which has a `write(Product)` method:

```
public class ProductService {
  public void write(Product product) {
    (...)
  }
}
```

You can reuse this class from an `ItemWriterAdapter`. The first step is to wire the existing bean to the adapter:

```
<bean id="productItemWriter"
      class="org.springframework.batch.item.
  ➥ adapter.ItemWriterAdapter">
  <property name="targetObject" ref="productService" />
  <property name="targetMethod" value="write" />
</bean>
<bean id="productService"
      class="com.manning.sbia.ch06.service.
  ➥ ProductService" />
```

You configure an `ItemWriterAdapter` with a `targetObject`, the service, and a `target-Method`, the target method of the service.

If the service method is more complex, Spring Batch provides another `ItemWriter` to extract properties from an item bean. Let's imagine another `ProductService` class with a `write` method that takes multiple arguments:

```
public class ProductService {
  public void write(String id, String name,
                    String description, BigDecimal price) {
(...)
  }
}
```

The `PropertyExtractingDelegatingItemWriter` class extracts data from an item and calls the target method with the extracted values. The following listing shows how to configure a `PropertyExtractingDelegatingItemWriter`.

Listing 6.23 Configuring a `PropertyExtractingDelegatingItemWriter`

```
<bean id="productItemWriter" class="org.
  ➥ springframework.batch.item.adapter.
  ➥ PropertyExtractingDelegatingItemWriter">
  <property name="targetObject" ref="productService" />
  <property name="targetMethod" value="write" />
  <property name="fieldsUsedAsTargetMethodArguments">
    <list>
      <value>id</value>
      <value>name</value>
      <value>description</value>
      <value>price</value>
```

❶ Declares ItemWriter

❷ Extracts data for arguments

```
        </list>
    </property>
</bean>

<bean id="productService"
      class="com.manning.sbia.ch06.service.
➥ ProductService" />
```

2 **Extracts data
for arguments**

You first define a `productWriter` bean **1** using a `PropertyExtractingDelegating-`
`ItemWriter`. The property `fieldsUsedAsTargetMethodArguments` defines the item
properties to use as arguments when calling the target method **2**.

The `ItemWriterAdapter` and `PropertyExtractingDelegatingItemWriter` help
reuse existing services. If this isn't enough for your use cases, you can create more
solutions by reusing existing services, as discussed in section 5.6.1, "Services as input."

Before describing custom writer implementations, we implement and configure
writing data using a message-oriented middleware (MOM) broker like JMS. We also see
how to send emails for items.

6.5   *Writing to JMS*

A MOM broker allows you to send messages asynchronously to other applications (see
figure 6.9). For example, a writer can send products to a billing information system.

Spring Batch includes the `JmsItemWriter` class, which you can use without writing
any Java code, only XML configuration, as shown in the following listing.

Listing 6.24   Configuring a `JmsItemWriter`

```
<amq:connectionFactory id="jmsFactory"
    brokerURL="tcp://localhost:61616"/>
<amq:queue id="productDestination"
           physicalName="destination.product" />

<bean id="jmsTemplate" class="org.springframework.jms.
  ➥ core.JmsTemplate">
  <property name="connectionFactory" ref="jmsFactory" />
  <property name="defaultDestination" ref="productDestination" />
  <property name="receiveTimeout" value="500" />
  <property name="sessionTransacted" value="true" />
</bean>

<bean id="productItemWriter" class="org.
  ➥ springframework.batch.item.jms.JmsItemWriter">
  <property name="jmsTemplate" ref="jmsTemplate" />
</bean>
```

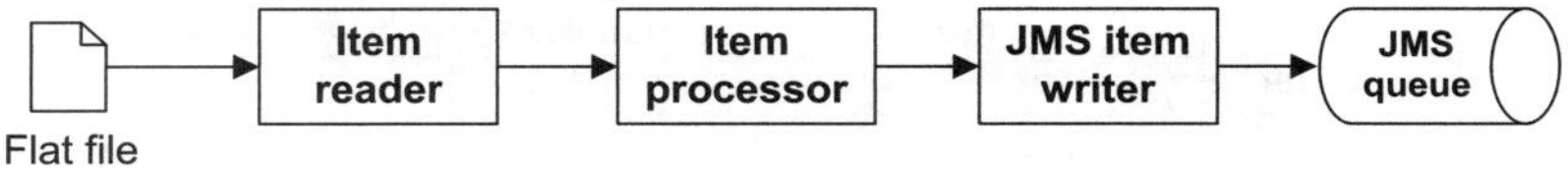

**Figure 6.9   An application puts messages on a JMS queue with a JMS item writer.
Applications often use JMS to communicate with each other in a decoupled and
asynchronous way.**

You first configure the connection parameters to the JMS Server and set the JMS queue name where the application will send JMS messages. You also create a Spring `JmsTemplate` to create JMS messages more easily. Finally, you configure an `ItemJmsWriter` with the `JmsTemplate`.

Spring Batch makes it easy to send items to other applications through a MOM broker. Before implementing a custom writer, we see how an item writer sends email messages.

6.6   *Sending email messages*

Spring Batch provides an `ItemWriter` to send emails, the `SimpleMailMessageItem-Writer`. For this use case, you have a file (it could also be a database table) containing information about new users, and you want to send each a welcome email message. The following snippet lists the content of the customer flat file:

```
CLIENT_ID,NAME,EMAIL
1,Mr. White,white@nowhere.com
2,Mr. Orange,orange@nowhere.com
3,Mr. Pink,pink@nowhere.com
4,Mr. Blue,blue@nowhere.com
5,Mr. Brown,brown@nowhere.com
```

Figure 6.10 illustrates a Spring Batch application that sends an email message for each customer in the input file.

The job reads the flat file and creates a `Customer` object for each input line. After that, you use an `ItemProcessor` to convert each `Customer` to a `SimpleMailMessage` (a Spring support class,) as described in the following listing.

Listing 6.25   Converting a `Customer` to `SimpleMailMessage`

```
public class CustomerItemProcessor implements
  ItemProcessor<Customer, SimpleMailMessage> {
  @Override
  public SimpleMailMessage process(Customer item)           ❶ Converts customer
        throws Exception {                                     to email message
    SimpleMailMessage msg = new SimpleMailMessage();
    msg.setFrom("springbatchinaction@test.com");
    msg.setTo(item.getEmail());
    msg.setSubject("Welcome message !!");
    msg.setText("Hello " + item.getName());
    return msg;
  }
}
```

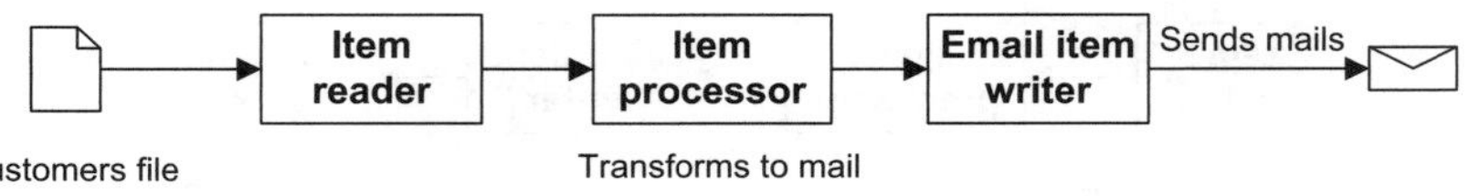

Figure 6.10   Sending an email message for each customer in an input file. Because Spring Batch's email item writer only takes care of sending email, it's common practice to use an item processor to convert read items into ready-to-be-sent `SimpleMailMessage` or `MimeMessage` objects.

You implement an `ItemProcessor` to create new `SimpleMailMessage` objects from `Customer` objects ❶. The `process` method takes a `Customer` item, creates a new email message, and sets the message fields `From`, `To`, `Subject`, and `Body`.

The following listing configures a `SimpleMailMessageItemWriter`.

Listing 6.26   Configuring a `SimpleMailMessageItemWriter`

```
<bean id="javaMailSender" class="org.springframework.                ❶ Creates
  ➥ mail.javamail.JavaMailSenderImpl">                                   JavaMailSender
  <property name="host" value="127.0.0.1" />
  <property name="port" value="3025" />
  <property name="defaultEncoding" value="UTF-8" />
</bean>

(...)
  <step id="readWrite">
    <tasklet>
      <chunk reader="customerItemReader"
             writer="mailMessageItemWriter"                         ❷ Configures
             processor="customerProcessor"                             chunk
             commit-interval="100" />
    </tasklet>
  </step>
(...)

<bean id="mailMessageItemWriter"
      class="org.springframework.batch.                            ❸ Creates mail
  ➥ item.mail.SimpleMailMessageItemWriter">                           item writer
  <property name="mailSender" ref="javaMailSender" />
</bean>

<bean id="customerProcessor"
      class="com.manning.sbia.ch06.mail.CustomerItemProcessor" />
```

First, you create a `JavaMailSenderImpl` ❶, a bean to send mail required for the writer. You configure a chunk with a processor to convert `Customer` items to `Simple-MailMessage` objects ❷. Finally, you configure the `SimpleMailMessageItemWriter` and its `mailSender` property ❸.

In this section, we saw how to send messages to a mail server. The next section focuses on implementing your own item writers.

6.7   *Implementing custom item writers*

If none of the built-in Spring Batch `ItemWriter`s matches your requirements, you can create your own. For example, you may want to create your own JDBC item writer. The following listing shows an example implementation.

Listing 6.27   Creating a custom JDBC `ItemWriter`

```
public class JdbcProductItemWriter implements ItemWriter<Product> {
  String INSERT_PRODUCT =
       "INSERT INTO PRODUCT (ID,NAME,DESCRIPTION,PRICE) VALUES(?,?,?,?)";
  String UPDATE_PRODUCT =
```

```
            "UPDATE PRODUCT SET NAME=?, DESCRIPTION=?, PRICE=? WHERE ID = ?";
    private JdbcTemplate jdbcTemplate;

    public void setJdbcTemplate(JdbcTemplate jdbcTemplate) {
      this.jdbcTemplate = jdbcTemplate;
    }

    @Override
    public void write(List<? extends Product> items) throws Exception {
      for (Product item : items) {
        int updated = jdbcTemplate.update(
                          UPDATE_PRODUCT,
                          item.getName(),
                          item.getDescription(),
                          item.getPrice(),
                          item.getId());
        if (updated == 0) {
          jdbcTemplate.update(
                          INSERT_PRODUCT,
                          item.getId(),
                          item.getName(),
                          item.getDescription(),
                          item.getPrice());
        }
      }
    }
  }
}
```

This JDBC example class implements the `ItemWriter` interface. The configuration injects a `JdbcTemplate` to take advantage of Spring JDBC. The `write` method updates or inserts a row in the product table. If the `UPDATE` statement returns zero rows affected, then you insert a new row in the table.

To be complete, the item writer should be restartable. Imagine the system crashes when a job is writing to a file. On a restart, if the reader can start reading where it left off, the writer should *also* be able to resume its writing exactly where it was interrupted. You should care about restartability on the writer side mainly for file-based writers (good news: the implementations Spring Batch provides are restartable). Database-based writers are usually automatically restartable: they just write the items the reader pushes. So restartability is a reader concern in this case.

This section completes our presentation of custom writers. The next section discusses advanced writing techniques.

6.8   *Advanced writing techniques*

You've seen how to use the item writers provided by Spring Batch and how to implement your own item writer. In this section, you learn more about Spring Batch item writers. To implement a complex job, it may be necessary to create something more complex than a custom item writer. You may need to chain writers to write to different targets. You may also need to choose between several writers, depending on the item.

6.8.1 *Composing item writers*

Spring Batch can configure only a single item writer for a chunk-oriented tasklet, and sometimes you need multiple writers for the same chunk. The classic Composite pattern provides this functionality. A composite wraps a set of objects and presents them as a single object. Figure 6.11 illustrates a Composite-ItemWriter containing a set of item writers.

Figure 6.11 A composite item writer delegates writing to a list of item writers. Use this pattern to send items to several targets, like a database and a file.

The following listing configures a CompositeItemWriter with two delegate item writers.

Listing 6.28 Configuring a CompositeItemWriter

```
<bean id="productItemWriter"
      class="org.springframework.
   batch.item.support.CompositeItemWriter">    ❶ Declares
  <property name="delegates">                       CompositeItemWriter
    <list>
      <ref local="delimitedProductItemWriter"/>   ❷ Adds item writer
      <ref local="fixedWidthProductItemWriter"/>     references
    </list>
  </property>
</bean>

<bean id="delimitedProductItemWriter"
      class="org.springframework.batch.item.file.FlatFileItemWriter">
(...)
</bean>

<bean id="fixedWidthProductItemWriter"
      class="org.springframework.batch.item.file.FlatFileItemWriter">
(...)
</bean>
```

You first create a CompositeItemWriter ❶ with its delegates property set to a list of a item writers ❷. This composite calls each item writer in the configured order. This technique allows the job to write items to multiple files in different formats. This technique also allows the job to write items in both files and relational databases, all from one composite item writer. The next section discusses a more complex topic: how to route an item to a specific item writer.

6.8.2 *Routing items to specific item writers*

In this section, we discuss a more complex use case: how to route items to specific item writers on the basis of some criteria. In the following input file, the column called OPERATION represents an operation to execute: C to create, U to update, and D to delete:

```
PRODUCT_ID,NAME,DESCRIPTION,PRICE,OPERATION
PR....210,BlackBerry 8100 Pearl,,124.60,C
PR....211,Sony Ericsson W810i,,139.45,D
PR....212,Samsung MM-A900M Ace,,97.80,U
PR....213,Toshiba M285-E 14,,166.20,C
```

For this use case, you want to route each product item to an item writer, depending on the value of a `Product`'s operation. The operation determines whether to create, update, or delete a product in a relational database. Figure 6.12 shows this use case.

One of the building blocks Spring Batch provides to implement this type of use case is an interface called `Classifier`. You implement a `Classifier` to map an input object of type C to another object of type T:

```
public interface Classifier<C, T> {
  T classify(C classifiable);
}
```

The `ClassifierCompositeItemWriter` class is an `ItemWriter` implementation that wraps a `Classifier`. This `Classifier` takes an object and returns an `ItemWriter` for objects of the same type.

The `BackToBackPatternClassifier` class is a `Classifier` implementation for mapping arbitrary objects to other objects using pattern matchers. We call this type of classifier a *router*.

Now that you have some good building blocks, let's see how to use these types for our use case. First, you create the router, which is a `Classifier`, to return the operation value for a given `Product`:

```
public class ProductRouterClassifier {
  @Classifier
  public String classify(Product classifiable) {
    return classifiable.getOperation();
  }
}
```

You can create a class that implements the `Classifier` interface or use the `@Classifier` annotation to return the product operation value. This example uses the `@Classifier` annotation.

You now have all the pieces needed to configure a `BackToBackPatternClassifier` to get an item writer for a given product operation:

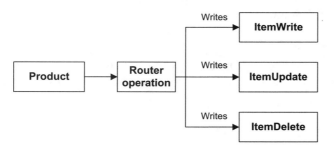

Figure 6.12   Routing a `Product` item to a specific writer

```
<bean class="org.springframework.batch.classify.
➥  BackToBackPatternClassifier">
  <property name="routerDelegate">
    <bean class="com.manning.sbia.ch06.advanced.
➥  ProductRouterClassifier" />
  </property>
  <property name="matcherMap">
    <map>
      <entry key="C"
             value-ref="insertJdbcBatchItemWriter" />
      <entry key="U"
             value-ref="updateJdbcBatchItemWriter" />
      <entry key="D"
             value-ref="deleteJdbcBatchItemWriter" />
    </map>
  </property>
</bean>
```

The BackToBackPatternClassifier uses a router to get a key value to get the matching item writer.

The following listing shows the complete configuration for your BackToBack-PatternClassifier routing use case.

Listing 6.29 Configuring a routing BackToBackPatternClassifier

```
<bean id="productItemWriter"                                    ❶ Creates Classifier-
      class="org.springframework.batch.item.support.              CompositeItemWriter
➥  ClassifierCompositeItemWriter">
  <property name="classifier">
    <bean class="org.springframework.batch.classify.
➥  BackToBackPatternClassifier">
      <property name="routerDelegate">                          ❷ Creates
        <bean class="com.manning.sbia.ch06.advanced.               router
➥  ProductRouterClassifier" />
      </property>
      <property name="matcherMap">
        <map>
          <entry key="C"
               value-ref="insertJdbcBatchItemWriter" />
          <entry key="U"                                        ❸ Creates
               value-ref="updateJdbcBatchItemWriter" />            writer map
          <entry key="D"
               value-ref="deleteJdbcBatchItemWriter" />
        </map>
      </property>
    </bean>
  </property>
</bean>
<bean id="insertJdbcBatchItemWriter">
  (...)
  <property name="sql"
    value="INSERT INTO PRODUCT(ID,NAME,PRICE) VALUES(:id,:name,:price)" />
</bean>
```

This configuration defines a `productItemWriter` bean as a `ClassifierComposite-`
`ItemWriter` ❶. This item writer sets its `classifier` property to a `BackToBack-`
`PatternClassifier`, which delegates to the router in the `routerDelegate` property
defined as a custom `ProductRouterClassifier` ❷. This router maps `Product` operations to an item writer that does the work ❸. Phew!

This section completes our presentation of advanced writing techniques. You can
now use and implement your own `ItemWriters`. You can also route domain objects to
specific item writers. Spring Batch can indeed deal with some complex writing use cases.

6.9   *Summary*

Writing data is the last step in a chunk-oriented tasklet. Spring Batch offers a simple
interface, the `ItemWriter`, to implement this task and provides implementations for
different delimited and fixed-width flat files, XML files, JDBC, and ORM. For ORM, we
saw how to write to Hibernate.

We studied how to write items reusing legacy services, how to write items to a JMS
queue, and how to send emails for items. We also saw how to implement a custom item
writer. Finally, we discussed advanced writing techniques, the use of the composite pattern, and how to route a domain object to an item writer on the basis of various criteria.

In chapter 7, you learn how to process data, the middle section of a chunk-
oriented step.

Processing data

This chapter covers
- Writing business logic in a chunk-oriented step
- Processing items in a chunk-oriented step
- Transforming items
- Filtering items
- Validating items

Chapters 5 and 6 focused heavily on Spring Batch input and output: how to read and write data from various types of data stores. You learned that Spring Batch enforces best practices to optimize I/O and provides many ready-to-use components. This is important for batch applications because exchanging data between systems is common. Batch applications aren't limited to I/O; they also have business logic to carry on: enforcing business rules before sending items to a database, transforming data from a source representation to one expected by a target data store, and so on.

In Spring Batch applications, you embed this business logic in the *processing phase*: after you read an item but before you write it. Thanks to its chunk-oriented architecture, Spring Batch provides first-class support for this type of processing in a dedicated component—the *item processor*—that you insert between the item reader and the item writer. After explaining item processing and its configuration in Spring Batch, we show you how to use item processors to modify, filter, and validate items. For validation, we examine two techniques: programmatic validation in Java and validation through configuration files using a validation language and validation annotations. Finally, we cover how to chain item processors following the composite design pattern. By the end of this chapter, you'll know exactly where and how to write the business logic for your batch application. You'll also learn about advanced topics, such as the distinction between filtering and skipping items. Let's start with processing items in Spring Batch.

7.1   Processing items

Spring Batch provides a convenient way to handle a large number of records: the chunk-oriented step. So far, we've covered the read and write phases of the chunk-oriented step; this section explains how to add a processing phase. This processing phase is the perfect place to embed your application-specific business logic. It also avoids tangling your business code in the reading and writing phases (input and output). We'll see what kind of business logic the processing phase can handle, how to configure an item processor in a chunk-oriented step, and the item processor implementations delivered with Spring Batch.

7.1.1   Processing items in a chunk-oriented step

Recall that a chunk-oriented step includes a reading component (to read items one by one) and a writing component (to handle writing several items in one chunk). The two previous chapters covered how to read and write items from different kinds of data stores and in various formats. Spring Batch can insert an optional processing component between the reading and writing phases. This component—the item processor—embeds some business logic, such as transforming or filtering items, between reading and writing. Figure 7.1 illustrates where item processing takes place in a chunk-oriented step.

   When a chunk-oriented step contains no processing phase, items read are sent as-is to the writer, and Spring Batch takes care of aggregating items in chunks. Now, imagine that an application can't allow writing items as-is because some kind of processing must be applied to the items first. Let's add a new business requirement to the online store example: you want to apply discounts to products before the job imports

Figure 7.1 Spring Batch allows insertion of an optional processing phase between the reading and writing phases of a chunk-oriented step. The processing phase usually contains some business logic implemented as an item processor.

them in the online store database. To do so, you must modify the products imported from the flat file in the item-processing phase.

7.1.2 Use cases for item processing

The processing phase is a good place for business logic. A common use case in Spring Batch is to use built-in readers and writers to deal with data stores—like flat files and databases—and to add an item processor to hold any custom business logic. Table 7.1 lists the categories of business logic that can take place in the item-processing phase.

Table 7.1 Categories of business logic in the item-processing phase

Category	Description
Transformation	The item processor transforms read items before sending them to the writer. The item processor can change the state of the read item or create a new object. In the latter case, written items may not be of the same type as read items.
Filtering	The item processor decides whether to send each read item to the writer.

The processing phase is an interesting link between the reading and writing phase. It allows you to go beyond the simple "read an item–write that item" pattern. The rest of this chapter examines the subtleties of item processing—with realistic use cases—to illustrate the many possibilities of this pattern. Let's start with the basic configuration of an item processor in Spring Batch.

7.1.3 Configuring an item processor

Spring Batch defines the item-processing contract with the `ItemProcessor` interface as follows:

```
package org.springframework.batch.item;

public interface ItemProcessor<I, O> {

  O process(I item) throws Exception;

}
```

The `ItemProcessor` interface uses two type arguments, `I` and `O`:

- Spring Batch passes a read item of type `I` to the `process` method. The type `I` must be compatible with the item reader type.
- The `process` method returns an item of type `O`, which Spring Batch in turn sends to the item writer, also of a type compatible with `O`.

You define the concrete types `I` and `O` in your `ItemProcessor` implementation. If the `process` method returns `null`, Spring Batch won't send the item to the writer, as defined by the filtering contract (filtering is different from skipping; more on this later). The following listing shows how to implement a filtering `ItemProcessor`.

Listing 7.1   Implementation of a filtering item processor

```
package com.manning.sbia.ch07;

import org.apache.commons.lang.math.NumberUtils;
import org.springframework.batch.item.ItemProcessor;
import com.manning.sbia.ch01.domain.Product;

public class FilteringProductItemProcessor implements        Receives and returns
            ItemProcessor<Product, Product> {                objects of same type

  @Override
  public Product process(Product item) throws Exception {
    return needsToBeFiltered(item) ? null : item;
  }

  private boolean needsToBeFiltered(Product item) {
    String id = item.getId();
    String lastDigit = id.substring(
      id.length()-1, id.length());
    if(NumberUtils.isDigits(lastDigit)) {                     Implements
      return NumberUtils.toInt(lastDigit) % 2 == 1;          filtering logic
    } else {
      return false;
    }
  }
}
```

This `ItemProcessor` implementation has the following characteristics:

- *No transformation*—The processor receives a `Product` object and returns a `Product` object. Therefore, the `I` and `O` type arguments of the `FilteringProduct-ItemProcessor` class both use the `Product` class.

- *Filtering*—Depending on the result of the `needsToBeFiltered` method, Spring Batch sends the item to the writer or discards it. The filtering logic is simple: if an item ID's last character is an even digit, the filter accepts the item.

Our `ItemProcessor` example isn't useful beyond showing you how to configure item processing in a chunk-oriented step. The following listing shows how to configure this item processor.

Listing 7.2   Configuring an item processor in a chunk-oriented step

```
<batch:job id="readWriteJob">
  <batch:step id="readWriteStep">
    <batch:tasklet>
      <batch:chunk
        reader="reader"                    Adds item processor to
        processor="processor"              chunk-oriented step
        writer="writer"
        commit-interval="100" />
    </batch:tasklet>
  </batch:step>
</batch:job>
```

```
<bean id="processor"
      class="com.manning.sbia.ch07.
  ➥ FilteringProductItemProcessor" />
<bean id="reader" (...) >
  (...)
</bean>
<bean id="writer" (...)>
  (...)
</bean>
```

**Defines item
processor bean**

Adding an item processor is straightforward with the Spring Framework and Spring Batch XML: you write a Spring bean that implements the `ItemProcessor` interface and then refer to it in your chunk-oriented step configuration with the `processor` attribute of a `chunk` element.

Now that you know the basics of item processing in Spring Batch, let's see what the framework offers in terms of ready-to-use `ItemProcessor` implementations.

7.1.4 *Item processor implementations*

As you saw in the previous section, implementing an `ItemProcessor` is simple, and it's usually what you end up doing to implement business logic. Nevertheless, Spring Batch provides implementations of `ItemProcessors` that can come in handy; table 7.2 lists these implementations.

Table 7.2 Spring Batch implementations of `ItemProcessor`

Implementation class	Description
ItemProcessorAdapter	Invokes a custom method on a delegate POJO, which isn't required to implement `ItemProcessor`
ValidatingItemProcessor	Delegates filtering logic to a `Validator` object
CompositeItemProcessor	Delegates processing to a chain of `ItemProcessors`

You'll have opportunities to use these `ItemProcessor` implementations later in the chapter. For now, let's dive into the details of transforming items.

7.2   *Transforming items*

Transforming read items and then writing them out is the typical use case for an item processor. In Spring Batch, we distinguish two kinds of transformation: changing the state of the read item, and producing a new object based on the read item. In the latter case, the object the processor returns can be of a different type than the incoming item.

We illustrate both kinds of transformation with our online store application. Imagine that the application is successful and that other companies ask ACME to add their products to the online catalog; for this service, ACME takes a percentage of each partner's product sold. For the application, this means importing products from different files: a file for its own catalog and a file for each partner catalog. With this use case in mind, let's first explore transforming the state of read items.

7.2.1   Changing the state of read items

ACME needs to import a flat file for each partner's product catalog. In our scenario, the model of the ACME product and of each partner product is similar, but some modifications must be made to all partners' imported products before they're written to the database. These modifications require some custom business logic, so you embed this logic in a dedicated application component. You then use this component from an item processor.

INTRODUCING THE USE CASE

The model of the ACME product and of each partner product is similar, but each partner maintains its own product IDs. ACME needs to map partner product IDs to its own IDs to avoid colli-

Figure 7.2   In the processing phase of a chunk-oriented step, you can choose to only change the state of read items. In this case, the item reader, processor, and writer all use the same type of object (illustrated by the small squares).

sions. Figure 7.2 shows that the item reader, processor, and writer of the chunk-oriented step all use the same type of object.

The custom mapping between partner IDs and online store IDs takes place in the `PartnerIdMapper` class, as shown in the following listing.

Listing 7.3   Mapping partner IDs with store IDs in a business component

```
package com.manning.sbia.ch07;

import javax.sql.DataSource;
import org.springframework.jdbc.core.JdbcTemplate;
import com.manning.sbia.ch01.domain.Product;

public class PartnerIdMapper {
  private static final String SQL_SELECT_STORE_PRODUCT_ID =
    "select store_product_id from partner_mapping " +
    "where partner_id = ? and partner_product_id = ?";

  private String partnerId;

  private JdbcTemplate jdbcTemplate;

  public Product map(Product partnerProduct) {
    String storeProductId=jdbcTemplate.queryForObject(
      SQL_SELECT_STORE_PRODUCT_ID,                         Finds product ID
      String.class,                                        in mapping table
      partnerId, partnerProduct.getId()
    );
    partnerProduct.setId(storeProductId);             Modifies
    return partnerProduct;                            incoming product
  }
```

```
public void setPartnerId(String partnerId) {
  this.partnerId = partnerId;
}
public void setDataSource(DataSource dataSource) {
  this.jdbcTemplate = new JdbcTemplate(dataSource);
}
}
```

To perform the product ID mapping, you search the product ID for the online store in a mapping database table, using the partner ID and product ID in the partner namespace as the criteria. In an alternative implementation, the PartnerIdMapper class could generate the ID on the fly and store it if it didn't find it in the mapping table.

> **NOTE** The PartnerIdMapper class is a POJO (plain old Java object): it doesn't depend on the Spring Batch API, but it does use the JdbcTemplate class from the Spring JDBC Core package. This is important because this class implements the business logic, and you don't want to couple it tightly to the Spring Batch infrastructure.

Let's now plug the business component into Spring Batch.

IMPLEMENTING A CUSTOM ITEM PROCESSOR

You implement a dedicated ItemProcessor with a plug-in slot for a PartnerIdMapper, as shown in the following snippet:

```
package com.manning.sbia.ch07;

import org.springframework.batch.item.ItemProcessor;
import com.manning.sbia.ch01.domain.Product;

public class PartnerIdItemProcessor implements
    ItemProcessor<Product, Product> {

  private PartnerIdMapper mapper;

  @Override
  public Product process(Product item) throws Exception {
    return mapper.map(item);                    ⬱ Delegates
  }                                                processing
                                                   to business
  public void setMapper(PartnerIdMapper mapper) {  component
    this.mapper = mapper;
  }

}
```

Now you need to wire these components together in the configuration of a chunk-oriented step, as shown in the following listing.

Listing 7.4 Configuring the dedicated item processor to map product IDs

```
<batch:job id="readWriteJob">
  <batch:step id="readWriteStep">
    <batch:tasklet>
```

```
        <batch:chunk reader="reader"
                     processor="processor"                          Sets item
                     writer="writer"                                processor in step
                     commit-interval="100" />
      </batch:tasklet>
    </batch:step>
  </batch:job>
                                                                    Injects ID
  <bean id="processor"                                              mapper
        class="com.manning.sbia.ch07.PartnerIdItemProcessor">      in item
    <property name="mapper" ref="partnerIdMapper" />                processor
  </bean>

  <bean id="partnerIdMapper"
        class="com.manning.sbia.ch07.PartnerIdMapper">
    <property name="partnerId" value="PARTNER1" />                 Declares ID
    <property name="dataSource" ref="dataSource" />                mapper bean
  </bean>

  <bean id="reader" (...)>
    (...)
  </bean>

  <bean id="writer" (...)>
    (...)
  </bean>
```

That's it! You configured processing that converts the IDs of the incoming products into the IDs that the online store uses. You isolated the business logic from Spring Batch—separation of concerns—but you had to implement a custom `ItemProcessor` to call your business logic. You can achieve the same goal without this extra custom class.

PLUGGING IN AN EXISTING COMPONENT WITH THE ITEMPROCESSORADAPTER

Sometimes an existing business component is similar to a Spring Batch interface like `ItemProcessor`, but because it doesn't implement the interface, the framework can't call it directly. That's why the `PartnerIdItemProcessor` class was implemented in the previous section: to be able to call business code from Spring Batch. It worked nicely, but isn't it a shame to implement a dedicated class to delegate a call? Fortunately, Spring Batch provides the `ItemProcessorAdapter` class that you can configure to call any method on a POJO. Using the `ItemProcessorAdapter` class eliminates the need to implement a class like `PartnerIdItemProcessor`. All you end up doing is a bit of Spring configuration. The following listing shows how to use the `ItemProcessor-Adapter` to call the `PartnerIdMapper` without a custom `ItemProcessor`.

Listing 7.5 Using the `ItemProcessorAdapter` to plug in an existing Spring bean

```
<batch:job id="readWriteJob">
  <batch:step id="readWriteStep">
    <batch:tasklet>
      <batch:chunk reader="reader"
                   processor="processor"
                   writer="writer"
                   commit-interval="100" />
```

```
        </batch:tasklet>
      </batch:step>
  </batch:job>

  <bean id="processor"
        class="org.springframework.batch.item.adapter.ItemProcessorAdapter">
    <property name="targetObject" ref="partnerIdMapper" />
    <property name="targetMethod" value="map" />
  </bean>

  <bean id="partnerIdMapper"
        class="com.manning.sbia.ch07.PartnerIdMapper">
    <property name="partnerId" value="PARTNER1" />
    <property name="dataSource" ref="dataSource" />
  </bean>

  <bean id="reader" (...)>
    (...)
  </bean>

  <bean id="writer" (...)>
    (...)
  </bean>
```

> **Sets target bean and method to call** (annotation pointing at the two `<property>` lines: `targetObject` and `targetMethod`)

Using an `ItemProcessorAdapter` should eliminate the need to implement a dedicated `ItemProcessor`. This reminds us that it's a best practice to have your business logic implemented in POJOs. The `ItemProcessorAdapter` class helps in reducing the proliferation of classes if you often need to use a processing phase.

The `ItemProcessorAdapter` class has a couple of drawbacks, though: it's not as type-safe as a dedicated `ItemProcessor` class, and you can make typos on the target method name when configuring it in XML. The good news is that the `ItemProcessor-Adapter` checks its configuration when it's created; you get an exception when the Spring application context starts and also at runtime.

We're done looking at a processing phase that changes the state of read items. We use such processing when read items are of the same type as written items but need some sort modification, such as the ID conversion for imported products. The next section covers a processing phase that produces a different type of object from the read item.

7.2.2 *Producing new objects from read items*

As ACME finds more partners, it must deal with different product lines as well as with mismatches between the partners' product models and its own product model. These model differences make the importing job more complex. You still base the import on an input flat file, but ACME needs a processing phase to transform the partners' products into products that fit in the online store database.

INTRODUCING THE USE CASE

The processing phase of your chunk-oriented step transforms `PartnerProduct` objects read by the `ItemReader` into `Product` objects that the `ItemWriter` writes into the online store database. This is a case where the reader, the processor, and the writer don't manipulate the same kind of objects at every step, as shown in figure 7.3.

Figure 7.3   The item processor of a chunk-oriented step can produce objects of a different type (represented by circles) than the read items (squares). The item writer then receives and handles these new objects.

The logic to transform a `PartnerProduct` object into an ACME `Product` object takes place in a dedicated business component—the `PartnerProductMapper` class—that implements the `PartnerProductMapper` interface:

```
package com.manning.sbia.ch07;

import com.manning.sbia.ch01.domain.Product;

public interface PartnerProductMapper {

  Product map(PartnerProduct partnerProduct);

}
```

We don't show an implementation of the `PartnerProductMapper` interface because it's all business logic not directly related to Spring Batch and therefore not relevant to our presentation of Spring Batch. You can find a simple implementation in the source code for this book. What we need to do now is to plug this business logic into a Spring Batch job.

What could the partner product mapper do?

Here's an example of what a `PartnerProductMapper` implementation could do in a real-world online store application. Up to now—for simplicity's sake—we've used a static structure for the products of our online store application. Most of the time, online store applications don't have a static structure for the products in their catalog: they use a metamodel configured with the structure of the products and a generic engine that uses this metamodel to display products dynamically. For example, a metamodel for products in a *book* category could have fields for author, title, publication date, and so on. We could imagine that the ACME online application uses such a metamodel but that the partners don't. The goal of the `PartnerProductMapper` would be to map statically structured partner products (from input flat files) to the online store's products model. Such a mapper would rely heavily on the metamodel to do its job.

Let's plug our `PartnerProductMapper` into an item processor.

IMPLEMENTING A CUSTOM ITEM PROCESSOR

Listing 7.6 shows a custom `ItemProcessor` called `PartnerProductItemProcessor` that calls the `PartnerProductMapper` class. This item processor is Spring Batch–specific because it implements `ItemProcessor` and delegates processing to its `Partner-ProductMapper`, itself a business POJO.

Listing 7.6 A dedicated item processor to call the partner product mapper

```
package com.manning.sbia.ch07;

import org.springframework.batch.item.ItemProcessor;
import com.manning.sbia.ch01.domain.Product;

public class PartnerProductItemProcessor implements
    ItemProcessor<PartnerProduct, Product> {

  private PartnerProductMapper mapper;

  @Override
  public Product process(PartnerProduct item) throws Exception {
    return mapper.map(item);                              ◁──┐ Delegates processing to
  }                                                           business component

  public void setMapper(PartnerProductMapper mapper) {
    this.mapper = mapper;
  }

}
```

Note that the actual argument types of the generic `ItemProcessor` interface now take two different types: `PartnerProduct` (for the input type) and `Product` (for the output type). Now that we have our `ItemProcessor`, let's see its configuration in the following listing.

Listing 7.7 Configuring an item processor to map partner products to store products

```
<batch:job id="readWriteJob">
  <batch:step id="readWriteStep">
    <batch:tasklet>
      <batch:chunk reader="reader"
                   processor="processor"
                   writer="writer"
                   commit-interval="100" />
    </batch:tasklet>
  </batch:step>
</batch:job>

<bean id="processor"
      class="com.manning.sbia.ch07.PartnerProductItemProcessor">
  <property name="mapper" ref="partnerProductMapper" />    ◁──┐ Injects product
</bean>                                                          mapper in item
                                                                processor
<bean id="partnerProductMapper"
      class="com.manning.sbia.ch07.
  ➥ SimplePartnerProductMapper" />

<bean id="reader" (...)>
  (...)
</bean>

<bean id="writer" (...)>
  (...)
</bean>
```

Thanks to the product mapping that takes place during the processing phase of this step, you can transform the partner product representation to the product representation expected by the online store application. If you need to perform a different conversion for another partner, you only need to implement another item processor and reuse the item reader and writer.

> **NOTE** As you did in the previous section, you can use the `ItemProcessor-Adapter` class to plug in the business component (`PartnerProductMapper`) in the processing phase, eliminating the need for the `PartnerProductItem-Processor` class.

Before ending this section on using the item-processing phase to modify or transform read items, let's see how to use an `ItemProcessor` to implement a common pattern in batch applications: the *driving query* pattern.

7.2.3 *Implementing the driving query pattern with an item processor*

The driving query pattern is an optimization pattern used with databases. The pattern consists of two parts:

- Execute one query to load the IDs of the items you want to work with. This first query—the driving query—returns N IDs.
- Execute queries to retrieve a database row for each item. In total, N additional queries load the corresponding objects.

This seems counterintuitive, but using this pattern can end up being faster than loading the whole content of each object in one single query. How is that possible?

Some database engines tend to use pessimistic locking strategies on large, cursor-based result sets. This can lead to poor performance or even deadlocks if applications other than the batch application access the same tables. The trick is to use a driving query to select the IDs and then load complete objects one by one. A single query can prevent the database from handling large datasets.

> **The driving query pattern and ORM tools**
>
> The driving query pattern works nicely with object-relational mapping (ORM) tools. A simple JDBC item reader reads IDs, and a custom item processor uses an ORM tool to load the objects. ORM tools like Hibernate use a built-in second-level cache to improve performance.

Spring Batch can easily match and implement the driving query pattern in a chunk-oriented step:

- An `ItemReader` executes the driving query.
- An `ItemProcessor` receives the IDs and loads the objects.
- The loaded objects go to the `ItemWriter`.

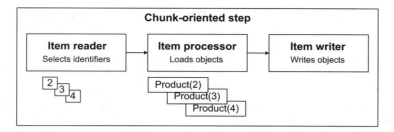

Figure 7.4 The driving query pattern implemented in Spring Batch. The item reader executes the driving query. The item processor receives the IDs and loads the objects. The item writer then receives these objects to, for example, write a file or update the database or an index.

Figure 7.4 illustrates the driving query pattern in Spring Batch.

Let's use the driving query pattern in our online application. Imagine the application features a search engine whose index needs to be updated from time to time (a complete re-indexing is rare because it takes too long). The indexing batch job consists of selecting recently updated products and updating the index accordingly. Because the online store is running during the indexing, you want to avoid locking overhead, so you shouldn't load large datasets; therefore, the driving query pattern is a good match. Let's see how to implement this with Spring Batch!

EXECUTING THE DRIVING QUERY WITH A JDBC ITEM READER

You use a Spring Batch cursor-based JDBC item reader to retrieve the product IDs. The product table contains an `update_timestamp` column updated each time a product row changes. Who performs the update? The application, a database trigger, or a persistence layer like Hibernate can perform the update. We use the `update_timestamp` column to select the products that the database must index. Listing 7.8 shows how to configure a `JdbcCursorItemReader` to execute the driving query for our use case.

Listing 7.8 Configuring an item reader to execute the driving query

```
<bean id="reader"
      class="org.springframework.batch.item.database.JdbcCursorItemReader">
  <property name="dataSource" ref="dataSource"/>
  <property name="sql"
            value="select id from product where update_timestamp &gt; ?" />
  <property name="preparedStatementSetter">
    <bean class="org.springframework.jdbc.core.
➥ ArgPreparedStatementSetter"
          scope="step">
      <constructor-arg
      value="#{jobParameters['updateTimestampBound']}"
      />
    </bean>
  </property>
  <property name="rowMapper">
    <bean class="org.springframework.jdbc.core.
➥ SingleColumnRowMapper">
```

❶ Assigns parameter to SQL query

❷ Returns a String for each row

```
      <constructor-arg value="java.lang.String" />
    </bean>
  </property>
</bean>
```

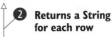 Returns a String for each row

If you're unfamiliar with the `JdbcCursorItemReader` class, please see chapter 5. You use the `JdbcCursorItemReader` `sql` property to set the SQL query to execute. This query selects the IDs of the products that were updated after a given date (by using the `where > ?` clause). To pass a parameter to the query, you set the `preparedStatement-Setter` property ❶ with an `ArgPreparedStatementSetter` (this is a class from the Spring Framework). You use the Spring Expression Language to get the date query parameter from the job parameters. To retrieve the IDs from the JDBC result set, you use the Spring class `SingleColumnRowMapper` ❷.

That's it! You configured your item reader to execute the driving query. Note that you didn't write any Java code: you configured only existing components provided by Spring Batch and the Spring Framework. Next, let's see how to load the products from their IDs within an item processor.

LOADING ITEMS IN AN ITEM PROCESSOR

You need to load a product based on its ID. This is a simple operation, and a data access object (DAO) used in the online store application already implements this feature. The following listing shows the implementation of this DAO.

Listing 7.9 Implementing a DAO to load a product from its ID

```java
package com.manning.sbia.ch07;

import javax.sql.DataSource;
import org.springframework.jdbc.core.JdbcTemplate;
import org.springframework.jdbc.core.RowMapper;
import com.manning.sbia.ch01.domain.Product;

public class JdbcProductDao implements ProductDao {

  private static final String SQL_SELECT_PRODUCT =
    "select id,name,description,price " +
    "from product where id = ?";

  private JdbcTemplate jdbcTemplate;

  private RowMapper<Product> rowMapper = new ProductRowMapper();

  @Override
  public Product load(String productId) {
    return jdbcTemplate.queryForObject(
      SQL_SELECT_PRODUCT, rowMapper, productId           // Loads entire object
    );                                                   // from database
  }

  public void setDataSource(DataSource dataSource) {
    this.jdbcTemplate = new JdbcTemplate(dataSource);
  }

}
```

You use a `ProductRowMapper` to map a JDBC result set to `Product` objects. Remember that the `RowMapper` is a Spring interface. You can use `RowMapper` implementations in a JDBC-based data access layer for your online applications. You can also use a `RowMapper` with a Spring Batch JDBC-based item reader.

What you need to do now is connect your data access logic with Spring Batch. This is what the item processor in the following listing does.

Listing 7.10   Implementing an item processor to call the DAO

```
package com.manning.sbia.ch07;

import org.springframework.batch.item.ItemProcessor;
import com.manning.sbia.ch01.domain.Product;

public class IdToProductItemProcessor implements
    ItemProcessor<String, Product> {

  private ProductDao productDao;

  @Override
  public Product process(String productId) throws Exception {
    return productDao.load(productId);
  }

  public void setProductDao(ProductDao productDao) {
    this.productDao = productDao;
  }

}
```

The class `IdToProductItemProcessor` delegates product loading to the product DAO. To avoid writing a dedicated class, you could have used an `ItemProcessorAdapter`, but with the `IdToProductItemProcessor` class, the input and output types are easier to picture: `String` for the IDs returned by the driving query (input), and `Product` instances loaded by the item processor (output).

CONFIGURING A CHUNK-ORIENTED STEP FOR THE DRIVING QUERY PATTERN

The configuration of a chunk-oriented step using the driving query pattern is like any other chunk-oriented step, except that it needs to have an item processor set. The following listing shows this configuration (we elided the reader and writer details).

Listing 7.11   Configuring a driving query

```
<batch:job id="readWriteJob">
  <batch:step id="readWriteStep">
    <batch:tasklet>
      <batch:chunk reader="reader"
                   processor="processor"
                   writer="writer"
                   commit-interval="100" />
    </batch:tasklet>
  </batch:step>
</batch:job>
```

```
<bean id="reader"
      class="org.springframework.batch.item.database.JdbcCursorItemReader">
   (...)
</bean>

<bean id="processor"
      class="com.manning.sbia.ch07.IdToProductItemProcessor">
   <property name="productDao" ref="productDao" />
</bean>

<bean id="productDao"
      class="com.manning.sbia.ch07.JdbcProductDao">
   <property name="dataSource" ref="dataSource" />
</bean>

<bean id="writer" (...)>
   (...)
</bean>
```

Injects product DAO in item processor

Declares product DAO bean

The implementation of the driving query pattern with Spring Batch ends this section. We covered how to use the processing phase of a chunk-oriented step as a way to modify read items and create new items. The next section covers how to use the processing phase as a way to filter read items before sending them to an item writer.

7.3   *Filtering and validating items*

The processing phase of a chunk-oriented step not only can modify read items but also can filter them. Imagine reading a flat file containing some products that belong in the database and some that don't. For example, some products don't belong to any of the categories of items sold in the store, some products are already in the database, and so on. You can use an item processor to decide whether to send a read item to the item writer, as shown in figure 7.5.

We cover how to implement a typical filtering item processor and how to filter using validation. We implement programmatic validation, but we also use declarative validation using integration between Spring Batch and the Spring Modules project. First, let's learn more about the filtering contract in the item-processing phase.

7.3.1   *Filtering in the item-processing phase*

The basic contract for filtering in an item processor is simple: if the item processor's process method returns null, the read item won't go to the item writer. This

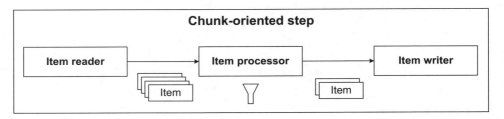

Figure 7.5   An item processor filters read items. It implements logic to decide whether to send a read item to the item writer.

defines the main contract, but there are subtleties; let's look at the filtering rules for item processors:

- If the process method returns null, Spring Batch filters out the item and it won't go to the item writer.
- Filtering is different from skipping.
- An exception thrown by an item processor results in a skip (if you configured the skip strategy accordingly).

The basic contract for filtering is clear, but we must point out the distinction between filtering and skipping:

- *Filtering* means that Spring Batch shouldn't write a given record. For example, the item writer can't handle a record.
- *Skipping* means that a given record is invalid. For example, the format of a phone number is invalid.

NOTE The job repository stores the number of filtered items for each chunk-oriented step execution. You can easily look up this information using a tool like Spring Batch Admin or by consulting the corresponding database table.

The last detail of the filtering contract we need to examine is that an item processor can filter items by returning null for some items, but it can also *modify* read items, like any other item processor. You shouldn't mix filtering and transformation in a same-item processor (separation of concerns), but it's your right to do so!

Best practice: separate filtering and transformation

If your application needs to both filter items and transform items, then follow the separation of concerns pattern by using two item processors: one to filter and one to transform.

Now that you know all about the filtering contract, let's see how to implement a filtering item processor.

7.3.2 Implementing a filtering item processor

Let's look back at the import products job from chapter 1 and see in which circumstances it could use filtering. Remember that this job consists of reading a flat file containing product records and creating or updating the database accordingly. You get into trouble if you execute the import job while the online store application hits the database: updating products from the job locks database rows and makes the online store less responsive. Nevertheless, you want the database to be as up to date as possible. A good compromise is to read the flat file and create new product records, but discard updating existing products. You can update existing products later, in a separate job, when there's less traffic in the online store.

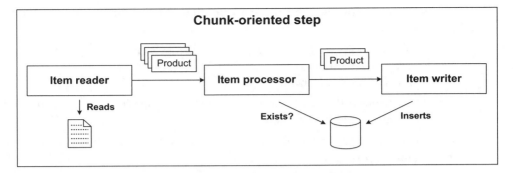

Figure 7.6   The filtering item processor discards products that are already in the database. This item writer only inserts new records and doesn't interfere with the online application. A different job updates existing records when there's less traffic in the online store.

You meet this requirement by inserting a filtering item processor between the reading of the flat file and the writing to the database. This item processor checks the existence of the record in the database and discards it if it already exists. Figure 7.6 illustrates how the import products job works with a filtering phase.

The following listing shows the implementation of the filtering item processor.

Listing 7.12   Filtering existing products with an item processor

```java
package com.manning.sbia.ch07;

import javax.sql.DataSource;
import org.springframework.batch.item.ItemProcessor;
import org.springframework.jdbc.core.JdbcTemplate;
import com.manning.sbia.ch01.domain.Product;

public class ExistingProductFilterItemProcessor implements
    ItemProcessor<Product, Product> {

  private static final String SQL_COUNT_PRODUCT =
    "select count(1) from product where id = ?";

  private JdbcTemplate jdbcTemplate;

  @Override
  public Product process(Product item) throws Exception {
    return needsToBeFiltered(item) ? null : item;       Filters existing
  }                                                      product records

  private boolean needsToBeFiltered(Product item) {
    return jdbcTemplate.queryForInt(                    Checks product
      SQL_COUNT_PRODUCT, item.getId()) != 0;            existence in database
  }

  public void setDataSource(DataSource dataSource) {
    this.jdbcTemplate = new JdbcTemplate(dataSource);
  }

}
```

NOTE A more advanced version of the filtering item processor could let record updates pass through in a given time window, such as between 2 a.m. and 4 a.m. when there isn't much activity in the online store. This would make the filtering more dynamic and could eliminate the need to have two distinct jobs (one for inserts only and one for inserts and updates).

The following listing shows the configuration of the import products job with the filtering item processor.

Listing 7.13 Configuring the filtering item processor

```
<batch:job id="readWriteJob">
  <batch:step id="readWriteStep">
    <batch:tasklet>
      <batch:chunk reader="reader"
                   processor="processor"         Sets filtering item
                   writer="writer"               processor in step
                   commit-interval="100" />
    </batch:tasklet>
  </batch:step>
</batch:job>

<bean id="reader"
    class="org.springframework.batch.item.file.FlatFileItemReader">
  (...)
</bean>

<bean id="processor" class="com.manning.sbia.ch07.
    ExistingProductFilterItemProcessor">           Declares filtering
  <property name="dataSource" ref="dataSource" />   item processor bean
</bean>

<bean id="writer"
    class="com.manning.sbia.ch01.batch.ProductJdbcItemWriter">
  <constructor-arg ref="dataSource" />
</bean>
```

The item processor implemented here is a typical case of using the item processor phase as a filter. The item processor receives valid items from the item reader and decides which items to pass to the item writer. The item processor effectively filters out the other items.

Let's now see another case where you can use item processing to prevent read items from reaching the item writer: validation.

7.3.3 *Validating items*

Because validation is business logic, the standard location to enforce validation rules is in the item-processing phase of a chunk-oriented step. A common practice in Spring Batch is for an item processor to perform validation checks on read items and decide whether to send the items to the item writer. As an example, let's see how to validate the price of imported products and check that prices aren't negative numbers (products with a negative price shouldn't reach the database—you don't want to credit your customers!). Should you consider an item that fails the validation check filtered or skipped? Skipping is semantically closer to a validation failure, but this remains questionable, and the business requirements usually lead to the correct answer.

A validation failure should lead to a skipped or filtered item, but what you care about is that the item writer doesn't receive the item in question. Remember that the corresponding step-execution metadata stored in the job repository is distinct (skip and filter count), and this distinction can be relevant for some use cases. If you want to enforce validation rules in your item processor, use the following semantics for validation failure in the item processor's `process` method:

- If validation means skip, throw a runtime exception
- If validation means filter, return `null`

What kind of validation can an item processor perform? You can do almost anything: state validation of the read object, consistency check with other data, and so forth. In the import products job, for example, you can check that the price of products from the flat file is positive. A well-formatted negative price would pass the reading phase (no parsing exception), but you shouldn't write the product to the database. The job of the item processor is to enforce this check and discard invalid products.

You can implement an item processor corresponding to this example and follow the semantics outlined here, but Spring Batch already provides a class called `ValidatingItemProcessor` to handle this task.

VALIDATION WITH A VALIDATINGITEMPROCESSOR

The Spring Batch class `ValidatingItemProcessor` has two interesting characteristics:

- It delegates validation to an implementation of the Spring Batch `Validator` interface.
- It has a `filter` flag that can be set to `false` to throw an exception (skip) or `true` to return `null` (filter) if the validation fails. The default value is `false` (skip).

By using the `ValidatingItemProcessor` class, you can embed your validation rules in dedicated `Validator` implementations (which you can reuse) and choose your validation semantics by setting the `filter` property.

The Spring Batch `Validator` interface is

```
package org.springframework.batch.item.validator;

public interface Validator<T> {

   void validate(T value) throws ValidationException;
}
```

When you decide to use the `ValidatingItemProcessor` class, you can either code your validation logic in `Validator` implementations or create a `Validator` bridge to a full-blown validation framework. We illustrate both next.

VALIDATION WITH A CUSTOM VALIDATOR

Let's say you want to check that a product doesn't have a negative price. The following snippet shows how to implement this feature as a Validator:

```
package com.manning.sbia.ch07.validation;

import java.math.BigDecimal;
import org.springframework.batch.item.validator.ValidationException;
import org.springframework.batch.item.validator.Validator;
import com.manning.sbia.ch01.domain.Product;

public class ProductValidator implements Validator<Product> {

  @Override
  public void validate(Product product) throws ValidationException {
    if(BigDecimal.ZERO.compareTo(product.getPrice()) >= 0) {
      throw new ValidationException("Product price cannot be negative!");
    }
  }

}
```

This validator isn't rocket science, but as you configure it with Spring, it benefits from the ability to use dependency injection to, for example, access the database through a Spring JDBC template. The configuration for this validating item processor example has some interesting aspects, so let's examine the following listing.

Listing 7.14 Configuring a validating item processor

```
<batch:job id="readWriteJob">
  <batch:step id="readWriteStep">
    <batch:tasklet>
      <batch:chunk reader="reader"
                   processor="processor"
                   writer="writer"
                   commit-interval="100"
                   skip-limit="5">
        <batch:skippable-exception-classes>
          <batch:include
            class="org.springframework.batch.item.
   ⇨ validator.ValidationException"/>
        </batch:skippable-exception-classes>
      </batch:chunk>
    </batch:tasklet>
  </batch:step>
</batch:job>

<bean id="processor" class="org.springframework.batch.item.validator.
   ⇨ ValidatingItemProcessor">
  <property name="filter" value="false" />
  <property name="validator">
    <bean class="com.manning.sbia.ch07.validation.ProductValidator" />
  </property>
</bean>

<bean id="reader" (...) >
```

Skips validation exceptions

Re-throws validation exceptions to enforce skipping

```
    (...)
</bean>

<bean id="writer" (...)>
    (...)
</bean>
```

Most of this configuration isn't elaborate: an XML chunk element for a chunk-oriented step, positioning of the item processor between the reader and the writer, and injection of the product validator in the `ValidatingItemProcessor`.

Because you set the `filter` property of the validating item processor to `false`—this is the default value, but we wanted to make this example explicit—the item processor rethrows any `ValidationException` thrown by its validator.

This implies the configuration of a skip strategy if you don't want to fail the whole job execution in case of a validation failure. The skip configuration consists of setting a skip limit and skipping `ValidationExceptions`.

If you were only to *filter* products that have a negative price, you would set the filter property of the `ValidatingItemProcessor` to `true` and wouldn't need any skip configuration.

Writing dedicated validator classes can be overkill and result in overall code bloat. An alternative is to make the validation *declarative*: instead of coding the validation in Java, you implement it with a dedicated validation language in the configuration file.

VALIDATION WITH THE VALANG VALIDATOR FROM SPRING MODULES

The Spring Modules project provides a simple yet powerful validation language: Valang (for *va*-lidation *lang*-uage). You can easily integrate Valang with Spring Batch to write your validation rules without Java code. For example, to verify that the product price isn't negative, you write the following rule in Valang (assuming the evaluation context is a `Product` object):

```
{ price : ? >= 0 : 'Product price cannot be negative!' }
```

Valang has a rich syntax to create validation expressions. We don't cover this syntax here; our point is to show how to integrate Valang rules within a validating item processor.[1]

Because Valang isn't Java code, we use the Spring configuration to implement validating the product price, as shown in the following listing.

> **Listing 7.15 Embedding validation logic in the configuration with Valang**

```
<batch:job id="readWriteJob">
  <batch:step id="readWriteStep">
    <batch:tasklet>
      <batch:chunk reader="reader"
                   processor="processor"
                   writer="writer"
                   commit-interval="100"
                   skip-limit="5">
```

---

[1] You can learn more about the Valang syntax at https://springmodules.dev.java.net/docs/reference/0.9/html/validation.html.

```
        <batch:skippable-exception-classes>
          <batch:include
            class="org.springframework.batch.item.
➥  validator.ValidationException"/>
          </batch:skippable-exception-classes>
        </batch:chunk>
      </batch:tasklet>
    </batch:step>
</batch:job>

<bean id="processor"class="org.springframework.batch.item.validator.
  ➥  ValidatingItemProcessor">
  <property name="filter" value="false" />
  <property name="validator" ref="validator" />
</bean>

<bean id="validator" class="org.springframework.batch.item.validator.
  ➥  SpringValidator">
  <property name="validator">
    <bean class="org.springmodules.validation.valang.ValangValidator">
      <property name="valang">
        <value><![CDATA[
{price : ? >= 0 : 'Product price cannot be negative!'}
        ]]></value>                                          ◁──┐ Uses Valang
      </property>                                                │ for validation
    </bean>
  </property>
</bean>

<bean id="reader" (...) >
  (...)
</bean>

<bean id="writer" (...)>
  (...)
</bean>
```

The key to this configuration is the link between the Spring Batch ValidatingItem-Processor class and the Spring Modules ValangValidator class. The Spring Batch ValidatingItemProcessor class needs a Spring Batch Validator, so you provide it a Spring Batch SpringValidator class, which itself needs a Spring Validator—the interface the ValangValidator class implements! In short, the Spring Batch Spring-Validator class is the bridge between the Spring Batch and Spring validation systems, and the ValangValidator builds on the Spring system (figure 7.7 illustrates the relationships between these interfaces and classes, and you can also read the note about validator interfaces if you want the whole story). The valang property of ValangValidator accepts one or more validation rules (we used only one in the example). We explicitly set the validating item processor to skip mode (the filter property is false), so we need to set up a skip strategy to avoid failing the job if the validation fails.

Valang works great and allows you to embed validation rules directly in your Spring configuration files. But what if you want to reuse your validation rules in different contexts, such as in your batch jobs and in a web application? You can do this with Valang, but the Bean Validation standard also offers a widespread and effective solution.

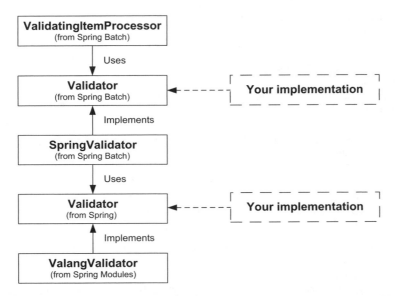

Figure 7.7   The relationships between Spring Batch, Spring, and your validation logic. Spring Batch provides a level of abstraction with its `Validator` **interface and an implementation (**`SpringValidator`**) that uses the Spring** `Validator` **interface. The** `ValangValidator` **implementation, from Spring Modules, depends on the Spring** `Validator` **interface. Both** `Validator` **interfaces are potential extension points for your own implementations.**

> ## Validator interfaces everywhere!
> Spring Batch doesn't intend for application-specific validators to be the only implementers of the Spring Batch `Validator` interface. It can also provide a level of indirection between Spring Batch and your favorite validation framework. Spring Batch provides one implementation of `Validator`: `SpringValidator`, which plugs in the Spring Framework's validation mechanism. Spring bases its validation mechanism on a `Validator` interface, but this one lies in the `org.springframework.validation` package and is part of the Spring Framework. This can look confusing, but the Spring Batch team didn't want to directly tie Spring Batch's validation system to Spring's. By using the Spring Batch `SpringValidator` class, you can use any Spring `Validator` implementation, like the one from Spring Modules for Valang.

VALIDATION WITH THE BEAN VALIDATION STANDARD

It's common to use the same validation constraints in multiple places: when an administrator updates the product catalog manually, they shouldn't be able to enter a negative price. In this case, the web framework enforces this constraint. Web frameworks like Spring MVC (Model-View-Controller) or JavaServer Faces (JSF) have dedicated support for validation. If you really want to avoid products with a negative price, you can also validate the objects when they're about to be persisted in the database. JPA—Java Persistence API, the Java standard for object-relational mapping—has some support to execute code before storing an object in the database. Finally, you also want to avoid negative prices when you import products with a Spring Batch job.

What you want is multiple processes—web, batch—with the same validation constraints. Is it possible to define constraints in one place and enforce them with an API from such different processes? Yes, thanks to the Bean Validation (JSR 303) standard!

The idea behind Bean Validation is simple but powerful: embed validation constraints with annotations on the classes you want to validate and enforce them anywhere you need to. The good news is that many frameworks support Bean Validation out of the box: they validate incoming objects transparently for you. That's the case with all the frameworks we just mentioned (Spring MVC, JSF, and JPA). Wouldn't it be nice to reuse all your Bean Validation constraints in your Spring Batch jobs? Let's see how to do this.

JSR 303: The Bean Validation standard

Bean Validation promotes a declarative and reusable way to validate Java objects. The idea is to use Java classes as the definitive repository for validation constraints. As soon as you have access to a Java object, you can validate it, because it contains its own validation rules. You express Bean Validation constraints with Java annotations, but you can also do so in XML. Bean Validation is becoming increasingly popular, and many frameworks integrate support for it. The reference implementation for Bean Validation is the Hibernate Validator project, which is at the origin of the standard.

Let's start with the `Product` class, which now contains the constraint for negative prices. The following listing shows the `Product` class with the Bean Validation annotations on the getter method for `price`.

Listing 7.16 Embedding validation constraint in the `Product` class

```
package com.manning.sbia.ch01.domain;

import java.math.BigDecimal;
import javax.validation.constraints.Min;
import javax.validation.constraints.NotNull;

public class Product {

  private String id;
  private String name;
  private String description;
  private BigDecimal price;

  @NotNull                                    Validation constraints
  @Min(0)                                     on the price property
  public BigDecimal getPrice() {
    return price;
  }

  public void setPrice(BigDecimal price) {
    this.price = price;
```

```
    }
    (...)
}
```

The validation constraints specify that the price can't be `null` or negative. These constraints are simple, but Bean Validation includes constraints that are more advanced and lets you also define your own.

   To use Bean Validation in your Spring Batch jobs, you only have to define a custom `Validator` that enforces the validation constraints on incoming items, as shown in the following listing.

Listing 7.17   A Spring Batch validator for Bean Validation

```
package com.manning.sbia.ch07.validation;

import java.util.Set;
import javax.validation.ConstraintViolation;
import javax.validation.Validation;
import javax.validation.ValidatorFactory;
import
  org.springframework.batch.item.validator.ValidationException;
import org.springframework.batch.item.validator.Validator;

public class BeanValidationValidator<T> implements Validator<T> {

  private ValidatorFactory factory =
    Validation.buildDefaultValidatorFactory();          Initializes Bean
                                                        Validation validator
  private javax.validation.Validator validator =
    factory.getValidator();

public void validate(T value) throws ValidationException {
    Set<ConstraintViolation<T>> violations =
      validator.validate(value);
    if(!violations.isEmpty()) {                         Enforces validation
      throw new ValidationException(                    constraints
        "Validation failed for " + value + ": " +
        violationsToString(violations));
    }
  }

  private String violationsToString(
    Set<ConstraintViolation<T>> violations) {           Produces readable
    (...)                                               String from violations
  }

}
```

The validator is straightforward to implement thanks to the Bean Validation API. You can inject an instance of the validator in the validator item processor that Spring Batch provides, as shown in the following snippet:

```
<bean id="validator"
  class="com.manning.sbia.ch07.validation.BeanValidationValidator" />

<bean id="processor"
```

```
class="org.springframework.batch.item.validator.ValidatingItemProcessor">
<property name="validator" ref="validator" />
</bean>
```

Using Bean Validation is particularly relevant if you use exactly the same classes in your batch jobs and in other applications. Many frameworks support Bean Validation, from the web layer to the persistence layer, and using it offers the best opportunity to reuse your validation constraints.

The integration between Spring Batch and the Bean Validation standard ends our coverage of the use of the item-processing phase for validation. Remember that you must follow strict rules if you don't want to confuse skip with filter when validating items. Spring Batch includes the `ValidatingItemProcessor` class that you can configure to skip or filter when validation fails. Finally, you can implement your validation rules programmatically—in Java—or choose a declarative approach with a validation language like Valang or with Bean Validation. Let's see now how to apply the composite pattern to chain item processors.

7.4   *Chaining item processors*

As we stated at the beginning of this chapter, the item-processing phase of a chunk-oriented step is a good place to embed business logic. Assuming that each item processor in your application implements one single business rule (this is simplistic but enough to illustrate our point), how could you enforce several business rules in the item-processing phase of a single step? Moreover, recall that you can insert only a single item processor between an item reader and an item writer. The solution is to apply the composite pattern by using a composite item processor that maintains a list of item processors (the delegates). The composite item processor delegates the calls to all the members in its list, one after the next. Figure 7.8 illustrates the model of a composite item processor.

When using a composite item processor, the delegates should form a type-compatible chain: the type of object an item processor returns must be compatible with the type of object the next item processor expects.

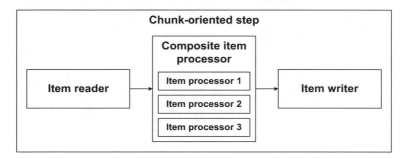

Figure 7.8   Using a composite item processor allows item processors to be chained in order to apply a succession of business rules, transformations, or validations.

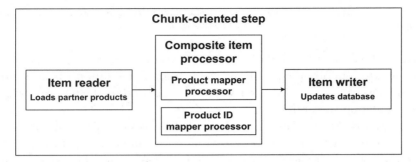

Figure 7.9   Applying the composite item processor pattern to the import products job. The first delegate item processor converts partner product objects into online store product objects. The second delegate item processor maps partner IDs with ACME IDs. You reuse and combine item processors without any modification.

Spring Batch provides the `CompositeItemProcessor` class, and we illustrate its use with the import of partner products into the online store. In section 7.2, we covered the transformation of read items, where we distinguished two types of transformations:

- *Changing the state of the read item*—We mapped the product ID in the partner's namespace to the product ID in the ACME system.
- *Producing another object from the read item*—We produced instances of the `Product` class from `PartnerProduct` objects (created by the item reader).

What do you do if your import job needs to do both? You use two item processors: the first item processor reads raw `PartnerProduct` objects from the flat file and transforms them into `Product` objects, and then the second item processor maps partner product IDs to ACME IDs. Figure 7.9 illustrates the sequence of the import step.

You already implemented all the Java code in section 7.2, so you only need to configure a Spring Batch `CompositeItemProcessor` with your two delegate item processors, as shown in the following listing.

Listing 7.18   Chaining item processors with the composite item processor

```
<batch:job id="readWriteJob">
  <batch:step id="readWriteStep">
    <batch:tasklet>
      <batch:chunk reader="reader"
                   processor="processor"
                   writer="writer"
                   commit-interval="100" />
    </batch:tasklet>
  </batch:step>
</batch:job>

<bean id="reader"
      class="org.springframework.batch.item.file.FlatFileItemReader">
  (...)
</bean>
```

```
<bean id="processor"
    class="org.springframework.batch.item.support.
➥ CompositeItemProcessor">
  <property name="delegates">
    <list>
      <ref bean="productMapperProcessor" />
      <ref bean="productIdMapperProcessor" />
    </list>
  </property>
</bean>
```

Sets two delegates to compose item processor

```
<bean id="productMapperProcessor"
    class="com.manning.sbia.ch07.
➥ PartnerProductItemProcessor">
  <property name="mapper">
    <bean class="com.manning.sbia.ch07.
➥ SimplePartnerProductMapper" />
  </property>
</bean>
```

Converts partner products to store products

```
<bean id="productIdMapperProcessor"
    class="com.manning.sbia.ch07.
➥ PartnerIdItemProcessor">
  <property name="mapper">
    <bean id="partnerIdMapper"
        class="com.manning.sbia.ch07.
➥ PartnerIdMapper">
      <property name="partnerId" value="PARTNER1" />
      <property name="dataSource" ref="dataSource" />
    </bean>
  </property>
</bean>
```

Maps partner product IDs to store product IDs

```
<bean id="writer"
    class="com.manning.sbia.ch01.batch.ProductJdbcItemWriter">
  <constructor-arg ref="dataSource" />
</bean>
```

This example shows the power of the composite pattern applied to building a processing chain: you didn't modify your two existing item processors, you reused them as is. Spring Batch encourages separation of concerns by isolating business logic in reusable item processors.

7.5 Summary

Spring Batch isn't only about reading and writing data: in a chunk-oriented step, you can insert an item processor between the item reader and the item writer to perform any kind of operation. The typical job of an item processor is to implement business logic. For example, an item processor can convert read items into other kinds of objects Spring Batch sends to the item writer. Because batch applications often exchange data between two systems, going from one representation to another falls into the domain of item processors.

Spring Batch defines another contract in the processing phase: filtering. For example, if items already exist in the target data store, the application shouldn't insert them again. You can filter items such that they'll never get to the writing phase. We made a clear distinction between filtering items and skipping items. Skipping denotes that an item is invalid. This distinction became even more relevant when we covered validation. Thanks to the Spring Batch `ValidatingItemProcessor` class, you can easily switch from skipping to filtering semantics. We used the `ValidatingItemProcessor` class to validate that the price of imported products isn't negative before the job writes the products to the database. We saw that we can isolate validation rules in dedicated validator components, and we used this feature to plug in two declarative validation frameworks, Valang and Bean Validation.

This chapter about data processing ends our coverage of the three phases of a chunk-oriented step: reading, processing, and writing. You now have all the information necessary to write efficient batch applications with Spring Batch. Chapter 8 introduces you to techniques used to make batch applications more robust, and you'll see that chunk-oriented processing plays an important role.

Implementing
bulletproof jobs

This chapter covers

- Handling errors with retry and skip
- Logging errors with listeners
- Restarting an execution after a failure

Batch jobs manipulate large amounts of data automatically. Previous chapters showed how Spring Batch helps to read, process, and write data efficiently and without much Java code, thanks to ready-to-use I/O components. It's time to deal with the automatic aspect of batch jobs. Batch jobs operate over long periods, at night, for example, and without human intervention. Even if a batch job can send an email to an operator when something's wrong, it's on its own most of the time. A batch job isn't automatic if it fails each time something goes wrong; it needs to be able to handle errors correctly and not crash abruptly. Perhaps you know how frustrating it is to sit at your desk in the morning and see that some nightly jobs have crashed because of a missing comma in an input file.

223

This chapter explains techniques to make your batch jobs more robust and reliable when errors occur during processing. By the end of this chapter, you'll know how to build bulletproof batch jobs and be confident that your batch jobs will succeed.

The first section of this chapter explains how a batch job should behave when errors or edge cases emerge during processing. Spring Batch has built-in support, its skip and retry features, to handle errors when a job is executing. Skip and retry are about avoiding crashes, but crashes are inevitable, so Spring Batch also supports restarting a job after a failed execution. Sections 8.2, 8.3, and 8.4 cover skip, retry, and restart, respectively.

By following the guidelines and the techniques in this chapter, you'll go from "my job failed miserably because of a missing comma" to "bring in your fancy-formatted input file—nothing scares my job anymore." Let's get bulletproof!

8.1 What is a bulletproof job?

A bulletproof job is able to handle errors gracefully; it won't fail miserably because of a minor error like a missing comma. It won't fail abruptly, either, for a major problem like a constraint violation in the database. Before reviewing some guidelines on the design of a robust job, let's consider some requirements that a job must meet.

8.1.1 What makes a job bulletproof?

A bulletproof batch job should meet the following general requirements:

- *Robust*—The job should fail only for fatal exceptions and should recover gracefully from any nonfatal exception. As software developers, we can't do anything about a power cut, but we can properly handle incorrectly formatted lines or a missing input file.
- *Traceable*—The job should record any abnormal behavior. A job can skip as many incorrectly formatted lines as it wants, but it should log to record what didn't make it in the database and allow someone to do something about it.
- *Restartable*—In case of an abrupt failure, the job should be able to restart properly. Depending on the use case, the job could restart exactly where it left off or even forbid a restart because it would process the same data again.

Good news: Spring Batch provides all the features to meet these requirements! You can activate these features through configuration or by plugging in your own code through extension points (to log errors, for example). A tool like Spring Batch isn't enough to write a bulletproof job: you also need to design the job properly before leveraging the tool.

8.1.2 Designing a bulletproof job

To make your batch jobs bulletproof, you first need to think about failure scenarios. What can go wrong in this batch job? Anything can happen, but the nature of the operations in a job helps to narrow the failure scenarios. The batch job we introduced in chapter 1 starts by decompressing a ZIP archive to a working directory before reading the lines of the extracted file and inserting them in the database. Many things can go wrong: the archive can be corrupt (if it's there!), the OS might not allow the process to write in the working directory, some lines in the files may be incorrectly formatted, and the list goes on.

Testing failure scenarios

Remember that Spring Batch is a lightweight framework. It means you can easily test failure scenarios in integration tests. You can simulate many failure scenarios thanks to testing techniques like mock objects, for example. Chapter 14 covers how to test batch applications. For JUnit testing techniques in general, you can also refer to *JUnit in Action* by Peter Tahchiev, Filipe Leme, Vincent Massol, and Gary Gregory (Manning Publications, 2011).

Once you've identified failure scenarios, you must think about how to deal with them. If there's no ZIP archive at the beginning of the execution, there's not much the job can do, but that's no reason to fail abruptly. How should the job handle incorrectly formatted lines? Should it skip them or fail the whole execution as soon as it finds a bad line? In our case, we could skip incorrect lines and ensure that we log them somewhere.

Spring Batch has built-in support for error handling, but that doesn't mean you can make batch jobs bulletproof by setting some magical attribute in an XML configuration file (even if sometimes that's the case). Rather, it means that Spring Batch provides infrastructure and deals with tedious plumbing, but you must always know what you're doing: when and why to use Spring Batch error handling. That's what makes batch programming interesting! Let's now see how to deal with errors in Spring Batch.

8.1.3 Techniques for bulletproofing jobs

Unless you control your batch jobs as Neo controls the Matrix, you'll always end up getting errors in your batch applications. Spring Batch includes three features to deal with errors: skip, retry, and restart. Table 8.1 describes these features.

Table 8.1 Error-handling support in Spring Batch

Feature	When?	What?	Where?
Skip	For nonfatal exceptions	Keeps processing for an incorrect item	Chunk-oriented step
Retry	For transient exceptions	Makes new attempts on an operation for a transient failure	Chunk-oriented step, application code
Restart	After an execution failure	Restarts a job instance where the last execution failed	On job launch

The features listed in table 8.1 are independent from each other: you can use one without the others, or you can combine them. Remember that skip and retry are about avoiding a crash on an error, whereas restart is useful, when a job has crashed, to restart it where it left off.

Skipping allows for moving processing along to the next line in an input file if the current line is in an incorrect format. If the job doesn't process a line, perhaps you can live without it and the job can process the remaining lines in the file.

Retry attempts an operation several times: the operation can fail at first, but another attempt can succeed. Retry isn't useful for errors like badly formatted input lines; it's useful for transient errors, such as concurrency errors. Skip and retry contribute to making job executions more robust because they deal with error handling during processing.

Restart is useful after a failure, when the execution of a job crashes. Instead of starting the job from scratch, Spring Batch allows for restarting it exactly where the failed execution left off. Restarting can avoid potential corruption of the data in case of reprocessing. Restarting can also save a lot of time if the failed execution was close to the end.

Before covering each feature, let's see how skip, retry, and restart can apply to our import products job.

8.1.4 *Skip, retry, and restart in action*

Recall our import products job: the core of the job reads a flat file containing one product description per line and updates the online store database accordingly. Here is how skip, retry, and restart could apply to this job.

- *Skip*—A line in the flat file is incorrectly formatted. You don't want to stop the job execution because of a couple of bad lines: this could mean losing an unknown amount of updates and inserts. You can tell Spring Batch to skip the line that caused the item reader to throw an exception on a formatting error.

- *Retry*—Because some products are already in the database, the flat file data is used to update the products (description, price, and so on). Even if the job runs during periods of low activity in the online store, users sometimes access the updated products, causing the database to lock the corresponding rows. The database throws a concurrency exception when the job tries to update a product in a locked row, but retrying the update again a few milliseconds later works. You can configure Spring Batch to retry automatically.

- *Restart*—If Spring Batch has to skip more than 10 products because of badly formatted lines, the input file is considered invalid and should go through a validation phase. The job fails as soon as you reach 10 skipped products, as defined in the configuration. An operator will analyze the input file and correct it before restarting the import. Spring Batch can restart the job on the line that caused the failed execution. The work performed by the previous execution isn't lost.

The import products job is robust and reliable thanks to Spring Batch. Let's study the roles of skip, retry, and restart individually.

8.2 *Skipping instead of failing*

Sometimes errors aren't fatal: a job execution shouldn't stop when something goes wrong. In the online store application, when importing products from a flat file, should you stop the job execution because one line is in an incorrect format? You could stop the whole execution, but the job wouldn't insert the subsequent lines from the file, which means fewer products in the catalog and less money coming in! A better solution is to skip the incorrectly formatted line and move on to the next line.

Whether or not to skip items in a chunk-oriented step is a business decision. The good news is that Spring Batch makes the decision of skipping a matter of configuration; it has no impact on the application code. Let's see how to tell Spring Batch to skip items and then how to tune the skip policy.

8.2.1 *Configuring exceptions to be skipped*

Recall that the import products job reads products from a flat file and then inserts them into the database. It would be a shame to stop the whole execution for a couple of incorrect lines in a file containing thousands or even tens of thousands of lines. You can tell Spring Batch to skip incorrect lines by specifying which exceptions it should ignore. To do this, you use the `skippable-exception-classes` element, as shown in the following listing.

Listing 8.1 Configuring exceptions to skip in a chunk-oriented step

```
<job id="importProductsJob">
  <step id="importProductsStep">
    <tasklet>
      <chunk reader="reader" writer="writer" commit-interval="100"
             skip-limit="10">
        <skippable-exception-classes>
          <include class="org.springframework.batch        ┃ Sets exceptions
➥ .item.file.FlatFileParseException" />                    ┃ to skip
        </skippable-exception-classes>
      </chunk>
    </tasklet>
  </step>
</job>
```

In the `skippable-exception-classes` element, you specify the exceptions to skip with the `include` element. You can specify several exception classes (with several `include` elements). When using the `include` element, you specify not only one class of exception to skip but also all the subclasses of the exception. Listing 8.1 configures Spring Batch to skip a `FlatFileParseException` and *all its subclasses*.

Note also in listing 8.1 the use of the `skip-limit` attribute, which sets the maximum number of items to skip in the step before failing the execution. Skipping is useful, but skipping too many items can signify that the input file is corrupt. As soon as Spring Batch exceeds the skip limit, it stops processing and fails the execution. When you declare an exception to skip, you must specify a skip limit.

The `include` element skips a whole exception hierarchy, but what if you don't want to skip all the subclasses of the specified exception? In this case, you use the `exclude` element. The following snippet shows how to skip `ItemReaderExceptions` but excludes `NonTransientResourceException`:

```
<skippable-exception-classes>
  <include
    class="org.springframework.batch.item.ItemReaderException"/>
  <exclude
    class="org.springframework.batch.item.NonTransientResourceException"/>
</skippable-exception-classes>
```

Figure 8.1 shows the relationship between `ItemReaderException` and `NonTransient-ResourceException`. With the settings from the previous snippet, a `FlatFileParse-Exception` triggers a skip, whereas a `NonTransientFlatFileException` doesn't. Expressing this requirement in English, we would say that we want to skip any error due to bad formatting in the input file (`ParseException`) and that we don't want to skip errors due to I/O problems (`NonTransientResourceException`).

Specifying exceptions to skip and a skip limit is straightforward and fits most cases. Can you avoid using a skip limit and import as many items as possible? Yes. When importing products in the online store, you could process the entire input file, no matter how many lines are incorrect and skipped. As you log these skipped lines, you can correct them and import them the next day. Spring Batch gives you full control over the skip behavior by specifying a *skip policy*.

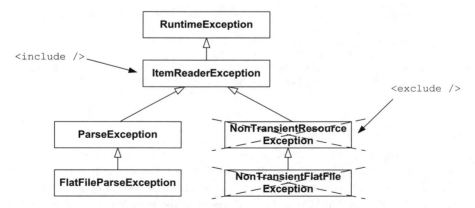

Figure 8.1   The `include` element specifies an exception class and all its subclasses. If you want to exclude part of the hierarchy, use the `exclude` element. The `exclude` element also works transitively, as it excludes a class and its subclasses.

Figure 8.2 When skip is on, Spring Batch asks a skip policy whether it should skip an exception thrown by an item reader, processor, or writer. The skip policy's decision can depend on the type of the exception and on the number of skipped items so far in the step.

8.2.2 Configuring a SkipPolicy for complete control

Who decides if an item should be skipped or not in a chunk-oriented step? Spring Batch calls the skip policy when an item reader, processor, or writer throws an exception, as figure 8.2 shows. When using the `skippable-exception-classes` element, Spring Batch uses a default skip policy implementation (`LimitCheckingItemSkipPolicy`), but you can declare your own skip policy as a Spring bean and plug it into your step. This gives you more control if the `skippable-exception-classes` and `skip-limit` pair isn't enough.

> **NOTE** The `skip-limit` attribute and the `skippable-exception-classes` tag have no effect as soon as you plug your own skip policy into a step.

Let's say you know exactly on which exceptions you want to skip items, but you don't care about the number of skipped items. You can implement your own skip policy, as shown in the following listing.

Listing 8.2 Implementing a skip policy with no skip limit

```
package com.manning.sbia.ch08.skip;

import org.springframework.batch.core.step.skip.SkipLimitExceededException;
import org.springframework.batch.core.step.skip.SkipPolicy;

public class ExceptionSkipPolicy implements SkipPolicy {

  private Class<? extends Exception> exceptionClassToSkip;

  public ExceptionSkipPolicy(
      Class<? extends Exception> exceptionClassToSkip) {
    super();
    this.exceptionClassToSkip = exceptionClassToSkip;
  }

  @Override
  public boolean shouldSkip(Throwable t, int skipCount)
      throws SkipLimitExceededException {
    return exceptionClassToSkip.isAssignableFrom(      ⟵ Skips on
      t.getClass()                                        Exception class
    );                                                     and subclasses
  }

}
```

Once you implement your own skip policy and you declare it as a Spring bean, you can plug it into a step by using the `skip-policy` attribute, as shown in the following listing.

Listing 8.3 Plugging in a skip policy in a chunk-oriented step

```
<bean id="skipPolicy" class="com.manning.sbia.ch08
   .skip.ExceptionSkipPolicy">
   <constructor-arg value="org.springframework.batch
   .item.file.FlatFileParseException" />
</bean>

<job id="importProductsJobWithSkipPolicy"
      xmlns="http://www.springframework.org/schema/batch">
   <step id="importProductsStepWithSkipPolicy">
      <tasklet>
         <chunk reader="reader" writer="writer" commit-interval="100"
               skip-policy="skipPolicy" />          ◁─┐ Sets skip
      </tasklet>                                        │ policy in step
   </step>
</job>
```

Table 8.2 lists the skip policy implementations Spring Batch provides. Don't hesitate to look them up before implementing your own.

Table 8.2 Skip policy implementations provided by Spring Batch

Skip policy class*	Description
LimitCheckingItemSkipPolicy	Skips items depending on the exception thrown and the total number of skipped items; this is the default implementation
ExceptionClassifierSkipPolicy	Delegates skip decision to other skip policies depending on the exception thrown
AlwaysSkipItemSkipPolicy	Always skips, no matter the exception or the total number of skipped items
NeverSkipItemSkipPolicy	Never skips

* From the org.springframework.batch.core.step.skip package.

When it comes to skipping, you can stick to the skippable-exception-classes and skip-limit pair, which have convenient behavior and are easy to configure, with dedicated XML elements. You typically use the default skip policy if you care about the total number of skipped items and you don't want to exceed a given limit. If you don't care about the number of skipped items, you can implement your own skip policy and easily plug it into a chunk-oriented step.

How Spring Batch drives chunks with skipped items

We focused on skipping items during the reading phase, but the skip configuration also applies to the processing and writing phases of a chunk-oriented step. Spring Batch doesn't drive a chunk-oriented step the same way when a skippable exception is thrown in the reading, processing, or writing phase.

(continued)

When an item reader throws a skippable exception, Spring Batch just calls the read method again on the item reader to get the next item. There's no rollback on the transaction. When an item processor throws a skippable exception, Spring Batch rolls back the transaction of the current chunk and resubmits the read items to the item processor, except for the one that triggered the skippable exception in the previous run. Figure 8.3 shows what Spring Batch does when the item writer throws a skippable exception. Because the framework doesn't know which item threw the exception, it reprocesses each item in the chunk one by one, in its own transaction.

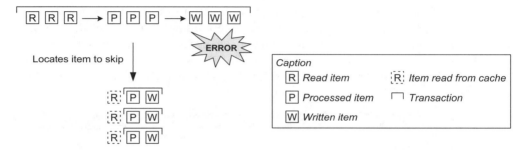

Figure 8.3 When a writer throws a skippable exception, Spring Batch can't know which item triggered the exception. Spring Batch then rolls back the transaction and processes the chunk item by item. Note that Spring Batch doesn't read the items again, by default, because it maintains a chunk-scoped cache.

Skipping incorrect items makes a job more robust, but you might want to keep track of these items. Let's see how Spring Batch lets you do that with a skip listener.

8.2.3 *Listening and logging skipped items*

Okay, your job doesn't fail miserably anymore because of a single incorrect line in your 500-megabyte input file, fine—but how do you easily spot these incorrect lines? One solution is to log each skipped item with the skip callbacks provided by Spring Batch. Once you have the skipped items in a file or in a database, you can deal with them: correct the input file, do some manual processing to deal with the error, and so on. The point is to have a record of what went wrong!

Spring Batch provides the SkipListener interface to listen to skipped items:

```
public interface SkipListener<T,S> extends StepListener {
  void onSkipInRead(Throwable t);
  void onSkipInProcess(T item, Throwable t);
  void onSkipInWrite(S item, Throwable t);
}
```

You can implement a skip listener and plug it into a step, as figure 8.4 shows. Spring Batch calls the appropriate method on the listener when it skips an item. To implement

Figure 8.4   Spring Batch lets you register skip listeners. Whenever a chunk-oriented step throws a skippable exception, Spring Batch calls the listener accordingly. A listener can then log the skipped item for later processing.

a skip listener, you can directly implement the `SkipListener` interface, but this implies implementing three methods, even if you expect skipped items only during the reading phase. To avoid implementing empty methods, you can inherit from the `SkipListener-Support` adapter class, which provides no-op implementations: you override only the method you need.

There's one more solution: using annotations on a simple class (no interface, no abstract class). Spring Batch provides one annotation for each method of the `Skip-Listener` interface: `@OnSkipInRead`, `@OnSkipInProcess`, and `@OnSkipInWrite`.

Next, you use the annotation solution with `@OnSkipInRead` to skip items during the reading phase. The following listing shows the skip listener, which logs the incorrect line to a database.

Listing 8.4   Logging skipped items with a skip listener

```
package com.manning.sbia.ch08.skip;

import javax.sql.DataSource;
import org.springframework.batch.core.annotation.OnSkipInRead;
import org.springframework.batch.item.file.FlatFileParseException;
import org.springframework.jdbc.core.JdbcTemplate;

public class DatabaseSkipListener {

  private JdbcTemplate jdbcTemplate;

  public DatabaseSkipListener(DataSource ds) {
    this.jdbcTemplate = new JdbcTemplate(ds);
  }
  @OnSkipInRead                                          ←┘ Uses annotation to
  public void log(Throwable t) {                            trigger callback
    if(t instanceof FlatFileParseException) {
      FlatFileParseException ffpe = (FlatFileParseException) t;
      jdbcTemplate.update(
        "insert into skipped_product " +                    Logs line information
        "(line,line_number) values (?,?)",                  in database
        ffpe.getInput(),ffpe.getLineNumber()
      );
    }
  }

}
```

The skip listener logs the incorrect line in the database, but it could use any other logging system, a logging framework like Java's own `java.util.logging`, Apache Log4J, or SLF4J, for example.

Once you implement the skip listener, you need to register it. The following listing shows how to register the skip listener on a step, using the `listeners` element in the `tasklet` element.

Listing 8.5 Registering a skip listener

```
<bean id="skipListener" class="com.manning
    .sbia.ch08.skip.DatabaseSkipListener">
  <constructor-arg ref="dataSource" />
</bean>

<job id="importProductsJob"
    xmlns="http://www.springframework.org/schema/batch">
  <step id="importProductsStep">
    <tasklet>
      <chunk reader="reader" writer="writer"
             commit-interval="100" skip-limit="10">
        <skippable-exception-classes>
          <include class="org.springframework.batch.item.file
    .FlatFileParseException" />
        </skippable-exception-classes>
      </chunk>
      <listeners>
        <listener ref="skipListener" />
      </listeners>
    </tasklet>
  </step>
</job>
```

> **Declares skip listener bean**

> **Registers skip listener**

A couple of details are worth mentioning in the skip listener configuration:

1. *You can have several skip listeners.* Only one skip listener was registered in the example, but you can have as many as you want.

2. *Spring Batch is smart enough to figure out the listener type.* The example used the generic `listener` element to register the skip listener. Spring Batch detects that it is a skip listener (Spring Batch provides many different kinds of listeners).

When does Spring Batch call a skip listener method? Just after the item reader, processor, or writer throws the to-be-skipped exception, you may think. But no, not just after. Spring Batch postpones the call to skip listeners until right before committing the transaction for the chunk. Why is that? Because something wrong can happen *after* Spring Batch skips an item, and Spring Batch could then roll back the transaction. Imagine that the item reader throws a to-be-skipped exception. Later on, something goes wrong during the writing phase of the same chunk, and Spring Batch rolls back the transaction and could even fail the job execution. You wouldn't want to log the skipped item during the reading phase, because Spring Batch rolled back the whole chunk! That's why Spring Batch calls skip listeners just before the commit of the chunk, when it's almost certain nothing unexpected could happen.

We're done with skipping, a feature Spring Batch provides to make jobs more robust when errors aren't fatal. Do you want your jobs to be even more robust? Perhaps skipping an item immediately is too pessimistic—what about making additional attempts before skipping? This is what we call *retry*, and Spring Batch offers first-class support for this feature.

8.3   Retrying on error

By default, an exception in a chunk-oriented step causes the step to fail. You can skip the exception if you don't want to fail the whole step. Skipping works well for deterministic exceptions, such as an incorrect line in a flat file. Exceptions aren't always deterministic; sometimes they can be *transient*. An exception is transient when an operation fails at first, but a new attempt—even immediately after the failure—is successful.

Have you ever used your cell phone in a place where the connection would arguably be bad? In a tunnel, for example, or on a ferry, sailing on the Baltic Sea on a Friday night while watching a Finnish clown show?[1] You start speaking on the cell phone, but the line drops out. Do you give up and start watching the clown show, or do you try to dial the number again? Maybe the connection will be better on the second attempt or in a couple of minutes. Transient errors happen all the time in the real world when using the phone or online conference tools like Skype. You usually retry several times after a failure before giving up and trying later if the call doesn't go through.

What are transient exceptions in batch applications? Concurrency exceptions are a typical example. If a batch job tries to update a row that another process holds a lock on, the database can cause an error. Retrying the operation immediately can be successful, because the other process may have released the lock in the meantime. Any operation involving an unreliable network—like a web service call—can also throw transient exceptions, so a new attempt, with a new request (or connection), may succeed.

You can configure Spring Batch to retry operations transparently when they throw exceptions, without any impact on the application code. Because transient failures cause these exceptions, we call them *retryable* exceptions.

8.3.1   Configuring retryable exceptions

You configure retryable exceptions inside the chunk element, using the retryable-exception-classes element, as shown in the following listing.

Listing 8.6   Configuring retryable exceptions

```
<job id="importProducsJob">
  <step id="importProductsStep">
    <tasklet>
      <chunk reader="reader" writer="writer" commit-interval="100"
             retry-limit="3">
        <retryable-exception-classes>
            <include class="org.springframework.dao              Sets exceptions
   .OptimisticLockingFailureException" />                         to retry on
        </retryable-exception-classes>
      </chunk>
    </tasklet>
  </step>
</job>
```

---

[1] It happened while one of the authors was working on this book!

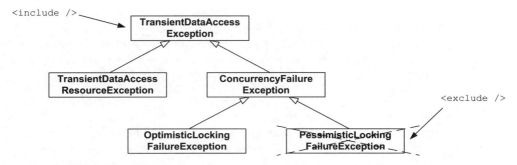

Figure 8.5 Spring Batch configured to retry exceptions: the include tag includes an exception class and all its subclasses. By using the exclude tag, you specify a part of the hierarchy that Spring Batch shouldn't retry. Here, Spring Batch retries any transient exception except pessimistic locking exceptions.

Notice the `retry-limit` attribute, used to specify how many times Spring Batch should retry an operation. Just as for skipping, you can include a complete exception hierarchy with the `include` element and exclude some specific exceptions with the `exclude` element. You can use both XML elements several times. The following snippet illustrates the use of the exclude element for retry:

```
<retryable-exception-classes>
  <include
    class="org.springframework.dao.TransientDataAccessException"/>
  <exclude
    class="org.springframework.dao.PessimisticLockingFailureException"/>
</retryable-exception-classes>
```

Figure 8.5 shows the relationship between the exceptions `TransientDataAccess-Exception` and `PessimisticLockingFailureException`. In the preceding snippet, you tell Spring Batch to retry when Spring throws transient exceptions unless the exceptions are related to pessimistic locking.

Spring Batch only retries the item processing and item writing phases. By default, a retryable exception triggers a rollback, so you should be careful because retrying too many times for too many items can degrade performance. You should use retryable exception only for exceptions that are nondeterministic, not for exceptions related to format or constraint violations, which are typically deterministic. Figure 8.6 summarizes the retry behavior in Spring Batch.

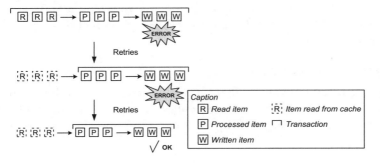

Figure 8.6 Spring Batch retries only for exceptions thrown during item processing or item writing. Retry triggers a rollback, so retrying is costly: don't abuse it! Note that Spring Batch doesn't read the items again, by default, because it maintains a chunk-scoped cache.

Override `equals()` **and** `hashCode()` **when using retry**

In a chunk-oriented step, Spring Batch handles retry on the item processing and writing phases. By default, a retry implies a rollback, so Spring Batch must restore the context of retried operations across transactions. It needs to track items closely to know which item could have triggered the retry. Remember that Spring Batch can't always know which item triggers an exception during the writing phase, because an item writer handles a list of items. Spring Batch relies on the identity of items to track them, so for Spring Batch retry to work correctly, you should override the `equals` and `hashCode` methods of your items' classes—by using a database identifier, for example.

COMBINING RETRY AND SKIP

You can combine retry with skip: a job retries an unsuccessful operation several times and then skips it. Remember that once Spring Batch reaches the retry limit, the exception causes the step to exit and, by default, fail. Use combined retry and skip when you don't want a persisting transient error to fail a step. The following listing shows how to combine retry and skip.

Listing 8.7   Combining retry and skip

```
<job id="job">
  <step id="step">
    <tasklet>
      <chunk reader="reader" writer="writer" commit-interval="100"
             retry-limit="3" skip-limit="10">
        <retryable-exception-classes>
          <include class="org.springframework.dao
➥ .DeadlockLoserDataAccessException" />        Specifies retryable
        </retryable-exception-classes>           and skippable
        <skippable-exception-classes>            exceptions
          <include class="org.springframework.dao
➥ .DeadlockLoserDataAccessException" />
        </skippable-exception-classes>
      </chunk>
    </tasklet>
  </step>
</job>
```

Automatic retry in a chunk-oriented step can make jobs more robust. It's a shame to fail a step because of an unstable network, when retrying a few milliseconds later could have worked. You now know about the default retry configuration in Spring Batch, and this should be enough for most cases. The next section explores how to control retry by setting a *retry policy*.

8.3.2   *Controlling retry with a retry policy*

By default, Spring Batch lets you configure retryable exceptions and the retry count. Sometimes, retry is more complex: some exceptions deserve more attempts than others do, or you may want to keep retrying as long as the operation doesn't exceed a given timeout. Spring Batch delegates the decision to retry or not to a *retry policy*. When configuring retry in Spring Batch, you can use the `retryable-exception-classes` element and `retry-limit` pair or provide a `RetryPolicy` bean instead.

Table 8.3 lists the `RetryPolicy` implementations included in Spring Batch. You can use these implementations or implement your own retry policy for specific needs.

Table 8.3 `RetryPolicy` implementations provided by Spring Batch

Class	Description
SimpleRetryPolicy	Retries on given exception hierarchies, a given number of times; this is the default implementation configured with `retryable-exception-classes/retry-limit`
TimeoutRetryPolicy	Stops retrying when an operation takes too long
ExceptionClassifierRetryPolicy	Combines multiple retry policies depending on the exception thrown

Let's see how to set a retry policy with an example. Imagine you want to use retry on concurrent exceptions, but you have several kinds of concurrent exceptions to deal with and you don't want the same retry behavior for all of them. Spring Batch should retry all generic concurrent exceptions three times, whereas it should retry the deadlock concurrent exceptions five times, which is more aggressive.

The `ExceptionClassifierRetryPolicy` implementation is a perfect match: it delegates the retry decision to different policies depending on the class of the thrown exception. The trick is to encapsulate two `SimpleRetryPolicy` beans in the `ExceptionClassifierRetryPolicy`, one for each kind of exception, as shown in the following listing.

Listing 8.8 Using a retry policy for different behavior with concurrent exceptions

```
<job id="retryPolicyJob"
     xmlns="http://www.springframework.org/schema/batch">
  <step id="retryPolicyStep">
    <tasklet>
      <chunk reader="reader" writer="writer" commit-interval="100"
          retry-policy="retryPolicy" />                              ◁──┐ Sets retry policy
    </tasklet>                                                           │ on chunk
  </step>
</job>

<bean id="retryPolicy" class="org.springframework
  ➥.batch.retry.policy.ExceptionClassifierRetryPolicy">
  <property name="policyMap">
    <map>
      <entry key="org.springframework.dao.ConcurrencyFailureException">
        <bean class="org.springframework.batch.retry
  ➥.policy.SimpleRetryPolicy">                                       Sets max attempts for
        <property name="maxAttempts" value="3" />         ◁──┘       concurrent exceptions
```

```
      </bean>
    </entry>
    <entry key="org.springframework.dao
  .DeadlockLoserDataAccessException">
      <bean class="org.springframework.batch.retry
  .policy.SimpleRetryPolicy">
        <property name="maxAttempts" value="5" />      ◁——┐  Sets max attempts for
      </bean>                                                deadlock exceptions
    </entry>
  </map>
</property>
</bean>
```

Listing 8.8 shows that setting a retry policy allows for flexible retry behavior: the number of retries can be different, depending on the kind of exceptions thrown during processing.

Transparent retries make jobs more robust. Listening to retries also helps you learn about the causes of retries.

8.3.3   *Listening to retries*

Spring Batch provides the `RetryListener` interface to react to any retried operation. A retry listener can be useful to log retried operations and to gather information. Once you know more about transient failures, you're more likely to change the system to avoid them in subsequent executions (remember, retried operations always degrade performance).

You can directly implement the `RetryListener` interface; it defines two lifecycle methods—`open` and `close`—that often remain empty, because you usually care only about the error thrown in the operation. A better way is to extend the `Retry-ListenerSupport` adapter class and override the `onError` method, as shown in the following listing.

Listing 8.9   Implementing a retry listener to log retried operations

```java
package com.manning.sbia.ch08.retry;

import org.slf4j.Logger;
import org.slf4j.LoggerFactory;
import org.springframework.batch.retry.RetryCallback;
import org.springframework.batch.retry.RetryContext;
import org.springframework.batch.retry.listener.RetryListenerSupport;

public class Slf4jRetryListener extends RetryListenerSupport {

  private static final Logger LOG =
    LoggerFactory.getLogger(Slf4jRetryListener.class);

  @Override
  public <T> void onError(RetryContext context, RetryCallback<T> callback,
      Throwable throwable) {
    LOG.error("retried operation",throwable);
  }

}
```

The retry listener uses the SLF4J logging framework to log the exception the operation throws. It could also use JDBC to log the error to a database. The following listing registers the listener in the step, using the `retry-listeners` XML element.

Listing 8.10 Registering a retry listener

```xml
<bean id="retryListener" class="com.manning.sbia.ch08          Declares retry
    .retry.Slf4jRetryListener" />                              listener bean

<job id="job" xmlns="http://www.springframework.org/schema/batch">
  <step id="step">
    <tasklet>
      <chunk reader="reader" writer="writer"
            commit-interval="10" retry-limit="3">
        <retryable-exception-classes>
          <include class="org.springframework.dao
    .OptimisticLockingFailureException" />
        </retryable-exception-classes>
        <retry-listeners>                                      Registers retry
          <listener ref="retryListener" />                     listener
        </retry-listeners>
      </chunk>
    </tasklet>
  </step>
</job>
```

Any time you need to know about retried operations—for example, to get rid of them!—Spring Batch lets you register retry listeners to log errors.

Retry is a built-in feature of chunk-oriented steps. What can you do if you need to retry in your own code, for example, in a tasklet?

8.3.4 *Retrying in application code with the RetryTemplate*

Imagine you use a web service in a custom tasklet to retrieve data that a subsequent step will then use. A call to a web service can cause transient failures, so being able to retry this call would make the tasklet more robust. You can benefit from Spring Batch's retry feature in a tasklet, with the `RetryOperations` interface and its `RetryTemplate` implementation. The `RetryTemplate` allows for programmatic retry in application code.

The online store uses a tasklet to retrieve the latest discounts from a web service. The discount data is small enough to keep in memory for later use in the next step. The `DiscountService` interface hides the call to the web service. The following listing shows the tasklet that retrieves the discounts (the setter methods are omitted for brevity). The tasklet uses a `RetryTemplate` to retry in case of failure.

Listing 8.11 Programmatic retry in a tasklet

```java
package com.manning.sbia.ch08.retry;

import java.util.List;
import org.springframework.batch.core.StepContribution;
```

```
import org.springframework.batch.core.scope.context.ChunkContext;
import org.springframework.batch.core.step.tasklet.Tasklet;
import org.springframework.batch.repeat.RepeatStatus;
import org.springframework.batch.retry.RetryCallback;
import org.springframework.batch.retry.RetryContext;
import org.springframework.batch.retry.policy.SimpleRetryPolicy;
import org.springframework.batch.retry.support.RetryTemplate;

public class DiscountsWithRetryTemplateTasklet implements Tasklet {

    private DiscountService discountService;
    private DiscountsHolder discountsHolder;

    @Override
    public RepeatStatus execute(StepContribution contribution,
        ChunkContext chunkContext) throws Exception {
      RetryTemplate retryTemplate = new RetryTemplate();
      SimpleRetryPolicy retryPolicy =
        new SimpleRetryPolicy();
      retryPolicy.setMaxAttempts(3);
      retryTemplate.setRetryPolicy(retryPolicy);
      List<Discount> discounts = retryTemplate.execute(
          new RetryCallback<List<Discount>>() {
        @Override
        public List<Discount> doWithRetry(
            RetryContext context)
          throws Exception {
          return discountService.getDiscounts();
        }
      });
      discountsHolder.setDiscounts(discounts);
      return RepeatStatus.FINISHED;
    }
    (...)
}
```

- Configures RetryTemplate
- Calls web service with retry
- Stores result for later use

The use of the RetryTemplate is straightforward. Note how the RetryTemplate is configured with a RetryPolicy directly in the tasklet. You could have also defined a RetryOperations property in the tasklet and used Spring to inject a RetryTemplate bean as a dependency. Thanks to the RetryTemplate, you shouldn't fear transient failures on the web service call anymore.

Use of the RetryTemplate is simple, but the retry logic is hardcoded in the tasklet. Let's go further to see how to remove the retry logic from the application code.

8.3.5 *Retrying transparently with the RetryTemplate and AOP*

Can you remove all the retry logic from the tasklet? It would make it easier to test, because the tasklet would be free of any retry code and the tasklet could focus on its core logic. Furthermore, a unit test wouldn't necessarily deal with all retry cases.

Spring Batch provides an AOP interceptor for retry called RetryOperationsInterceptor. By using this interceptor, the tasklet can use a DiscountService object directly. The interceptor delegates calls to the real DiscountService and handles the retry logic. No more dependency on the RetryTemplate in the tasklet—the code

Aspect-oriented programming (AOP)

Aspect-oriented programming is a programming paradigm that allows modularizing crosscutting concerns. The idea of AOP is to remove crosscutting concerns from an application's main logic and implement them in dedicated units called *aspects*. Typical crosscutting concerns are transaction management, logging, security, and retry. The Spring Framework provides first-class support for AOP with its interceptor-based approach: Spring intercepts application code and calls aspect code to address crosscutting concerns. Thanks to AOP, boilerplate code doesn't clutter the application code, and code aspects address crosscutting concerns in their own units, which also prevents code scattering.

becomes simpler! The following listing shows the new version of the tasklet, which doesn't handle retries anymore.

Listing 8.12 Calling the web service without retry logic

```
package com.manning.sbia.ch08.retry;

import java.util.List;
import org.springframework.batch.core.StepContribution;
import org.springframework.batch.core.scope.context.ChunkContext;
import org.springframework.batch.core.step.tasklet.Tasklet;
import org.springframework.batch.repeat.RepeatStatus;

public class DiscountsTasklet implements Tasklet {

  private DiscountService discountService;
  private DiscountsHolder discountsHolder;

  @Override
  public RepeatStatus execute(StepContribution contribution,
      ChunkContext chunkContext) throws Exception {
    List<Discount> discounts = discountService.getDiscounts();
    discountsHolder.setDiscounts(discounts);
    return RepeatStatus.FINISHED;
  }
  (...)
}
```

If you want to keep the tasklet this simple, you need the magic of AOP to handle the retry transparently. Spring AOP wraps the target `DiscountService`—the one that makes the web service call—in a proxy. This proxy handles the retry logic thanks to the retry interceptor. The tasklet ends up using this proxy. The following listing shows the Spring configuration for transparent, AOP-based retry.

Listing 8.13 Configuring transparent retry with Spring AOP

```
<bean id="discountService" class="com.manning.sbia        | Declares target
  ➥ .ch08.retry.DiscountServiceImpl" />                    | discount service

<bean id="retryAdvice"                                     | Declares retry
    class="org.springframework.batch.retry               | interceptor with
  ➥ .interceptor.RetryOperationsInterceptor">              | RetryTemplate
```

```
    <property name="retryOperations">
      <bean class="org.springframework.batch.retry.support.RetryTemplate">
        <property name="retryPolicy">
          <bean class="org.springframework.batch.retry.policy
  ➥ .SimpleRetryPolicy">
            <property name="maxAttempts" value="3" />
          </bean>
        </property>
      </bean>
    </property>
  </bean>

  <aop:config>
    <aop:pointcut id="retriedOperations"
      expression="execution(* com.manning.sbia.ch08
  ➥ .retry.DiscountService.*(..))" />          Applies
    <aop:advisor pointcut-ref="retriedOperations"     interceptor on
                 advice-ref="retryAdvice" />          target service
  </aop:config>

  <bean class="com.manning.sbia.ch08.retry.DiscountsTasklet">
    <property name="discountService" ref="discountService" />
    <property name="discountsHolder" ref="discountsHolder" />
  </bean>

  <bean id="discountsHolder"
        class="com.manning.sbia.ch08.retry.DiscountsHolder" />
```

That's it! Not only should you no longer fear transient failures when calling the web service, but the calling tasklet doesn't even know that there's some retry logic on the DiscountService. In addition, retry support isn't limited to batch applications: you can use it in a web application whenever a call is subject to transient failures.

This ends our coverage of retry. Spring Batch allows for transparent, configurable retry, which lets you decouple the application code from any retry logic. Retry is useful for transient, nondeterministic errors, like concurrency errors. The default behavior is to retry on given exception classes until Spring Batch reaches the retry limit. Note that you can also control the retry behavior by plugging in a retry policy.

Skip and retry help prevent job failures; they make jobs more robust. Thanks to skip and retry, you'll have fewer red-light screens in the morning. But crashes are inevitable. What do you do when a job runs all night and crashes two minutes before reaching the end? If you answer, "I restart it and wait another day," keep on reading; the next section teaches you that you can answer, "I restart it and it's going to take two minutes."

8.4   *Restart on error*

Okay, your job is running, there are some transient errors, retry comes to the rescue, but these errors aren't that transient after all. The job ends up skipping the errors. Is the job finished? Not yet. More errors come up, and the job finally reaches the skip limit. Spring Batch must fail the job! Despite all of your bulletproofing techniques, jobs can't dodge bullets forever—they can fail. Can't developers honor the exchange format you spent weeks to establish?

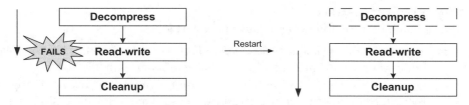

Figure 8.7 If a job fails in the middle of processing, Spring Batch can restart it exactly where it left off.

There's still hope, because Spring Batch lets you restart a job exactly where it left off. This is useful if the job was running for hours and was getting close to the end when it failed. Figure 8.7 illustrates a new execution of the import products job that continues processing where the previous execution failed.

8.4.1 *How to enable restart between job executions*

How does Spring Batch know where to restart a job execution? It maintains metadata for each job execution. If you want to benefit from restart with Spring Batch, you need a persistent implementation for the job repository. This enables restart across job executions, even if these executions aren't part of the same Java process. Chapter 2 shows how to configure a persistent job repository and illustrates a simple restart scenario. It also discusses Spring Batch metadata and job executions, as figure 8.8 shows.

Spring Batch has a default behavior for restart, but because there's no one-size-fits-all solution for batch jobs, it provides hooks to control exactly how a restarted job execution should behave. Let's focus first on the default restart behavior.

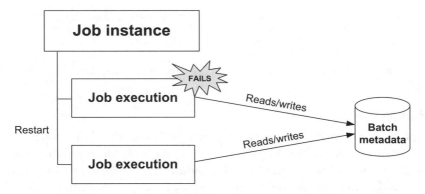

Figure 8.8 Restart is possible thanks to batch metadata that Spring Batch maintains during job executions.

DEFAULT RESTART BEHAVIOR

Spring Batch uses the following defaults to restart jobs:

- *You can only restart a failed job execution.* This seems obvious but has the following implications: you must provide the job launcher with the job and the exact same job parameters as the failed execution you want to restart. Using Spring Batch terminology: when using restart, you start a new job execution of an existing, uncompleted job instance.
- *You can restart any job.* You can start a new execution for any failed job instance. You can disable restart for a specific job, but you need to disable it explicitly.
- *A job restarts exactly where the last execution left off.* This implies that the job skips already completed steps.
- *You can restart a job as many times as you want.* Well, almost—the limit is a couple of billion restarts.

You can override the defaults, and Spring Batch lets you change the restart behavior. Table 8.4 summarizes the restart settings available in the configuration of a job. The defaults for these settings match the default behavior we described.

Table 8.4 Configuration of the restart behavior

Attribute	XML element	Possible values	Description
`restartable`	`job`	`true` / `false`	Whether the job can be restarted; default is `true`
`allow-start-if-complete`	`tasklet`	`true` / `false`	Whether a step should be started even if it's already completed; default is `false`
`start-limit`	`tasklet`	Integer value	Number of times a step can be started; default is `Integer.MAX_VALUE`

Let's learn more about restart options in Spring Batch by covering some typical scenarios.

8.4.2 No restart please!

The simplest restart option is *no restart*. When a job is sensitive and you want to examine each failed execution closely, preventing restarts is useful. After all, a command-line mistake or an improperly configured scheduler can easily restart a job execution. Forbid restart on jobs that are unable to restart with correct semantics. Forbidding an accidental restart can prevent a job from processing data again, potentially corrupting a database.

To disable restart, set the attribute `restartable` to `false` on the job element:

```
<job id="importProductsJob"
    restartable="false">
  (...)
</job>
```

Remember that jobs are restartable by default. If you're worried that you'll forget that, set the `restartable` flag explicitly on all your jobs.

Restart is a nice feature, so let's assume now that our jobs are restartable and explore more scenarios.

8.4.3 Whether or not to restart already completed steps

Remember that the import products job consists of two steps: the first decompresses a ZIP archive, and the second reads products from the decompressed file and writes into the database. Imagine the first step succeeds and the second step fails after several chunks. When restarting the job instance, should you re-execute the first step or not? Figure 8.9 illustrates both alternatives. There's no definitive answer to such questions; this is a business decision, which determines how to handle failed executions.

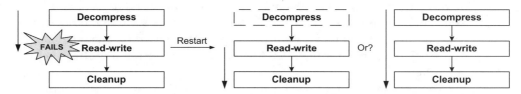

Figure 8.9 Spring Batch lets you choose if it should re-execute already completed steps on restart. Spring Batch doesn't re-execute already completed steps by default.

When is skipping the first, already completed step a good choice? If you check the Spring Batch logs and fix the decompressed input file after the failure, restarting directly on the second step is the way to go. The chunk-oriented step should complete correctly, or at least not fail for the same reason. If you stick to this scenario, you have nothing to do: skipping already completed steps is the default restart behavior.

Let's consider now re-executing the first, already completed step on restart. When the batch operator sees that the execution failed during the second step, their reaction may be to send the log to the creator of the archive and tell them to provide a correct one. In this case, you should restart the import for this specific job instance with a new archive, so re-executing the first step to decompress the new archive makes sense. The second step would then execute and restart exactly on the line where it left off (as long as its item reader can do so and assuming the input has no lines removed, moved, or added).

To re-execute a completed step on a restart, set the `allow-start-if-complete` flag to `true` on the `tasklet` element:

```
<job id="importProductsJob">
  <step id="decompressStep" next="readWriteProductsStep">
    <tasklet allow-start-if-complete="true">          ⊲┐ Sets step to
      (...)                                              │ re-execute
    </tasklet>                                           ┘ on restart
  </step>
  <step id="readWriteProductsStep" next="cleanStep">
```

```
    <tasklet>
      (...)
    </tasklet>
  </step>
  <step id="cleanStep">
    <tasklet>
      (...)
    </tasklet>
  </step>
</job>
```

Restarting a job is like many things: don't do it too often. Let's see how to avoid restarting a job indefinitely.

8.4.4 Limiting the number of restarts

Repeatedly restarting the same job instance can mean there's something wrong and you should simply give up with this job instance. That's where the restart limit comes in: you can set the number of times a step can be started for the same job instance. If you reach this limit, Spring Batch forbids any new execution of the step for the same job instance.

You set the start limit at the step level, using the start-limit attribute on the tasklet element. The following snippet shows how to set a start limit on the second step of the import products job:

```
<job id="importProductsJob">
  <step id="decompressStep" next="readWriteProductsStep">
    <tasklet>
      (...)
    </tasklet>
  </step>
  <step id="readWriteProductsStep">
    <tasklet start-limit="3">
      (...)
    </tasklet>
  </step>
</job>
```

Let's see a scenario where the start limit is useful. You launch a first execution of the import products job. The first decompression step succeeds, but the second step fails after a while. You start the job again. This second execution starts directly where the second step left off. (The first step completed, and you didn't ask to execute it again on restart.) The second execution also fails, and a third execution fails as well. On the fourth execution—you're stubborn—Spring Batch sees that you've reached the start limit (3) for the step and doesn't even try to execute the second step again. The whole job execution fails and the job instance never completes. You need to move on and create a new job instance.

Spring Batch can restart a job exactly at the step where it left off. Can you push restart further and restart a chunk-oriented step exactly on the item where it failed?

8.4.5 *Restarting in the middle of a chunk-oriented step*

When a job execution fails in the middle of a chunk-oriented step and has already processed a large amount of items, you probably don't want to reprocess these items again on restart. Reprocessing wastes time and can duplicate data or transactions, which could have dramatic side effects. Spring Batch can restart a chunk-oriented step exactly on the chunk where the step failed, as shown in figure 8.10, where the item reader restarts on the same input line where the previous execution failed.

   The item reader drives a chunk-oriented step and provides the items to process and write. The item reader is in charge when it comes to restarting a chunk-oriented step. Again, the item reader knows where it failed in the previous execution thanks to metadata stored in the step execution context. There's no magic here: the item reader must track what it's doing and use this information in case of failure.

> **NOTE** Item writers can also be restartable. Imagine a file item writer that directly moves to the end of the written file on a restart.

A restartable item reader can increment a counter for each item it reads and store the value of the counter each time a chunk is committed. In case of failure and on restart, the item reader queries the step execution context for the value of the counter. Spring Batch helps by storing the step execution context between executions, but the item reader must implement the restart logic. After all, Spring Batch has no idea what the item reader is doing: reading lines from a flat file, reading rows from a database, and so on.

> **WARNING** When using a counter-based approach for restart, you assume that the list of items doesn't change between executions (no new or deleted items, and the order stays the same).

Most of the item readers that Spring Batch provides are restartable. You should always carefully read the Javadoc of the item reader you're using to know how it behaves on restart. How the item reader implements its restart behavior can also have important

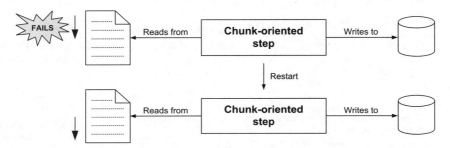

Figure 8.10   A chunk-oriented step can restart exactly where it left off. The figure shows an item reader that restarts on the line where the previous execution failed (it assumes the line has been corrected). To do so, the item reader uses batch metadata to store its state.

consequences. For example, an item reader may not be thread-safe because of its restart behavior, which prevents multithreading in the reading phase. Chapter 13 covers how to scale Spring Batch jobs and the impacts of multithreading on a chunk-oriented step.

What if you write your own item reader and you want it to be restartable? You must not only read the items but also access the step execution context to store the counter and query it in case of failure. Spring Batch provides a convenient interface—Item-Stream—that defines a contract to interact with the execution context in key points of the step lifecycle.

Let's take an example where an item reader returns the files in a directory. The following listing shows the code of the FilesInDirectoryItemReader class. This item reader implements the ItemStream interface to store its state periodically in the step execution context.

Listing 8.14   Implementing `ItemStream` to make an item reader restartable

```java
package com.manning.sbia.ch08.restart;

import java.io.File;
import java.io.FileFilter;
import java.util.Arrays;
import org.apache.commons.io.comparator.NameFileComparator;
import org.apache.commons.io.filefilter.FileFilterUtils;
import org.springframework.batch.item.ExecutionContext;
import org.springframework.batch.item.ItemReader;
import org.springframework.batch.item.ItemStream;
import org.springframework.batch.item.ItemStreamException;
import org.springframework.batch.item.NonTransientResourceException;
import org.springframework.batch.item.ParseException;
import org.springframework.batch.item.UnexpectedInputException;

public class FilesInDirectoryItemReader
        implements ItemReader<File>, ItemStream {

  private File [] files;

  private int currentCount;

  private String key = "file.in.directory.count";

  public void setDirectory(String directory) {
    this.files = new File(directory).listFiles(
      (FileFilter) FileFilterUtils.fileFileFilter()
    );
    Arrays.sort(files, new NameFileComparator());
  }

  @Override
  public void open(ExecutionContext executionContext)
     throws ItemStreamException {
    currentCount = executionContext.getInt(key, 0);
  }

  @Override
```

❶ Initializes file array to read from

❷ Initializes file array counter

```
public File read() throws Exception, UnexpectedInputException,
    ParseException, NonTransientResourceException {
  int index = ++currentCount - 1;
  if(index == files.length) {
    return null;
  }
  return files[index];
}

@Override
public void update(ExecutionContext executionContext)
    throws ItemStreamException {
  executionContext.putInt(key, currentCount);
}

@Override
public void close() throws ItemStreamException { }
}
```

❸ Increments counter on read

❹ Stores counter in step context

The reader implements both the ItemReader (read method) and ItemStream (open, update, and close methods) interfaces. The code at ❶ initializes the file array to read files, where you would typically set it from a Spring configuration file. You sort the file array because the order matters on a restart and the File.listFiles method doesn't guarantee any specific order in the resulting array. When the step begins, Spring Batch calls the open method first, in which you initialize the counter ❷. You retrieve the counter value from the execution context, with a defined key. On the first execution, there's no value for this key, so the counter value is zero. On a restart, you get the last value stored in the previous execution. This allows you to start exactly where you left off. In the read method, you increment the counter ❸ and return the corresponding file from the file array. Spring Batch calls the update method just before saving the execution context. This typically happens before a chunk is committed. In update, you have a chance to store the state of the reader, the value of the counter ❹. ItemStream provides the close method to clean up any resources the reader has opened (like a file stream if the reader reads from a file). You leave the method empty, as you have nothing to close.

Listing 8.14 shows you the secret to restarting in a chunk-oriented step. You can achieve this thanks to the ItemStream interface. ItemStream is one kind of listener that Spring Batch provides: you can use the interface for item processors, writers, and on plain steps, not only chunk-oriented steps. To enable restart, ItemStream defines a convenient contract to store the state of a reader at key points in a chunk-oriented step. Note that Spring Batch automatically registers an item reader that implements ItemStream.

NOTE You implement the FilesInDirectoryItemReader class mainly to illustrate creating a custom, restartable item reader. If you want an item reader to read files, look at the more powerful MultiResourceItemReader provided by Spring Batch.

This ends our tour of restart in Spring Batch. Remember that Spring Batch can restart a job instance where the last execution left off thanks to the metadata it stores in the job repository. Spring Batch has reasonable defaults for restart, but you can override them to re-execute an already completed step or limit the number of executions of a step. Restarting in the middle of a chunk-oriented step is also possible if the item reader stores its state periodically in the execution context. To use this feature, it's best to implement the `ItemStream` interface.

Remember that restart makes sense only when a job execution fails. You can configure restart to prevent reprocessing, potentially avoiding data corruption issues. Restart also avoids wasting time and processes the remaining steps of a failed job execution. Skip and retry are techniques to use before relying on restart. Skip and retry allow jobs to handle errors safely and prevent abrupt failures.

Congratulations for getting through this chapter! You're now ready to make your Spring Batch jobs bulletproof.

8.5   Summary

Spring Batch has built-in support to make jobs more robust and reliable. Spring Batch jobs can meet the requirements of reliability, robustness, and traceability, which are essential for automatic processing of large amounts of data. This chapter covered a lot of material, but we can summarize this material as follows:

- Always think about failure scenarios. Don't hesitate to write tests to simulate these scenarios and check that your jobs behave correctly.
- Use skip for deterministic, nonfatal exceptions.
- Use retry for transient, nondeterministic errors, such as concurrency exceptions.
- Use listeners to log errors.
- Make a job restartable in case of failure if you're sure it won't corrupt data on restart. Many Spring Batch components are already restartable, and you can implement restartability by using the execution context.
- Disable restart on a job that could corrupt data on a restart.

Another key point to consider when you want to implement bulletproof jobs is transaction management. Proper transaction management is essential to a batch application because an error during processing can corrupt a database. In such cases, the application can trigger a rollback to put the database back in a consistent state. The next chapter covers transactions in Spring Batch applications and is the natural transition after the coverage of the bulletproofing techniques in this chapter. So keep on reading for extra-bulletproof jobs!

Transaction management

Chapter 8 introduced techniques like skip and restart to make batch jobs robust and reliable. This chapter complements the last one by covering another topic critical to batch jobs: transaction management. As batch jobs interact with transactional resources like databases, proper transaction management is crucial to make batch applications robust and reliable. Because an error can occur at any time during batch processing, a job needs to know if it should roll back the current transaction to avoid leaving data in an inconsistent state or if it can commit the transaction to persist changes.

This chapter starts with a quick transaction primer. Section 9.2 explains how Spring Batch handles transactions. How does Spring Batch manage transactions in a tasklet and in a chunk-oriented step? When and why does Spring Batch trigger a rollback? Section 9.2 answers these questions. Once we show the transaction management defaults in Spring Batch, section 9.3 explains why and how to override them. It also shows you how to avoid common pitfalls related to using declarative transactions and transactional readers.

251

Section 9.4 covers patterns that help you tackle tricky transaction scenarios in batch applications. You use these patterns to deal with global transactions—transactions spanning multiple resources—and batch jobs that interact with JMS queues.

Why should you read this chapter? Spring Batch has reasonable defaults for simple jobs. To implement complex jobs, you need to know more about transaction management. That's what this chapter is about: explaining how Spring Batch handles transactions and providing you with guidelines and ready-to-use solutions to deal with challenging jobs.

9.1   *A transaction primer*

Transactions make the interactions between an application and a data store reliable. When writing batch applications, you need to know exactly what you're doing with transactions, because they affect the robustness of your batch jobs and even their performance. With a transaction, you can safely interact with a data store. An interaction consists of one or more operations—SQL statements if the data store is a database. "Safely" means that the transaction is atomic, consistent, isolated, and durable. We commonly refer to these kinds of transactions as having ACID properties. Here is what an ACID transaction requires:

- *Atomicity*—All the operations in the transaction are successful, or none is.
- *Consistency*—A transaction always leaves the data store in a consistent state.
- *Isolation*—An ongoing transaction can't see partial data of other ongoing transactions.
- *Durability*—A committed transaction survives any system failure.

A transaction often scopes to a business use case, and its ACID properties apply to the affected data. For example, for the use case of a money transfer between two bank accounts, we have the following operations: select both accounts, debit one account, and credit the other. The debit and credit should both happen; otherwise, money disappears (or appears, depending on the order of the operations); this illustrates the atomicity property. The balance between the two accounts should be the same before and at the end of the transfer (again, no money appears or disappears); this is the consistency property. Isolation is about how other transactions can see or even update the same data at the same time. Isolation deals with concurrent access and can affect performance; a high isolation level translates to poor performance. As soon as a data store tells you it committed a transaction, it should never lose the transacted data, even in case of a severe failure; this is the durability property.

In most applications, you choose how to drive transactions by using programmatic transaction demarcations or declarative transaction management (as the Spring Framework provides). It's not the same in a Spring Batch job: Spring Batch drives the flow and the transactions. Batch applications don't follow the request-response flow of typical web applications; this makes transaction management in batch jobs more complicated. The next section explains the default Spring Batch behavior that drives transactions.

9.2   *Transaction management in Spring Batch components*

Spring Batch handles transactions at the step level. This means that Spring Batch will never use only one transaction for a whole job (unless the job has a single step). Remember that you're likely to implement a Spring Batch job in one of two ways: using a tasklet or using a chunk-oriented step. Let's see how Spring Batch handles transactions in both cases.

9.2.1   *Transaction management in tasklets*

You use a tasklet whenever you need custom processing. This differs from the usual read-process-write behavior that Spring Batch's chunk-oriented step handles well. Here are cases where you can use a tasklet: launching a system command, compressing files in a ZIP archive, decompressing a ZIP archive, digitally signing a file, uploading a file to a remote FTP server, and so on. The `Tasklet` interface is

```
public interface Tasklet {
  RepeatStatus execute(StepContribution contribution,
      ChunkContext chunkContext) throws Exception;
}
```

By default, the `execute` method of a tasklet is transactional. *Each invocation of* `execute` *takes place in its own transaction.* Here's a simple example implementation:

```
class MyTasklet implements Tasklet {

  @Override
  public RepeatStatus execute(
      StepContribution contribution,
      ChunkContext chunkContext) throws Exception {    Called in a
    // your custom processing here                     transaction
    return RepeatStatus.FINISHED;
  }

}
```

A tasklet is repeatable: Spring Batch calls the `execute` method of a tasklet as long as the method returns `RepeatStatus.CONTINUABLE`. As we mentioned, each `execute` invocation takes place in its own transaction. When the `execute` method returns `RepeatStatus.FINISHED` or `null`, Spring Batch stops calling it and moves on to the next step.

> **NOTE** Be careful when implementing repeatable tasklets, because Spring Batch creates a new transaction for each invocation to the `execute` method. If a tasklet doesn't use a transactional resource—like when decompressing a ZIP archive—you can set the propagation level to `PROPAGATION_NEVER`. Section 9.3.1 covers modifying transaction attributes.

To summarize, a tasklet is a potentially repeatable transactional operation. Let's now see how Spring Batch handles transactions in a chunk-oriented step.

9.2.2   *Transaction management in chunk-oriented steps*

A chunk-oriented step follows the common read-process-write behavior for a large number of items. You know by now that you can set the chunk size. Transaction management depends on the chunk size: Spring Batch uses a transaction for each chunk. Such transaction management is

- *Efficient*—Spring Batch uses a single transaction for all items. One transaction per item isn't an appropriate solution because it doesn't perform well for a large number of items.
- *Robust*—An error affects only the current chunk, not all items.

When does Spring Batch roll back a transaction in a chunk? Any exception thrown from the item processor or the item writer triggers a rollback. This isn't the case for an exception thrown from the item reader. This behavior applies regardless of the retry and skip configuration.

You can have transaction management in a step; you can also have transaction management *around* a step. Remember that you can plug in listeners to jobs and step executions, to log skipped items, for example. If logging to a database, for example, logging needs proper transaction management to avoid losing data or logging the wrong information.

9.2.3   *Transaction management in listeners*

Spring Batch provides many types of listeners to respond to events in a batch job. When Spring Batch skips items from an input file, you may want to log them. You can plug in an `ItemSkipListener` to the step. How does Spring Batch handle transactions in these listeners? Well, it depends (the worst answer a software developer can get). There's no strict rule on whether or not a listener method is transactional; you always need to consider each specific case. Here's one piece of advice: always check the Javadoc (you're in luck; the Spring Batch developers documented their source code well).

If we take the `ChunkListener` as an example, its Javadoc states that Spring Batch executes its `beforeChunk` method in the chunk transaction but its `afterChunk` method out of the chunk transaction. Therefore, if you use a transaction resource such as a database in a `ChunkListener`'s `afterChunk` method, you should handle the transaction yourself, using the Spring Framework's transaction support.

Spring Batch also includes listeners to listen to phases for item reading, processing, and writing. Spring Batch calls these listeners before and after each phase and when an error occurs. The error callback is transactional, but it happens in a transaction that Spring Batch is about to roll back. Therefore, if you want to log the error to a database, you should handle the transaction yourself and use the `REQUIRES_NEW` propagation level. This allows the logging transaction to be independent from the chunk and the transaction to be rolled back.

Now that we've completed this overview of transaction management in Spring Batch jobs, let's study how to tune transactions during job executions. Setting transaction attributes like the isolation level is common in batch applications because it can provide better performance.

9.3 Transaction configuration

Spring Batch uses reasonable defaults for transaction management, but you can't use these defaults for all batch jobs. This section explains why and how to override these defaults and how to avoid common pitfalls.

9.3.1 Transaction attributes

You learned in chapter 3 that you can use the `transaction-attributes` element in a `tasklet` element to set a transaction's attributes, such as the propagation level, isolation level, and timeout. This allows you to have transaction attributes for a specific chunk different from the default attributes provided by a data source (which are commonly `REQUIRED` for the propagation level and `READ_COMMITED` for the isolation level).

> **NOTE** We don't provide an in-depth explanation of transaction attributes. If you want to learn more about this topic, please see *Spring in Action* by Craig Walls (Manning Publications, 2011).

Most of the time, default transaction attributes are fine, so when would you need to override these defaults? It depends on the use case. Some batch jobs can work concurrently with online applications, for example. The isolation level dictates the visibility rules between ongoing, concurrent transactions. Table 9.1 lists isolation levels, from the least isolated—`READ_UNCOMMITTED`—to the most isolated—`SERIALIZABLE`.

Table 9.1 Isolation levels for transactions

Isolation level	Description
READ_UNCOMMITTED	A transaction sees uncommitted changes from other transactions. Dirty reads, nonrepeatable reads, and phantom reads may occur.
READ_COMMITTED	A transaction sees only committed changes from other transactions. No dirty reads are possible. Nonrepeatable reads and phantom reads may occur.
REPEATABLE_READ	A transaction can read identical values from a field multiple times. Dirty reads and nonrepeatable reads don't occur. Phantom reads may occur.
SERIALIZABLE	Dirty reads, nonrepeatable reads, and phantom reads don't occur. Performance can be poor.

When a batch job works concurrently with an online application, *increasing* the isolation level can ensure that the batch job and the online application properly read and update data, but at the cost of lower performance.

Alternatively, a batch job can be the only process working on the data, so *decreasing* the isolation level can result in faster processing than with the default isolation level. The following snippet shows how to set the isolation level to the lowest level, `READ_UNCOMMITTED`:

```
<job id="importProductsJob">
  <step id="importProductsStep">
    <tasklet>
      <chunk reader="reader" writer="writer" commit-interval="100" />
      <transaction-attributes
        isolation="READ_UNCOMMITTED" />
    </tasklet>
  </step>
</job>
```

In this snippet, you ask the database to provide the lowest isolation guarantee, but because the batch job is the only one working on the data, you don't care about concurrent access.

That's it for transaction attributes: override them only when you must. Let's now see how a powerful Spring feature—declarative transaction management—can have catastrophic consequence when used in Spring Batch.

9.3.2 *Common pitfalls with declarative transactions*

Spring provides declarative transaction management: you say what you want to be transactional and Spring demarcates transactions for you. You can configure transactions using the @Transactional annotation or XML. This is convenient for online applications, like web applications: application code doesn't depend on transaction management because Spring adds it transparently at runtime. Transactions become a *crosscutting concern*.

In a Spring Batch application, Spring Batch is in charge of transactions. If at any time Spring Batch calls application code annotated with @Transactional, the transaction for this code uses the transaction managed by Spring Batch. Because it's using the default propagation level—REQUIRED—the transaction that @Transactional uses is the same as the Spring Batch transaction. Figure 9.1 illustrates how application code annotated with @Transactional can interfere with the chunk transaction in a Spring Batch job.

The following are guidelines to avoid conflict between Spring Batch–managed and Spring-managed transactions:

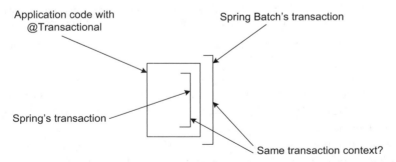

Figure 9.1   Be careful when using Spring's declarative transaction in a Spring Batch job. Depending on the transaction attributes, the Spring-managed transaction can participate (or not) with the Spring Batch–managed transaction.

- *Disable Spring's declarative transactions for your batch application*—Don't use the `tx:annotation-driven` element or any XML configuration related to declarative transaction management.
- *Be careful using propagation levels if declarative transactions are on*—If you call transactional classes from a Spring Batch job, Spring's transaction propagation can interfere with the Spring Batch transaction because of the propagation level. The `REQUIRES_NEW` propagation level could typically cause problems because the application code runs in its own transaction, independent of the Spring Batch transaction.

In short, be careful with declarative transactions. One of your best friends in online applications can become your worst enemy in offline applications! Let's now meet another friend, the transactional reader.

9.3.3 *Transactional reader and processor*

Spring Batch can perform optimizations at any time. For example, Spring Batch buffers read items for a chunk so that, in case of a retryable error during writing, it can roll back the transaction and get the read items from its cache to submit to the writer instead of reading them again from the item reader. This behavior works perfectly if you read items from a data source like a database: Spring Batch reads a record, that's it. The transaction rollback has no effect on the record read by Spring Batch: the database doesn't care.

The story isn't the same with a Java Message Service (JMS) queue. You not only read a message from a queue, you *dequeue* it: you read a message and remove it from the queue at the same time. Reading and removing a message must be atomic. In message-oriented middleware (MOM) and JMS terms, you also say that you *consume* a message. When there's a transaction rollback, JMS returns the read messages to the queue. If the processing of the messages failed, the messages must stay on the queue. In the case of a JMS reader, buffering the read items is a bad idea: if a rollback occurs, the messages go back to the queue, Spring Batch then resubmits the items to the writer using its cache, and the writing succeeds. This is a bad combination: the processing succeeded but the messages are still on the queue, ready for Spring Batch to read and to trigger the processing...again!

Figure 9.2 illustrates the difference between a nontransactional and a transactional reader. The nontransactional reader can read from a database (the database doesn't care about clients reading it). The transactional reader gets items from the data source and puts them back in case of an error. The cache Spring Batch maintains for read items prevents the transactional reader from getting items again after a failure, so you should disable it when the reader is transactional.

To avoid processing messages several times because of Spring Batch's cache, set the `reader-transactional-queue` attribute of the `chunk` element to `true` (the default is `false`), as the following snippet demonstrates:

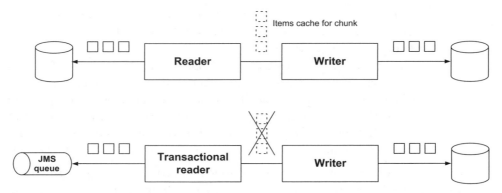

Figure 9.2   The difference between nontransactional and transactional readers. By default, Spring Batch maintains a cache of read items for retries. You must disable this cache when the reader is transactional, so Spring Batch can read the items again in case of a rollback. A JMS item reader is an example of a transactional reader because reading a message from a JMS queue removes it from the queue. A database reader is a nontransactional reader, because reading rows from a database doesn't modify the database.

```
<job id="importProductsJob">
  <step id=" importProductsStep">
    <tasklet>
      <chunk reader="reader" writer="writer"
             commit-interval="100" skip-limit="5"
             reader-transactional-queue="true">           Specifies reader
        <skippable-exception-classes>                      is transactional
          <include class="org.springframework.dao
    .DeadlockLoserDataAccessException" />
        </skippable-exception-classes>
      </chunk>
    </tasklet>
  </step>
</job>
```

Setting the `reader-transactional-queue` attribute to `true` disables Spring Batch's chunk cache. Spring Batch sends messages back to the queue on a rollback and reads them again if it attempts to process the chunk again.

> **NOTE**   The `processor-transactional` attribute allows for the same settings as `reader-transactional-queue`, but for the processor. The default value is `true`, which implies always re-executing the processor before sending items to the writer.

The only known use case of a transactional reader is JMS, but if you come up with a new one, don't forget to set the `reader-transactional-queue` flag attribute to `true`! Let's now see how to avoid transaction rollbacks.

9.3.4   *To roll back or not to roll back*

In a chunk-oriented step, Spring Batch rolls back a chunk transaction if an error occurs in the item processor or in the item writer. This seems safe because an error could have corrupted the state of the transaction, so a rollback ensures data isn't in an inconsistent state. Sometimes you're sure that a specific error didn't corrupt the transaction, so Spring Batch can retry the operation or skip the item. This saves a rollback and therefore a new transaction. Having fewer transactions is better because transactions are costly.

Use the `no-rollback-exception-classes` element in the `tasklet` element to cause Spring Batch to avoid triggering a rollback on specific exceptions, as shown in the following listing.

Listing 9.1 Avoiding a rollback for an exception

```
<job id="importProductsJob">
  <step id="importProductsStep">
    <tasklet>
      <chunk reader="reader" writer="writer"
             commit-interval="100" skip-limit="5">
        <skippable-exception-classes>
          <include class="org.springframework.batch
    ➥.item.validator.ValidationException" />
        </skippable-exception-classes>
      </chunk>
      <no-rollback-exception-classes>
        <include class="org.springframework          Avoids rollbacks
    ➥.batch.item.validator.ValidationException"/>      on exception
      </no-rollback-exception-classes>
    </tasklet>
  </step>
</job>
```

Use the `no-rollback-exception-classes` feature only when you're sure that an exception can't corrupt a transaction; consider yourself warned!

You now know a lot about transaction management in Spring Batch and related configuration options. Robust batch applications sometimes need more than tuning. The next section explores transaction management patterns for real-world batch scenarios.

9.4   Transaction management patterns

This section covers commons challenges related to transaction management in batch applications. We look at guidelines and patterns using the Spring Framework and Spring Batch to overcome these challenges. By the end of this section, you'll have a clear understanding of global transactions (transactions spanning multiple resources). We also see how to deal with global transactions when a database and a JMS queue are involved.

9.4.1   Transactions spanning multiple resources: global transactions

Applications sometimes need to perform transactional operations spanning multiple resources. We call these types of transactions *global* or *distributed* transactions. For example, such resources can be two databases, or a database and a JMS queue. Such transactional operations must meet the ACID properties we previously listed.

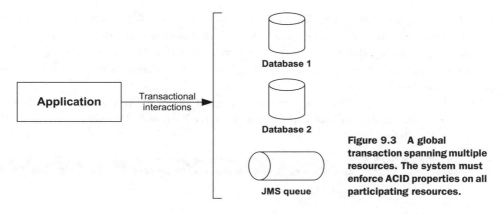

Figure 9.3   A global transaction spanning multiple resources. The system must enforce ACID properties on all participating resources.

In the case of two databases and the classic money transfer example, imagine that the credited account is in a first database and the debited account in a second database. The consistent state—*C* in *ACID*—spans both databases.

For a database and a JMS queue, the reception of the message and its processing must be atomic. We don't want to lose the message if the processing fails. Figure 9.3 shows an application that uses transactions over multiples resources.

LOCAL TRANSACTIONS

Global transactions are different from local transactions, where only one resource is involved and the application directly communicates with the resource to demarcate transactions, as shown in figure 9.4.

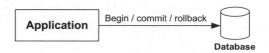

Figure 9.4   Local transactions between an application and a resource. The application directly communicates with the resource to demarcate transactions. Try to use local transactions as much as possible: they're fast, simple, and reliable.

Local transactions are the most common case. You should strive to use local transactions as much as possible because they're simple to set up, reliable, and fast. Always consider if you need a JMS queue or a second database in your application. The Spring Framework provides support for local transactions for various data access technologies such as JDBC, Hibernate, Java Persistence API (JPA), and JMS. Spring Batch benefits directly from this support.

TRANSACTION MANAGERS AND GLOBAL TRANSACTIONS

Support for global transactions is a different beast. Global transactions are too difficult for an application to deal with, so an application relies on a dedicated component called a *transaction manager*. This transaction manager component implements a special protocol called XA. In this case, a third-party component handles the transactions, so we call such transactions *managed transactions*. In Java, to perform global transactions using the XA protocol, we need the following:

1. *A JTA transaction manager*—It implements the Java Transaction API (JTA) specification, which requires the implementation of the XA protocol. Such a transaction manager is included in a Java EE application server or is available as a standalone component.

2. *XA-aware drivers*—The resources must provide XA-compliant drivers so the transaction manager can communicate with the resources using the XA protocol. Practically speaking, this implies the drivers provide implementations of interfaces like `javax.sql.XAConnection`. Thanks to these interfaces, the JTA transaction manager can enlist the resources in distributed transactions, as shown in figure 9.5.

All Java EE application servers include a JTA transaction manager (Glassfish, JBoss, WebSphere, and so on; forgive us if we don't list the others). Standalone JTA transaction managers also exist: Atomikos, Java Open Transaction Manager (JOTM), and the Bitronix Transaction Manager are some examples. You can plug in a standalone transaction manager in a web container like Tomcat and Jetty to provide JTA transactions. You can also use a standalone JTA transaction manager in a standalone process, like a batch application. Figure 9.5 shows an application using a JTA transaction manager to demarcate transactions spanning multiple resources.

If you want to use global transactions, the database or the JMS provider you're using must have an XA-compliant driver available. Most of the popular databases and JMS providers have XA drivers.

If an application wants to use global transactions, it doesn't need to write any global transaction–specific code: the transaction manager and the resources handle all the heavy lifting. The application only needs to use the JTA, or it can use an abstraction, like the one provided by Spring with the `PlatformTransactionManager` interface and the `JtaTransactionManager` implementation.

> **WARNING** Spring doesn't provide a JTA transaction manager. The Spring `JtaTransactionManager` class is only a bridge between Spring's transaction management support and a full-blown JTA transaction manager.

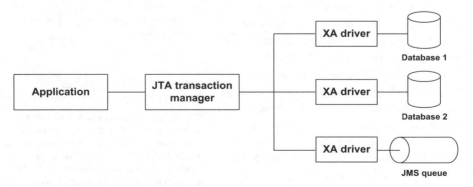

Figure 9.5 An application can use a JTA transaction manager to handle global transactions. The resources must provide XA drivers to communicate with the transaction manager using the XA protocol.

Make no mistake: global transactions are tricky. First, the configuration can be difficult. Second, some implementations (transaction managers and XA drivers) remain buggy. Third, XA is inherently slower than local transactions because the strong transactional guarantees it provides imply some overhead (the transaction manager and the resources need to maintain precise logs of what they're doing, for instance).

> **NOTE**   The source code for this chapter contains an example of using Spring Batch with a standalone JTA transaction manager (the Bitronix Transaction Manager). This is appropriate for integration tests. If your jobs are running inside a Java EE application server, consider using that server's transaction manager.

We're not saying that using JTA for global transactions is a bad solution. It provides strong guarantees, but they come at a price. JTA has the advantage of working in all cases, as long you meet its requirements: a transaction manager and XA drivers. XA isn't the only solution for global transactions. Depending on the context and resources involved, other techniques are viable alternatives to XA; they involve coding and usually perform better than XA.

   We examine the following two patterns: the *shared resource transaction* pattern when two databases are involved, and the *best effort* pattern when a database and a JMS queue are involved. You can use both in batch applications by leveraging the Spring Framework and Spring Batch.

9.4.2   *The shared resource transaction pattern*

Sometimes, the same physical resource backs multiple logical resources. For example, two JDBC `DataSources` can point to the same database instance. Using Oracle terminology, we say that you refer to schema B from schema A by using the same connection. You also need to define synonyms in schema A for schema B's tables. This enables real global transactions using the same mechanism as for local transactions. The overhead is a little more than for true local transactions but less than with XA.

   Figure 9.6 shows a use case of the shared resource pattern, where a database schema contains tables for a first application and Spring Batch's tables. Another database schema contains tables for a second application. A Spring Batch job executes against both applications' tables, but using only one connection, with the use of synonyms.

   Applying the shared resource transaction pattern can have some limitations, depending on the database engine. For

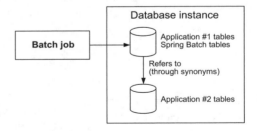

Figure 9.6   Use the shared resource transaction pattern when a common resource hosts the transactional resources. In this example, two Oracle database schemas exist in the same database instance. The first schema refers to the second schema's tables using synonyms. This allows the application to use local transactions.

The shared resource transaction pattern for batch metadata

Here's an example of the shared resource transaction pattern applied to Spring Batch. People are sometimes reluctant to host the batch execution metadata in the same database as the business data (they don't want to mix infrastructure and business concerns, which makes sense). Therefore, Spring Batch must span transactions over two databases for the execution metadata and the business data to ensure proper counts of skipped items, retries, and so on. You can use the shared resource transaction pattern to host batch execution metadata and business data in different databases. The pattern keeps your batch metadata and business data separate and properly synchronized, and you can stick to local transactions.

example, you may need to change some application or configuration code to add a schema prefix to refer explicitly to the correct schema.

Even when this pattern applies in a specific context, it generally provides better throughput and needs less configuration than an XA solution. Let's now see the best effort pattern, which applies to a database and a JMS queue.

9.4.3 *The best effort pattern with JMS*

Reading messages from a JMS queue and processing them in a database is a common scenario for a batch application. For example, our online store could accumulate orders in a JMS queue and read them periodically to update its inventory. This solution allows for full control over the processing of messages, including postponing processing to periods when the system isn't under heavy load. Note that this example solution doesn't exclude processing the messages as they're arriving by plugging in a queue listener. Figure 9.7 illustrates a chunk-oriented step that reads from a queue and updates a database during the writing phase.

WHAT CAN GO WRONG ON MESSAGE DELIVERY

This pattern requires two resources—a JMS queue and a database—and must be transactional. What can go wrong? Let's look at the two cases:

1 *Losing the message*—The application receives a message, acknowledges it, but fails to process it. The message is no longer on the queue, and there's been no processing in the database: the message is lost.

2 *Receiving and processing the same message twice*—The application receives a message and processes it, but the acknowledgment fails. The JMS broker delivers the message again, and the application processes it again. We call this a *duplicate message.*

Figure 9.7   The best effort pattern can apply when reading from a JMS queue and writing to a database.

Back to the inventory update example: losing messages means that orders arrive but the application doesn't update the inventory. The inventory ends up with more products than it should. Perhaps the company won't be able to provide customers with their ordered items. Processing orders multiple times means that the inventory runs out of products faster. Perhaps you'll lose orders because customers won't buy items that aren't virtually in stock. Perhaps the company will ask to resupply its stock when it doesn't need to. All these scenarios could put the company in a world of hurt. You want to avoid that.

JMS message acknowledgment

Acknowledging a message means that you tell the JMS provider that you processed the message you received. Once you acknowledge a message, the JMS provider removes it from the queue. JMS has two techniques to acknowledge messages: one is using JMS in acknowledgment mode, and the other is using a local JMS transaction. The two techniques are exclusive. JMS has three acknowledgment modes: acknowledge messages as soon as they're received (AUTO_ACKNOWLEDGE), let the application acknowledge messages explicitly (CLIENT_ACKNOWLEDGE), and lazily acknowledge the delivery of messages (DUPS_OK_ACKNOWLEDGE). This last acknowledgment mode is faster than the auto acknowledgment mode but can lead to duplicate messages. When using a local JMS transaction for acknowledgment, you start a transaction in a JMS session, receive one or more messages, process the messages, and commit the transaction. The commit tells the JMS broker to remove the messages from the queue.

We could use XA to avoid both problems, but remember that we can do without XA sometimes. Let's see how Spring helps us avoid losing messages.

AVOIDING LOSING MESSAGES WITH TRANSACTION SYNCHRONIZATION

To avoid losing messages, Spring synchronizes the local JMS transaction with the database transaction. Spring commits the JMS transaction immediately after the commit of the database transaction. We call this the best effort pattern. Spring does the synchronization transparently as long as you use the correct settings. This synchronization is a Spring feature; you can use it in any kind of application, and Spring Batch jobs are no exception. Figure 9.8 shows how Spring synchronizes a local JMS transaction with a chunk transaction.

To benefit from transaction synchronization, you need to tell Spring to use a local JMS transaction with a JmsTemplate to receive messages. Listing 9.2 sets up a JmsTemplate and a JMS item reader to use a local JMS transaction and so benefits from the automatic transaction synchronization feature. Note that the session-Transacted flag is set to true in the JmsTemplate, which instructs Spring to use a local JMS transaction.

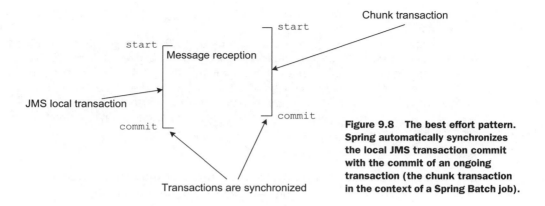

Figure 9.8 The best effort pattern. Spring automatically synchronizes the local JMS transaction commit with the commit of an ongoing transaction (the chunk transaction in the context of a Spring Batch job).

Listing 9.2   Using transaction synchronization to avoid losing messages

```
<bean id="jmsTemplate" class="org.springframework.jms.core.JmsTemplate">
  <property name="connectionFactory" ref="connectionFactory" />
  <property name="defaultDestination" ref="orderQueue" />
  <property name="receiveTimeout" value="100" />
  <property name="sessionTransacted" value="true" />
</bean>
<bean id="jmsReader" class="org.springframework.batch.item.jms
➥ .JmsItemReader">
  <property name="jmsTemplate" ref="jmsTemplate" />
</bean>
```

Remember that it's not only thanks to local JMS transactions that you avoid losing messages; it's also due to the transaction synchronization that Spring performs transparently.

The JmsTemplate uses the AUTO_ACKNOWLEDGE mode by default, but don't use this default; set the sessionTransacted flag to true to use local JMS transactions. Remember that the acknowledgment mode and the use of a JMS transaction are exclusive: you choose one or the other (JMS brokers usually ignore the acknowledgment mode when you ask for a transacted JMS session).

NOTE   When using a JMS item reader, remember to set the reader-transactional-queue flag to true in the chunk XML element.

Synchronizing the commit of the local JMS transaction with the database transaction commit ensures that the application acknowledges the message only if processing is successful. No more lost messages, no more lost inventory updates!

Does the best effort pattern apply only to JMS?

You can apply the best effort pattern to any resources that have transaction-like behavior. Spring Batch uses the best effort pattern when writing files. Do you remember the transactional flag in the FlatFileItemWriter? It applies to the buffer Spring Batch maintains for the output file.

> **(continued)**
> If this flag is set to true (the default), Spring Batch flushes the buffer only after the transaction commit (once it's sure the chunk completed successfully). It does this by synchronizing the flush with the database commit (it's the same when synchronizing a JMS commit with a database commit). The flush is the file equivalent of the transaction commit in a database. We resort to the best effort pattern for file writing because there's no support—like JTA—for true distributed transactions over a database and a file system.

But the best effort pattern isn't perfect, and the next subsection covers its shortcomings. Don't worry: we'll see techniques to address these shortcomings.

AVOIDING DUPLICATE MESSAGES

Let's consider the following vicious failure scenario. The JMS item reader reads messages, the item writer processes the chunk, and Spring Batch commits the chunk transaction. The JMS transaction is then committed because it's synchronized with the chunk transaction commit. What happens if the JMS transaction commit fails because of a network failure? Remember what a JMS transaction rollback means for the JMS broker: the application says the processing of the messages failed. The JMS broker then puts back the messages read during the transaction on the queue. The messages are then ready to be read and processed again. Figure 9.9 illustrates this failure scenario, where the best effort pattern shows its limitation.

The best effort pattern isn't bulletproof because of the small window it leaves open between the commit of the two transactions. You won't lose messages, thanks to the best effort pattern, but you still need to deal with duplicate messages. Let's now see two solutions to deal with duplicate messages.

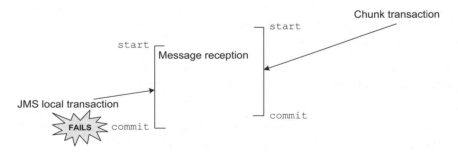

Figure 9.9   When the best effort pattern fails. The database commit works, but the JMS commit fails. JMS puts the message back on the queue, and the batch job processes it again. Even if such duplicate messages are rare, they can corrupt data because of repeated processing.

9.4.4 *Handling duplicate messages with manual detection*

When you use the best effort pattern, you need to avoid processing duplicate messages. This is easily doable, but you need some extra code in your application. This extra code has two parts:

1 *Tracking messages during processing*—The tracking mechanism can be a dedicated database table that flags messages as processed. Tracking must be part of the database transaction.

2 *Detecting previously processed messages and filtering them out*—The application must perform this check before processing by using a tracking system.

You have everything you need to build such a tracking system in Spring Batch. In a chunk-oriented step, the item writer processes messages by updating the database and takes care of tracking by adding a row in the tracking table. An item processor is in charge of filtering out duplicate, already-processed messages by checking the tracking table. Remember that an item processor can transform read items before Spring Batch passes them to an item writer, but it can also filter out items by returning null. Figure 9.10 shows a chunk-oriented step that reads JMS messages, filters out duplicate messages, and implements processing in the writing phase.

Let's get back to the inventory example to see how to implement the detection of duplicate messages.

JMS MESSAGES AND DOMAIN OBJECTS

The online store accumulates orders in a JMS queue, and a batch job reads the messages to update the inventory table. A JMS message contains an Order, which itself contains a list of OrderItems. The following listing shows the definition of the Order and OrderItem classes.

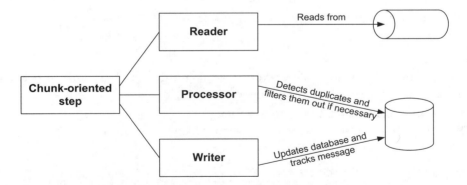

Figure 9.10 Detecting duplicate messages and filtering them out with an item processor in a chunk-oriented job. The item writer must track whether a processor processed each message. The best effort pattern combined with this filtering technique prevents a processor from processing duplicate messages.

Listing 9.3   A JMS message containing an `Order` object

```
package com.manning.sbia.ch09.domain;

import java.io.Serializable;
import java.util.Collections;
import java.util.List;

public class Order implements Serializable {

  private String orderId;
  private List<OrderItem> items;

  public Order(String orderId, List<OrderItem> items) {
    this.orderId = orderId;
    this.items = Collections.unmodifiableList(items);
  }

  public String getOrderId() { return orderId; }

  public List<OrderItem> getItems() { return items; }

  (...)

}

package com.manning.sbia.ch09.domain;

import java.io.Serializable;

public class OrderItem implements Serializable {

  private String productId;
  private short quantity;

  public OrderItem(String productId, short quantity) {
    this.productId = productId;
    this.quantity = quantity;
  }

  public String getProductId() { return productId; }

  public short getQuantity() { return quantity; }

  (...)

}
```

equals and
hashCode
methods
omitted for
brevity

You now know what kind of objects you're dealing with. Let's look at the processing by implementing the corresponding item writer.

WRITING AND TRACKING ITEMS IN AN ITEM WRITER

The following listing shows how the `InventoryOrderWriter` processes and then tracks orders.

Listing 9.4   Processing and tracking orders in an item writer

```
package com.manning.sbia.ch09.batch;

import java.util.Date;
import java.util.List;
import javax.sql.DataSource;
import org.springframework.batch.item.ItemWriter;
import org.springframework.jdbc.core.JdbcTemplate;
```

```
import com.manning.sbia.ch09.domain.Order;
import com.manning.sbia.ch09.domain.OrderItem;

public class InventoryOrderWriter implements ItemWriter<Order> {

  private JdbcTemplate jdbcTemplate;

  public InventoryOrderWriter(DataSource dataSource) {
    this.jdbcTemplate = new JdbcTemplate(dataSource);
  }

  @Override
  public void write(List<? extends Order> orders) throws Exception {
    for(Order order: orders) {
      updateInventory(order);
      track(order);                                       Tracks        Processes
    }                                                  2  order      1  order
  }

  private void updateInventory(Order order) {
    for(OrderItem item : order.getItems()) {
      jdbcTemplate.update(
        "update inventory set quantity = quantity - ? where product_id = ?",
        item.getQuantity(),item.getProductId()
      );
    }
  }

  private void track(Order order) {
    jdbcTemplate.update(
      "insert into inventory_order "+                        3  Uses dedicated
      "(order_id,processing_date) values (?,?)",                table for tracking
      order.getOrderId(),new Date()
    );
  }

}
```

For each order, the InventoryOrderWriter first handles the processing ❶, which consists of removing the items from the inventory. Then, the writer tracks that the order has been processed ❷. To track the processing, the system uses a dedicated database table to store the order ID ❸.

> **NOTE** You're lucky in this case to have a unique business ID. If you don't have access to a unique ID for your custom processing, use the JMS message ID.

You also store the timestamp of the processing. This can be useful to purge the table from time to time.

You now have the first part of your mechanism to detect duplicate messages. The second part detects redelivered messages and checks to see if the job has already processed a redelivered message.

DETECTING AND FILTERING OUT DUPLICATE MESSAGES WITH AN ITEM PROCESSOR
The following listing shows the item processor code that detects and filters out duplicate messages.

Listing 9.5 Detecting and filtering out duplicate messages with an item processor

```
package com.manning.sbia.ch09.batch;

import javax.jms.JMSException;
import javax.jms.Message;
import javax.jms.ObjectMessage;
import javax.sql.DataSource;
import org.springframework.batch.item.ItemProcessor;
import org.springframework.jdbc.core.JdbcTemplate;
import org.springframework.jms.support.converter
    .MessageConversionException;
import com.manning.sbia.ch09.domain.Order;

public class DuplicateOrderItemProcessor implements
    ItemProcessor<Message, Order> {

  private JdbcTemplate jdbcTemplate;

  public DuplicateOrderItemProcessor(DataSource dataSource) {
    this.jdbcTemplate = new JdbcTemplate(dataSource);
  }

  @Override
  public Order process(Message message) throws Exception {      ❶ Checks if JMS
    Order order = extractOrder(message);                            redelivered a
    if(message.getJMSRedelivered()) {                               message
      if(orderAlreadyProcessed(order)) {             ❷ Checks if
        order = null;                                    message
      }                                                  already
    }                                                  ❷ processed
    return order;
  }

  private Order extractOrder(Message message) {
    if(message instanceof ObjectMessage) {
      try {
        return (Order) ((ObjectMessage) message).getObject();
      } catch (JMSException e) {
        throw new MessageConversionException("couldn't extract order", e);
      }
    }
    return null;
  }

  private boolean orderAlreadyProcessed(Order order) {
    return jdbcTemplate.queryForInt("select count(1) "+          ❸ Queries
    " from inventory_order where order_id = ?",                     tracking table
      order.getOrderId()) > 0;
  }

}
```

When a JMS broker redelivers a message, it sets the message object's redelivered flag
to true. You use this flag ❶ to avoid querying the database, an optimization. If the
message isn't a redelivery, you let it go to the writer. In the case of a redelivered message, you check ❷ whether you've already processed the message. The check consists

of querying the tracking table to see if it contains the order ID ❸. The detection of a duplicate is simple and cheap, and duplicate messages are rare. This solution also performs better than the equivalent using XA.

CONFIGURING A JOB TO DETECT DUPLICATE MESSAGES

The following listing shows the relevant portion of the job configuration (we skipped the infrastructure configuration for brevity).

Listing 9.6   Configuring the duplicates detection job

```
<job id="updateInventoryJob"
    xmlns="http://www.springframework.org/schema/batch">
  <step id="updateInventoryStep">
    <tasklet>
      <chunk reader="reader" processor="processor" writer="writer"
        commit-interval="100"
        reader-transactional-queue="true" />
    </tasklet>
  </step>
</job>

<bean id="reader" class="org.springframework.batch.item.jms.JmsItemReader">
  <property name="jmsTemplate" ref="jmsTemplate" />
  <property name="itemType"
          value="javax.jms.Message" />
</bean>

<bean id="jmsTemplate" class="org.springframework.jms.core.JmsTemplate">
  <property name="connectionFactory" ref="connectionFactory" />
  <property name="defaultDestination" ref="orderQueue" />
  <property name="receiveTimeout" value="100" />
  <property name="sessionTransacted" value="true" />
</bean>

<bean id="processor"
      class="com.manning.sbia.ch09.batch.DuplicateOrderItemProcessor">
  <constructor-arg ref="dataSource" />
</bean>

<bean id="writer" class="com.manning.sbia.ch09.batch.InventoryOrderWriter">
  <constructor-arg ref="dataSource" />
</bean>
```

❶ Specifies reader is transactional

❷ Passes plain JMS message to item processor

❸ Uses local JMS transaction

This configuration is typical for a chunk-oriented step, but it contains a couple of subtleties. Note the use of the `reader-transactional-queue` attribute ❶. This flag should always be set to `true` for a JMS item reader. At ❷, you ask the JMS item reader to pass the plain JMS message—no extraction of the body—to the item processor. Remember that you need the JMS message in the item processor to check the redelivered flag. Because you want to use the best effort pattern, you use local JMS transactions with the JMS template for message acknowledgment ❸.

That's it; you detect duplicate messages with your filtering item processor. By also using the best effort pattern, you enforce atomicity in your global transaction without using XA. This solution is straightforward to implement thanks to Spring Batch and the Spring Framework, and it avoids the overhead of an XA solution. Your inventory is now safe!

Next, we see how to deal with duplicate messages without any extra code.

9.4.5   *Handling duplicate messages with idempotency*

In the inventory update example, you want to avoid duplicate messages because you can't afford to process messages multiple times. You need this functionality because processing removes ordered items from the inventory. What if processing a message multiple times is harmless? When an application can apply an operation multiple times without changing the result, we say it's *idempotent*.

WHAT IS IDEMPOTENCY?

Idempotency is an interesting property for message processing. It means that we don't care about duplicate messages! Always think about idempotency when designing a system: idempotent operations can make a system much simpler and more robust.

IDEMPOTENT OPERATIONS IN A BATCH JOB

Let's see an example of an idempotent operation in the online store application. The shipping application—a separate application—sends a message on a JMS queue for each shipped order. The online store keeps track of the state of orders to inform customers of their orders. A batch job reads messages from the shipped order queue and updates the online store database accordingly. Figure 9.11 illustrates this batch job.

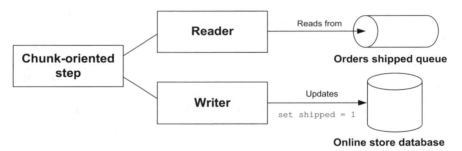

Figure 9.11   When performing an idempotent operation on the reception of a message, there's no need to detect duplicate messages. The best effort pattern combined with an idempotent operation is an acceptable solution.

The processing is simple: it consists only of setting the shipped flag to `true`. The following listing shows the item writer in charge of updating shipped orders.

Listing 9.7   Updating the shipped order (idempotent processing)

```
package com.manning.sbia.ch09.batch;

import java.sql.PreparedStatement;
import java.sql.SQLException;
import java.util.List;
```

```
import javax.sql.DataSource;
import org.springframework.batch.item.ItemWriter;
import org.springframework.jdbc.core.BatchPreparedStatementSetter;
import org.springframework.jdbc.core.JdbcTemplate;
import com.manning.sbia.ch09.domain.Order;

public class ShippedOrderWriter implements ItemWriter<Order> {

  private JdbcTemplate jdbcTemplate;

  public ShippedOrderWriter(DataSource dataSource) {
    this.jdbcTemplate = new JdbcTemplate(dataSource);
  }

  @Override
  public void write(final List<? extends Order> items) throws Exception {
    jdbcTemplate.batchUpdate(
      "update orders set shipped = ?",
      new BatchPreparedStatementSetter() {

        @Override
        public void setValues(PreparedStatement ps,
                              int i)
              throws SQLException {            Performs
          ps.setBoolean(1, true);            idempotent
        }                                     update

        @Override
        public int getBatchSize() {
          return items.size();
        }
      }
    );
  }
}
```

Because the message processing is idempotent—setting the shipped flag to true in the database—you don't need to handle duplicate messages. You can kiss goodbye any tracking system and filtering item processors. This only works for idempotent operations!

This completes our coverage of transaction management patterns. You now know how to implement global transactions in Spring Batch. A use case must meet specific conditions to apply these patterns successfully, and it's up to you to design your system in a manner suitable to apply these patterns. We saw how the shared transaction resource pattern applies when a transaction spans two schemas that belong to the same database instance. Spring implements the best effort pattern—synchronizing the local JMS transaction with the database transaction commit—but you need to be careful using it. You must detect duplicate messages by using a tracking system if the message processing isn't idempotent. You don't have to worry if the processing is idempotent.

Transaction management in batch application holds no secrets for you anymore!

9.5   *Summary*

Transaction management is a key part of job robustness and reliability. Because errors happen, you need to know how Spring Batch handles transactions, figure out when a failure can corrupt data, and learn to use appropriate settings. Remember the following about transaction management in batch applications, and don't hesitate to go back to the corresponding sections for more details:

- Spring Batch handles transactions at the step level. A tasklet is transactional; Spring Batch creates and commits a transaction for each chunk in a chunk-oriented step.

- Be careful with declarative transaction management (with XML or the `Transactional` annotation); it can interfere with Spring Batch and produce unexpected results.

- When a batch application interacts with more than one transactional resource and these interactions must be globally coordinated, use JTA or one of the patterns we've discussed.

- JTA is a bulletproof solution for global transactions, but it can be complex to set up and adds overhead.

- The alternative techniques for handling global transactions without JTA work only in specific contexts and can add extra logic to the application.

With the previous chapter on bulletproofing jobs and this chapter on transaction management, you now know the techniques to write truly bulletproof jobs.

Remember an interesting feature Spring Batch provides: skipping. In a chunk-oriented step, Spring Batch can skip exceptions to avoid failing a whole step. When the step reaches the skip limit, Spring Batch fails the step. Does Spring Batch cause the failure of the whole job? By default, yes, but you can override this behavior. Instead of failing the whole job immediately, for example, you can execute a tasklet to create and email a report on the execution of the job to an operator. If you're interested in discovering how you can choose between different paths for steps in a Spring Batch job, please continue on to the next chapter, which covers how Spring Batch handles the execution of steps inside a job.

Part 3

Advanced Spring Batch

The previous chapters provide enough information to write complete batch applications using Spring Batch. This final part guides you through advanced techniques and scenarios to make your batch architecture even more powerful.

If your batch jobs are made of complex, nonlinear flows of steps, chapter 10 is definitely for you. It shows you how to decide which step to execute next when a step ends. It also explains how to transmit data between steps and interact with a Spring Batch execution context.

Chapter 11 takes a Spring Batch job on a tour around the world of enterprise integration. Don't think batch jobs are isolated pieces of software running alone at night. In this chapter, a batch job meets exciting technologies like REST and Spring Integration to cover a real-world enterprise integration scenario with Spring technologies.

Is there a more beautiful sight than green lights saying that all your job executions are successful? Chapter 12 guides you through different techniques to monitor your Spring Batch architecture: building your own interface from Spring Batch monitoring components, using JMX, and using the Spring Batch Admin web console.

Chapter 13 presents techniques to make your job execution scale. You'll discover which strategies Spring Batch provides to parallelize job executions on multiple threads and even on multiple nodes, thanks to JMS and Spring Integration.

Chapter 14 covers testing. You can test pretty much everything in a Spring Batch job: readers, writers, converters, listeners, and so on. This chapter shows you why and how to test your Spring Batch jobs using unit and integration tests.

Following part 3 are two appendixes: one to set up your development with the SpringSource Tool Suite and Maven, and another to configure the Spring Batch Admin web console.

Controlling execution 10

This chapter covers

- Controlling a job's execution path
- Sharing data between job steps at runtime
- Externalizing job definitions for reuse
- Choosing how to stop a job after executing a step

Writing batch applications isn't an easy task. Previous chapters covered how to read and write data efficiently with Spring Batch. These chapters also covered error handling during processing by skipping errors or retrying operations transparently. This chapter covers mastering job execution with Spring Batch. What do we mean by job execution?

A job consists of steps, and *execution* refers to the sequence of steps that run when a job starts. In simple jobs, the sequence of steps is linear. In complex jobs, execution can take multiple paths, and the sequence is no longer linear. Figure 10.1 shows the structure of a simple, linear job and a more complex, nonlinear job.

Because batch jobs must run automatically, without human intervention, we need a way to configure a step sequence so that a job knows which step to execute next.

In an ideal world, steps are independent of each other: they don't need to share data at runtime. This happens when the execution of a first step has no impact on

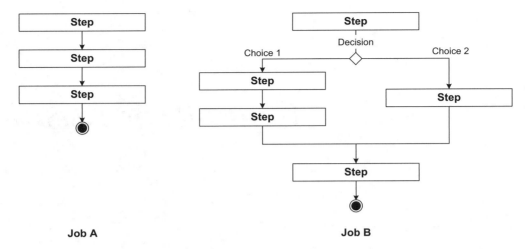

Figure 10.1   Jobs with linear and nonlinear flows. Job A, on the left, has a simple linear flow. Job B, on the right, isn't linear because there are multiple execution paths.

the execution of a second step. A job is simpler to implement when it's made of independent steps. You can easily test the steps independently, and you can even think about reusing them in another job. Having only independent steps isn't always possible: a time will come when a step needs data computed in a previous step.

If your jobs require complex flows or the need to share data between steps, this chapter helps you to fulfill these requirements. You're on your way to learning how to master complex execution scenarios in your batch applications. The next section gives a detailed overview of the features covered in this chapter. We base this overview on a real-world scenario: an advanced version of the import products job for our online store application.

10.1   *A complex flow in the online store application*

The flow of a job isn't always simple. In chapter 1, we introduced our online store example application, whose main job is to import products into a database. The job is simple: a first step decompresses a ZIP archive, and a chunk-oriented step reads the extracted file in order to import it in the database. Even though the job is simple, it's realistic; but not all jobs are that simple. Figure 10.2 shows an advanced version of our import products job.

This new version of the job is more demanding in terms of features: it has a more complex flow, one step requires data computed in a previous step, and the job execution can end after the first step if there's no ZIP to download (whereas a job usually completes with the end of the last step). Table 10.1 gives a detailed view of this new version of the import products job and lists the corresponding Spring Batch features used to fulfill its requirements.

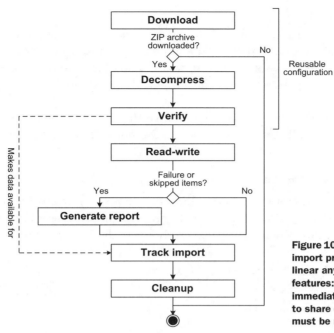

Figure 10.2 In this advanced version of the import products job, the flow of steps isn't linear anymore and requires more complex features: job execution can end immediately after the first step, steps need to share data, and part of the configuration must be reusable by other jobs.

Table 10.1 Requirements and features of the new version of the import products job

Requirement	Description	Spring Batch feature
Nonlinear flow	If the job skips lines in the read or write step or if the step fails, a report must be generated by a dedicated step.	Use conditional flow and custom exit statuses.
Sharing data	A step extracts metadata, and another step needs it to track the import.	Use execution context and data holder.
Reuse of configuration	Part of the job configuration should be reusable as-is by other jobs.	Use externalized flows and jobs.
Early completion	If the job didn't download an archive, the job should complete immediately.	Use XML elements end, stop, and fail.

That's many new requirements! Now, those are common requirements in batch applications, and, good news, Spring Batch has everything in its toolbox to fulfill them.

NOTE We cover these features separately for clarity, but you can combine them. This chapter focuses on job execution, so don't be surprised if you don't find details on step implementations (tasklets, readers, writers, and so on).

Now that you have an overview of the new features of our advanced version of the import products jobs, let's start with creating nonlinear flows.

10.2   *Driving the flow of a job*

Not all jobs are linear: their steps don't always execute one after the other in a simple sequence. Jobs can take multiple paths: depending on the result of a step, you can choose to execute one step or another. In our new version of the import products job, the job executes an optional step to generate a report if something goes wrong in the read-write step.

This section covers how Spring Batch lets you configure such nonlinear jobs. By the end of this section, you'll know how to escape the simple linear job scenario and create complex flows for your jobs.

10.2.1   *Choosing one path over another*

Until now, we've focused on jobs with linear flows: the steps execute one after another in a linear fashion. For linear flows, only the next attribute in the step element needs to be set and must indicate which step is next, as shown in the following snippet:

```
<job id="importProducts">
  <step id="decompress" next="readWriteProducts">
    <tasklet>(...)</tasklet>
  </step>
  <step id="readWriteProducts" next="clean">
    <tasklet>(...)</tasklet>
  </step>
  <step id="clean">
    <tasklet>(...)</tasklet>
  </step>
</job>
```

Uses next attribute for transition

Note that the last step in a job doesn't need a next attribute: step completion indicates the end of the job execution. How would we define a nonlinear flow? Imagine that you don't want the job to fail when the read-write step fails; instead, you want to generate a report and then execute a cleanup step. Figure 10.3 illustrates this flow.

To configure a nonlinear flow like the one in figure 10.3, use the nested next element in the step. The condition of the transition is set with the attribute on. The to attribute points to the next step to execute, as shown in the following listing.

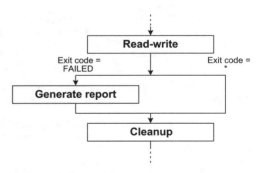

Figure 10.3   A nonlinear flow. If the read-write step fails, the execution shouldn't end; instead, the job should generate a report. For all other cases, the execution proceeds directly to the cleanup step.

Listing 10.1   Configuring a nonlinear flow

```
<job id="importProducts">
  <step id="decompress" next="readWriteProducts">
```

```
    <tasklet>(...)</tasklet>
  </step>
  <step id="readWriteProducts" next="clean">
    <tasklet>(...)</tasklet>
    <next on="*" to="clean" />
    <next on="FAILED" to="generateReport"/>
  </step>
  <step id="generateReport" next="clean">
    <tasklet>(...)</tasklet>
  </step>
  <step id="clean">
    <tasklet>(...)</tasklet>
  </step>
</job>
```

**Generates report
in case of failure**

What is the value of the on attribute in this example? It matches the exit status of the step (we'll see more on the exit status concept in the upcoming subsection). You can use exact values in the on attribute and special characters to define patterns. Table 10.2 shows examples of exact values and the special characters Spring Batch accepts.

Table 10.2   Syntax for the step attribute on

Value/special character	Description	Examples
String	Exact value of the step exit status	COMPLETED FAILED
*	Matches 0 or more characters	* (matches any value) COMPLETED* (matches COMPLETED and COMPLETED WITH SKIPS)
?	Matches exactly one character	C?T (matches CAT but not COUNT)

Note that Spring Batch is smart enough to order transitions from the most to the least specific automatically. This means the order of the next tags in the configuration doesn't matter; you can define transitions with wildcards first (less specific) and transitions with exact values last (more specific).

> **WARNING**   Be careful when transitioning to a step using the * special character. If the * matches the FAILED exit status (because there's no more specific match), the next step is executed even if the current step fails. Perhaps this isn't what you want; you may want to fail the job execution when a step fails. When using conditional transitions, you must handle failed steps yourself. Refer to section 10.5 to see how to cause a job execution to fail in a transition decision.

You can now configure conditional execution by matching the exit status of a step with the next step to execute. What exactly is the exit status, and what kind of value can it take?

10.2.2 Batch status vs. exit status: what's the deal?

Spring Batch uses two concepts to represent the status of an execution: the batch status and the exit status. Both step execution and job execution have their own batch and exit statuses property. The batch status describes the status of the execution of a job or a step. The exit status represents the status of the job/step once the execution is finished. The difference between both statuses isn't obvious, mainly because Spring Batch defines both as a status.

> **BATCH STATUS VS. EXIT STATUS**   The batch status represents the status of an execution, whereas the exit status is more like a literal exit status.

Table 10.3 lists other differences between the batch status and exit status.

Table 10.3   Differences between batch status and exit status

Status	Type	Description
Batch	`BatchStatus*` (enumeration)	Enumerates a finite set of statuses. A batch status is persisted in the batch metadata as the overall status of a job or step execution.
Exit	`ExitStatus*` (class)	Defines constants values. Also defines custom values and descriptions. An exit status is persisted in the batch metadata as the exit status of a job or step execution. Used for transition between steps.

* Defined in the org.springframework.batch.core package

To see the values a batch status can take, look at the `BatchStatus` enumeration; example values are `COMPLETED`, `STARTED`, `FAILED`, and `STOPPED`. The `ExitStatus` class has predefined values defined as constants. `ExitStatus` values roughly match those of the `BatchStatus`, but because it's a class, you can define your own instances. What's the point of defining your own `ExitStatus`? You can define your own exit statuses to create a set of options to manage your job flows. Remember that a transition bases its decision on the value of an exit status. For complex conditional flows, you can use your own exit status instances to choose where to go next. You aren't limited to predefined values, and you can use exit statuses like `COMPLETED WITH SKIPS`, which carry more semantics than `COMPLETED`.

If you're now asking, "How can I choose the exit status returned by a step?" and "How can I use this exit status to decide which step to execute next?" then read the next section.

10.2.3 Choosing the exit status

Let's go back to the import products job and imagine you want to generate a report if the read-write step skips input lines. Figure 10.4 illustrates this conditional flow.

You configure the transition decision using the `next` element and the `on/to` attributes, but there's no ready-to-use exit status to express that the step skipped some items. Wouldn't it be nice to configure the transition as follows?

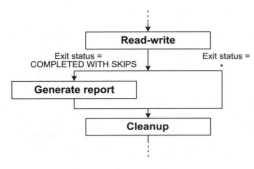

Figure 10.4 A nonlinear flow using a custom exit status. Custom exit statuses carry more semantics than standard exit statuses (COMPLETED, FAILED, and so on), which is helpful in making complex flow decisions.

```
<step id="readWrite">
  <tasklet>(...)</tasklet>
  <next on="COMPLETED WITH SKIPS" to="generateReport" />
  <next on="*" to="clean" />
</step>
```

How can you get a COMPLETED WITH SKIPS exit status at the end of this step? The solution is to execute code immediately after the execution of the step. This code checks the number of skipped items and returns the appropriate custom exit status. You have two ways to do this; the first is by using a step execution listener.

EMBEDDING THE DECISION LOGIC IN A STEP EXECUTION LISTENER

Spring Batch lets the developer plug in listeners to react to events during job execution. One of these listeners is the step execution listener: Spring Batch calls it before and after the execution of a step. The after-execution callback is interesting in our case because it has access to the step execution object and can decide which exit status to return. By using this after-execution callback, you see the step execution—skipped items or not—and return a custom exit status. The job then uses this custom exit status to decide which step to execute next. Figure 10.5 illustrates this mechanism.

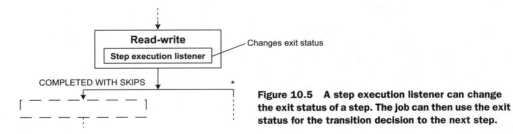

Figure 10.5 A step execution listener can change the exit status of a step. The job can then use the exit status for the transition decision to the next step.

You have your solution using a custom exit status—COMPLETED WITH SKIPS—to decide whether or not to generate a report. The following listing shows the step execution listener that chooses which exit status to return.

Listing 10.2 Choosing the exit status for a step with a step execution listener

```
package com.manning.sbia.ch10.listener;

import org.springframework.batch.core.ExitStatus;
import org.springframework.batch.core.StepExecution;
```

```
import org.springframework.batch.core.StepExecutionListener;

public class SkippedItemsStepListener implements StepExecutionListener {

  @Override
  public void beforeStep(StepExecution stepExecution) { }

  @Override
  public ExitStatus afterStep(StepExecution stepExecution) {
    if(!ExitStatus.FAILED.equals(
           stepExecution.getExitStatus()) &&
        stepExecution.getSkipCount() > 0) {
      return new ExitStatus("COMPLETED WITH SKIPS");
    } else {
      return stepExecution.getExitStatus();
    }
  }

}
```

Returns custom status for skipped items

Returns default status

Because the listener has access to the StepExecution, it knows if Spring Batch skipped items during processing and decides which exit status to return. Note that the listener returns the default exit status if there are no skipped items.

The following listing shows the corresponding XML configuration that plugs in the listener and specifies the transitions.

Listing 10.3 Conditional flow with custom exit status using a step execution listener

```
<bean id="skippedItemsStepListener"
      class="com.manning.sbia.ch10.listener
   .SkippedItemsStepListener" />

<job id="importProductsJob"
     xmlns="http://www.springframework.org/schema/batch">
  (...)
  <step id="readWriteStep">
    <tasklet>
      <chunk reader="reader" writer="writer"
             commit-interval="100" skip-limit="5">
        <skippable-exception-classes>
          <include class="org.springframework.batch.item.file
   .FlatFileParseException" />
        </skippable-exception-classes>
      </chunk>
      <listeners>
        <listener ref="skippedItemsStepListener" />
      </listeners>
    </tasklet>
    <next on="COMPLETED WITH SKIPS"
          to="generateReportStep" />
    <next on="*" to="cleanStep" />
  </step>
  <step id="generateReportStep" next="cleanStep">
    <tasklet>(...)</tasklet>
  </step>
  <step id="cleanStep">
```

Declares listener bean

Registers listener

Defines transition decisions

```
    <tasklet>(...)</tasklet>
  </step>
</job>
```

That's it! With a step execution listener, you can cause a step execution to return a custom exit status. Using this exit status, you can configure which step the job should execute next. This allows for nonlinear job flows.

Using a step execution listener is one solution to using custom exit statuses to control job flow, but Spring Batch also provides a dedicated component to determine the flow of a job: the job execution decider.

EMBEDDING THE DECISION LOGIC IN A JOB EXECUTION DECIDER

Spring Batch defines the `JobExecutionDecider` interface to control the flow of a job. Whereas a step execution listener is a generic-purpose component—among others—that you can use to set the exit status of a step, the only goal in the life of a job execution decider is to return an exit status. Contrary to a step execution listener, a job execution decider isn't part of a step; it's a dedicated component in the job flow, as illustrated in figure 10.6.

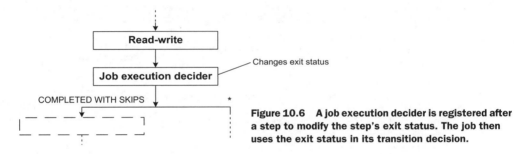

Figure 10.6 A job execution decider is registered after a step to modify the step's exit status. The job then uses the exit status in its transition decision.

Let's look at our flow requirement to illustrate the use of a job execution decider: you want the job to transition to generate a report step if the read-write step skipped items.

The following listing shows a `JobExecutionDecider` implementation that checks if the read-write step skipped items and returns an appropriate exit status.

Listing 10.4 Controlling job flow with a job execution decider

```
package com.manning.sbia.ch10.decider;

import org.springframework.batch.core.ExitStatus;
import org.springframework.batch.core.JobExecution;
import org.springframework.batch.core.StepExecution;
import org.springframework.batch.core.job.flow.FlowExecutionStatus;
import org.springframework.batch.core.job.flow.JobExecutionDecider;

public class SkippedItemsDecider implements JobExecutionDecider {

  @Override
  public FlowExecutionStatus decide(JobExecution jobExecution,
      StepExecution stepExecution) {
```

```
    if(!ExitStatus.FAILED.equals(
        stepExecution.getExitStatus()) &&
      stepExecution.getSkipCount() > 0) {
      return new FlowExecutionStatus(
        "COMPLETED WITH SKIPS"
      );
    } else {
      return new FlowExecutionStatus(
        jobExecution.getExitStatus().toString()
      );
    }
  }
}
```

Returns custom status for skipped items

Returns default status

A `JobExecutionDecider` returns a `FlowExecutionStatus`. This data structure is roughly equivalent to a plain `ExitStatus`. The job bases its transition decision on the string value used to create the `FlowExecutionStatus`.

You register a job execution decider as a standalone component, in the flow of the job, as shown in the following listing.

Listing 10.5   Configuring a conditional flow with a job execution listener

```
<bean id="skippedItemsDecider"
    class="com.manning.sbia.ch10.decider
  .SkippedItemsDecider" />

<job id="importProductsJob"
    xmlns="http://www.springframework.org/schema/batch">
  (...)
  <step id="readWriteStep" next="skippedItemsDecision">
    <tasklet>
      <chunk reader="reader" writer="writer"
          commit-interval="100" skip-limit="5">
        <skippable-exception-classes>
          <include class="org.springframework.batch.item.file
  .FlatFileParseException" />
        </skippable-exception-classes>
      </chunk>
    </tasklet>
  </step>
  <decision id="skippedItemsDecision"
          decider="skippedItemsDecider">
    <next on="COMPLETED WITH SKIPS"
        to="generateReportStep" />
    <next on="*" to="cleanStep" />
  </decision>
  <step id="generateReportStep" next="cleanStep">
    <tasklet>(...)</tasklet>
  </step>
  <step id="cleanStep">
    <tasklet>(...)</tasklet>
  </step>
</job>
```

Declares decider bean

Transitions to decider

Defines transition decisions

Listing 10.5 shows that a job execution decider has its own place in the definition of the flow. The decider has an ID, and the step transitions to it by using this ID in its `next` attribute.

You achieve the same goal with a job execution decider as with a step execution listener: you set the exit status by querying the execution of the previous step. By using transition decisions in the XML configuration, you can define which step to execute next. Because you have two ways of achieving the same goal, let's define some guidelines to help you decide when to use each solution.

STEP EXECUTION LISTENER OR JOB EXECUTION DECIDER?

Let's be frank: the choice you're about to make between a step execution listener and a job execution decider for your conditional flow won't change your life. The solutions are quite similar. Here are some considerations to help you choose the appropriate solution depending on your context:

- *Using the step execution listener affects the batch metadata of the step execution.* If you return a custom exit status in the step execution listener, Spring Batch persists it in the batch metadata. This can be helpful for monitoring. Spring Batch doesn't track anything about a job execution decider in the batch metadata.

- *Late binding isn't available with a job execution decider.* You can't refer to job parameters in the XML configuration when using a job execution decider (by using the `#{jobParameters['someKey']}` Spring Expression Language [SpEL] syntax). Because a step execution listener is part of the step execution, this feature is available for its configuration.

- *The usefulness of a job execution decider is obvious and makes the configuration more readable.* As soon as you see a job execution decider in a job configuration, you know that there's logic defining a conditional flow. This isn't as obvious with a step execution listener, which you can use for other purposes. By using a job execution decider over a step execution listener, you follow the principle of least astonishment.

You know now how to control the flow of steps inside a job. A job can base its transition decisions on the current execution, like skipped items in the previous step, or on anything available in the execution context. The next section expands on job executions by exploring how steps can share data, so that a step can access and use data computed in any previous step.

10.3 *Sharing data between steps*

In a Spring Batch job, each step has its own task to fulfill. To know what it must do, a step can use job parameters. For example, the decompress step uses a ZIP archive location parameter to know which file to decompress. In this case, you know the required input for the step when you launch the job. Sometimes, you can't know the inputs for a step when the job starts because a previous step must compute these inputs. In such circumstances, the calculating step and the receiving step must find a way to share data.

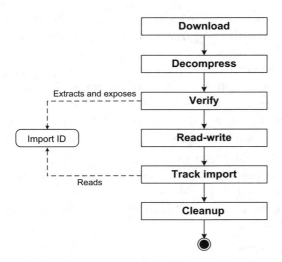

Figure 10.7 The verify step checks the integrity of the extracted files and extracts import metadata needed by the track import step. These steps need a way to communicate this information.

Let's use the import products job as an example. Imagine that the ZIP archive processed by the job contains not only a flat file with the products to import but also a text file that provides information about the import: the ID and date of the import, a list of input files in the archive, and a digest for each archived file used to validate it. Let's call this information the import metadata. Figure 10.7 shows the job flow and the information that the two steps need to share.

The job starts with the decompress step. The second step checks the integrity of the decompressed files using the import metadata. Notice the track import step after the read-write step: it stores in the database confirmation that the job processed this particular import. To do so, the track import step needs the import ID, which is read previously by the verify step. This import ID is the data you want to share between steps.

We cover different techniques to share this import ID between the two steps. This example is simple, but the principles remain identical with more complex data structures.

> **WARNING** As soon as steps share data, that data couples the steps to each other. Strive to make steps as independent as possible. If you can't make them independent, use the techniques presented here. You should consider data sharing as a fallback pattern when you can't build independent steps.

You can share data in batch applications in many ways, and you can implement them all using Spring Batch. For example, you can use a database as a shared repository between steps: a step stores shared data in the database, and the receiving step reads them from the database. Such a solution is straightforward to implement with Spring Batch using custom tasklets or chunk-oriented steps, but that's not what we show here. This section covers techniques that leverage special features of Spring Batch and of the Spring Framework. Table 10.4 lists these techniques.

Table 10.4　Techniques for sharing data between steps

Technique	Principle
Execution context	Use a Spring Batch execution context as a container for user data. A step writes to the execution context; then another step reads from the execution context.
Holder	Use a Spring bean and dependency injection. Spring injects a holder bean in the communicating beans. A first step sets values in the holder; another step reads values from the holder.

Let's start with using the Spring Batch execution context to share data.

10.3.1　*Using the execution context to share data*

You must know by now that Spring Batch maintains metadata on job executions. This batch metadata allows for features like restart because the data is stored permanently in a database. The batch developer can also use part of this batch metadata to store a job's own data. The data is then available across executions—for restart—as well as in the same execution, and that's exactly what you need. As soon as your application gains access to the execution context from a job artifact (tasklet, reader, processor, writer, or listener), you can use it to share data.

What exactly is the execution context? The class ExecutionContext represents the execution context, which acts as a map (of key-value pairs) but with an API better suited to batch applications. Here's an example of writing and reading data to and from ExecutionContext:

```
executionContext.putString("importId", importId);
String importId = jobExecutionContext.getString("importId");
```

An execution context exists only as part of a job execution, and there are different kinds of execution contexts.

JOBS AND STEPS HAVE THEIR OWN EXECUTION CONTEXT

Spring Batch provides two kinds of execution contexts: the job execution context and the step execution context. They're both of the same type—ExecutionContext—but they don't have the same scope. Figure 10.8 illustrates both kinds of execution contexts in a job execution. Note the visibility rules between execution contexts.

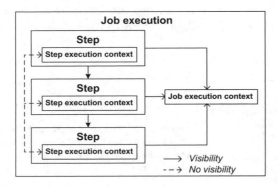

Figure 10.8　A job execution has its own execution context. Within a job execution, each step also has its own execution context. Spring Batch stores execution contexts across executions.

How do you gain access to an execution context? You need a reference to the corresponding execution: a JobExecution if you want to access a job execution context, or a StepExecution if want to access a step execution context. Nearly all Spring Batch artifacts can easily access either a JobExecution or a StepExecution. The unlucky artifacts without this access are the item reader, processor, and writer. If you need access to an execution context from an item reader, processor, or writer, you can implement a listener interface that provides more insight into the execution, such as an Item-Stream. The following listing shows an ItemReader that implements the ItemStream interface to gain access to the execution context.

Listing 10.6   Implementing a listener interface to access the execution context

```
public class FilesInDirectoryItemReader implements
    ItemReader<File>, ItemStream {

  @Override
  public void open(ExecutionContext executionContext)
      throws ItemStreamException { }

  @Override
  public void update(ExecutionContext executionContext)
      throws ItemStreamException { }

  @Override
  public void close() throws ItemStreamException { }

  @Override
  public File read() throws Exception, UnexpectedInputException,
      ParseException, NonTransientResourceException { (...) }

}
```

Now that you have enough background information on execution contexts, let's see the first technique used to exchange data between steps by using an execution context.

USING THE JOB EXECUTION CONTEXT TO SHARE DATA BETWEEN STEPS
You can use the job execution context to share data between steps. A first step writes data to the job execution context, and another step reads the data from the execution context. Figure 10.9 illustrates this technique.

In our example, the verify tasklet not only verifies the integrity of the decompressed files but also extracts the import metadata and stores the import ID in the job

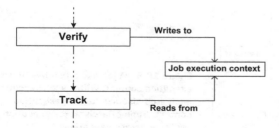

Figure 10.9   Sharing data through the job execution context. A first step writes data in the job execution context for a subsequent step to read.

execution context. The following listing shows the verify tasklet code (setter methods are omitted for brevity).

Listing 10.7 Writing data in the job execution context from a tasklet

```
package com.manning.sbia.ch10.tasklet;

import org.springframework.batch.core.StepContribution;
import org.springframework.batch.core.scope.context.ChunkContext;
import org.springframework.batch.core.step.tasklet.Tasklet;
import org.springframework.batch.item.ExecutionContext;
import org.springframework.batch.repeat.RepeatStatus;
import com.manning.sbia.ch10.batch.BatchService;
import com.manning.sbia.ch10.batch.ImportMetadata;

public class VerifyStoreInJobContextTasklet implements Tasklet {

  private String outputDirectory;
  private BatchService batchService;

  @Override
  public RepeatStatus execute(StepContribution contribution,
      ChunkContext chunkContext) throws Exception {
    batchService.verify(outputDirectory);
    ImportMetadata importMetadata = batchService
      .extractMetadata(outputDirectory);
    ExecutionContext jobExecutionContext =
      chunkContext.getStepContext()                        Gets job execution
        .getStepExecution().getJobExecution()              context
        .getExecutionContext();
    jobExecutionContext.putString("importId",              Writes import ID in
      importMetadata.getImportId());                       execution context
    return RepeatStatus.FINISHED;
  }
  (...)
}
```

You can see in listing 10.7 that the job execution context is accessible through the ChunkContext parameter of the tasklet's execute method. We'll admit the code path isn't obvious! Figure 10.10 helps you visualize the succession of calls.

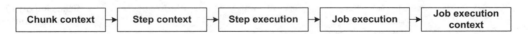

Figure 10.10 The succession of calls needed to access the job execution context from a tasklet

> **NOTE** The tasklet delegates the business logic to a BatchService. Try to use this kind of delegation in your tasklets because it avoids embedding too much business logic in the tasklet (a batch artifact) and promotes reusability of your business services. This delegation also makes the tasklet easier to test because you can use a mock object for the BatchService in integration tests. Figure 10.11 illustrates business delegation in a batch artifact.

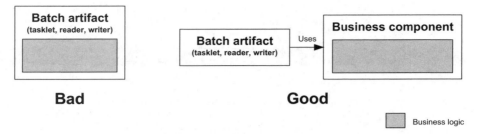

Figure 10.11   A batch artifact such as a tasklet shouldn't embed too much business logic. Instead, it should use a dedicated business component. Such delegation allows for better reusability of business logic and makes business components easier to test because they don't depend on the batch environment.

Once the import ID is available in the job execution context, the track import tasklet can read and use it, as shown in the following listing.

Listing 10.8   Reading data from the job execution context in a tasklet

```
package com.manning.sbia.ch10.tasklet;

import org.springframework.batch.core.StepContribution;
import org.springframework.batch.core.scope.context.ChunkContext;
import org.springframework.batch.core.step.tasklet.Tasklet;
import org.springframework.batch.item.ExecutionContext;
import org.springframework.batch.repeat.RepeatStatus;
import com.manning.sbia.ch10.batch.BatchService;

public class TrackImportFromJobContextTasklet implements Tasklet {

  private BatchService batchService;

  @Override
  public RepeatStatus execute(StepContribution contribution,
      ChunkContext chunkContext) throws Exception {
    ExecutionContext jobExecutionContext =
      chunkContext.getStepContext()                       Gets job execution
        .getStepExecution().getJobExecution()             context
        .getExecutionContext();
    String importId = jobExecutionContext.getString(      Reads import ID from
      "importId");                                        execution context
    batchService.track(importId);
    return RepeatStatus.FINISHED;
  }
  (...)
}
```

When using the job execution context as a container to share data, the writing and reading components must agree on a key used to access the context map. In our example, the key is the hardcoded String `"importId"`, used mainly to make the code more readable and easier to understand. The key could be configurable as a `String` property in both tasklets and set in the XML configuration.

Whatever way the job configures the key, be careful that another component using the same key for another purpose doesn't erase the value. Remember that the job execution context is global to the job: all batch artifacts can access it. Don't hesitate to use prefixes in your keys. In our case, we could have used `importMetadata.importId` instead of `importId`. The reverse domain name notation is also a good choice to avoid collisions: we could have also used `com.acme.onlinestore.importId`.

Giving steps access to the job execution context directly couples them quite tightly. Nevertheless, it's a straightforward solution for many use cases. The next section covers a technique also based on the job execution context but provides more flexibility at the price of being more complex to configure.

USING THE STEP EXECUTION CONTEXT AND PROMOTING THE DATA TO THE JOB EXECUTION CONTEXT
The technique we show next is less straightforward than writing to and reading from the job execution context. It requires that a step writes data in its own execution context and that a listener promotes the data to the job execution context, such that the data can be accessible to anyone. Figure 10.12 illustrates this process; notice that a step listener promotes the data transparently.

The solution used to promote data from a step's scope to a job's scope consists of two parts: you programmatically make the data available in the step execution context and promote this data to the job execution context through configuration. This solution looks complex, but it confines the data exposure to the step and makes the choice of exposing the data a configuration choice. The communicating steps aren't as tightly coupled with each other as in the pure job execution context solution. Imagine that you write jobs by assembling existing tasklets. In some cases, you need to share data between steps, and in other cases, you don't need to share data. By using

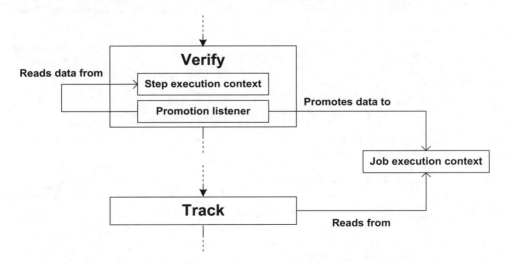

Figure 10.12 Sharing data by writing into the step execution context and promoting data to the job execution context. The receiving step then has access to the data.

the promotion approach, you can choose to conceal data from the step execution context or to expose the data transparently only when you need to.

Going back to our example, the writing tasklet now writes in its own execution context, as shown in the following listing.

Listing 10.9   Writing data in the step execution context from a tasklet

```java
public class VerifyStoreInStepContextTasklet implements Tasklet {

  @Override
  public RepeatStatus execute(StepContribution contribution,
      ChunkContext chunkContext) throws Exception {
    batchService.verify(outputDirectory);
    ImportMetadata importMetadata = batchService
      .extractMetadata(outputDirectory);
    ExecutionContext stepExecutionContext =
      chunkContext.getStepContext().getStepExecution()     // Gets step
      .getExecutionContext();                              // execution context
    stepExecutionContext.putString("importId",             // Writes import ID in
      importMetadata.getImportId());                       // execution context
    return RepeatStatus.FINISHED;
  }
  (...)
}
```

How does the data end up in the job execution context? Spring Batch provides a ready-to-use step listener for that, the ExecutionContextPromotionListener. All you need to do is register the step listener on the writing step and set which key(s) you want to promote. The following shows how to use the promotion step listener.

Listing 10.10   Promoting data from the step to the job execution context

```xml
<bean id="promotionListener"
      class="org.springframework.batch.core.listener
  ➥ .ExecutionContextPromotionListener">                    Declares promotion
  <property name="keys" value="importId" />                 step listener
</bean>

<job id="importProductsJob"
    xmlns="http://www.springframework.org/schema/batch">
  (...)
  <step id="verifyStep" next="readWriteStep">
    <tasklet ref="verifyTasklet">
      <listeners>
        <listener ref="promotionListener" />                Registers listener
      </listeners>                                           on writing step
    </tasklet>
  </step>
  (...)
  <step id="trackImportStep" next="cleanStep">
    <tasklet ref="trackImportTasklet" />
  </step>
  (...)
</job>
```

What happens in the receiving step? The code of its tasklet doesn't change; it remains the same as in listing 10.8. The receiving tasklet reads data from the job execution context, so it sees the data that the listener promoted.

Configuration drives the promotion approach more than the solution relying on purely using a job execution context. Promotion provides more flexibility but needs the configuration of a listener. The next solution is even more configuration driven and leaves the code less dependent on the execution context.

WRITING IN THE JOB EXECUTION CONTEXT AND READING USING LATE BINDING

This approach consists of writing in the job execution context and then referring to the data from the XML configuration, using late binding. The writing tasklet writes in the job execution context, so it remains the same as in listing 10.7. The receiving tasklet doesn't read from any execution context: it reads its own property, as shown in the following listing.

Listing 10.11 A tasklet reading data from its own property

```java
public class TrackImportTasklet implements Tasklet {

  private BatchService batchService;
  private String importId;

  @Override
  public RepeatStatus execute(StepContribution contribution,
      ChunkContext chunkContext) throws Exception {
    batchService.track(importId);                    // Tracks import ID
    return RepeatStatus.FINISHED;
  }

  public void setImportId(String importId) {         // Declares setter for
    this.importId = importId;                        // dependency injection
  }

  public void setBatchService(BatchService batchService) {
    this.batchService = batchService;
  }
}
```

The good news about this new version of the receiving tasklet is that it doesn't depend on the Spring Batch runtime anymore. This makes the tasklet easier to test: you don't have to recreate the execution context; all you need to do is set the tasklet property. This is a benefit of using dependency injection over a lookup mechanism. Speaking of dependency injection, the responsibility of setting the property correctly now belongs to Spring, with help from the step scope and SpEL:

```xml
<bean id="trackImportTasklet"
      class="com.manning.sbia.ch10.tasklet.TrackImportTasklet"
      scope="step">
  <property name="batchService" ref="batchService" />
  <property name="importId"
            value="#{jobExecutionContext['importId']}" />
</bean>
```

The # character triggers the evaluation of an expression. Our expression refers to the importId key in the jobExecutionContext variable. This implicit variable is available only for a step-scoped Spring bean running in a step! Spring Batch creates the instance at the last moment, when the step is about to run. That's why we call it *late binding*.

This solution, combining the job execution context to store data and SpEL, is elegant and frees part of the application code from a reference to the runtime environment. As long as you can use late binding in a step scope, you should prefer this solution to the previous two. But the step scope isn't always available: imagine you want to share data between a step and a job execution decider (for a conditional flow). The step scope isn't available in the decider because it's not part of a step. You would need to use the job execution context in the decider code.

Okay, we're not done yet with sharing data techniques, but we're getting close to the end. The next section covers yet another category of techniques to share data in a job. If the previous category was Spring Batch–oriented—using the Spring Batch runtime—this new category is more Spring-oriented. It's based on the definition of holder classes whose instances are used as Spring beans. These techniques are more type-safe than the ones using execution contexts, but they require writing dedicated classes and rely on Spring for dependency injection.

10.3.2 *Sharing data using Spring holder beans*

The concept of a holder bean in a job is simple: the data that a step creates and wants to share is set inside a Spring bean—a holder for this data—and the step that wants to read the data is injected with the holder bean. Figure 10.13 illustrates the concept of a holder bean shared between steps.

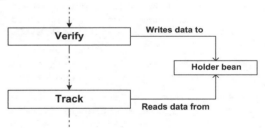

The holder is empty when the Spring application context is created, a step writes data to the holder, and another step reads the data.

Figure 10.13 Using a Spring bean as a holder to share data. Spring injects the holder as a dependency into the batch artifacts that want to share data. An artifact then writes data in the holder, and the receiving artifact reads the data from the holder.

> **WARNING** When using the holder technique, beware of conflicts on the same holder between different job instances or even different jobs. If job instances run in the same process—because you embedded Spring Batch in a web container—don't let a job instance use the values from any previous job instance. A job should clean the holder it uses once it's done using it. This warning doesn't apply if you launch jobs from the command line, because you'll have a different instance of the holder for each execution.

Remember the use case on sharing data: you extract some metadata from the verify step, and the job must make this metadata available to the track step. In our example, the `ImportMetadata` class represents the metadata. The `ImportMetadata` class contains only properties and corresponding getter and setter methods. One of these properties is the one you're interested in: the import ID. You define an `ImportMeta-dataHolder` class whose only goal in life is to hold on to and provide access to an `ImportMetadata` object. You then configure an `ImportMetadataHolder` Spring bean that Spring injects into the interested batch components (tasklets in this case). The following snippet shows the holder code for the import metadata:

```
package com.manning.sbia.ch10.batch;

public class ImportMetadataHolder {

  private ImportMetadata importMetadata;

  public ImportMetadata get() {
    return importMetadata;
  }
  public void set(ImportMetadata importMetadata) {
    this.importMetadata = importMetadata;
  }

}
```

You now know enough to learn a first technique based on the use of a holder to share data between steps. The second technique uses advanced features like SpEL and late binding.

WRITING AND READING WITH HOLDERS

When using a holder, the writing and reading components both refer to the holder. The following listing shows the new version of the tasklets that now depend on the `ImportMetadataHolder`. Note that the listing includes the normally omitted setter methods to highlight their importance: Spring uses injection to set their values.

Listing 10.12 Tasklets communicating through a holder

```
public class VerifyTasklet implements Tasklet {

  private String outputDirectory;
  private BatchService batchService;
  private ImportMetadataHolder importMetadataHolder;

  @Override
  public RepeatStatus execute(StepContribution contribution,
      ChunkContext chunkContext) throws Exception {
    batchService.verify(outputDirectory);
    importMetadataHolder.set(                          Writes data
      batchService.extractMetadata(outputDirectory)    in holder
    );
    return RepeatStatus.FINISHED;
  }
  public void setBatchService(BatchService batchService) {
    this.batchService = batchService;
  }
  public void setOutputDirectory(String outputDirectory) {
```

```
      this.outputDirectory = outputDirectory;
    }

    public void setImportMetadataHolder(
        ImportMetadataHolder importMetadataHolder) {
      this.importMetadataHolder = importMetadataHolder;
    }

}

public class TrackImportWithHolderTasklet implements Tasklet {

    private BatchService batchService;
    private ImportMetadataHolder importMetadataHolder;

    @Override
    public RepeatStatus execute(StepContribution contribution,
        ChunkContext chunkContext) throws Exception {
      batchService.track(
        importMetadataHolder.get().getImportId()
      );
      return RepeatStatus.FINISHED;
    }

    public void setBatchService(BatchService batchService) {
      this.batchService = batchService;
    }

    public void setImportMetadataHolder(
        ImportMetadataHolder importMetadataHolder) {
      this.importMetadataHolder = importMetadataHolder;
    }

}
```

> **Reads data from holder** — `importMetadataHolder.get().getImportId()`

Now both tasklets depend only on the holder and no longer on the Spring Batch runtime. The following listing shows the straightforward required configuration: it declares the beans and wires them together.

Listing 10.13   Configuring tasklets to use a holder

```xml
<bean id="importMetadataHolder"
      class="com.manning.sbia.ch10.batch
    .ImportMetadataHolder" />

<bean id="verifyTasklet"
      class="com.manning.sbia.ch10.tasklet.VerifyTasklet">
  <property name="batchService" ref="batchService" />
  <property name="outputDirectory" value="/tmp/batch" />
  <property name="importMetadataHolder"
            ref="importMetadataHolder" />
</bean>

<bean id="trackImportTasklet"
      class="com.manning.sbia.ch10.tasklet.TrackImportWithHolderTasklet">
  <property name="batchService" ref="batchService" />
  <property name="importMetadataHolder"
            ref="importMetadataHolder" />
</bean>
```

> **Declares holder bean**

> **Injects holder into tasklet**

> **Injects holder into tasklet**

The holder technique is simple and type-safe. It has a couple of disadvantages: you need to create an extra holder class, and the batch artifacts depend on it. The holder technique also introduces the risk of concurrent access to the holder (an execution could see the values from the previous execution).

Let's see a variation on the holder technique, which gets rid of the dependency on the holder in the receiving tasklet.

WRITING TO THE HOLDER AND USING LATE BINDING TO READ FROM THE HOLDER
Using this pattern, the writing tasklet fills in the holder as usual, but Spring creates and injects the receiving tasklet using late binding and SpEL. By doing so, the receiving tasklet no longer depends on the holder: it depends on a `String` property, which is set by Spring when the tasklet is created, before its execution. The tasklet is less tightly coupled to the sharing data pattern than it is using the previous technique because it depends only on a primitive type, not on a holder class. The writing tasklet remains the same as in listing 10.12; it depends only on the holder. The receiving tasklet reads the import ID from a property, like in listing 10.11. The following listing shows the corresponding configuration.

Listing 10.14 Referring to the holder using late binding

```
<bean id="importMetadataHolder"
      class="com.manning.sbia.ch10.batch.ImportMetadataHolder" />

<bean id="verifyTasklet"
      class="com.manning.sbia.ch10.tasklet.VerifyTasklet">
  <property name="batchService" ref="batchService" />
  <property name="outputDirectory" value="/tmp/batch" />
  <property name="importMetadataHolder" ref="importMetadataHolder" />
</bean>

<bean id="trackImportTasklet"
      class="com.manning.sbia.ch10.tasklet.TrackImportTasklet"      ◁─┐ Uses step
      scope="step">                                                    │ scope
  <property name="batchService" ref="batchService" />
  <property name="importId" value="
➥ #{importMetadataHolder.get().getImportId()}" />                      │ Refers to holder
</bean>                                                                 │ bean with SpEL
```

This one is tricky, so let's study what is happening:

1 Spring creates beans, but the creation of the verify tasklet is deferred because it's a step-scoped bean.
2 The verify tasklet is called and writes the import ID to the holder.
3 Once the job gets to the track step, the track tasklet is created and initialized with the value returned by the call on the holder.
4 The job calls the track tasklet, and it uses the value of the `importId` property.

The key part of this technique is the creation of the step-scoped track tasklet: Spring initializes it at the last moment, once the holder already contains the import ID. This last technique frees the receiving tasklet from any dependency on the holder. The price you pay is a more complex configuration and—let's admit it—an initialization mechanism more difficult to understand.

This ends our coverage of patterns used to share data in a job. We distinguish two main pattern categories: the first relies on Spring Batch's notion of the execution context. This works great but couples your batch components with the runtime environment. The second group of patterns introduces data holder objects that batch artifacts use to share data. This technique is more type-safe but requires the creation of dedicated holder classes. Both techniques are roughly equivalent; choosing one over the other is a matter of preference.

Our preference goes to holders when we have enough energy to write holder classes and configure Spring beans. We tend to use execution contexts when we're tired or feel lazy.

We're done with sharing data; the next section still deals with job execution but takes a more configuration-oriented point of view. It covers how to reuse parts of your flow configuration across jobs. This feature comes in handy when some of your jobs share the same sequence of steps. You can configure these common steps once and reuse the configuration across other jobs. If your job configuration contains a lot of duplicate code, you should definitely read the next section to find ways to get rid of it!

10.4 *Externalizing flow definitions*

Reusability is the Holy Grail of software engineering. Spring Batch is part of this quest when it comes to reusing batch components and job configurations. Indeed, portions of a job configuration can be generic and reused across jobs. In the advanced version of our import products job, before reading and writing products from a flat file, preliminary steps prepare the ground for the import: a first step downloads the ZIP archive, a second step decompresses the archive, and a third step checks the integrity of the decompressed files. These preliminary steps are generic and could be useful to other jobs: it's common for a batch job to import data from a file it has downloaded. Why not externalize this flow and reuse it in other jobs? Figure 10.14 illustrates the process of reusing a flow in multiple jobs.

The following listing shows how to define a standalone flow—also called an *externalized* flow—and how to reuse this definition in a job.

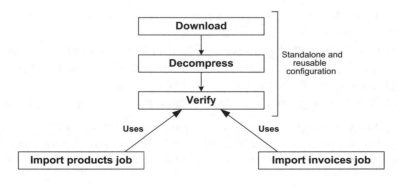

Figure 10.14   A flow of steps can be defined as a standalone entity so that other jobs can reuse it. This promotes reusability of code and configuration.

Listing 10.15 Externalizing a flow definition for reuse

```
<flow id="prepareInputFileFlow">
  <step id="downloadStep" next="decompressStep">
    <tasklet ref="downloadTasklet" />
  </step>
  <step id="decompressStep" next="verifyStep">
    <tasklet ref="decompressTasklet" />
  </step>
  <step id="verifyStep">
    <tasklet ref="verifyTasklet" />
  </step>
</flow>

<job id="importProductsJob">
  <flow parent="prepareInputFileFlow"
      id="importProducts.prepareInputFileFlow"
      next="readWriteStep" />
  <step id="readWriteStep" next="trackImportStep">
    <tasklet>(...)</tasklet>
  </step>
  (...)
</job>
```

> Defines
> externalized flow

> Uses flow
> definition in job

Because the prepareInputFileFlow is generic, we define it as a standalone entity. Jobs can then use it if they need to download, decompress, and verify an input file. Think about another scenario: testing. You want to test the import products job, but the test effort should be on the core part of the job—the import—not on the preparation of the input file. You can define a dummy, empty prepareInputFileFlow bean and set up the test fixture—an input flat file copied in some working directory—and you'll be able to test the core part of the import products job. You don't need to bother preparing a ZIP archive for the test!

You can push further the idea of externalized flow by reusing a whole job. The following listing shows the preliminary steps of our advanced import job set up in a standalone job. The core import job then refers to this job definition.

Listing 10.16 Reusing a job definition in another job

```
<job id="prepareInputFileJob">
  <step id="downloadStep" next="decompressStep">
    <tasklet ref="downloadTasklet" />
  </step>
  <step id="decompressStep" next="verifyStep">
    <tasklet ref="decompressTasklet" />
  </step>
  <step id="verifyStep">
    <tasklet ref="verifyTasklet" />
  </step>
</job>

<job id="importProductsJob">
  <step id="importProducts.prepareInputFileJob" next="readWriteStep">
    <job ref="prepareInputFileJob" />
```

> Defines
> job

> Uses job definition
> in other job

```
  </step>
  <step id="readWriteStep" next="trackImportStep">
    <tasklet>(...)</tasklet>
  </step>
  (...)
</job>
```

> **NOTE** By default, Spring Batch passes all job parameters of the surrounding job to the externalized job. You can have control over these job parameters by registering a `JobParametersExtractor` bean. A job parameters extractor implements a translation strategy between the owning step execution and the job parameters to pass to the subjob. Spring Batch provides a `DefaultJobParametersExtractor` implementation, which pulls all the job parameters from the surrounding job to the subjob.

The externalization of flows and jobs promotes the reusability of flow code and configurations. It's also a nice feature to simplify integration tests.

> **NOTE** Some batch systems use a scheduler to orchestrate the execution of jobs one after another. Jobs return exit statuses, and the scheduler knows which job to execute next by using a mapping between exit statuses and jobs. When using externalized jobs in a Spring Batch system, you orchestrate jobs by reusing job configurations. If you choose to orchestrate your job executions with a scheduler and exit statuses, see section 4.2.1 on using Spring Batch's `CommandLineJobRunner` to customize exit statuses.

With the externalization of flows and jobs, you now have a new way to orchestrate job executions. The next section shows how to get even more control over a job execution by allowing the job execution to stop after a step. If you want to learn how to control your jobs and to decide if a job should fail, stop, or complete, keep on reading!

10.5 *Stopping a job execution*

Until now, our jobs end when you reach the last step, the processing throws an exception, or we stop the execution by sending an interrupt signal. Table 10.5 summarizes these three alternatives, which are the default mechanisms to end a job execution.

The defaults shown in table 10.5 make sense, but a job flow isn't always that simple. An exception thrown in a step doesn't always mean that the whole job execution must

Table 10.5 Default behaviors that end a job execution

Behavior	Batch status	Description
Last step reached	COMPLETED	The last step completes successfully, which ends the job execution.
Error	FAILED	Processing throws an unexpected exception.
Interrupt signal	STOPPED	Interrupt signal sent from an admin console like Spring Batch Admin or programmatically.

fail. Perhaps the job should take another path (section 10.2 shows how to do that with conditional flows). Perhaps the step failure isn't critical, so the application can consider the job execution complete.

In the advanced version of the import products job, the first step consists of downloading a ZIP archive. If there's no ZIP archive, what should you do? Should you end the job execution because there's nothing to import today? Should you stop the execution and try to work out the situation by finding the ZIP archive somewhere else? Should you fail the execution because you're supposed to have new products every day? This is more of a business decision, and Spring Batch lets you define the job behavior declaratively. Figure 10.15 illustrates the "what will be the status of my job execution after this step" problem.

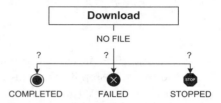

To decide on the status of a job execution after the end of a step, Spring Batch provides three XML elements. You use them, along with transition decisions, inside a `step` or `decision` element. Table 10.6 describes these three elements.

Figure 10.15 When a step ends, Spring Batch lets you choose if you want to complete, fail, or stop the job execution. In the case of the import products job, if the job didn't download a ZIP archive, it makes sense to consider the job execution complete.

Table 10.6 The `end`, `fail`, and `stop` elements

XML element	Batch status	Description
end	COMPLETED	Spring Batch completes the job after the step execution. Spring Batch can't restart the job instance. You can use an optional `exit-code` attribute to customize the `ExitCode`.
fail	FAILED	Spring Batch fails the job after the step execution. Spring Batch can restart the job instance. You can use an optional `exit-code` attribute to customize the `ExitCode`.
stop	STOPPED	Spring Batch stops the job after the step execution. Spring Batch can restart the job instance after a manual operation, for instance. Requires a `restart` attribute to specify on which step the execution should resume.

The `end`, `fail`, and `stop` elements have some special attributes of their own, but they all require an `on` attribute. The value of the `on` attribute matches the value of the step exit status. The following listing shows how to use the `stop` and `fail` elements after the download step in the import products job.

Listing 10.17 Choosing how to end a job after a step execution

```
<job id="importProductsJob" xmlns="http://www.springframework.org/schema/
    batch">
  <step id="downloadStep">
    <tasklet ref="downloadTasklet">
```

```
        <listeners>
          <listener ref="fileExistsStepListener" />
        </listeners>
      </tasklet>
      <end on="NO FILE" />
      <next on="FILE EXISTS" to="decompressStep"/>
      <fail on="*" />
    </step>
    <step id="decompressStep" next="verifyStep">
      <tasklet ref="decompressTasklet" />
    </step>
    (...)
</job>
```

> **Ends, fails, or moves on to next step**

Listing 10.17 shows that you choose to complete the job if there's no archive, move on to the next step if the archive exists, and fail the job in all other cases. These decisions are based on custom exit statuses set by a step listener after the end of the step. You can use the `end`, `fail`, and `stop` elements for any exit statuses, and you could have stuck to exit statuses like `COMPLETED` and `FAILED`. In this case, you need more semantics—you have an archive file or you don't—which is why you use custom exit statuses.

The `end`, `fail`, and `stop` elements bring a lot of flexibility to job flows. With them, you can escape from the simple "the last step completed successfully completes the job" scenario. Combined with conditional flows, which help you go beyond linear jobs, you can create job scenarios with complex step sequences.

You now know everything you need to create, control, and configure job execution flows; let's wrap everything up.

10.6   *Summary*

This chapter covered patterns and techniques used to control precisely the execution of the steps inside your jobs. Always keep things simple, but follow these guidelines when facing complex execution scenarios:

- Control the sequence of steps using conditional flows—Spring Batch lets you choose declaratively which step to execute next on the basis of the exit status of the previous step.
- Define custom exit statuses for complex flow decisions when you reach the limit of default exit statuses (`COMPLETED`, `FAILED`, and so on). Use your own exit statuses with a step execution listener or a job execution decider.
- Use the execution context or holder beans to exchange data between steps—when a step needs data computed by a previous step, use the execution context to make the data accessible between steps. If you don't want to depend on the batch runtime, inject holder beans inside the batch artifacts that need to share data.
- Reuse configuration. You can externalize definitions of flows or of whole jobs and reuse them across jobs.
- End the execution of a job declaratively after any step—use the `end`, `fail`, and `stop` elements to end a job with an appropriate batch status at the end of a step.

With all this new knowledge, you're now ready to start one of the most exciting parts of this book. Chapter 11 shows how Spring Batch fits in a real-world integration scenario. Be prepared to leverage your Spring Batch skills but also to discover new content on enterprise integration styles, REST, and technologies like Spring Integration.

Enterprise integration

IT systems are complex beasts: they can consist of hundreds of applications that don't work in isolation and need to communicate with each other. An example of Spring Batch helping applications communicate is a batch job processing files from one application and writing data into the database of another application. The term *enterprise integration* refers to such communication techniques between applications. Because batch processes are often central to enterprise integration projects, this chapter is dedicated to explaining how to use Spring Batch and other Spring-related technologies in such projects. The online store application we use in this book is a typical enterprise integration project: the application imports product data from various systems (ACME and its partners) so that customers can browse and purchase products through the online store web interface. Figure 11.1 illustrates how enterprise integration fits between the online store application and other systems.

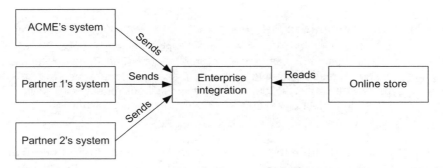

Figure 11.1 The online store application uses enterprise integration techniques to import product data from other systems.

Enterprise integration is a broad topic, and trying to cover all of it would require a whole book, much less one chapter. Instead of thinly covering as much as possible, this chapter uses a practical approach and implements a realistic enterprise integration scenario for the online store application. By the end of this chapter, you'll have an overview of enterprise integration and techniques used to tackle its challenges. These techniques rely on technologies like Representational State Transfer (REST), messaging, and batch processes, and use frameworks like Spring MVC, Spring Integration, and Spring Batch.

All of the chapters in this book focus on Spring Batch, but this chapter isn't only about Spring Batch: it covers other Spring frameworks. The point is to show you how Spring Batch combines with other frameworks as a key component in real-world enterprise projects. Let's start by learning more about enterprise integration.

11.1 *What is enterprise integration?*

Even if we know that enterprise integration includes making applications communicate with each other, the term is vague. This section gives a more comprehensive and practical definition of enterprise integration, along with some use case examples. This section also covers integration styles that deal with enterprise integration challenges and we'll see what roles Spring Batch can play in this world.

11.1.1 *Enterprise integration challenges*

Enterprise integration is a set of techniques and practices for connecting enterprise applications. Most of the time, these applications don't share the same data, don't use the same technologies internally, or don't even run on the same network. Despite these differences, these applications need to communicate to fulfill business requirements.

Is there always a need to make applications work together? Can't a company use a single application? The answer is often, if not always, no. A company—even small— doesn't run its whole business on a single, monolithic application. It chooses a distinct application for each of its business functions and allows picking a best-of-breed solution for each situation (homemade applications and ready-to-use products). We're

The *Enterprise Integration Patterns* book

We consider *Enterprise Integration Patterns* by Gregor Hohpe and Bobby Woolf (Addison-Wesley, 2004) one of the canons of enterprise integration. The book focuses on solutions based on messaging and describes message-oriented patterns for enterprise integration. We strongly recommend reading this book for anyone involved in enterprise integration projects. We refer to it as *the EIP book* in this chapter.

describing applications within the same company; what about applications in different companies? To work with partners, a company must open parts of its IT system, and when a company doesn't control the applications of its business partners, it needs to integrate with them.

Enterprise integration should be clearer now. Let's look at a couple of typical enterprise integration projects.

INFORMATION PORTAL

The first type of integration project we consider is the *information portal* (as named in the EIP book). Imagine a user wants to check the status of an order. This request can access data from multiple applications: the order management application, the customer directory, and the inventory application. An information portal gathers all this information in one place so that the end user doesn't have to access each application and track the necessary data spread over each application. Figure 11.2 illustrates an information portal.

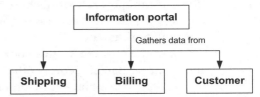

Figure 11.2   **An information portal is a typical enterprise integration project. It gathers data from several applications and makes it available in one place to the end user.**

DATA REPLICATION

Another example of enterprise integration is *data replication*. Applications often use the same data (like customers) but use their own data stores because they need a specific representation of the data. For example, a shipping application doesn't need the same customer data as a billing application. One application holds the reference data ("the truth"), and the system propagates any update to this reference data to the other applications. Figure 11.3 illustrates data replication in an enterprise.

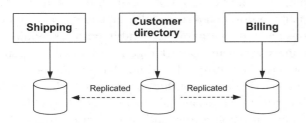

Figure 11.3   **Data replication in an enterprise integration project. In this example, the customer directory holds the reference data for anything related to customers. The billing and shipping applications need this information. The system replicates data from the customer directory to the shipping and billing data stores.**

Considering these two typical enterprise integration patterns, the information portal and data replication, presents us with the following challenges:

- Enforcing complex business rules that emerge from combining services
- Replicating large amounts of data
- Working with different technologies, such as programming languages

The list could go on; no two enterprise integration projects are the same, and you don't know what applications you'll need to integrate with your system.

Now that you have a better understanding of enterprise integration and the challenges it presents, let's see some ways to deal with these issues.

11.1.2 Styles of enterprise integration

We use four main approaches to solve enterprise integration challenges. Per the EIP book, we refer to these as *styles*:

- *File transfer*—One application writes a file, and another application reads the file.
- *Shared database*—Applications share the same database: there is no transfer.
- *Remote procedure invocation*—An application exposes part of its functionality so that other applications can invoke it remotely.
- *Messaging*—An application publishes messages on a channel, and other applications can read these messages at their convenience.

Each integration style has its advantages, disadvantages, and limitations. No one integration style is better than another. Each specific situation dictates which one to choose or even which combination of styles to use. Table 11.1 lists some of the pros and cons of each integration style. Note that these tables are by no means exhaustive!

Table 11.1 Advantages and disadvantages of integration styles

Integration style	Advantages	Disadvantages
File transfer	Simple, interoperable	Not transactional, not real-time
Shared database	Simple, transactional	Can be slow, schema hard to evolve
Remote procedure invocation	Simple, can be fast	Not interoperable, synchronous, tightly coupled
Messaging	Asynchronous, scalable	Complex

Spring offers support for each integration style. Table 11.2 lists the Spring technologies to use for each integration style.

Table 11.2 Integration styles and corresponding Spring technologies

Integration style	Spring technologies
File transfer	Spring resource abstraction, Spring Batch
Shared database	Spring data access (JDBC, Object-Relational Mapping, transaction)

Table 11.2   Integration styles and corresponding Spring technologies *(continued)*

Integration style	Spring technologies
Remote procedure invocation	Spring remoting (Remote Method Invocation, HttpInvoker, Hessian, Burlap)
Messaging	Spring `JmsTemplate`, Spring message container listeners, Spring Integration

Table 11.2 shows that Spring Batch matches the file transfer style. Since this is a book about Spring Batch, let's talk a bit more about this so we can understand how Spring Batch fits in enterprise integration.

11.2   Spring Batch and enterprise integration

By now, you know that Spring Batch is good at reading and writing large amounts of data in an efficient and reliable way. You also know that Spring Batch has sophisticated support for files of any kind (text files, XML files). This makes Spring Batch a perfect tool for file transfer integration. Because Spring Batch provides support for databases, an application can read data from its database and write to files, and another application can do the mirror operation—all of this using Spring Batch!

Spring Batch can integrate applications using file transfer, database access, and much more. You can also combine Spring Batch with other technologies—especially Spring technologies—to implement advanced enterprise integration solutions.

11.2.1   An enterprise integration use case

In chapter 1, we introduced the online store application. This web application sells products from the ACME Corporation and its partners. ACME and its partners (the *clients* of the application) send files every day that a Spring Batch job imports every night into the online store database. This is a typical example of file transfer integration, illustrated by figure 11.4.

Unfortunately, the pace of imports isn't fast enough for some partners: they would like to see their products available for sale as quickly as possible. One solution is to accept small-to-midsized imports from clients and import them as quickly as possible (an hour between the submission and import is acceptable).

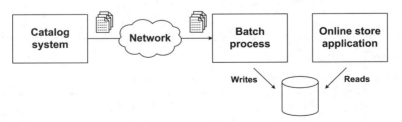

Figure 11.4   The online store application uses transfer file integration to synchronize its catalog with partner catalogs. The corresponding batch process is the basis of our enterprise integration scenario.

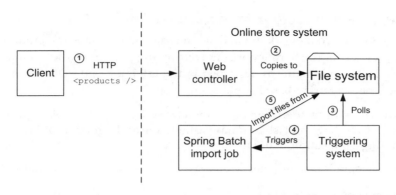

Figure 11.5 A client submits products to import over HTTP. The system copies the import data into a file. A triggering system—like a scheduler—can then launch a Spring Batch job to read the file and update the database accordingly. Clients update the store catalog more frequently, but the application controls the frequency.

ACME has decided to improve the online store backend to meet these requirements with the following architecture:

- Clients submit imports as XML documents over HTTP.
- The application stores the XML documents on the file system.
- A Spring Batch job is triggered to import the files in the store catalog.

Figure 11.5 illustrates this architecture. This figure shows Spring Batch as one of many components in ACME's enterprise integration scenario. A single framework couldn't fulfill all the tasks in this scenario by itself. You need components other than Spring Batch to implement this scenario. The Spring MVC web framework will help you receive import requests, and you'll use techniques related to messaging integration to interact with the file system using Spring Integration. Table 11.3 matches the use case tasks with Spring technologies.

Task	Technology
Receiving import submissions	Spring MVC
Copying imports to the file system	Spring Integration
Polling file system to trigger jobs	Spring Integration
Triggering jobs	Spring Integration
Importing products	Spring Batch

Table 11.3 Use case tasks and matching Spring technologies

As you can see from table 11.3, Spring Integration plays an important role in our scenario. Spring Integration deals with messaging enterprise integration and deserves its own section, as described next.

11.3   *Spring Integration, a toolbox for enterprise integration*

Spring Integration is a framework to facilitate messaging enterprise integration. Like Spring Batch, it's part of the Spring portfolio. Spring Integration provides support for the enterprise integration patterns described in the EIP book and makes using these patterns easier for any Spring-based application.

> **TIP**   To learn everything there is to know about Spring Integration, read *Spring Integration in Action* by Mark Fisher, Jonas Partner, Marius Bogoevici, and Iwein Fuld (Manning Publications, 2011).

Message-based integration is difficult, so let's see how Spring Integration helps.

11.3.1   *The Spring Integration project*

The Spring Integration framework aims at applying the Spring programming model to message-based enterprise integration applications. It enables messaging *within* Spring applications and provides adapters to integrate with external systems, using various technologies (file system, Java Message Service [JMS], HTTP, Remote Method Invocation [RMI], and so forth). Applications that communicate with messages are more decoupled and therefore easier to integrate. For example, an ordering application doesn't directly communicate with a billing application: it sends a message for an order, and the billing application handles the message when it sees fit.

Don't confuse Spring Integration with an enterprise service bus (ESB). Spring Integration is a framework that you embed in your applications, not a container that runs your application code. Figure 11.6 illustrates how you can use Spring Integration in your applications.

Spring Integration provides support for enterprise integration patterns and simplifies message handling: routing, transforming, splitting, and aggregating are all operations you can easily perform on messages with Spring Integration. Note that the Spring Integration messaging infrastructure is agnostic to any backing technology: messages can come from any source (a file dropped on the file system or a JMS queue,

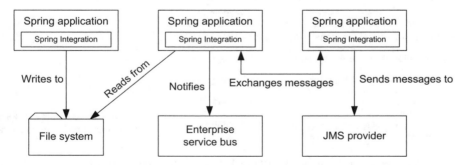

Figure 11.6   Spring Integration enables messaging within Spring applications. It can be embedded in any Spring application and can integrate with external systems using built-in adapters for various technologies, such as HTTP, JMS, file systems, and RMI.

for example), be routed through the application thanks to the messaging bus, and then be sent to any target. This makes applications that use Spring Integration decoupled from their surrounding environment.

If the usefulness of Spring Integration is still in doubt, don't worry: we'll dive into some examples soon. First, let's examine the relationship between Spring Integration and Spring Batch.

11.3.2 Combining Spring Integration and Spring Batch

Because enterprise integration patterns are mainly message driven and Spring Integration supports messaging, you might think Spring Integration and Spring Batch wouldn't need each other. After all, the Spring Batch integration style is file transfer, not messaging. But these two frameworks are complementary, and Spring developers who deal with enterprise integration should have both in their toolbox. If frameworks had astrological signs, Spring Integration and Spring Batch would be compatible!

> **NOTE** Dave Syer—the Spring Batch project lead—posted an article on his blog on the practical use of Spring Batch and Spring Integration.[1] This post inspired the Spring Integration quick-start section in this chapter.

Spring Integration is complementary to Spring Batch: it adds the messaging integration style to the Spring Batch file transfer style. An enterprise integration solution can use multiple integration styles, making Spring Integration and Spring Batch appealing solutions for the two most popular integration styles: messaging and file transfer.

Developers can implement solutions using these two frameworks, but Spring Batch can also use Spring Integration for internal tasks like retry and distributing chunks (in a step) on multiple nodes. See chapter 13 to learn how to scale batch processes using these techniques.

The remainder of this chapter addresses the integration use case introduced in section 11.2.1, with Spring Integration playing an important role in creating a solution. Because Spring Integration is a newcomer to this book, we give you a quick-start guide next. You'll learn the basics of Spring Integration, and you'll see Spring Integration and Spring Batch working together. Let's see how to use the Spring Integration messaging system to launch Spring Batch jobs.

11.3.3 Spring Integration quick-start: launching a Spring Batch job

We introduce Spring Integration by implementing a generic Spring Batch job launcher. The goal of this quick-start is twofold: discovering Spring Integration and implementing a component to use in our use case. The principle of the job launcher is simple: allow wrapping job launch requests in Spring Integration messages. Such messages then trigger the launch of Spring Batch jobs, as shown in figure 11.7.

---

[1] http://blog.springsource.com/2010/02/15/practical-use-of-spring-batch-and-spring-integration/

Figure 11.7   The Spring Integration quick-start uses Spring Integration messages to trigger Spring Batch jobs.

Because Spring Integration provides adapters for many message sources (HTTP, file system, JMS, and so on), you can launch jobs using various technologies. Let's start by defining a job launch request with a Java class.

JAVA REPRESENTATION OF A JOB LAUNCH REQUEST

To launch a Spring Batch job, you need the name of the job and some (optional) job parameters. Let's gather this information in a Java class. The following listing shows our custom Java representation of a job launch request.

Listing 11.1   Java representation of a job launch request

```java
package com.manning.sbia.ch11.integration;

import java.util.Collections;
import java.util.HashMap;
import java.util.Map;

public class JobLaunchRequest {

  private String jobName;

  private Map<String,String> jobParameters;

  public JobLaunchRequest(String jobName) {
    this(jobName,Collections.EMPTY_MAP);
  }

  public JobLaunchRequest(String jobName, Map<String,String> jobParams) {
    super();
    this.jobName = jobName;
    this.jobParameters = jobParams;
  }

  public String getJobName() {
    return jobName;
  }

  public Map<String,String> getJobParameters() {
    return jobParameters == null ? Collections.EMPTY_MAP :
      Collections.unmodifiableMap(jobParameters);
  }

}
```

The JobLaunchRequest class is a wrapper. It doesn't depend on the Spring Batch API: no one using the JobLaunchRequest class will know that you're using Spring Batch at the end of the processing chain.

You now need to write the code to launch a Spring Batch job from a `JobLaunchRequest`. The following listing shows the Java class in charge of adapting a `JobLaunchRequest` instance to the Spring Batch launching API (we elided Java imports for brevity).

Listing 11.2 Launching a Spring Batch job from a `JobLaunchRequest` object

```
package com.manning.sbia.ch11.integration;

(...)

public class JobLaunchingMessageHandler {

  private JobRegistry jobRegistry;

  private JobLauncher jobLauncher;

  public JobLaunchingMessageHandler(JobRegistry jobRegistry,
      JobLauncher jobLauncher) {
    super();
    this.jobRegistry = jobRegistry;
    this.jobLauncher = jobLauncher;
  }

  public JobExecution launch(JobLaunchRequest request)
      throws JobExecutionAlreadyRunningException, JobRestartException,
      JobInstanceAlreadyCompleteException, JobParametersInvalidException,
      NoSuchJobException {
    Job job = jobRegistry.getJob(            Looks up
      request.getJobName()                   job object
    );
    JobParametersBuilder builder = new JobParametersBuilder();
    for(Map.Entry<String,String> entry :
        request.getJobParameters().entrySet()) {    Converts job
      builder.addString(                             parameters
        entry.getKey(), entry.getValue()
      );
    }
    return jobLauncher.run(job, builder.toJobParameters());    Launches
  }                                                             job

}
```

The `JobLaunchingMessageHandler` class works with `JobParameters` and `JobLauncher` objects, familiar Spring Batch classes by now. It also uses a less commonly used Spring Batch type that deserves some explanation: the `JobRegistry` interface. A job registry allows looking up a `Job` object by name. It's used here because the `JobLaunchRequest` class contains only the name of the job, and you want to keep this class independent from the Spring Batch API. The following snippet declares a `jobRegistry` in Spring:

```
<bean id="jobRegistry"
      class="org.springframework.batch.core.configuration.support.
  ➥ MapJobRegistry" />
<bean class="org.springframework.batch.core.configuration.support.
  ➥ JobRegistryBeanPostProcessor">
  <property name="jobRegistry" ref="jobRegistry" />
</bean>
```

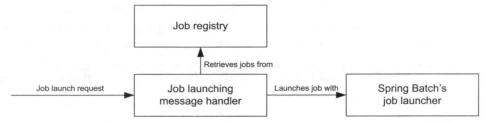

Figure 11.8   The job launching message handler receives job launch request messages and uses Spring Batch's job launcher to effectively launch jobs. It retrieves job beans from the job registry—an infrastructure bean that Spring Batch provides.

Figure 11.8 illustrates the interaction of the job launching message handler with Spring Batch's job registry and job launcher.

Whereas the `JobLaunchRequest` is a plain old Java object (POJO), the `JobLaunchingMessageHandler` class relies on Spring Batch components. This makes sense: the `JobLaunchingMessageHandler` is a bridge between the POJO-based messaging world and the Spring Batch launch API. Note that you use a `JobLaunchingMessageHandler` with Spring Integration, but it doesn't depend on the Spring Integration API. The Spring Integration framework uses the `JobLaunchingMessageHandler` on its message bus, but the class remains independent from any messaging infrastructure. Later, we'll send messages containing `JobLaunchRequest` objects and see Spring Integration handle routing, extracting `JobLaunchRequests`, and calling the `JobLaunchingMessage-Handler` launch method.

You now have the necessary classes to launch Spring Batch jobs in a generic manner. Let's create a simple job to illustrate our quick-start with Spring Integration.

A SIMPLE JOB TO DISPLAY JOB PARAMETERS

Our sample job contains only a `Tasklet` that echoes its parameters to the console. This job is simple but enough to make our Spring Integration quick-start complete. The following listing shows the `Tasklet` code.

Listing 11.3   The echo `Tasklet`

```
package com.manning.sbia.ch11;

import org.springframework.batch.core.StepContribution;
import org.springframework.batch.core.scope.context.ChunkContext;
import org.springframework.batch.core.step.tasklet.Tasklet;
import org.springframework.batch.repeat.RepeatStatus;

public class EchoJobParametersTasklet implements Tasklet {

  @Override
  public RepeatStatus execute(StepContribution contribution,
      ChunkContext chunkContext) throws Exception {
    System.out.println(chunkContext.getStepContext().getJobParameters());
    return RepeatStatus.FINISHED;
  }

}
```

The EchoJobParametersTasklet lets you check (on the console) that Spring Batch received the job parameters you passed through a JobLaunchRequest. Let's now see the configuration of Spring Integration for this Tasklet.

CONFIGURING SPRING INTEGRATION TO LAUNCH A JOB

Spring Integration relies on Spring for its configuration. Listing 11.4 shows the configuration to connect an input channel for job requests to the JobLaunchingMessage-Handler and echo the JobExecution returned on the console. For brevity's sake, we elided the configuration of the batch infrastructure: the job launcher, job repository, and job registry.

Listing 11.4   Spring Integration configuration to launch jobs

```
<int:channel id="job-requests" />                              ⊲⎯  Defines input
                                                                   message channel
<int:service-activator
    input-channel="job-requests"
    output-channel="job-executions">
  <bean class="com.manning.sbia.ch11.integration.             ⎯  Launches job on
 ➥   JobLaunchingMessageHandler">                                incoming message
    <constructor-arg ref="jobRegistry" />
    <constructor-arg ref="jobLauncher" />
  </bean>
</int:service-activator>

<int-stream:stdout-channel-adapter         ⎮  Outputs job
    id="job-executions" />                 ⎮  execution on console

<batch:job id="echoJob">
  <batch:step id="echoStep">
    <batch:tasklet>
      <bean class="com.manning.sbia.ch11.EchoJobParametersTasklet" />
    </batch:tasklet>
  </batch:step>
</batch:job>
```

In listing 11.4, you first define a job-requests message channel. You use this channel to send messages containing JobLaunchRequest objects. Spring Integration takes care of routing these messages to the *service activator* you defined. A service activator connects the messaging infrastructure with an application service (a JobLaunchingMessage-Handler bean in this case). Note that the Spring Integration service activator is two-way: it passes incoming messages to the application service and sends the object returned by the application service to an output channel. Because the JobLaunchingMessage-Handler returns JobExecution objects, Spring Integration wraps them into messages and sends them to the job-executions channel. You connect this channel to a console output adapter, with the stdout-channel-adapter XML element. You can then monitor JobExecution objects on the console.

In figure 11.9, we use enterprise integration pattern icons to represent the flow of messages configured in listing 11.4.

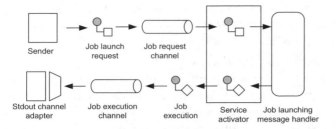

Figure 11.9   The flow of messages represented with enterprise integration pattern icons. Job launch requests are sent and received by the service activator, which unwraps them from messages and calls the job launching message handler. The service activator retrieves the job executions and sends them on a dedicated channel, where Spring Batch outputs them to the console.

Spring Integration XML namespaces

Spring Integration relies on XML namespaces for configuration. The framework includes a namespace to define generic messaging components (channel, service activator, and so on) and namespaces for the different kinds of adapters (file system, JMS, RMI, and so forth). Because namespace declarations are verbose (but easy to achieve with tools like SpringSource Tool Suite), we elide them in the listings and snippets for this chapter.

NOTE   You can find descriptions of each icon in the EIP book and on the Enterprise Integration Patterns website: www.enterpriseintegrationpatterns .com. SpringSource Tool Suite uses these icons for its Spring Integration graphical editor.

Figure 11.9 depicts your complete message flow. but one component doesn't appear in the Spring configuration: the sender. This is because you use Java code to send messages. Next, you write and run this program.

SENDING A JOB LAUNCH REQUEST WITH SPRING INTEGRATION

The Spring Integration message bus runs in a plain Spring application context. You only need to bootstrap a Spring application context, get the inbound message channel bean, and send messages using it, as shown in the following listing

Listing 11.5   Launching a job with Spring Integration

```
ApplicationContext ctx = new ClassPathXmlApplicationContext(
  "spring-integration-quick-start.xml"
);
JobLaunchRequest jobLaunchRequest =
  new JobLaunchRequest(
      "echoJob",
      Collections.singletonMap("param1", "value1")
);
Message<JobLaunchRequest> msg = MessageBuilder
```

```
        .withPayload(jobLaunchRequest).build();
MessageChannel jobRequestsChannel = ctx.getBean(
    "job-requests",MessageChannel.class);
jobRequestsChannel.send(msg);
```

In listing 11.5, you create a `JobLaunchRequest` (to launch your `echoJob` job) and wrap the request object in a Spring Integration message. Spring Integration provides the `MessageBuilder` class to create the message. You use it to set the *payload* (or body) of the message with the job launch request. Once you create the message, you can look up the `job-requests` channel from the application context and send the request. If you execute the code from listing 11.5, you'll see output like the following on the console:

```
{param1=value1}
JobExecution: id=1, startTime=Tue Jul 27 11:07:33 CEST 2010,
    endTime=Tue Jul 27 11:07:33 CEST 2010,
    lastUpdated=Tue Jul 27 11:07:33 CEST 2010, status=COMPLETED,
    exitStatus=exitCode=COMPLETED;exitDescription=,
    job=[JobInstance: id=1,JobParameters=[{param1=value1}],Job=[echoJob]]
```

The first line of output on the console comes from the `EchoJobParametersTasklet`. The second line is the job execution displayed by the console channel adapter. This means that your job launch with Spring Integration is a success!

Wrapping and unwrapping messages with Spring Integration

When you send the job launch request, you wrap it in a Spring Integration message, even though the `JobLaunchingMessageHandler` uses a `JobLaunchRequest` object. You do this because Spring Integration automatically unwraps the payload from the message. The framework analyzes the signature of the message handler and is smart enough to call the handler's method with the payload as the parameter. You didn't even specify a method to call in the `service-activator` XML element! You can also use annotations on the message handler to help Spring Integration extract information from the message: `@ServiceActivator` specifies which method to call on an incoming message, and `@Header` extracts a header from the message. With Spring Integration, message handlers can have flexible method signatures.

NOTE Application code should remain agnostic to the messaging infrastructure. This isn't the case in listing 11.5 where you refer directly to the Spring Integration API. But thanks to Spring Integration features (wrapping/unwrapping, gateways), application components can work directly with application classes. Spring Integration adapts the messaging infrastructure behavior to the application code.

This completes our quick-start guide to Spring Integration. You know the framework basics and saw the construction of a component you'll reuse in the use case: a message handler to launch Spring Batch jobs. Any Spring Integration message containing a `JobLaunchRequest` as its payload can trigger a job launch. Spring Integration provides many ready-to-use message adapters for varied message sources (JMS, HTTP, file system, and so on) and all the features required to route and transform messages. You now have many options to launch Spring Batch jobs.

> **Do Spring Batch and Spring Integration overlap?**
>
> No, Spring Batch and Spring Integration don't overlap. This question comes up quite often when exploring these frameworks, mainly because both provide support to connect to external resources: files (flat or XML), JMS queues, databases, and so on. Remember that Spring Batch is good at bulk processing: it can efficiently and reliably read flat files with hundreds of thousands of lines, for example. Spring Integration is more event driven: it can generate a message when it discovers a new file in a directory or on a remote FTP server. Spring Integration also provides support to route and transform messages. How can the frameworks work together? Spring Integration can work *before* Spring Batch to trigger an event that will start a job (dropping in a new input file). This is what we do next in this chapter. You can also find Spring Integration *in* Spring Batch: the remote chunking–scaling strategy that chapter 13 covers builds on top of Spring Integration.

You made two Spring-based projects work together—and how seamlessly! Our horoscope metaphor makes more sense now, and this is only the beginning: the Spring Integration–based job launcher is a reusable tool, and you can now start the implementation of your use case. Fasten your seat belt and get ready to receive import job submissions thanks to Spring MVC.

11.4 *RESTful job submission with Spring MVC*

In figure 11.8, the first step in our use case is to receive job submissions for the import products job through HTTP. A submission will contain a client-defined import identifier (to track the status of the import) and the products to import, all as an XML document such as this:

```xml
<?xml version="1.0" encoding="UTF-8"?>
<products import-id="partner1-1">
  <product>
    <id>216</id>
    <name>CN Clogs Beach/Garden Clog</name>
    <description>CN Clogs Beach/Garden Clog</description>
    <price>190.70</price>
  </product>
  <product>
    <id>217</id>
    <name>ATT 8525 PDA</name>
    <description>ATT 8525 PDA</description>
    <price>289.20</price>
  </product>
</products>
```

Because this kind of job submission works for small-to-midsized files (tens or even hundreds of megabytes, but not more!), you can go from one large, nightly import to several smaller, more frequent imports.

> ## Spring MVC and REST
>
> Spring MVC is the web framework bundled with Spring. It's a simple yet powerful, command-based web framework, equivalent to web frameworks like Struts 1 and Struts 2. You can write web applications using Spring MVC with features like validation, binding, and separation between request processing and view generation. As of Spring 3.0, it also supports REST.
>
> What is REST? REST stands for *Representational State Transfer* and is a style of architecture. The most famous implementation of REST is the World Wide Web; the HTTP specification follows all REST semantics. REST enforces practices like statelessness and use of a uniform interface (HTTP operations like POST, GET, and PUT). Servers and clients communicate through the transfer of representation of *resources*.

Clients send XML job submissions over HTTP—using REST semantics—and the system routes these XML documents to the file system, where another part of the system picks them up and sends them to Spring Batch (as we'll see). Table 11.4 lists the tasks involved in handling job submissions and the corresponding technologies we use to implement them.

Table 11.4 Tasks and corresponding technologies to handle job submissions

Task	Technologies
Receiving job submissions	REST, Spring MVC
Tracking job submissions	Database, Spring JDBC, and transaction support
Routing job submission messages	Spring Integration
Copying job submissions to file system	Spring Integration file system support

The first task uses Spring MVC to handle HTTP job submissions. Let's start by deploying Spring—along with Spring MVC—in a web application.

11.4.1 Deploying Spring in a web application

In our deployment, a Spring MVC controller handles job submissions coming in as HTTP requests. The controller delegates tracking to a repository and routing to a Spring Integration gateway. Figure 11.10 illustrates this process.

To deploy Spring MVC controllers, you need a DispatcherServlet. The Spring beans related to data access and Spring Integration are deployed in the *root application context* of the web application. You end up with two Spring application contexts: one

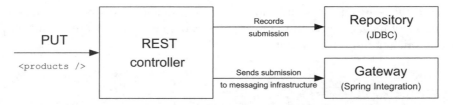

Figure 11.10   Job submissions come in as HTTP PUT requests. The Spring MVC controller uses a repository to record each submission in a database. The controller then sends submissions to the Spring Integration messaging infrastructure through a gateway.

for the `DispatcherServlet` and another for the whole web application. This structure is typical of web applications using Spring MVC as their web container. The two application contexts share a parent-child relationship: the `Dispatcher-Servlet` application context sees all the beans from the root application context, but not the other way around. Figure 11.11 illustrates the two application contexts, their relationship, and the kinds of Spring beans they typically own.

The configuration has two steps: configuring the root application context and configuring the

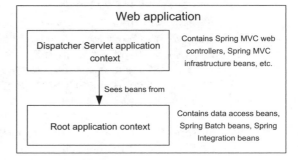

Figure 11.11   In a web application, a `DispatcherServlet` (the heart of Spring MVC) has its own Spring application context, which can see beans from the root application context. The scope of the root application context is the entire web application and contains beans for data access, business services, and all the beans from frameworks like Spring Batch and Spring Integration.

Spring MVC `DispatcherServlet`. Chapter 4 covers both steps, so please refer to section 4.4.1, and in section 4.4.2, the section "Configuring Spring MVC."

Table 11.5 displays the locations of Spring configuration files for both application contexts in our application.

Table 11.5   Location of Spring configuration files in the web application

Configuration	Location
Spring MVC application	/WEB-INF/sbia-servlet.xml
Root application context	/WEB-INF/applicationContext.xml

Unless specified, all Spring configurations in the next snippets and listings take place in the configuration file for the root application context (you'll see that there's not much in the Spring MVC configuration). You're now ready to implement the REST controller.

11.4.2 *Writing the REST web controller*

Starting with Spring 3.0, Spring MVC provides support for REST. If you're familiar with Spring MVC, the programming model for REST support is the same as for traditional, annotation-based Spring MVC applications. If you're new to Spring MVC, a REST controller is a POJO with Spring annotations.

But using a REST framework isn't enough to be truly RESTful: you need to follow strict REST semantics, as defined by the HTTP specification. Our RESTful job submission follows these rules:

- *Operations will be accessible on the /product-imports URL*—REST is all about resources; our resource is an import products document.
- *Clients must* PUT *product imports on the /product-imports/{importId} URL*—The {importId} element is the import identifier. Clients generate import Ids, and an ID must start with the name of the client in order to avoid collisions. An example of a product import URL is /product-imports/partner1-1.
- *The import content is in the body of the request*—The body of the HTTP request contains the XML document describing the products to import. HTTP requests with a nonempty body are rare in traditional web applications, but that's not the case in RESTful applications.
- *The system returns an appropriate status code to inform the client of whether the import was accepted*—A 202 status code is returned if the system accepts the job submission. The system can return a 409 status code if a client tries to submit the same import multiple times. This makes job submissions *idempotent*—a client can resubmit an import if it didn't get a response. This is useful because the HTTP protocol doesn't provide any guarantee of delivery.

Figure 11.12 captures all these requirements.

> **WARNING** We don't secure the REST controller, mainly for brevity, but we could do so with a framework like Spring Security.

If you think that fulfilling all these requirements is difficult, don't worry: Spring MVC makes the implementation of the REST controller a breeze!

Figure 11.12   The job submission enforces REST rules. Clients must send an HTTP PUT to import products on a specific URL, which identifies the import as a resource. The REST controller sends back appropriate status codes: 202 if the submission is accepted, 409 if the server already accepted the import.

IMPLEMENTATION OF THE REST WEB CONTROLLER

Implementing the REST web controller by following the rules listed previously will make you a good citizen in the REST world. You also get all the benefits of REST: the simplicity and reliability of the HTTP protocol and interoperability with large amounts of client technologies. Spring MVC helps to enforce these rules through its REST support. The following listing shows our job submission REST controller; this leverages some of the REST features of Spring MVC.

Listing 11.6   Receiving job submissions with a REST web controller

```
package com.manning.sbia.ch11.web;

import org.springframework.beans.factory.annotation.Autowired;
import org.springframework.dao.DuplicateKeyException;
import org.springframework.http.HttpStatus;
import org.springframework.stereotype.Controller;
import org.springframework.web.bind.annotation.ExceptionHandler;
import org.springframework.web.bind.annotation.PathVariable;
import org.springframework.web.bind.annotation.RequestBody;
import org.springframework.web.bind.annotation.RequestMapping;
import org.springframework.web.bind.annotation.RequestMethod;
import org.springframework.web.bind.annotation.ResponseStatus;

import com.manning.sbia.ch11.integration.ProductImport;
import com.manning.sbia.ch11.integration.ProductImportGateway;
import com.manning.sbia.ch11.repository.ProductImportRepository;

@Controller
public class ImportProductsController {

    @Autowired
    private ProductImportRepository productImportRepository;

    @Autowired
    private ProductImportGateway productImportGateway;        ❶ Maps HTTP request
                                                                to controller method
    @RequestMapping(
      value="/product-imports/{importId}",
      method=RequestMethod.PUT)                               ❷ Handles response
    @ResponseStatus(HttpStatus.ACCEPTED)                        status code
    public void importProducts(
        @PathVariable String importId,          ◁——❸ Binds import ID from URL path
        @RequestBody String content) {                              ◁
      productImportRepository.createProductImport(importId);   ❹ Binds HTTP
      productImportGateway.importProducts(content);              request content
    }

    @ExceptionHandler(DuplicateKeyException.class)
    @ResponseStatus(                                           ❺ Handles
      value=HttpStatus.CONFLICT,                                 resubmission
      reason="Import already submitted.")
    public void duplicateImport() { }
}
```

For the `DispatcherServlet` to pick up the REST controller, you annotate it with `@Controller`. Because the controller is a Spring-managed bean, it can benefit from dependency injection using the `@Autowired` annotation for its two collaborators. The `importProducts` method handles job submissions and uses Spring MVC annotations to map the HTTP request to the method and to handle the HTTP response. The `@RequestMapping` annotation ❶ maps the URL and the `PUT` operation to the method. The `@ResponseStatus` annotation ❷ sets which status code to send back to the client. At ❸, you bind part of the URL to the first parameter of the controller's `importProducts` method with the `@PathVariable` annotation. Spring MVC automatically fills in this parameter representing the import ID, as defined by the value of the `@RequestMapping` annotation. In the String `"/product-imports/{imported}"`, the `{importId}` placeholder refers to the name of the parameter in the Java method. At ❹, using the `@RequestBody` annotation, you bind the body of the HTTP request with the second parameter of the controller's `importProducts` method. Before we see how to handle the job submission, let's study ❺, where exceptions are handled. By using the `@ExceptionHandler` annotation with a list of exception classes on a controller method, you direct Spring MVC to call this method whenever a controller throws an exception. This means that if Spring MVC catches a `DuplicateKeyException` from the `importProducts` method, it calls the `duplicateImport` method and sends back a 409 status code ("conflict").

> **NOTE** If you want to learn more about Spring MVC and its REST support, read *Spring in Action, Third Edition*, by Craig Walls (Manning Publications, 2011).

Where does a `DuplicateKeyException` come from? It comes from handling the job submission. In figure 11.8, we show two steps to handle submissions: first, we record the import request, and then we send it to the messaging infrastructure. Let's study the first step, where the system can throw a `DuplicateKeyException`.

TRACKING THE JOB SUBMISSIONS WITH A JDBC-BASED REPOSITORY

The system must track job submissions such that system administrators and clients can monitor the lifecycle of each import. The following listing shows how each product import ID is stored in the database thanks to a JDBC-based repository.

Listing 11.7 Tracking job submissions with a JDBC-based repository

```
package com.manning.sbia.ch11.repository.jdbc;

import java.util.Date;
import javax.sql.DataSource;
import org.springframework.dao.DuplicateKeyException;
import org.springframework.jdbc.core.JdbcTemplate;
import org.springframework.stereotype.Repository;
import org.springframework.transaction.annotation.Transactional;
import com.manning.sbia.ch11.repository.ProductImportRepository;

@Repository
@Transactional
public class JdbcProductImportRepository
    implements ProductImportRepository {

  private JdbcTemplate jdbcTemplate;
```

```
public JdbcProductImportRepository(DataSource dataSource) {
  this.jdbcTemplate = new JdbcTemplate(dataSource);
}

@Override
public void createProductImport(String importId)
    throws DuplicateKeyException {
  int count = jdbcTemplate.queryForInt(
    "select count(1) from product_import "+
    "where import_id = ?",importId);
  if(count > 0) {
    throw new DuplicateKeyException(
      "Import already exists: "+importId);
  }
  jdbcTemplate.update(
    "insert into product_import "+
    "(import_id,creation_date) values (?,?)",
    importId,new Date());
}

}
```

> **Checks import existence** *(annotation pointing to the count query block)*
>
> **Inserts import ID in database** *(annotation pointing to the insert block)*

Note that the repository throws a DuplicateKeyException if there's already an import with the same ID in the database. Spring MVC then catches this exception and sends a 409 status code to the client because the web controller's method is annotated with @ExceptionHandler. Listing 11.7 shows the first version of the products import repository; we'll improve it later to map a product import with its corresponding Spring Batch job instance. Let's now see the second step in handling the submission: the Spring Integration gateway.

GETTING ON THE SPRING INTEGRATION BUS THROUGH A GATEWAY

If you go back to the REST controller code in listing 11.6, you see that it sends the XML content of the job submission to a ProductImportGateway. The following snippet shows the definition of the ProductImportGateway interface:

```
package com.manning.sbia.ch11.integration;

public interface ProductImportGateway {

  void importProducts(String content);

}
```

The gateway is an enterprise integration pattern: it allows an application to access the messaging system transparently. The XML content of the job submission goes on the Spring Integration messaging bus, but the REST controller doesn't know anything about it. This makes the REST controller easier to test and more flexible because it can be used in a nonmessaging system by providing it an appropriate ProductImport-Gateway implementation.

But what about our ProductImportGateway messaging implementation, the one that sends the XML content to the messaging bus? We have good news: there won't be any implementation! Spring Integration provides the implementation dynamically. This is the Spring configuration we cover next.

CONFIGURING THE CONTROLLER, REPOSITORY, AND GATEWAY WITH SPRING

It's time to configure the components used to receive product import submissions. If you guessed that we use Spring for this configuration, you're correct. Let's start by registering the Spring MVC REST controller. This configuration must take place in the file /WEB-INF/sbia-servlet.xml. The following XML snippet shows the configuration of the REST controller:

```xml
<?xml version="1.0" encoding="UTF-8"?>
<beans xmlns="http://www.springframework.org/schema/beans"
  xmlns:xsi="http://www.w3.org/2001/XMLSchema-instance"
  xmlns:context="http://www.springframework.org/schema/context"
  xsi:schemaLocation="http://www.springframework.org/schema/beans
    http://www.springframework.org/schema/beans/spring-beans-3.0.xsd
    http://www.springframework.org/schema/context
    http://www.springframework.org/schema/context/spring-context-3.0.xsd">

  <context:component-scan
    base-package="com.manning.sbia.ch11.web" />

</beans>
```

> Registers REST controller with component scanning

That's it! Spring detects the REST controller because you use component scanning and annotate the controller class with `@Controller`. Spring then wires the controller dependencies. Let's now see the configuration for the repository and gateway.

Component scanning

Spring can autodetect beans from classes annotated with specific Spring annotations. This feature is called *component scanning* because Spring scans the classpath to discover candidate classes. The annotations that trigger component scanning are *stereotype* annotations: they also denote the use of the class (web controller or business service, for example). Spring provides annotations like `@Controller`, `@Service`, and `@Repository`, and you can even create your own by annotating them with `@Component`. This allows creating your own stereotypes, also eligible for component scanning.

The repository and gateway are part of the root application context. The following listing shows their configuration along with other infrastructure beans, such as the transaction manager.

Listing 11.8 Declaring the gateway and repository in the root application context

```xml
<?xml version="1.0" encoding="UTF-8"?>
<beans (...)>

  <bean id="productImportRepository"
      class="com.manning.sbia.ch11.repository.jdbc.
  JdbcProductImportRepository">
    <constructor-arg ref="dataSource" />
  </bean>
```

> ❶ Declares repository

```
<int:gateway id="productImportGateway"
  service-interface="com.manning.sbia.ch11.
  ➥  integration.ProductImportGateway"
  default-request-channel="product-imports-as-string"
  />

<int:channel id="product-imports-as-string" />

<int-stream:stdout-channel-adapter
    channel="product-imports-as-string"/>

  <bean id="dataSource"
        class="org.apache.commons.dbcp.
  ➥  BasicDataSource">
    (...)
  </bean>

  <jdbc:initialize-database data-source="dataSource">
    (...)
  </jdbc:initialize-database>

  <bean id="transactionManager"
        class="org.springframework.jdbc.datasource.
  ➥  DataSourceTransactionManager">
    <constructor-arg ref="dataSource" />
  </bean>

  <tx:annotation-driven />

</beans>
```

❷ Declares gateway

❸ Outputs content to console for testing

❹ Declares and initializes data source

❺ Sets up transaction infrastructure

The configuration starts with the repository declaration ❶. This is a plain Spring bean, not much to say. The most interesting part is the gateway declaration ❷. You tell Spring Integration to create an object implementing ProductImportGateway (in the service-interface attribute). This creates a Spring bean that you can inject in any other bean. If you call a method on this bean, Spring Integration wraps the method argument in a message and sends it to the channel set up with the default-request-channel attribute. Remember that the gateway pattern allows application code to access the messaging system transparently. This is a common requirement, and Spring Integration provides a dynamic implementation of this pattern, so you don't need to write any Java code. Spring Integration sends the content of each job submission to the product-imports-as-string channel. At ❸, you send this content to the console. Because this is for testing purpose, you don't wire content transfer to the file system (you'll do that in a later example). Finally, you configure a DataSource ❹ and the transaction infrastructure ❺.

You're done with the configuration, and although the system isn't functional yet, you can easily test it. Let's see how this works.

TESTING A JOB SUBMISSION WITH CURL

The test checks that the REST controller receives a job submission correctly and sends it through the gateway such that the content of the request is output on the console.

All you have to do is send an HTTP PUT request with some content. To do that, you use the command-line tool curl. You create a products.xml file with some valid XML content and execute the following command:

```
curl http://localhost:8080/enterpriseintegration/product-imports/partner1-1
    -H 'Content-type:text/xml;charset=utf-8' -X PUT
    --data-binary @products.xml
```

This command sends an HTTP request with the content of the products.xml file in the body of the request. You should see the content of the file output on the console, due to the stdout-channel-adapter you configured (temporarily) in listing 11.8 at ❸.

As an alternative to curl, let's see a Java solution using the Spring class RestTemplate.

TESTING A JOB SUBMISSION WITH RESTTEMPLATE

Spring MVC not only provides REST support on the server side (see the REST controller), it also provides REST support on the client side. The Spring class RestTemplate is used to consume RESTful web services. In the following snippet, you use the REST template to submit a PUT request with a small XML document in its body:

```
RestTemplate restTemplate = new RestTemplate();
restTemplate.put(
    "http://localhost:8080/enterpriseintegration/product-imports/{importId}",
    "<products />",
    "partner1-1"
);
```

The first parameter of the put method is the URL of the web service. The second parameter is the body of the request (a string with some XML in this case). You can then pass any number of additional parameters for the RestTemplate to bind in the requested URL (in this case, only one, the import ID). By executing the code in the previous snippet, you should see the content of the import—<products />—output on the console.

> **Any other REST clients out there?**
> There are graphical alternatives to curl and to the RestTemplate. Firefox has a helpful plug-in called Poster for performing REST requests. The rest-client (hosted on Google Code) project also provides a graphical Java-based application to test a variety of HTTP communications.

You're getting close to the end of handling a job submission. Next, you need to do something with the content of the submission, namely, the XML document contained in the body of the request. You're going to copy the XML document to a file so that the system picks up the file later and submits it to Spring Batch.

11.4.3 Writing the import file in a directory with Spring Integration

You received a job submission and want to store the products to import in the file system. Because you use a Spring Integration gateway, the content of the import is now

Figure 11.13   The file-writing channel adapter receives messages and copies their payload to the file system. It delegates filename creation to a filename generator (an example of the strategy pattern).

on the messaging bus as an XML document. You could write a custom message handler to receive the content, create a file, and copy the content into it, but as a Java programmer, you know that file I/O in Java is cumbersome. Moreover, writing the content of a message to the file system is a common requirement, so Spring Integration provides a ready-to-use file-writing channel adapter. Figure 11.13 illustrates how the file-writing channel adapter works in the case of our import job submission.

Let's see now how to configure the file-writing channel adapter.

CONFIGURING A FILE-WRITING CHANNEL ADAPTER

Spring Integration provides a dedicated XML element to declare a file-writing channel adapter, as shown in the following XML fragment:

```
<int:channel id="product-imports-as-string" />

<int-file:outbound-channel-adapter
  directory="file:/var/sbia/dropin"
  auto-create-directory="true"
  channel="product-imports-as-string"
  filename-generator="productImportFileNameGenerator"
  />

<bean id="productImportFileNameGenerator"
    class="com.manning.sbia.ch11.integration.
  ProductImportFileNameGenerator" />
```

Copies messages' content on file system

With the outbound-channel-adapter element, a file-writing channel adapter is simple to declare; its XML attributes are self-explanatory.

> **NOTE**   The file-writing channel adapter replaces the stdout-channel-adapter you configured previously to consume job submission messages.

We should point out the default behavior of the file-writing channel adapter: it takes the String payload of incoming messages and uses it as the content of the output file. This is a reasonable default, but the channel adapter needs some help to choose the name of the output file. It delegates this job to a filename generator that you plug in using the filename-generator attribute. This is an example of Spring Integration implementing boilerplate code (file I/O) and letting you plug in your business logic (filename generation).

Next, you create a custom implementation of a filename generator, which uses the import ID as part of the filename.

CREATING THE DESTINATION FILE NAME

You're about to copy the XML document containing the job submission to a file, but you need to be careful about the name of this file, mainly to avoid collisions. Fortunately, each import has a unique ID. Recall the structure of an import file:

```
<?xml version="1.0" encoding="UTF-8"?>
<products import-id="partner1-1">
  (...)
</products>
```

By using this ID in the name of the file, you should be able to avoid duplicate filenames. Spring Integration allows plugging in a filename generation component in its file-writing channel adapter by implementing the `FileNameGenerator` interface. The following listing shows the filename generator implementation, which uses the import ID to generate filenames.

Listing 11.9 Implementing the filename generation strategy

```
package com.manning.sbia.ch11.integration;

import org.springframework.integration.Message;
import org.springframework.integration.file.FileNameGenerator;
import org.springframework.util.Assert;

public class ProductImportFileNameGenerator implements FileNameGenerator {

  @Override
  public String generateFileName(Message<?> message) {
    Assert.notNull(message.getPayload());
    Assert.isInstanceOf(String.class, message.getPayload());
    String payload = (String) message.getPayload();
    return ProductImportUtils.extractImportId(payload)        // Uses import ID
      +".xml";                                                 // for filename
  }

}
```

The `ProductImportFileNameGenerator` class extracts the import ID from the XML document and adds an XML extension to generate the name of the file. A static method in the `ProductImportUtils` class encapsulates the import ID extraction. This method contains some boilerplate XPath code to retrieve the value of the `import-id` attribute (this code isn't worth showing here).

You've completed the handling of import job submissions. Clients can send HTTP PUT requests, and the system tracks each import submission and copies its content to the file system. You can test the submission chain with curl or the `RestTemplate` class and see if the system creates the files in the target directory (assuming that you send a valid XML file with a `products` element and an `import-id` attribute).

Now that the import submissions are safely stored on the file system, you need to send them to a Spring Batch job for processing. The next section covers how to achieve this with Spring Integration.

11.5   *Triggering jobs from file system events*

Our system handles job submissions by receiving them over HTTP and storing them on the file system in a specific target directory. How should the system process these files? You can launch a Spring Batch job every hour to retrieve all files from the directory and import their contents in the database. This is an easy task with a scheduler. But what about *reacting* to a *new* import file in the directory? If you use an event-driven system, files can be imported as soon as they arrive in the directory.

Spring Integration provides a file message source that does exactly that: it polls a file system directory and creates a message for each new file created in this directory. If you can notify the system when a new import file is available, you can trigger a Spring Batch job to import it.

You implemented a message-driven Spring Batch job launcher in the Spring Integration quick-start. The only thing you need to add is functionality to adapt the message coming from the file system to a request message to launch a job. Figure 11.14 illustrates this flow of messages.

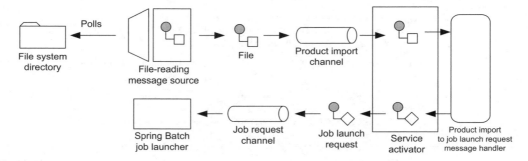

Figure 11.14   Triggering the import job when an import file is created in the submission directory. The Spring Integration inbound file message source polls the submission directory and sends messages for each new file. A custom message handler converts the file messages into job launch messages. Our message-driven job launcher receives these messages to trigger Spring Batch jobs.

In the rest of this section, we cover the configuration of the file-reading message source, the conversion between file messages and job launch messages, and the configuration of the Spring Batch import job. Let's get started.

11.5.1   *Scanning the input directory with Spring Integration*

Spring Integration provides the `inbound-channel-adapter` XML element to declare a message source for reading files. The following snippet shows how to use it to poll our submission directory for new files every second (expressed as 1,000 milliseconds):

```
<int-file:inbound-channel-adapter
    directory="file:/var/sbia/dropin"
    channel="product-imports"
    auto-create-directory="true"
```

```
      filename-pattern="*.xml">
  <int:poller fixed-rate="1000" />
</int-file:inbound-channel-adapter>
```

Every time the inbound file message source detects a new file in the submission directory, it sends a Spring Integration message with a File payload. This message contains
enough information to trigger the import job, but it needs some transformation
before going into our generic job launcher.

11.5.2 Converting a file into a job launch request

Our goal now is to create a Message<JobLaunchRequest> object from a Mes-
sage<File> object. Figure 11.15 illustrates this conversion.

  We haven't implemented the import job yet, but you can guess from figure 11.15
that its name will be importProducts and that it will need the import ID and the path
to the import file as parameters. The following snippet shows the Java class that does
the conversion between the two types of messages:

```java
package com.manning.sbia.ch11.integration;

import java.io.File;
import java.util.HashMap;
import java.util.Map;
import org.apache.commons.io.FilenameUtils;

public class ProductImportToJobLaunchRequestHandler {

  public JobLaunchRequest adapt(File products) {
    String importId = FilenameUtils.getBaseName(
      products.getAbsolutePath()
    );
    Map<String, String> jobParams = new HashMap<String, String>();
    jobParams.put("importId", importId);
    jobParams.put("inputFile", products.getAbsolutePath());
    return new JobLaunchRequest("importProducts",jobParams);
  }

}
```

The ProductImportToJobLaunchRequestHandler class is a POJO, which doesn't know
anything about messaging. You should now know enough about Spring Integration
not to be surprised: we rely on Spring Integration to wrap and unwrap our application
objects around and from messages automatically. You shouldn't be surprised either to

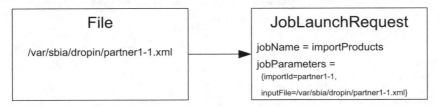

**Figure 11.15   The conversion between a file message and a job launch request message.
The latter then goes to the generic job launcher to trigger the import job.**

learn that a service activator will plug our handler into the messaging infrastructure, as shown in the following snippet:

```
<int:service-activator
    input-channel="product-imports"
    output-channel="job-requests">
  <bean class="com.manning.sbia.ch11.integration.
  ➥ ProductImportToJobLaunchRequestHandler" />
</int:service-activator>
```

That's it; the whole job submission chain is connected to the job launcher! Remember, we started from a REST request, went through the file system, and finally reused our message-driven job launcher. At the end of this chain lies the import job itself, so let's see some Spring Batch code to implement it.

11.5.3 *Implementing the import job*

The import job reads the input XML file and updates the database accordingly. It looks like something Spring Batch can easily handle. Nevertheless, you must implement a preliminary step: mapping the import with the job instance. Why do you need to do that? Imagine you want to know if the partner1-1 import completed successfully. You track imports by inserting their IDs in the database—mainly to avoid resubmissions—but you don't store anything about the status of imports. Spring Batch maintains metadata about

everything it does, so by mapping an import with a job instance, you know the status of the import. Nice, isn't?

Figure 11.16 shows the two steps of the import job.

Let's start at the beginning: the tasklet that maps the import with the job instance.

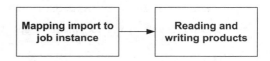

Figure 11.16 The import job has two steps. The first step maps the import to the job instance, which gives you access to the import status. The second step reads the XML file and updates the database.

MAPPING THE IMPORT WITH THE JOB INSTANCE

A custom tasklet is in charge of mapping the import with the job instance. The product_import database table stores the mapping, so you only need to update it. The JdbcProductImportRepository centralizes the operation on the product_import table, so you modify it to add the mapping method, as shown in the following listing.

> Listing 11.10 Updating the repository to map the import with the job instance

```
package com.manning.sbia.ch11.repository.jdbc;

(...)

@Repository
@Transactional
public class JdbcProductImportRepository
    implements ProductImportRepository {

  (...)
```

```
@Override
public void mapImportToJobInstance(String importId, Long jobInstanceId) {
  jdbcTemplate.update(
    "update product_import set job_instance_id = ? where import_id = ?",
    jobInstanceId, importId);
}

}
```

Because a Spring Batch step can't manipulate the repository, you implement the custom `Tasklet` shown in the following listing.

Listing 11.11 Tasklet to map the import with the job instance

```
package com.manning.sbia.ch11.batch;

import org.springframework.batch.core.StepContribution;
import org.springframework.batch.core.scope.context.ChunkContext;
import org.springframework.batch.core.step.tasklet.Tasklet;
import org.springframework.batch.repeat.RepeatStatus;
import org.springframework.beans.factory.InitializingBean;
import org.springframework.util.Assert;
import com.manning.sbia.ch11.repository.ProductImportRepository;

public class ImportToJobInstanceMappingTasklet
    implements Tasklet, InitializingBean {

  private String productImportId;

  private ProductImportRepository productImportRepository;

  @Override
  public RepeatStatus execute(StepContribution contribution,
      ChunkContext chunkContext) throws Exception {
    Long jobInstanceId = chunkContext.getStepContext()           Gets job instance
      .getStepExecution().getJobExecution()                      from runtime
      .getJobInstance().getId();
    productImportRepository.mapImportToJobInstance(              Maps import with
      productImportId, jobInstanceId                             job instance
    );
    return RepeatStatus.FINISHED;
  }

  public void setProductImportId(String productImportId) {
    this.productImportId = productImportId;
  }

  public void setProductImportRepository(
      ProductImportRepository productImportRepository) {
    this.productImportRepository = productImportRepository;
  }

  @Override
  public void afterPropertiesSet() throws Exception {
    Assert.notNull(productImportId);
  }

}
```

The first step of the job is complete. Let's now see how to read products from XML and write them to the database.

READING XML AND WRITING INTO THE DATABASE

The second step is a traditional read-write scenario, so the import isn't a big deal to implement with Spring Batch. You use Spring Batch's XML support to read the XML file and do some configuration. To update the database, you reuse the JDBC writer implemented in chapter 1. Recall that this writer only inserts or updates products in the database, depending on whether those products already exist. You don't write any new code for the writing phase, but you have to do some configuration work.

Spring Batch provides support to map XML fragments with Java objects. The framework integrates with a Spring module called Spring OXM to do this job. Spring OXM is mostly an abstraction that can plug into existing marshalling libraries. We use Castor here, but XStream, JAXB 2, or XMLBeans would work as well.

Castor needs metadata to map an XML fragment to a Java class. The metadata can be in an XML document, as shown in the following listing.

Listing 11.12 Configuring Castor to map XML to the `Product` class

```
<mapping>

  <class name="com.manning.sbia.ch01.domain.Product" identity="id">
    <map-to xml="product" />
    <field name="id" type="string">
      <bind-xml name="id" node="element" />
    </field>
    <field name="name" type="string">
      <bind-xml name="name" node="element" />
    </field>
    <field name="description" type="string">
      <bind-xml name="description" node="element" />
    </field>
    <field name="price" type="big-decimal">
      <bind-xml name="price" node="element"/>
    </field>
  </class>

</mapping>
```

You can then declare a Spring OXM marshaller that points to this mapping file:

```
<bean id="marshaller"
      class="org.springframework.oxm.castor.CastorMarshaller">
  <property name="mappingLocation"
    value="classpath:/com/manning/sbia/ch11/batch/castor-xml-mapping.xml"
    />
</bean>
```

The Spring Batch XML reader needs a reference to this marshaller bean to create product Java objects from the incoming XML file. Let's put all of this together by configuring the job.

CONFIGURING THE JOB

The following listing shows the job configuration, where you wire together the steps and their components: mapping tasklet, reader, and writer.

Listing 11.13 Configuring the import products job

```
<batch:job id="importProducts"
  xmlns="http://www.springframework.org/schema/batch">
  <step id="mapImportToJobInstanceStep"
        next="readWriteProductsStep">
    <tasklet ref="mapImportToJobInstanceTasklet" />
  </step>
  <step id="readWriteProductsStep" >                         Configures
    <tasklet>                                                job
      <chunk reader="productsReader"
             writer="productsWriter"
             commit-interval="100" />
    </tasklet>
  </step>
</batch:job>

<bean id="mapImportToJobInstanceTasklet"
      class="com.manning.sbia.ch11.batch.
  ➥ImportToJobInstanceMappingTasklet"
      scope="step">                                          Declares
  <property name="productImportId"                           mapping tasklet
           value="#{jobParameters['importId']}" />
  <property name="productImportRepository"
           ref="productImportRepository" />
</bean>

<bean id="productsReader"
      class="org.springframework.batch.item.xml.
  ➥ StaxEventItemReader"
      scope="step">
  <property name="unmarshaller" ref="marshaller" />
  <property name="fragmentRootElementName"
            value="product" />
  <property name="resource"                                  Declares reader
       value="file:#{jobParameters['inputFile']}" />         and writer
</bean>

<bean id="productsWriter"
      class="com.manning.sbia.ch01.batch.
  ➥ProductJdbcItemWriter">
  <constructor-arg ref="dataSource" />
</bean>
```

If you're this deep in the book, listing 11.13 should be clear (wink!). You configure the job with a plain `Tasklet` step and a chunk-oriented step. You also use late binding with the step scope to refer to job parameters. Don't hesitate to refer to chapter 5 if you want a quick reminder of an XML reader configuration.

This time, this is it; you completed the import of products! You used enterprise integration techniques to make the update of the online application event driven. Not only do nightly imports update the catalog, but clients can choose to submit updates through HTTP and see results quickly. Spring Batch lives at the end of this chain but fits nicely with REST and event-driven technologies like Spring MVC and Spring Integration.

Now that the import works, we can easily improve the system by adding monitoring features. Next, we provide access to the status of imports through REST.

11.6   *RESTful job monitoring with Spring MVC*

The online store application can now receive updates more frequently; you implemented this feature in the previous section. But the system is a black box to the client that submits imports. How can clients know that the application received and successfully processed the imports they submitted? It's time to complement the REST interface of our new system by communicating the status of imports.

Remember the first step of the import job: mapping the import to the job instance in the database. Spring Batch maintains metadata about the executions of batch processes—this is a key feature for monitoring but also for restarting jobs—so accessing the metadata is useful to communicate the state of an import job to a client.

Our goal is for clients and system administrators to be able to access the status of any import job. The REST controller is the entry point; it retrieves the information from the database thanks to an improved version of the JDBC repository. Figure 11.17 illustrates the architecture of our monitoring feature.

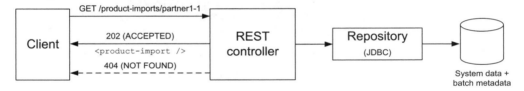

Figure 11.17   A client can find out the status of an import from the REST controller. The controller consults the repository, which uses system data and Spring Batch metadata to communicate the status of import jobs.

Adding this feature requires modifying the JDBC repository, the REST controller, and some configuration in the Spring MVC servlet (but these modifications are minor). Let's start by improving the repository.

11.6.1   *Getting access to the job metadata in the repository*

The `JdbcProductImportRepository` communicates the state of imports through `ProductImport` objects. The following listing shows the implementation of the `Product-Import` class.

> **Listing 11.14   Representing the status of an import in the `ProductImport` class**

```
package com.manning.sbia.ch11.integration;

public class ProductImport {
```

```
private String importId;

private String state;

public ProductImport() { }

public ProductImport(String importId, String state) {
  super();
  this.importId = importId;
  this.state = state;
}

// getters and setters
(...)

}
```

The ProductImport class is a POJO; its only goal is to encapsulate data. You'll see later that the system serializes instances of this class to XML and sends them to the client. For now, you're going to modify the JDBC repository to load ProductImport objects from the database, as shown in the following listing.

Listing 11.15 Retrieving the status of imports from the repository

```
package com.manning.sbia.ch11.repository.jdbc;

import org.springframework.batch.core.JobExecution;
import org.springframework.batch.core.JobInstance;
import org.springframework.batch.core.explore.JobExplorer;
import org.springframework.dao.EmptyResultDataAccessException;
import com.manning.sbia.ch11.integration.ProductImport;
import com.manning.sbia.ch11.repository.ProductImportRepository;
(...)
@Repository
@Transactional
public class JdbcProductImportRepository
    implements ProductImportRepository {

  private JdbcTemplate jdbcTemplate;

  private JobExplorer jobExplorer;

  public JdbcProductImportRepository(
      DataSource dataSource,JobExplorer jobExplorer) {
    this.jdbcTemplate = new JdbcTemplate(dataSource);
    this.jobExplorer = jobExplorer;
  }

  (...)

  @Override
  public ProductImport get(String importId) {
    int count = jdbcTemplate.queryForInt(
      "select count(1) from product_import "+
      "where import_id = ?",importId);
    if(count == 0) {
      throw new EmptyResultDataAccessException(
        "No import with this ID: "+importId,1);
    }
```

 ① Checks import existence

```
    String status = "PENDING";
    Long instanceId = jdbcTemplate.queryForLong(
      "select job_instance_id from product_import "+
      "where import_id = ?",importId);
    JobInstance jobInstance = jobExplorer
      .getJobInstance(instanceId);
    if(jobInstance != null) {
      JobExecution lastJobExecution = jobExplorer
        .getJobExecutions(jobInstance).get(0);
      status = lastJobExecution.getStatus().toString();
    }
    return new ProductImport(importId, status);
  }

}
```

➊ Sets default import status

➌ Gets job instance status

Listing 11.15 shows a new repository class dependency: JobExplorer. The Spring Batch JobExplorer interface provides easy access to batch metadata. The repository uses it to retrieve job instances and job executions. The repository's get method contains the logic to communicate the status of an import. It starts by checking the existence of the import the caller is querying ➊. If the method finds no corresponding import, it throws an exception. Once you know the import exists, you can start thinking about communicating its status. At ➋, you define the default status—PENDING—which means the import exists but no corresponding job instance exists yet (the import file is in the submission directory, waiting for Spring Integration to pick it up). At ➌, you try to find the corresponding job instance, and if it exists, you retrieve the status of its last execution.

> **NOTE**   The repository only communicates the status of the import, but it could also communicate any information available in the batch metadata, such as duration of the import and number of records written and skipped.

The new version of the repository is a good example of using Spring Batch beans to access batch metadata. Because the repository now depends on the job explorer, it requires a modification in its Spring configuration. The following snippet shows how to declare the job explorer and how to inject it in the repository:

```
<bean id="jobExplorer"
      class="org.springframework.batch.core.explore.support.
    ➥ JobExplorerFactoryBean">
  <property name="dataSource" ref="dataSource" />
</bean>
<bean id="productImportRepository"
      class="com.manning.sbia.ch11.repository.jdbc.
    ➥ JdbcProductImportRepository">
  <constructor-arg ref="dataSource" />
  <constructor-arg ref="jobExplorer" />
</bean>
```

Now that the repository connects the application and Spring Batch, let's see how to leverage this information in the web controller.

11.6.2 Communicating job status from a web controller

To communicate the status of an import, the REST web controller needs to follow the strict semantics illustrated back in figure 11.17:

- Answering GET operations from a resource URL
- Sending back a 200 (OK) status code if everything goes fine
- Sending back a 404 (NOT FOUND) status code if there's no import for the requested URL

The following listing shows how to fulfill these requirements with Spring MVC REST.

Listing 11.16 Communicating the status of an import with the web controller

```
package com.manning.sbia.ch11.web;

import org.springframework.beans.factory.annotation.Autowired;
import org.springframework.dao.EmptyResultDataAccessException;
import org.springframework.http.HttpStatus;
import org.springframework.web.bind.annotation.ExceptionHandler;
import org.springframework.web.bind.annotation.PathVariable;
import org.springframework.web.bind.annotation.RequestMapping;
import org.springframework.web.bind.annotation.RequestMethod;
import org.springframework.web.bind.annotation.ResponseBody;
import org.springframework.web.bind.annotation.ResponseStatus;
import com.manning.sbia.ch11.integration.ProductImport;
import com.manning.sbia.ch11.repository.ProductImportRepository;
(...)
@Controller
public class ImportProductsController {

  @Autowired
  private ProductImportRepository productImportRepository;

  (...)

  @RequestMapping(
    value="/product-imports/{importId}",
    method=RequestMethod.GET)                      Sends back
  @ResponseBody                                    product
  public ProductImport getProductImport(          import status
      @PathVariable String importId) {
    return productImportRepository.get(importId);
  }

  @ExceptionHandler(
    EmptyResultDataAccessException.class)          Sends 404 if no
  @ResponseStatus(value=HttpStatus.NOT_FOUND,      import found
    reason="No product import for this ID.")
  public void noImportFound() { }

}
```

The web controller delegates the retrieval of the ProductImport to the repository. If everything goes well, the system sends the ProductImport object to the response-rendering mechanism. Remember that the repository throws an EmptyResultData-AccessException if there's no import for the given ID. Such an exception triggers the exception-handling mechanism in Spring MVC, which calls the noImportFound method (annotated with @ExceptionHandler). The noImportFound method sends back a 404 (NOT FOUND) status code, following REST semantics.

But what happens to the ProductImport returned by the getProductImport method? You want the framework to serialize a ProductImport object to XML and send it back to the client in the response body. Spring MVC can do that, but it needs some hints. The first hint is the @ResponseBody annotation on the getProduct-Import method to trigger a special, REST-oriented rendering of the response in Spring MVC.

This rendering mechanism is based on message converters (HttpMessageConverter is the corresponding Spring interface) whose goal (among others) is to stream a Java object in the HTTP response. Spring MVC registers some default message converters, but you'll need to override them if you want to convert the ProductImport object into XML properly. Fortunately, Spring MVC integrates nicely with Spring OXM to do this job. Recall that in section 11.5.3, where Castor was used to import the XML products file into the database, you complemented the mapping information with instructions for the ProductImport class and plugged the Castor marshaller into Spring MVC.

The following listing shows how to provide the mapping information to Castor for converting a ProductImport object to XML.

Listing 11.17 Completing the Castor configuration to map the ProductImport class

```
<mapping>

  <class name="com.manning.sbia.ch01.domain.Product" identity="id">
    (...)
  </class>

  <class name="com.manning.sbia.ch11.integration.ProductImport">
    <map-to xml="product-import" />
    <field name="importId" type="string">
      <bind-xml name="import-id" node="element" />
    </field>
    <field name="state" type="string">
      <bind-xml name="state" node="element" />
    </field>
  </class>

</mapping>
```

Spring MVC needs to know about the Castor marshaller you defined earlier. This means registering an XML-based message converter using the marshaller and plugging this message converter into Spring MVC's HandlerAdapter. The following listing shows the necessary configuration to make Spring MVC use the XML message converter. Because this is a Spring MVC configuration, it should take place in the file /WEB-INF/sbia-servlet.xml.

Listing 11.18 Using the XML message converter with Spring MVC

```xml
<?xml version="1.0" encoding="UTF-8"?>
<beans (...)>

  <bean class="org.springframework.web.servlet.mvc.annotation.
➥ AnnotationMethodHandlerAdapter">
    <property name="messageConverters">
      <list>
        <bean class="org.springframework.http.converter.
➥ StringHttpMessageConverter" />
        <bean class="org.springframework.http.converter.xml.
➥ MarshallingHttpMessageConverter">
          <constructor-arg ref="marshaller" />
        </bean>
      </list>
    </property>
  </bean>

  <context:component-scan base-package="com.manning.sbia.ch11.web" />

</beans>
```

The Spring configuration in listing 11.18 is complex. Read the corresponding sidebar to learn more details about Spring MVC, handler adapters, and message converters.

Spring MVC, handler adapters, and message converters

The `DispatcherServlet` class is at the heart of the Spring MVC framework. It delegates work to infrastructure beans that include a handler adapter. The `Annotation-MethodHandlerAdapter` is a handler adapter implementation that allows using all of the annotations we've seen on Spring MVC web controllers. The `Dispatcher-Servlet` has such a handler adapter set up by default, but you can override it by declaring your own in the Spring application context for the servlet. That's exactly what you do in listing 11.18, because the default `AnnotationMethodHandlerAdapter` doesn't use Castor to serialize objects into XML returned by web controllers. Message converters registered on the handler adapter perform this serialization. You use a `MarshallingHttpMessageConverter` to use the Castor marshaller. But how can you refer to this Castor marshaller bean? Remember, the root application context defines the marshaller, whose beans are all visible from the application context of a `DispatcherServlet`.

Testing the monitoring feature is easy: first, submit an import to the system (see the source code for this book). Let's assume you submit a `partner1-1` import: you can use curl (or a web browser) to access it:

```
curl http://localhost:8080/enterpriseintegration/product-imports/partner1-1
```

The response (formatted for readability) should look like the following:

```
<?xml version="1.0" encoding="UTF-8"?>
<product-import>
  <import-id>partner1-1</import-id>
  <state>COMPLETED</state>
</product-import>
```

Congratulations, you completed the entire use case! This monitoring feature is the final touch on our enterprise integration system. Clients can now interact and control everything in the system, from import submissions to job monitoring.

11.7   *Summary*

This was quite a journey! Spring Batch can do so much more than handle large amounts of data through nightly cron jobs. Spring Batch is flexible enough to be part of an enterprise integration project that uses the messaging integration style. The scenario used in this chapter illustrates how different systems can communicate using lightweight and effective techniques and stay loosely coupled. Because of our new client submission architecture for imports to the online store, clients can update the catalog more frequently, in a simple way. Implementing our integration use case involved technologies like REST, file manipulation, messaging, and batch processes. Spring technologies—Spring MVC, Spring Integration, and Spring Batch—facilitated this implementation.

We finished by using Spring Batch job metadata to communicate the status of imports to clients. This monitoring feature rounds out our use case and, in chapter 12, you'll discover more monitoring techniques.

Monitoring jobs

12

This chapter covers

- Understanding the job metadata managed by Spring Batch
- Using Spring Batch objects to interact with the job metadata
- Monitoring jobs

In the real world, errors occur when running batch jobs. Batch jobs exchange data between different information systems and tools, and it's not always easy to guarantee consistency among these systems. Detecting job errors is more difficult because jobs don't require user interaction during execution. Detecting errors is also more challenging because applications generally execute batch jobs in the background.

In some cases, rerunning batch jobs is enough to solve problems, such as when a system like a database is temporarily down. When errors are caused by bad data, running the batch job again won't solve the problem. Because batch jobs run mainly in the background, receiving notifications when errors occur is critical. How do you solve this problem? You provide support in your application for batch monitoring and management.

Batch monitoring tracks batch job executions. Spring Batch makes it possible to monitor a job because it collects data on job and step executions and saves it to a database. Spring Batch provides classes to access the database and acts as the foundation for monitoring tools.

In this chapter, we cover what monitoring is and how to monitor job executions in Spring Batch. We then go through the different ways to monitor batch job executions as supported by the job repository database. First, let's see what monitoring is.

12.1   *Introducing monitoring*

In the scope of computer science, the word *monitoring* is used in different contexts: network, system, and website monitoring, for example. In all cases, monitoring aims to detect problems automatically and notify administrators through dedicated consoles and applications. This is a best practice used to detect errors that may occur in an application. For Spring Batch applications, this means detecting errors in jobs and notifying administrators.

In this section, we show what monitoring looks like at a high level and see its function in the context of batch job executions.

12.1.1   *Monitoring overview*

Before we get into the benefits of monitoring, let's first look at a high-level example by monitoring a web application. The goal is to make sure the application is reachable and that it responds to requests within a given time limit. Figure 12.1 depicts monitoring a web application.

For this use case, you can imagine a monitoring tool that checks that the web server process is up, the web application is available through HTTP, and the application responds to requests within a given time limit. This tool displays its results through a web page that it updates periodically and notifies administrators via email when problems occur.

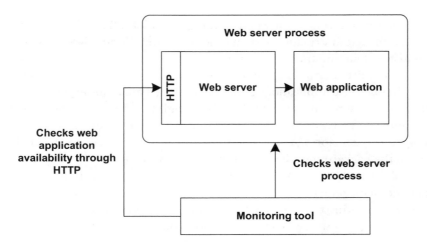

Figure 12.1   Monitoring a web application and checking its availability

A monitoring tool has two main features: detection and notification. The tool detects job execution errors and automatically sends notifications to application administrators depending on the severity of the problem. We call these notifications *alerts*. A tool can send an alert using email, Short Message Service (SMS), instant messaging, and so on. Monitoring an application warns you quickly of errors and provides information to allow you to diagnose and solve problems. This improves applications' availability.

You now have a high-level view of monitoring. Let's see how monitoring works with batch jobs in Spring Batch.

12.1.2 Batch jobs and monitoring

Monitoring is particularly useful and even essential in the context of batch jobs because applications execute jobs in the background without a user interface.

Monitoring is possible with Spring Batch because it records everything that happens during batch job executions in a job repository database. Figure 12.2 shows interactions between batch job executions and monitoring tools using the job repository database.

In figure 12.2, you can see that Spring Batch stores everything that happens during job execution in the job repository database; tools also access the job repository

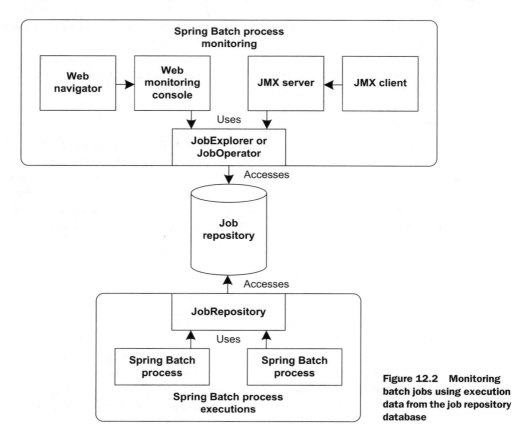

Figure 12.2   Monitoring batch jobs using execution data from the job repository database

database to provide monitoring and management. The repository tracks not only the whole batch job but also its component steps. This makes it possible to know precisely when and where errors occur.

You now know what monitoring is and what it looks like in general, as well as how it applies to batch jobs. It's time to get to the meat of the chapter by focusing on the job repository and detecting errors. Next, we describe accessing the job repository database from Java applications using the Spring Batch API. We also use Spring Batch Admin and JMX to monitor batch job executions.

When executing batch jobs, Spring Batch records information about what happens in the job repository database. This information is the foundation used to monitor executions.

12.2 *Accessing batch execution data*

As described in the previous section, monitoring uses data from the job repository database managed by the Spring Batch infrastructure. The first step in monitoring batch job executions is to understand the Spring Batch database schema. You'll then learn how to access the data using Spring Batch.

In this section, you use a database-based repository with JDBC. You should use an in-memory repository only for tests, not in production environments. Spring Batch provides a set of Data Access Objects (DAOs) that every class interacting with the persistent job repository uses internally. First, we look at the job database schema used by Spring Batch for a persistent job repository. Learning about this schema helps you understand how to monitor applications.

12.2.1 *Job database schema*

Spring Batch includes a built-in database schema for persistent job repositories but doesn't provide automatic schema creation. Spring Batch does, however, contain all the necessary scripts used to create this schema depending on your database. The scripts are located in the org.springframework.batch.core package. Spring Batch uses JDBC to interact with the job repository database. You use Spring's JDBC facilities and its JDBC XML vocabulary to create the database structure, as in following snippet:

```
<bean id="dataSource" class="(...)"> (...) </bean>

<jdbc:initialize-database data-source="dataSource">
  <jdbc:script
    location="classpath:/org/springframework/batch/core/schema-h2.sql"/>
  <!-- Additional scripts for application -->
  <jdbc:script location="classpath:/create-tables.sql"/>
</jdbc:initialize-database>
```

After configuring the data source to access the job repository, you specify the class path location of the H2 database script. Script filenames follow the pattern schema-<DATABASE-TYPE>.sql. All SQL scripts create the tables described in figure 12.3. Notice that Spring Batch also provides cleanup scripts for dropping the tables. These

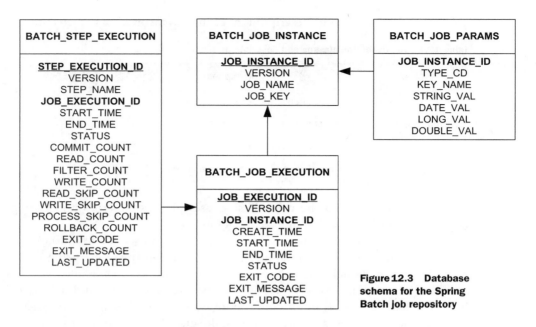

Figure 12.3 Database schema for the Spring Batch job repository

scripts are located in the same package and follow the pattern schema-drop-<DATA-BASE-TYPE>.sql.

Figure 12.4 shows the Spring Batch classes that carry the same data as the database tables. These classes store everything that happens during batch job executions. Because they provide an object-oriented representation of the tables they map, we use these classes to describe the schema.

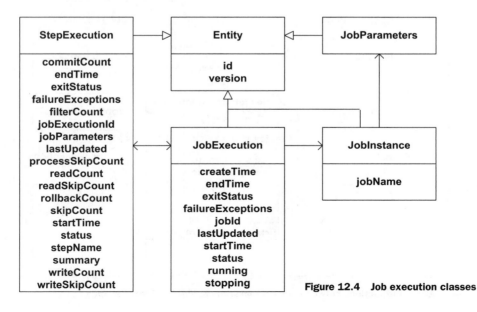

Figure 12.4 Job execution classes

Table 12.1 provides a short description of each class involved in job executions.

Table 12.1   Job execution classes and descriptions

Class	Description
JobInstance	A job instance with a set of parameters
JobParameters	The parameters of a job instance
JobExecution	An execution of a job instance
StepExecution	An execution of a step within a job execution

To help you understand the roles these classes play, we describe how Spring Batch populates these objects when it executes a job.

When Spring Batch launches a job, it first checks to see if a job instance exists. A job instance includes a set of parameters. With this information, Spring Batch determines if it can launch the job. Spring Batch then creates a job execution that includes information like the creation timestamp, start time, and a link to its job instance. The last task is to execute the job steps. After Spring Batch executes each job step, the exit status is set on each step; the global exit status for the job is set after all steps are executed.

Figure 12.5 shows the interactions between a job's lifecycle and the job repository.

You now know what happens during job execution and how Spring Batch populates data in the job repository. It's time to see what data is present in the job repository database after an execution of the imports products job from our case study. As

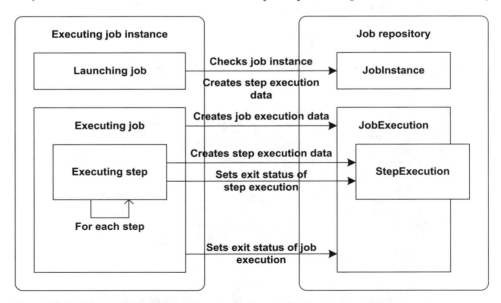

Figure 12.5   Interactions between job and repository during batch execution

JOB INSTANCE ID	VERSION	JOB NAME	JOB KEY
1	0	importProductsJob	eb11e6a10180f...
2	0	importProductsJob	b978628fe2d72f...
3	0	importProductsJob	f8acd1ef3e70fc...
4	0	importProductsJob	147fd7e660593...

Figure 12.6   Contents of the BATCH_JOB_INSTANCE table

you may recall, the job consists of a single step: read products from a file and insert them in a database table.

You launch the job `importProductsJob` four times with different parameters. Figure 12.6 shows the contents of the BATCH_JOB_INSTANCE table.

Because you launched the job `importProductsJob` four times, you have four rows in the BATCH_JOB_INSTANCE table. For each job instance, you execute the job only once, so you find one job execution row per job instance in the BATCH_JOB_EXECUTION table, for four rows, as shown in figure 12.7. In addition to the start and end times of the execution, you can also see the status and exit codes and that only one execution completed successfully; the other three failed.

JOB EXECUTION ID	VERSION	JOB INSTANCE ID	START TIME	END TIME	STATUS	EXIT CODE
1	2	1	2010-10-21 ...	2010-10-2...	FAILED	FAILED
2	2	2	2010-10-21 ...	2010-10-2...	FAILED	FAILED
3	2	3	2010-10-21 ...	2010-10-2...	COMPLETED	COMPLETED
4	2	4	2010-10-21 ...	2010-10-2...	FAILED	FAILED

Figure 12.7   Contents of the BATCH_JOB_EXECUTION table

The BATCH_STEP_EXECUTION table provides an additional level of detail. You can see which steps the job executed for each job execution, as described in figure 12.8. Because there's only a single step in the `importProductsJob` job, you find four rows for the executions (one per execution) and see that only a single step ended successfully. The exit codes of these step executions correspond to the exit codes of the job executions.

These database tables let you follow the execution of batch jobs and see what happens at both the job and step levels. You can easily get into the database with a tool like Squirrel—a universal SQL client for JDBC—but Spring Batch provides entities and facilities to access and visualize the data from Java applications and monitoring tools.

In the next section, we describe how to explore the job repository using Spring Batch facilities and how to detect problems in batch job executions.

STEP ...	...	STEP NAME	START TIME	END TIME	...	COMMI...	READ...	...	...	...	...	ROLLBACK...	EXIT CODE
1	2	readWrite	2010-10-2...	2010-10-2...	...	0	2	0	0	0	0	1	FAILED
2	2	readWrite	2010-10-2...	2010-10-2...	...	0	2	0	0	0	0	1	FAILED
3	3	readWrite	2010-10-2...	2010-10-2...	...	1	7	0	7	1	0	0	COMPLETED
4	2	readWrite	2010-10-2...	2010-10-2...	...	0	7	0	0	1	0	2	FAILED

Figure 12.8   Contents of the BATCH_STEP_EXECUTION table

12.2.2 *Accessing data from the job repository*

In addition to providing data structures for job metadata, Spring Batch provides entities that provide easy access to the job repository. In chapter 2, we introduced the JobRepository interface. In chapter 3, section 3.3, we showed how to configure a repository but not how to use it in detail. In this section, we explore this subject and describe different ways to interact with the job repository. We begin by using the JobRepository interface.

USING THE JOBREPOSITORY INTERFACE

Spring Batch defines the JobRepository interface for its internal infrastructure use when executing batch jobs. Spring Batch uses a JobRepository to interact with the job repository during batch job execution. Spring Batch also uses a JobRepository to check parameters when starting jobs and storing information corresponding to job and step executions. You configure a JobRepository and reference it from the job configuration.

This section presents an overview of the services the JobRepository interface offers. We describe how to use a JobRepository during batch execution, but we don't use it for batch monitoring. The following listing shows the JobRepository interface.

Listing 12.1   The JobRepository interface

```
public interface JobRepository {
  boolean isJobInstanceExists(String jobName, JobParameters jobParameters);
  JobExecution createJobExecution(
      String jobName, JobParameters jobParameters)
      throws JobExecutionAlreadyRunningException, JobRestartException,
          JobInstanceAlreadyCompleteException;
  void update(JobExecution jobExecution);
  void add(StepExecution stepExecution);
  void update(StepExecution stepExecution);
  void updateExecutionContext(StepExecution stepExecution);
  void updateExecutionContext(JobExecution jobExecution);
  StepExecution getLastStepExecution(
                JobInstance jobInstance, String stepName);
  int getStepExecutionCount(JobInstance jobInstance, String stepName);
  JobExecution getLastJobExecution(
                String jobName, JobParameters jobParameters);
}
```

Spring Batch defines the JobRepository interface for use by the job infrastructure to populate the job repository with job and step execution data. We don't recommend using a JobRepository outside the Spring Batch infrastructure. Fortunately, Spring Batch provides other objects for such use cases. The first one we discuss, the Job-Explorer interface, lets you explore the job repository content in read-only mode.

EXPLORING THE JOB REPOSITORY

The Spring Batch infrastructure uses the JobRepository interface during batch job execution to store job and step data. But JobRepository methods aren't well suited to exploring the job repository.

To explore the job repository, Spring Batch provides a dedicated interface, the JobExplorer, which offers methods to get information about job and step executions for both running and completed jobs and steps. The JobExplorer interface defines methods to get job execution, step execution, and job instance data, as described in the following listing.

Listing 12.2 The `JobExplorer` interface

```
public interface JobExplorer {
  Set<JobExecution> findRunningJobExecutions(String jobName);
  JobExecution getJobExecution(Long executionId);
  List<JobExecution> getJobExecutions(JobInstance jobInstance);
  JobInstance getJobInstance(Long instanceId);
  List<JobInstance> getJobInstances(
                      String jobName, int start, int count);
  List<String> getJobNames();
  StepExecution getStepExecution(
                  Long jobExecutionId, Long stepExecutionId);
}
```

As for the JobRepository interface, Spring Batch provides a built-in default implementation based on JDBC and previously described DAOs. To facilitate configuring a JobExplorer, Spring Batch provides the JobExplorerFactoryBean class. This factory class requires only a data source and a large object (LOB) handler for configuration. This allows the explorer to configure DAOs to save execution contexts automatically.

The following snippet configures a job explorer using the JobExplorerFactory-Bean class.

```
<bean id="jobExplorer"
      class="org.springframework.batch.core
                 .explore.support.JobExplorerFactoryBean">      Configures
  <property name="dataSource" ref="dataSource"/>               job explorer
  <property name="lobHandler" ref="lobHandler"/>
</bean>

<bean id="dataSource" class="(...)"> (...) </bean>
<bean id="lobHandler"
      class="org.springframework.jdbc.support.lob.DefaultLobHandler"/>
```

Now that you've configured a JobExplorer entity, let's see how you can use it. Table 12.2 describes each method of the JobExplorer interface. These methods act as the foundation for the next section, which describes how to detect job execution problems.

Table 12.2 `JobExplorer` interface methods

Method	Description
getJobNames	Gets the names of running or completed jobs. Use the names returned by this method to find job instances.
findRunningJobExecutions	Finds all currently running job executions.

Table 12.2   `JobExplorer` **interface methods** *(continued)*

Method	Description
getJobExecution	Returns a job execution based on an identifier. Use this method with a job execution identifier from the getJobExecutions method.
getJobExecutions	Gets all job executions for a job instance.
getJobInstance	Gets a job instance for an identifier.
getJobInstances	Gets all job instances for a job name.
getStepExecution	Gets a job execution for a job and step execution identifier. The JobExplorer interface doesn't have a method to return all step executions. Use the JobExecution class to do this.

The following snippet describes how to use the `JobExplorer` interface to find all currently running job instances.

```
List<JobExecution> runningJobInstances = new ArrayList<JobExecution>();
List<String> jobNames = jobExplorer.getJobNames();
for (String jobName : jobNames) {
  Set<JobExecution> jobExecutions
        = jobExplorer.findRunningJobExecutions(jobName);
  runningJobInstances.addAll(jobExecutions);
}
```

The `JobExplorer` interface is the root interface used to browse data contained in the job repository. The `JobOperator` interface let's you interact with and control job executions using job metadata. We cover this interface, which can also stop jobs, in chapter 4, section 4.5.1.

The `JobOperator` interface is similar to the `JobExplorer` interface but uses simpler types. The `JobOperator` interface also includes methods to start and stop jobs. The following listing shows the `JobOperator` interface.

Listing 12.3   **The** `JobOperator` **interface**

```
public interface JobOperator {
  List<Long> getExecutions(long instanceId);
  List<Long> getJobInstances(String jobName, int start, int count);
  Set<String> getJobNames();
  String getParameters(long executionId);
  Set<Long> getRunningExecutions(String jobName);
  Map<Long,String> getStepExecutionSummaries(long executionId);
  String getSummary(long executionId);
  Long restart(long executionId);
  Long start(String jobName, String parameters);
  Long startNextInstance(String jobName);
  boolean stop(long executionId);
}
```

As you can see, the JobOperator interface is similar to the JobExplorer interface, but it uses String and Long identifiers instead of Spring Batch metadata objects. Note the difference in the behavior of the getJobNames methods: the JobExplorer method looks at the repository and returns a sorted list of unique job instance names. The JobOperator method returns the available job names you can launch with the start method.

The JobOperator interface is lightweight and particularly suitable for monitoring technologies like JMX, which we examine in section 12.5.

Using what we've learned in this section, particularly the JobExplorer interface, we see next how to address real-life use cases monitoring batch jobs.

DETECTING PROBLEMS DURING JOB EXECUTIONS

As emphasized early in this chapter, the primary goal of job monitoring is to find out if, when, and where something went wrong. In this section, we present a practical example to detect problems and their causes. In sections 12.4 and 12.5, we follow the same pattern to find problems.

A common use case in monitoring is detecting batch job failures. You detect failed jobs by iterating over all job names and then finding job executions for job instances that end with a failed exit status. The following listing shows how to implement this detection algorithm using the JobExplorer interface. You use this code to iterate over the job names retrieved with the getJobNames method.

Listing 12.4 Detecting failed job instances

```
public List<JobExecution> getFailedJobExecutions(String jobName) {
  List<JobExecution> failedJobExecutions = new ArrayList<JobExecution>();

  int pageSize = 10;
  int currentPageSize = 10;
  int currentPage = 0;

  while (currentPageSize == pageSize) {                          ❶ Gets job instances for job
    List<JobInstance> jobInstances
                = jobExplorer.getJobInstances(
                        jobName, currentPage * pageSize, pageSize);
    currentPageSize = jobInstances.size();
    currentPage++;
    for (JobInstance jobInstance : jobInstances) {               ❷ Gets job executions for instance
      List<JobExecution> jobExecutions
                = jobExplorer.getJobExecutions(jobInstance);
      for (JobExecution jobExecution : jobExecutions) {
        if (jobExecution.getExitStatus().equals(                 ❸ Detects execution failures
                        ExitStatus.FAILED)) {
          failedJobExecutions.add(jobExecution);
        }
      }
    }
  }
}
```

First, you use the job name to get job instances, in pages, using the getJobInstances method ❶ from the JobExplorer interface. You call this method until you get to the last page. Using the job instance list, you then get the corresponding job executions with the getJobExecutions method ❷. By checking the exit status of each job execution, you can find which jobs ended in failure. You use the getExitStatus of the JobExecution class ❸ to check the exit status.

When you detect failed batch jobs, you investigate causes. Failures can occur at two levels during batch execution: job and step. After identifying the failed job execution, you can collect errors at both the job execution and step execution levels. The Job-Execution and StepExecution classes can also provide this information using the getExitStatus and getFailureExceptions methods, as described in table 12.3.

Table 12.3 JobExecution and StepExecution methods related to failures

Method	Description
getFailureExceptions	Returns the list of exceptions that caused the execution failure. Spring Batch populates this list during batch execution.
getExitStatus	Returns the execution exit code. The method returns an ExitStatus, which contains both the exit code and exit description.

These methods provide information on what went wrong during job executions. Exceptions are accessible through the getFailureExceptions method. The following listing describes how to query a failed job execution to get to the exceptions that caused the failures.

Listing 12.5 Getting exceptions that cause job execution failure

```
private List<Throwable> getFailureExceptions(JobExecution jobExecution) {
  List<Throwable> failureExceptions = new ArrayList<Throwable>();

  if (!jobExecution.getExitStatus().equals(ExitStatus.FAILED)) {
    return failureExceptions;
  }
  List<Throwable> jobFailureExceptions
                  = jobExecution.getFailureExceptions();
  failureExceptions.addAll(jobFailureExceptions);

  for (StepExecution stepExecution : jobExecution.getStepExecutions()) {
    List<Throwable> stepFailureExceptions
                    = stepExecution.getFailureExceptions();
    failureExceptions.addAll(stepFailureExceptions);
  }
  return failureExceptions;
}
```

❶ Gets failure exceptions for job

❷ Gets failure exceptions for steps

After checking the exit status to see if the job execution failed, you get a list of failure exceptions for this execution ❶. You then iterate over executed steps for the job execution and get the corresponding failure exceptions ❷. You add all exceptions to a List returned by the method.

Because Spring Batch doesn't save these exceptions in the job repository, this information is reachable only from the same process that runs the job execution. If you want to find the cause of a job execution failure after the job completes, you need to use the description of the exit status. The following listing describes how to retrieve all failure descriptions for a job execution.

Listing 12.6 Getting descriptions of problems that cause job execution failure

```
private List<String> getFailureExitDescriptions(
                     JobExecution jobExecution) {
  List<String> exitDescriptions = new ArrayList<String>();

  if (!jobExecution.getExitStatus().equals(ExitStatus.FAILED)) {
    return exitDescriptions;
  }
  String jobExitStatus                                          ❶ Gets exit
          = jobExecution.getExitStatus();                          description for job
  if (jobExitStatus.getExitDescription().isEmpty()) {
    exitDescriptions.add(jobExitStatus.getExitDescription());
  }

  for (StepExecution stepExecution : jobExecution.getStepExecutions()) {
    ExitStatus stepExitStatus
                  = stepExecution.getExitStatus();                ❷ Gets exit descriptions
    if (stepExitStatus.equals(ExitStatus.FAILED)                    for steps
            && !"".equals(stepExitStatus.getExitDescription())) {
      exitDescriptions.add(stepExitStatus.getExitDescription());
    }
  }

  return exitDescriptions;
}
```

The implementation of the getFailureExitDescriptions method is similar to the implementation of the getFailureExceptions method. After using the exit status to check that the job execution failed, you get the exit status description for the failed execution ❶. You then iterate over executed steps for the job execution and get the corresponding failure exit descriptions ❷. You add all descriptions to a List returned by the method.

In some cases, it's interesting to get execution information even if the executions are successful. It's particularly interesting when skips or retries occur. This makes it possible, for example, to detect whether or not skips are normal. The getSkipCount method of the StepExecution class provides information on the number of processed skips during execution, as described in the following snippet:

```
private boolean hasSkipsDuringExecution(JobExecution jobExecution) {
  for (StepExecution stepExecution : jobExecution.getStepExecutions()) {
    if (stepExecution.getSkipCount() > 0) {                        ❶ Check skip
      return true;                                                    count
```

```
      }
    }
    return false;
}
```

By iterating over all executed steps for a job execution, the method checks if the step execution contains skips using the JobExecution getSkipCount method ❶. If the returned value is greater than zero, the job contains at least one skip.

You can translate this processing using the JobOperator interface. Because Job-Operator methods deal only with simple types, you must use the summary methods, getSummary and getStepExecutionSummaries, to get details on errors or skip counts. In section 12.5, we describe how to use the JobOperator methods to monitor job executions.

You can use the JobExplorer and JobOperator interfaces to monitor job executions. You can also use tools to save time, receive notifications, and explore the job repository. Next, we describe how to receive notifications using a listener.

12.3   *Monitoring with listeners*

You can use two approaches to monitor jobs: active and passive. In this section, we show how to implement passive monitoring to send notifications when something goes wrong during batch job executions. We base our implementation on the Spring Batch listener feature.

We also describe how to implement and configure a generic monitoring listener for any use case. In this example, monitoring doesn't use data from the job repository but uses in-memory objects for the current batch job execution. When the listener receives failure notifications, you can then query the repository for more information.

12.3.1 *Implementing a monitoring listener*

The batch listener triggers notifications when failures occur during batch executions. Because you want to support different notification mechanisms (in our examples, email and Spring messaging), you create a general-purpose interface called Batch-MonitoringNotifier. By using this interface with a notification listener, you keep the listener generic and configurable.

The BatchMonitoringNotifier interface defines a single method named notify, which takes one argument: the current JobExecution instance. The job execution contains the job instance and failure exceptions. The following snippet shows the BatchMonitoringNotifier interface:

```
public interface BatchMonitoringNotifier {
  void notify(JobExecution jobExecution);
}
```

With this interface defined, you can build a generic monitoring listener. This listener uses the notifier when a job execution fails. The following listing provides an implementation of such a listener using Spring Batch annotations.

Listing 12.7 Implementation of the monitoring execution listener

```
public class MonitoringExecutionListener {
  private BatchMonitoringNotifier monitoringNotifier;           ◁─┐  References
                                                                 ❶  monitoring notifier
  @BeforeJob
  public void executeBeforeJob(JobExecution jobExecution) {
    //Do nothing
  }

  @AfterJob
  public void executeAfterJob(JobExecution jobExecution) {
    if(jobExecution.getStatus() == BatchStatus.FAILED) {        ◁─┐  Notifies
      //Notify when job fails                                    ❷  failures
      monitoringNotifier.notify(jobExecution);
    }
  }

  public void setMonitoringNotifier(
                  BatchMonitoringNotifier monitoringNotifier) {
    this.monitoringNotifier = monitoringNotifier;
  }
}
```

The `BatchMonitoringNotifier` interface is an instance variable ❶ in the `MonitoringExecutionListener` class. When Spring Batch calls this listener after a job executes, if the status of the job execution is `FAILED` ❷, the listener calls the monitoring notifier with the current `JobExecution` instance as its parameter.

The configuration of this execution listener follows the same rules as described in chapter 3, section 3.4.3. The following listing uses the `listeners` XML element to register the monitoring notifier in the `importProductsJob` job.

Listing 12.8 Configuring the monitoring listener

```
<batch:job id="importProductsJob">
  <batch:step id="readWrite">
    (...)
  </batch:step>
  <batch:listeners>                                              ❶  Registers
    <batch:listener ref="monitoringJobListener"/>         ◁─┘       listener for job
  </batch:listeners>
</batch:job>
                                                           ❷  Defines listener
<bean id="monitoringJobListener"                     ◁─┘      as bean
     class="com.manning.sbia.ch12.notifier.MonitoringExecutionListener">
  <property name="monitoringNotifier"                      ◁─┐  Sets
          ref="monitoringNotifier"/>                        ❸  notifier
</bean>

<bean id="monitoringNotifier"
     class="com.manning.sbia.ch12.notifier.BatchMonitoringNotifierImpl">
  (...)
</bean>
```

You use the listener XML element ❶ to register the listener in the job with a bean reference. You then define the listener ❷. You also define a property of type Batch-MonitoringNotifier and inject it in the listener configuration ❸.

You have implemented a generic framework to trigger notifications when failures occur; you can now implement some notifiers. You start with a JavaMail notifier, which sends emails when the listener detects a problem.

12.3.2   *Notifying using emails*

Our first notification use case is sending emails when failures occur. In this case, the application administrator receives emails containing error descriptions for failed jobs. This implementation is based on the JavaMail API and the corresponding Spring support.

This example uses a Spring MailSender to send an email and a Spring Simple-MailMessage to build the message content. The following listing describes this MonitoringNotifier implementation.

Listing 12.9   JavaMail failure notifier

```
public EmailMonitoringNotifier implements BatchMonitoringNotifier {
  private MailSender mailSender;
  private SimpleMailMessage templateMessage;

  private String formatExceptionMessage(Throwable exception) {
    ByteArrayOutputStream baos = new ByteArrayOutputStream();
    exception.printStackTrace(new PrintStream(baos));
    return baos.toString();
  }

  private String createMessageContent(JobExecution jobExecution) {
    List<Throwable> exceptions = jobExecution.getFailureExceptions();
    StringBuilder content = new StringBuilder();
    content.append("Job execution #");
    content.append(jobExecution.getId());
    content.append(" of job instance #");
    content.append(jobExecution.getJobInstance().getId());
    content.append(" failed with following exceptions:");
    for (Throwable exception : exceptions) {
      content.append("");
      content.append(formatExceptionMessage(exception));
    }
    return content.toString();
  }

  public void notify(JobExecution jobExecution) {
    SimpleMailMessage msg = new SimpleMailMessage(
      this.templateMessage
    );
    msg.setTo("batch-administrator@example.com");         ❶ Defines email
    String content = createMessageContent(                  message
      jobExecution
    );
    msg.setText(content);
```

❶ Defines email message

```
    try{
      mailSender.send(msg);
    } catch(MailException ex) { (...) }
  }
  (...)
}
```

◁─┐ **Sends**
❷ **message**

In the `notify` method, you create an email message using the `SimpleMailMessage` class. You set the recipient address and the plain text content created from data contained in the job execution ❶. You then use the injected `MailSender` instance to send the message ❷.

To configure this notifier, you define a Spring JavaMail sender and a template for messages. The following listing describes how to configure the email-based notifier.

Listing 12.10 Configuration of the JavaMail failure notifier

```
<bean id="mailSender"
      class="org.springframework.mail.javamail.JavaMailSenderImpl">
  <property name="host" value="mail.manning.com"/>
</bean>
<bean id="templateMessage"
      class="org.springframework.mail.SimpleMailMessage">
  <property name="from" value="batch-notifier@example.com"/>
</bean>
<bean id="emailMonitoringNotifier"
      class="com.manning.sbia.ch12.notifier.EmailMonitoringNotifier">
  <property name="mailSender" ref="mailSender"/>
  <property name="templateMessage" ref="templateMessage"/>
</bean>
```

◁─┐
Defines JavaMail ❶
entity
◁─┘

❷ **Injects**
entities

You first define JavaMail entities using Spring support ❶ and then inject them in the email-based notifier ❷.

Because Spring provides a generic messaging mechanism between beans configured in application contexts, it's also possible to provide a `BatchMonitoringNotifier` implementation that triggers events in this system rather than using JavaMail. This mechanism provides the ability to implement transparent bridges between technologies. In the next section, we describe how to implement a monitoring notifier that creates and sends messages using Spring messaging.

12.3.3 Notifying using Spring messaging

Sending email messages is good, but it's specific to a single messaging technology. Using the generic messaging feature in Spring opens the door to using other technologies for failure notifications like Java Management Extension (JMX). This feature is built in to the `ApplicationContext` and allows beans to send messages to each other. This corresponds to implementing the listener pattern in the Spring container. The Spring container itself uses this generic messaging framework to notify entities it manages of events like container initialization and finalization.

The two key messaging types are the `ApplicationEventPublisher` interface for sending messages and the `ApplicationEvent` class for consuming them. In order to notify, you configure Spring to inject an `ApplicationEventPublisher` instance in the notifier, which must also implement the Spring `ApplicationEventPublisher-Aware` interface. The following listing shows the implementation of a Spring messaging notifier.

Listing 12.11 Spring messaging notifier

```
public class ApplicationEventMonitoringNotifier
        implements ApplicationEventPublisherAware, MonitoringNotifier {
  private ApplicationEventPublisher applicationEventPublisher;

  (...)

  public void notify(JobExecution jobExecution) {
    String content = createMessageContent(jobExecution);
    applicationEventPublisher. publishEvent(
        new SimpleMessageApplicationEvent(this, content));
  }

  public void setApplicationEventPublisher(
          ApplicationEventPublisher applicationEventPublisher) {
    this.applicationEventPublisher = applicationEventPublisher;
  }
}
```

❶ Sends message

In this example, the `notify` method uses the `ApplicationEventPublisher` instance (configured through injection) to send a message ❶ to other beans present in the Spring application context. You create the message using the Spring `SimpleMessage-ApplicationEvent` class.

Configuration of the `ApplicationEventMonitoringNotifier` class is simple because all you do is define the notifier as a bean:

```
<bean id="applicationEventMonitoringNotifier"
      class="com.manning.sbia.ch12.notification
              ➥  .ApplicationEventMonitoringNotifier"/>
```

As you can see, this mechanism is generic and dispatches events from batch jobs in the Spring configuration, but this isn't all you can do. You can also plug in a listener using the `ApplicationListener` interface.

We've now finished our overview of the API used to implement monitoring of batch job executions. Choosing this low-level approach can be a bit tedious. We focus next on higher-level tools to monitor batch jobs. We begin with Spring Batch Admin.

12.4   *Web monitoring with Spring Batch Admin*

Spring Batch Admin is the monitoring web console that ships with Spring Batch. It provides a quick and convenient way to explore the job repository using a web browser. This approach falls into the active monitoring category because you need to use the tool to see if something went wrong; it doesn't provide notifications. We introduced this

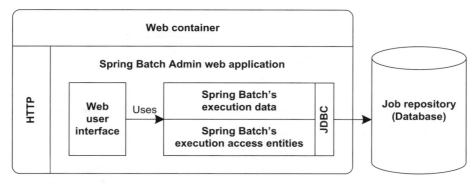

Figure 12.9 Overview of the Spring Batch Admin architecture

tool briefly in chapter 2 to display batch execution results. Appendix B covers how to install and set up Spring Batch Admin.

Figure 12.9 provides an overview of Spring Batch Admin and shows the tool running in a Java web server using Spring Batch execution data and JDBC-based DAOs to access the job repository.

Because Spring Batch Admin maps batch execution concepts and data into its UI, the information displayed will be familiar when using the tool. You can find batch execution problems with the same concepts as when using the Spring Batch API. In this section, we first provide an overview of the tool's capabilities and then describe how to detect problems.

12.4.1 *Feature overview*

You can look at Spring Batch Admin as an application layer on top of the job explorer described in section 12.2.2. Figure 12.10 shows how to navigate Spring Batch Admin.

One feature of Spring Batch Admin is the ability to import job configuration files. This feature makes it possible to manage executions (start, stop, and so on) directly through the web console. This section concentrates on how to use the tool to access information on job executions.

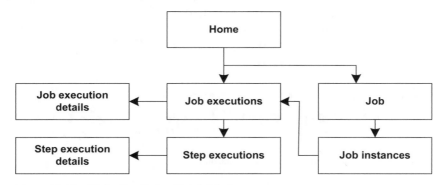

Figure 12.10 Navigating Spring Batch Admin

Job Names Registered

Name	Description	Execution Count	Launchable	Incrementable
infinite	No description	0	true	true
job1	No description	0	true	true
job2	No description	0	true	false
importProductsJob	No description	1	false	false

Rows: 1-4 of 4   Page Size: 20

Figure 12.11   Job names registered

Job Instances for Job (importProductsJob)

ID		JobExecution Count	Last JobExecution	Parameters
1	executions	1	COMPLETED	{date=1287995689949}

Rows: 1-1 of 1   Page Size: 20

Figure 12.12   Job instances for a given job

Recent and Current Job Executions

[Stop All]

ID	Instance	Name	Date	Start	Duration	Status	ExitCode
1	1	importProductsJob	2010-10-25	10:34:50	00:00:00	COMPLETED	COMPLETED

Rows: 1-1 of 1   Page Size: 20

Figure 12.13 Recent and current job executions

You execute the importProductsJob job from our case study, which contains a step named readWrite. When the job execution is in progress or is finished, the corresponding job and job instance are present in the UI, as shown in figures 12.11 and 12.12.

Figure 12.12 shows that the job instance contains the execution you launched and that it completed successfully. You can quickly see that the last execution completed successfully. You can then go to the recent and current job executions page and click on the job execution to see its details, as shown in figures 12.13 and 12.14.

The last details you can get to are those of step executions. You reach these pages by following the link on the job execution details page from figure 12.14. This gives you access to the information illustrated in figures 12.15 and 12.16.

Details for Job Execution

[Stop]

Property	Value
ID	1
Job Name	importProductsJob
Job Instance	1
Job Parameters	date(date)=2010/10/25
Start Date	2010-10-25
Start Time	10:34:50
Duration	00:00:00
Status	COMPLETED
Exit Code	COMPLETED
Step Executions Count	1
Step Executions	[readWrite]

Figure 12.14   Details for a job execution

Step Executions for Job = importProductsJob, JobExecution = 1

ID		Job Execution	Name	Date	Start	Duration	Status	Reads	Writes	Skips	ExitCode
1	detail	1	readWrite	2010-10-25	08:34:50	00:00:00	COMPLETED	8	8	0	COMPLETED

Figure 12.15   Step execution list for the job execution

The Spring Batch Admin tool lets you quickly access information on batch job executions. It provides a job list and the ability to drill down to details, all from a web browser. This is a great tool for monitoring batch jobs remotely. The main benefit is that you now have a way to detect failures.

12.4.2 Detecting problems encountered during batch executions

In the previous section, the tables in the figures contained fields named *Status* and *ExitCode*, which tell you about the success and failure of job and step executions.

If you see FAILED, you can conclude that something went wrong during an execution. As when using the job explorer, you look at the job and step details to know more about what failed. As an example of finding a failure, we introduce a malformed field in the input file of the importProductsJob batch job of our case study. Execute the job again, and you'll see in the job executions list and details that there was a problem, as shown in figures 12.17 and 12.18.

Details for Step Execution

Property	Value
ID	1
Job Execution	1
Job Name	importProductsJob
Step Name	readWrite
Start Date	2010-10-25
Start Time	08:34:50
Duration	00:00:00
Status	COMPLETED
Reads	8
Writes	8
Filters	0
Read Skips	0
Write Skips	0
Process Skips	0
Commits	1
Rollbacks	0
Exit Code	COMPLETED
Exit Message	

Figure 12.16   Details of the step execution

Recent and Current Job Executions for Job = importProductsJob, instanceId = 2

Stop All

ID	Instance	Name	Date	Start	Duration	Status	ExitCode
2	2	importProductsJob	2010-10-25	12:16:55	00:00:00	FAILED	FAILED

Figure 12.17   Recent and current job executions containing a failed job execution

Because the error occurs while importing the input file, you can't see the details of this error at the job execution level. You must look at the details of the corresponding step. This is the readWrite step from our case study, the only step in the importProductsJob job.

When displaying the step details, you see the corresponding error in the exit message field. This message corresponds to the exception thrown when trying to parse the malformed field. This exception is a FlatFileParseException, as shown in figure 12.19.

Figure 12.19 shows the step execution details page, which displays information related to failures and skips. This makes it possible to detect

Details for Job Execution

Abandon

Restart

Property	Value
ID	2
Job Name	importProductsJob
Job Instance	2
Job Parameters	date(date)=2010/10/25
Start Date	2010-10-25
Start Time	12:16:55
Duration	00:00:00
Status	FAILED
Exit Code	FAILED
Step Executions Count	1
Step Executions	[readWrite]

Figure 12.18   Details of a failed job execution

Details for Step Execution

Property	Value
ID	2
Job Execution	2
Job Name	importProducts.Job
Step Name	readWrite
Start Date	2010-10-25
Start Time	10:41:47
Duration	00:00:00
Status	FAILED
Reads	0
Writes	0
Filters	0
Read Skips	0
Write Skips	0
Process Skips	0
Commits	0
Rollbacks	1
Exit Code	FAILED
Exit Message	org.springframework.batch.item.file.FlatFileParseException: Parsing error at line: 2, input=[PR....210,BlackBerry 8100 Pearl,,124.60dd] at org.springframework.batch.item.file.mapping.DefaultLineMapper.mapLine(DefaultLineMapper.java:49) at org.springframework.batch.item.file.FlatFileItemReader.doRead(FlatFileItemReader.java:188) at org.springframework.batch.item.support.AbstractItemCountingItemStreamItemReader.read(AbstractItemCountingItemStreamItemReader.java:85

Figure 12.19   Details of a step execution failure include a stack trace in the exit message.

when skips occur during executions if they occur using the read skips, write skips, and process skips properties.

Using tools like Spring Batch Admin layered on top of Spring Batch to access the job repository saves you a lot of time. Spring Batch Admin uses the Spring Batch low-level API to provide a web console to monitor batch jobs. Next, we use JMX, the Java technology dedicated to management, to monitor our application.

12.5   *Monitoring with JMX*

JMX supplies management and monitoring tools for applications and devices (like printers). JMX represents resources with objects called *MBeans* (Managed Beans).

The success of JMX is such that Sun integrated it in J2SE as of version 5.0. Today, many Java EE application servers and frameworks use JMX. Applications that implement JMX provide access to information about application resources and provide administrative operations for live applications.

To understand how Spring Batch integrates with JMX, you must understand the JMX architecture. The layered architecture of JMX exposes application resources as MBeans through the *instrumentation* layer. The *MBean server* is responsible for handling resources exposed as remote resources through the *distributed services* layer. Figure 12.20 shows the layers of the JMX architecture. JMX clients like JConsole or applications can connect to agents through server-side connectors using client-side connectors.

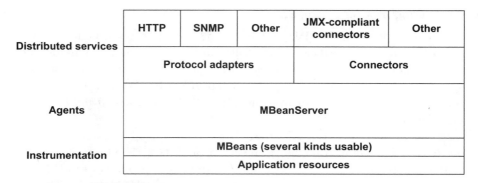

HTTP	SNMP	Other	JMX-compliant connectors	Other

Distributed services

Protocol adapters	Connectors

Agents — MBeanServer

Instrumentation

MBeans (several kinds usable)

Application resources

Figure 12.20 JMX architecture

Integrating Spring Batch with JMX involves exposing Spring Batch resources as JMX-managed resources. Spring provides support to expose any POJO as an MBean. Although exporting jobs is possible, you normally expose JobOperator entities as MBeans. Note that using a JobExplorer through JMX isn't great because it exposes complex objects, not simple ones like a JobOperator.

The JMX launcher configures and registers a JobOperator with JMX for running jobs asynchronously. Monitoring clients can then access the JobOperator through JMX. Clients include the standard Java *jconsole* application and any clients accessing entities remotely through JMX connectors. Figure 12.21 illustrates this architecture.

As shown in the figure, the first step is to define the Spring Batch monitoring process that configures Spring Batch's entities for JMX monitoring. This means configuring the JobOperator entity and exporting it as an MBean in the JMX server through Spring's JMX support. Although not mandatory, you commonly define batch structures at this level to manage them (start, stop, and so on) directly through JMX via a JobOperator. Next, we describe how to access and use entities present in the JMX server. Based on these entities, we monitor batch jobs and their executions.

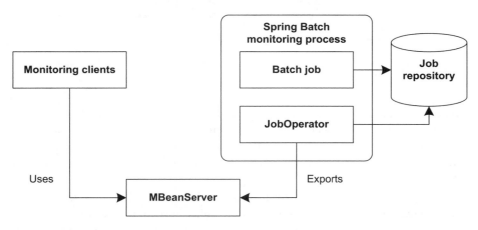

Figure 12.21 Using JMX with Spring Batch

12.5.1 *Configuring JMX for Spring Batch*

The main type in Spring JMX is the MBeanExporter class, which is responsible for transparently creating MBeans from POJOs and determining which fields and methods are reachable through JMX. Because Spring JMX is out of the scope of this book, we focus only on how to use Spring JMX to export Spring Batch entities through JMX. If you want to go deeper, refer to Craig Walls' *Spring in Action, Third Edition* (Manning Publications, 2010).

We describe how to configure the JobOperator entity in chapter 4, listing 4.6. Based on this configuration, you export objects through JMX. The first step is to define the bean corresponding to the JobOperator in the beans property of the MBeanExporter that defines beans to export and their corresponding JMX identifiers. The second step uses the assembler property to determine which data to export through JMX. The following listing shows how export a JobOperator bean through JMX.

Listing 12.12 Exporting a JobOperator through JMX

```
<bean class="org.springframework.jmx.export.MBeanExporter">
  <property name="beans">
    <map>
      <entry key="spring:service=batch,bean=jobOperator">        ① Exports job operator
        <bean class="org.springframework.aop.framework.ProxyFactoryBean">
          <property name="target" ref="jobOperator"/>
          <property name="interceptorNames" value="exceptionTranslator" />
        </bean>
      </entry>
    </map>
  </property>
  <property name="assembler">                                     ② Defines elements to export
    <bean class="org.springframework.jmx.export
                     .assembler.InterfaceBasedMBeanInfoAssembler">
      <property name="interfaceMappings">
        <map>
          <entry key="spring:service=batch,bean=jobOperator"
              value="org.springframework.batch.core.launch.JobOperator"/>
        </map>
      </property>
    </bean>
  </property>
</bean>
(...)
```

When you reference the jobOperator bean in the beans property of the MBean-Exporter bean, you specify its corresponding object name in JMX ①. In the case of the jobOperator bean, the domain is spring with two key-value property pairs. The first property specifies that the object be relative to a batch. The second property is the bean name.

Within the assembler property, you use the InterfaceBasedMBeanInfoAssembler class, which uses beans to define which fields and methods are reachable through JMX ②. For the previous JMX path, you specify use of the JobOperator interface.

> **JMX object names**
>
> A JMX object name is an MBean identifier and must conform to the syntax defined by the JMX specification. This syntax is a domain name and a colon, followed by a comma-separated list of key-value pairs. For example:
>
> ```
> spring:service=batch,bean=jobOperator.
> ```

The configuration doesn't define an MBean server for the MBeanExporter bean. The MBeanExporter bean can detect the current MBean server automatically from the JVM process. For example, Spring uses the MBean server from the JVM process with no additional configuration.

You access JMX remotely because the MBean server doesn't run on the same machine as the clients (by design). Therefore, you must configure a JMX *server connector*, which the JMX specification defines to allow remote access to JMX agents. JMX supports Remote Method Invocation (RMI) natively, and you can configure Spring JMX using its ConnectorServerFactoryBean class, as shown in the following listing. In this case, JMX manages RMI transparently for remote access.

Listing 12.13 Configuring a JMX server connector

```
<bean id="registry"                                      ◁──❶ Defines RMI registry
      class="org.springframework. remoting.rmi.RmiRegistryFactoryBean">
  <property name="port" value="1099"/>
</bean>                                                  ❷ Configures JMX
                                                     ◁──┘  connector
<bean id="serverConnector"
      class="org.springframework.jmx.support.ConnectorServerFactoryBean">
  <property name="objectName" value="connector:name=rmi"/>
  <property name="serviceUrl"
            value="service:jmx:rmi://localhost/jndi/
         ➥  rmi://localhost:1099/myconnector"/>
  <property name="threaded" value="true"/>
</bean>
```

You create the RMI registry with the Spring RmiRegistryFactoryBean class ❶ and set the RMI port. You then configure a JMX server connector with the ConnectorServerFactoryBean class ❷. After defining the path of the connector in JMX with the objectName property, you specify the address to access the JMX server through RMI with the serviceUrl property.

At this point, you've configured everything to monitor Spring Batch jobs through JMX. The next section focuses on how to explore batch execution data and find problems.

12.5.2 *Monitoring with JMX consoles*

Starting with Java 5, JMX, an MBean server, and JConsole are built into the Java platform. You launch JConsole using the jconsole command on the command line.

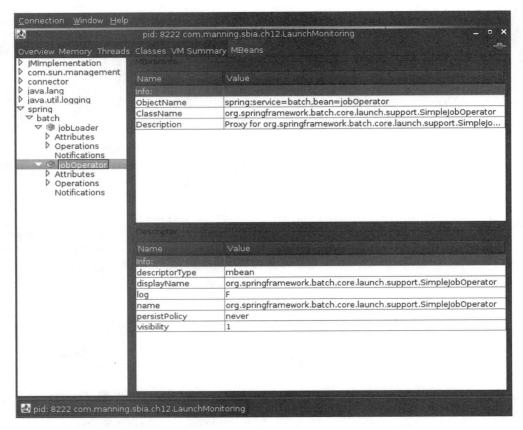

Figure 12.22   Monitoring batch jobs using JConsole

JConsole provides monitoring information on the Java process, its memory usage, thread and class information, and MBeans. JConsole displays both internal and user-defined MBeans. For JMX configurations used to monitor batch jobs in JConsole, corresponding MBeans are located under the spring/batch tree node of the MBean explorer tree in the left pane, as shown in figure 12.22.

Each MBean has a set of attributes and operations. In the case of the JobOperator MBean, these operations allow retrieving execution data, as shown in figure 12.23.

Using these methods, you monitor and manage a Spring Batch job, its instances, and its failures. This section follows the same use case as in

Figure 12.23   Viewing JobOperator operations (methods) in JConsole

the Spring Batch Admin section. First, you get job instances based on a job name, `importProductsJob` for the case study, as described in figure 12.24. The `getJobInstances` method returns job instance identifiers. Remember that the `JobInstance` class uses simple types exclusively. Using these identifiers, you can retrieve identifiers corresponding to job executions with the `getExecutions` methods, as shown in figure 12.25.

Figure 12.24 Getting job instance identifiers for a job name

Using a job execution identifier, you can use the `getSummary` and `get-StepExecutionSummaries` methods to get detailed information of what happened during execution at both the job and step execution levels. These two methods return a `String` containing information on executions, including the exit status and exit

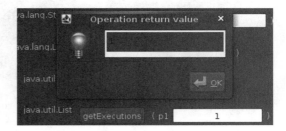

Figure 12.25 Getting job execution identifiers for a job instance

description, which you can use to detect errors and their causes.

Figures 12.26 and 12.27 describe calls to the methods `getSummary` and `getStepExecutionSummaries`. Figures 12.18 and 12.19 show the same information.

Spring Batch integrates well with JMX, the Java standard management technology, for monitoring purposes. Using Spring JMX support, you can expose `JobOperator`

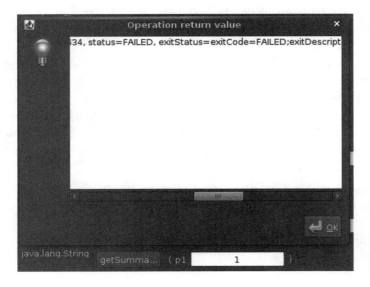

Figure 12.26 Displaying the summary of a job execution

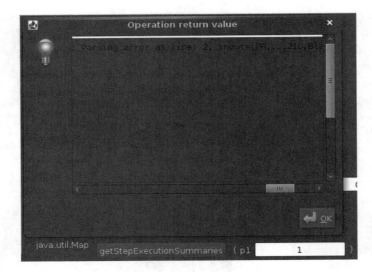

Figure 12.27   Displaying summaries for all step executions of a job execution

objects and interact with the job repository. You can then access these objects remotely through a JMX console like JConsole to remotely execute operations, get execution information, and manage batch job executions.

12.6   *Summary*

Monitoring is an important aspect of working with batch jobs because it lets you see what happens during job executions and detect failures. All through this chapter, we focused on which features and tools Spring Batch provides to monitor batch job executions and detect failures.

Spring Batch offers various ways to monitor batch job executions:

- *Directly browse the job repository database*—The most basic approach is to browse history data directly in the job repository database using a SQL client and executing SQL requests.
- *Access execution history using the Spring Batch API*—The `JobExplorer` and `JobOperator` interfaces implement a thin object-oriented layer on top of the job repository database.
- *Use Spring Batch Admin*—Spring Batch provides the Spring Batch Admin web console used to monitor batch job executions based on the job repository database.
- *Monitor with JMX*—You can use Spring Batch and JMX together to expose Spring Batch entities and access job execution history.

We don't recommend using the Spring Batch API directly in most cases. A better approach is to use high-level tools like Spring Batch Admin or JMX through a console like JConsole. In chapter 13, we focus on advanced features of Spring Batch used to improve performance: scaling jobs and parallelizing executions.

Scaling and parallel processing

13

This chapter covers
- Introducing scaling concepts
- Deciding when and where to use scaling
- Learning how to scale batch jobs
- Exploring scaling patterns and techniques

Now that you have some real batch jobs under your belt, you can test them for performance in a development or testing environment. But what do you do when performance isn't good enough?

You implement scaling and partitioning! Spring Batch provides several scaling techniques to improve performance without making code changes. You implement scaling by reconfiguring jobs, not changing code. For partitioning, you implement code to divide work between a master and slave nodes.

In this chapter, we discuss general scaling concepts for batch processing and, in particular, the Spring Batch model for scaling and partitioning. We look at the different ways to scale applications à la Spring Batch and describe various solutions.

We finish with guidelines for choosing the most efficient techniques to improve the performance of your batch job.

13.1   Scaling concepts

Before tackling scaling in Spring Batch, we describe what scaling is and how it can generally help improve the performance of your applications. We then see how to apply scaling concepts in the context of batch jobs.

Spring Batch provides a scaling framework and various implementations to improve the performance of jobs and steps through configuration changes without modifying code.

13.1.1   Enhancing performance by scaling

Batch jobs are a bit particular with regard to scaling because they run in the background and don't require user interaction. For this reason, measuring the response time for user requests isn't an applicable performance metric. Batch jobs do have constraints on the time it takes to process an entire job. Batch applications usually run at night and have a limited time window to complete. The goal of scaling a batch job is to meet execution time requirements.

As with any application, you can tune the step and application algorithms. This is the first step to consider, but processing can still take too much time even after such improvements. You must then consider scaling your batch applications.

Scaling is the capability of a system to increase total throughput under an increased load when you add resources (typically hardware). You can consider several approaches to implement scaling for your applications:

- *Vertical scaling (scale up)*—Getting a bigger, better, and faster machine that hosts the application to reach the desired performance.
- *Horizontal scaling (scale out)*—Adding more processing nodes (or machines) to a system to handle load. This approach aims to distribute processing remotely on several nodes.

With vertical scaling, you work at the computer and system levels to achieve what is also called *local scaling*. Such an approach is particularly interesting if you want to leverage multicore or multiprocessor hardware, as illustrated in figure 13.1. Local scaling is suitable if processing implies a lot of I/O.

Horizontal scaling uses another approach by distributing processing over several nodes, as shown in figure 13.2. Each node supports a portion of the processing load. In this

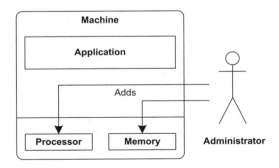

Figure 13.1   Vertical scaling (scaling up) migrates an application to more powerful hardware.

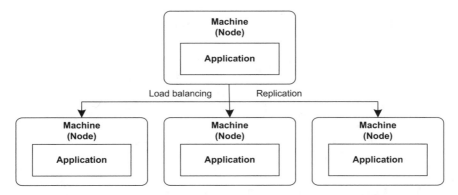

Figure 13.2 Horizontal scaling splits application processing on different nodes and requires load balancing.

scenario, computers don't necessarily need to be as powerful as in the vertical approach. Horizontal scaling commonly integrates mechanisms like load balancing, replication, and remote scaling.

Horizontal scaling can leverage grid and cloud computing in order to implement remote processing.

This concludes our brief overview of scaling concepts. We now have a high-level view of the two techniques we use to improve batch job performance: horizontal and vertical scaling. Next, we see how to implement horizontal and vertical scaling with minimum impact on applications.

13.1.2 *The Spring Batch scaling model*

As described in the early chapters of this book, Spring Batch offers a generic frame-work to support batch job concepts. Job, Step, Tasklet, and Chunk are all domain objects in the batch job world. These types define a job and its parts. By default, Spring Batch executes all jobs sequentially.

Scaling in Spring Batch defines how to execute processing in parallel, locally, or on other machines. Scaling takes place mainly at the step level, and you can use different strategies to define at which level you want to split processing. You can choose to par-allelize whole steps or only parts of their processing. You can also define datasets and process them in parallel locally or remotely. The best technique (or combination of techniques) is the one that allows your application to meet your performance expecta-tions. Figure 13.3 depicts Spring Batch local scaling, and figure 13.4 shows Spring Batch remote scaling.

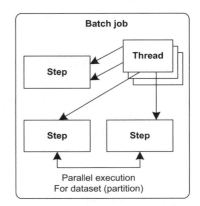

Figure 13.3 Local scaling in a single process executes batch job steps in parallel.

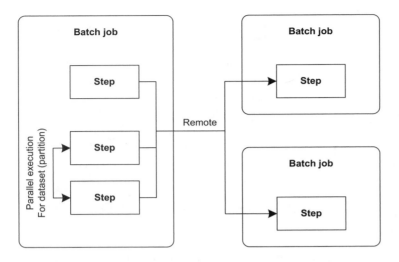

Figure 13.4   Remote scaling in more than one process executes batch job steps in parallel.

You can implement batch job scaling through configuration by using the Spring Batch XML vocabulary for multithreading and parallel step execution. For more advanced uses, you must configure steps with additional specialized objects.

Table 13.1 lists all scaling strategies provided by Spring Batch, shows if the strategy supports local or remote scaling, and describes its main feature.

Table 13.1   Scaling strategies provided by Spring Batch

Strategy	Local/Remote	Description
Multithreaded step	Local	A step is multithreaded.
Parallel step	Local	Executes steps in parallel using multithreading.
Remote chunking	Remote	Distributes chunk processing to remote nodes.
Partitioning step	Local and remote	Partitions data and splits up processing.

Before exploring each scaling strategy provided by Spring Batch, let's look at the features of local and remote scaling and the use of the Spring task executor.

LOCAL AND REMOTE SCALING

As noted in table 13.1, Spring Batch supports both local and remote scaling. Implementing scaling on a single machine uses multithreading through the Spring task executor abstraction that we describe in the next section. Spring Batch natively supports this feature without any advanced configuration. When specified, multithreading is automatically performed when executing steps.

Remote scaling is more complex: it requires a remoting technology like Java Messaging Service (JMS) or GridGain, and you must plug in scaling to batch processing using Spring Batch hooks. This allows you to remotely execute a step or process a chunk. Remote scaling is more complex to configure and use but it provides higher scalability.

Spring Batch doesn't provide implementations for remoting; it provides only the generic framework to plug in different service providers. The Spring Batch Admin module Spring Batch Integration aims to fill this void using Spring Integration facilities. We look at Spring Batch Integration in the remote chunking and partitioning sections.

THE SPRING TASK EXECUTOR ABSTRACTION

The Spring framework provides a Java 5–independent abstraction for using thread pools called the *task executor*. This abstraction is identical to the concept of the executor introduced in Java 5 and uses the same contract.

Concurrency and Java 5

Java 5 introduced the java.util.concurrent package, which includes classes commonly useful in concurrent programming. The package uses hardware-level constructs to allow efficient use of concurrency in Java programs without resorting to native code. The package provides classes and interfaces for collections (map, queue, list, and so on), executors (threads), synchronizers (semaphore), and timing.

The Spring task executor lets you execute a task according to a strategy by implementing the `java.lang.Runnable` interface. The following snippet lists the Spring Task-Executor interface:

```
public interface TaskExecutor {
  void execute(Runnable task);
}
```

This interface is used internally by Spring and its portfolio projects, but it can also be used for your own needs. It specifies execution of `Runnable` code in a multithreaded environment. The implementation is responsible for implementing the appropriate strategy. The following snippet describes how to use the `TaskExecutor` interface in an application. The first line creates the task executor, and the last line executes the task:

```
TaskExecutor taskExecutor = createTaskExecutor();
for(int i = 0; i<25; i++) {
  String message = "Execution " + i);
  taskExecutor.execute(new SampleTask(message));
}
```

The following listing shows the `SampleTask` class that implements the `Runnable` interface and prints a message to the console from its run method.

Listing 13.1 Implementing the `Runnable` interface

```
public class SampleTask implements Runnable {
  private String message;

  public SampleTask(String message) {
    this.message = message;
  }
```

```
public void run() {
    System.out.println(message);
  }
}
```

This technique simplifies multithreading usage in an application. It provides a simple contract and hides complexity in the implementations. Table 13.2 lists the main Spring `TaskExecutor` implementations.

Table 13.2   Main Spring `TaskExecutor` implementations

Implementation	Description
SimpleAsyncTaskExecutor	Starts a new thread for each invocation. Supports a concurrency limit, which blocks any invocations that are over the limit until a slot is free.
ThreadPoolTaskExecutor	Wraps and configures a Java 5 ThreadPoolExecutor class, which manages the thread pool.
WorkManagerTaskExecutor	Wraps and configures a CommonJ WorkManager class, which provides support for executing concurrent tasks.

Each of these `TaskExecutor` implementations can be configured as a bean in the Spring configuration and injected in other Spring-powered plain old Java objects (POJOs). The following snippet describes how to configure a `TheadPoolTaskExecutor`. It first defines a task executor bean and then specifies task executor properties:

```
<bean id="taskExecutor"
  class="org.springframework.scheduling.concurrent.ThreadPoolTaskExecutor">
  <property name="corePoolSize" value="5"/>
  <property name="maxPoolSize" value="10"/>
  <property name="queueCapacity" value="25"/>
</bean>
```

The Spring `TaskExecutor` interface provides a uniform way to add concurrent processing to Spring applications. Spring Batch uses a `TaskExecutor` to enable multithreading in batch jobs. This feature is particularly useful to scale applications locally and enable parallel processing. Practically speaking, when scaling locally, you declare a `TaskExecutor` bean and plug it into Spring Batch.

Now that you know the core concepts behind scaling, let's see the Spring Batch techniques for implementing it. For each technique, we describe its features, configuration, and when it applies. We start by adding multithreading to an application.

13.2   *Multithreaded steps*

By default, Spring Batch uses the same thread to execute a batch job from start to finish, meaning that everything runs sequentially. Spring Batch also allows multithreading at the step level. This makes it possible to process chunks using several threads.

> **Spring Batch entities and thread safety**
>
> Make sure you check the documentation of the readers and writers you use before configuring a step for multithreading. Most of the built-in Spring Batch readers and writers aren't thread-safe and therefore are unsafe for use in a multithreaded step. If the Javadoc for a class doesn't document thread safety, you need to look at the implementation to determine thread safety and make sure the code is stateless. You can still work with thread-safe (stateless) readers and writers; see the Spring Batch `parallelJobs` example, which demonstrates using a progress indicator for reading items from a database.

You can use multithreading to avoid waiting on one object (reader, processor, or writer) to finish processing one chunk in order to process another. Reading, processing, and writing chucks can take place in separate execution threads. This technique may not improve performance and is useful only if multithreading is supported by the hardware. Your mileage may vary. For example, performance wouldn't increase on a machine with one processor core and a job doing a huge amount of processing, but the technique would be more efficient for a job performing a lot of I/O.

Figure 13.5 illustrates how a step handles reading and writing using multiple threads.

One consequence of this approach is that the step doesn't necessarily process items in order. There's no guarantee as to the item processing order, so you should consider the order random or undefined. We look at this aspect of multithreading later in this section with an example.

We're done with multithreaded step concepts, so let's dive into configuration and usage.

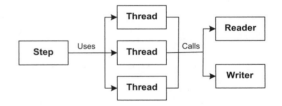

Figure 13.5   A step reading and writing using multiple threads

13.2.1   Configuring a multithreaded step

Configuring a multithreaded step in Spring Batch is simple because it involves only specifying a task executor for the step's tasklet. Spring Batch then automatically enables multithreading for the step and uses the task executor to process chunks.

The following listing describes how to configure and add multithreading to our `readWriteProductsStep` used to import products. For this example, we rename it `readWriteProductsMultiThreadedStep`.

Listing 13.2   Configuring a multithreaded step

```
<batch:job id="importProductsMultiThreadedJob">
  <batch:step id="readWriteProductsMultiThreadedStep">
    <batch:tasklet task-executor="taskExecutor">
```

```
        <batch:chunk reader="reader" writer="writer" commit-interval="10"/>
      </batch:tasklet>
    </batch:step>
  </batch:job>

  <bean id="taskExecutor"
    class="org.springframework.scheduling.concurrent.ThreadPoolTaskExecutor">
    <property name="corePoolSize" value="5"/>
    <property name="maxPoolSize" value="5"/>
  </bean>
```

The XML `tasklet` element sets the `task-executor` attribute, which is used to specify a `TaskExecutor` implementation configured as a Spring bean. Using this attribute automatically enables multithreading for the step.

Because understanding what happens when multithreading is involved is a bit difficult, let's see how it works by running an import of 100 products. You add trace statements in the reader and writer to see which thread executes read and write operations. The following listing shows a portion of the console output.

Listing 13.3   Console output when importing products using threads

```
(...)
thread #5 - read product with product id #51
thread #5 - read product with product id #52
thread #5 - read product with product id #53
thread #3 - read product with product id #54
thread #5 - read product with product id #55
thread #3 - read product with product id #56
thread #5 - read product with product id #57
thread #3 - read product with product id #58
thread #5 - read product with product id #59
thread #3 - read product with product id #60
thread #5 - read product with product id #61
thread #3 - read product with product id #62
thread #5 - read product with product id #63
thread #3 - read product with product id #64
thread #5 - read product with product id #65
thread #3 - read product with product id #66
thread #5 - read product with product id #67
thread #3 - read product with product id #68
thread #3 - read product with product id #69
thread #5 - write products with product ids #51, #52, #53,
  ➡ #55, #57, #59, #61, #63, #65, #67
thread #3 - read product with product id #70
thread #3 - write products with product ids #54, #56, #58,
  ➡ #60, #62, #64, #66, #68, #69, #70
(...)
```

Listing 13.3 shows items processed in separate execution threads. The main consequence of this approach is that Spring Batch doesn't read items sequentially; chunks may contain items that aren't consecutive because threads read input data progressively and concurrently. Each thread builds its own chunk using a reader and passes this chunk to the writer. When a thread reaches the commit interval for a chunk,

Spring Batch creates a new chunk. Because you're using stock Spring Batch readers and writers that aren't thread-safe, you must read, process, and write items from the same thread. Furthermore, out-of-order item processing must be supported for the application if you want to use this technique. Listing 13.3 also shows that each chunk built by a reader on a thread contains the number of items specified in the commit interval, except for the last items.

When configured for multithreading, the `tasklet` element also accepts an additional attribute called the `throttle-limit`. This attribute configures the level of thread concurrency and has a default value of 6. This is particularly useful to ensure that Spring Batch fully utilizes the thread pool. You must check that this value is consistent with other pooling resources such as a data source or thread pool. A thread pool might prevent the throttle limit from being reached. Ensure the core pool size is larger than this limit.

The following listing uses the `throttle-limit` attribute to configure a multithreaded step.

Listing 13.4 Setting the throttle limit of a multithreaded step

```
<batch:job id="importProductsMultiThreadedJob">
  <batch:step id="readWriteProductsMultiThreadedStep">
    <batch:tasklet task-executor="taskExecutor"
                   throttle-limit="5">           ◁—┐ Sets throttle
      (...)                                         │ limit to 5
    </batch:tasklet>
  </batch:step>
</batch:job>
(...)
```

This approach is particularly interesting to get several threads to process chunks in parallel and save execution time. Multithreading also has its drawbacks, because it implies concurrent access of readers, processors, and writers. Such issues can be problematic when the implementations aren't thread-safe. The next section focuses on these multithreading issues.

13.2.2 Multithreading issues

Spring Batch frees you from thread management in your code, but the nature of operating in a multithreaded environment means that you must be aware of its limitations and requirements. This is a similar situation as with Java EE environments and servlets. All objects shared by threads must be thread-safe to insure correct behavior. The bad news here is that most Spring Batch readers and writers aren't thread-safe. We call such objects *stateful*.

The most problematic classes regarding thread safety in Spring Batch are `Item-Reader` implementations because they commonly manage the state of processed data to make jobs restartable. To understand this better, take the example of a non-thread-safe `ItemReader` implementation, the `JdbcCursorItemReader` class. This class uses a JDBC `ResultSet` to read data and carries no thread-safety guarantee. For this reason

Thread safety

Thread safety describes the behavior of code when several threads access it concurrently. We say code (like a class) is thread-safe if you can use it in a multithreaded environment and it still produces correct results. This mainly means that conflicts don't arise when using its static and instance variables. Accessing static and instance variables from several threads can cause problems, so this type of code usually isn't thread-safe.

Such issues can also create additional problems during concurrent accesses of methods that use static variables without multithreading support.

Instance variables aren't free from concurrent access problems either. If one thread sets an instance variable, it can cause problems for another thread reading or writing it.

Classes can support multithreading using facilities provided by the Java platform, such as the `synchronized` keyword, the `ThreadLocal` class, and the Java 5 java .util.concurrent package.

In general, insuring thread safety is challenging.

and because the class doesn't implement concurrency management, you can't use it from multiple threads.

IMPLEMENTING A THREAD-SAFE ITEM READER

We have solutions to work around these thread safety issues. The first one is to implement a synchronizing delegator for the `ItemReader` interface that adds the synchronized keyword to the `read` method. Reading is usually cheaper than writing, so synchronizing the reading isn't that bad: one thread reads (quickly) a chunk and hands it off to another thread that handles the (time-consuming) writing. The writing thread is busy for a while, at least long enough for the reading thread to read another chunk and for another thread to write the new chunk. To summarize, threads won't fight for reading, because they're busy writing. The following listing shows how to implement a synchronized reader.

Listing 13.5   Implementation of a synchronized reader

```
public SynchronizingItemReader implements ItemReader<Product>, ItemStream {
  private ItemReader<Product> delegate;

  public synchronized Product read()                        ❶ Synchronizes
                    throws Exception {                          read method
    return delegate.read();
  }

  public void close() throws ItemStreamException {          ❷ Delegates for state
    if (this.delegate instanceof ItemStream) {                 management
      ((ItemStream)this.delegate).close();
    }
```

```
    }
    public void open(ExecutionContext context)
                    throws ItemStreamException {
      if (this.delegate instanceof ItemStream) {
        ((ItemStream)this.delegate).open(context);
      }
    }
    public void update(ExecutionContext context)
                    throws ItemStreamException {
      if (this.delegate instanceof ItemStream) {
        ((ItemStream)this.delegate).update(context);
      }
    }
    (...)
}
```

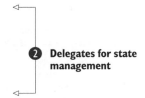

❷ Delegates for state management

First, you mark your product item reader's read method ❶ with the synchronized keyword and delegate processing to the delegate item reader. Because the target reader can potentially implement the ItemStream interface to manage state, you also need to implement this interface and delegate to its corresponding methods ❷.

Another solution is to add finer synchronization to processing and handle state yourself. After adding the synchronize keyword to the reader, you deactivate the Spring Batch step state management. You configure the ItemReader bean with the saveState attribute for built-in Spring Batch item readers. For custom implementations, you implement the update method from the ItemStream interface to do nothing if the class implements the ItemReader interface. Because you manage state yourself, you can restart the job.

IMPLEMENTING THE PROCESS INDICATOR PATTERN

Let's implement a thread-safe reader that applies the process indicator pattern. To apply this pattern, you add a dedicated column to the input data table to track processed products. For our use case, you use a column called processed from the Product table as the process indicator. The first step is to implement a thread-safe item reader. To do that, you reuse the SynchronizingItemReader class described in the previous section. The target item reader manages state on its own. In this simple scenario, the item writer sets the processed indicator flag to true after writing the item, as shown in figure 13.6.

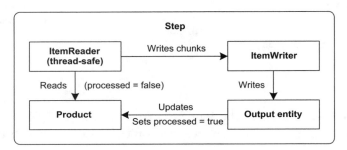

Figure 13.6 Implementation of the process indicator pattern in a step

The following listing describes how to make a `JdbcCursorItemReader` thread-safe and configure it to manage state.

Listing 13.6   Configuring a thread-safe `JdbcCursorItemReader` with an indicator

```
<bean id="productItemReader"
      class="com.manning.sbia.ch13.SynchronizingItemReader">
  <property name="delegate" ref="targetProductItemReader"/>
</bean>

<bean id="targetProductItemReader"
      class="org.springframework.batch.item.database.JdbcCursorItemReader">
  <property name="dataSource" ref="dataSource"/>
  <property name="sql"
            value="select id, name, description, price
                     from product where processed=false"/>
  <property name="saveState" value="false"/>
  <property name="rowMapper" ref="productRowMapper"/>
</bean>

(...)
```

You start by configuring a `SynchronizingItemReader` bean to make the delegate item reader thread-safe. The synchronized item reader uses the `delegate` property to reference the delegate item reader. You then use the `processed` indicator column in the SQL statement to read data. A `processed` value of `false` causes the database to return only unprocessed rows. Finally, you disable Spring Batch state management. This is the other requirement to make the item reader thread-safe (with the synchronization of the read method). But by doing that, you lose the reader's restartability feature, because the item reader won't know where it left off after a failure. Luckily, the process indicator is there to enable restartability: the reader reads only unprocessed items.

     The item writer then needs to flag the product as handled using the `processed` column and then write the item, as described in the following listing.

Listing 13.7   Implementing a JDBC `ItemWriter` with a SQL indicator

```
public class ProductItemWriter extends JdbcDaoSupport
                      implements ItemWriter<Product> {
  (...)
  public void  write(List<Product> items) throws Exception {
    for (Product product : items) {
      getJdbcTemplate().update(
        "update product set processed=true where id=?",          ◁── ❶ Marks item
                                      product.getId());                  as processed
      //Writing the product content
      (...)
    }
  }
}
```

In the `write` method, each item in the loop is tagged as processed ❶ by setting the `processed` column to `true`. The item reader won't process products with the

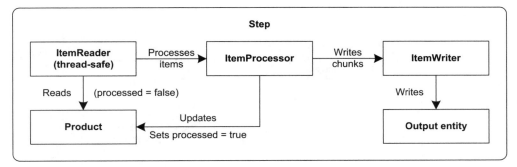

Figure 13.7   The process indicator pattern for a step using an `ItemProcessor`

`processed` column value set to `true`. This technique allows managing state and makes the job restartable.

Notice that the writer needs to extend a Spring Batch built-in writer like `Jdbc-BatchItemWriter` to specify processing and set the processed `column` to true when an item is processed. To go further and be nonintrusive, you add an item processor that manages the indicator column, as illustrated in figure 13.7.

You can imagine that implementing your own state management is more difficult with files as input. A common technique is to import data from a file into a dedicated staging database table. The import is fast, even when not multithreaded. The job then bases its data processing on this staging database table, using a parallelized step and the process indicator pattern.

We've begun to parallelize the processing using multithreading and focusing on chunk processing. This is an interesting way to improve performance but holds limitations due to multithreading and thread-safety issues. Let's turn our attention to a new technique that also uses multithreading to parallel processing, but at the step level, and eliminates these types of problems.

13.3   *Parallelizing processing (single machine)*

Based on the previous section, multithreading is far from good enough. We can now see that the key to scaling is to find a suitable technique to parallelize batch processing.

Spring Batch provides a convenient way to organize steps for parallel execution. Spring Batch XML supports this feature directly at the configuration level. The feature also relates to the job flow feature. We focus here on the capability of a job flow to split step processing. This aspect is useful for scaling batch jobs because it allows executing several steps in parallel, as illustrated in figure 13.8 where Spring Batch executes dedicated steps in parallel to process products, books, and mobile phones.

A Spring Batch job can define a set of steps that execute in a specific order. In chapter 10, we configure Spring Batch with advanced flows to control which steps to execute and in what order. Spring Batch flow support provides the `split` element as a child of the `job` element. The `split` element specifies parallel execution of its containing steps.

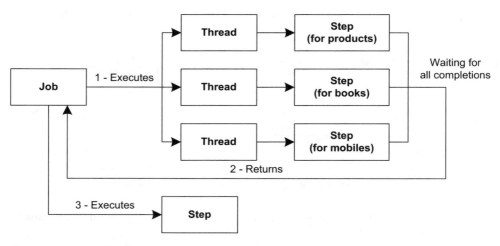

Figure 13.8   Executing steps in parallel using dedicated threads

13.3.1 *Configuring parallel steps*

Configuring steps for parallel execution is simple and natural in Spring Batch XML. In a split XML element, you add flows to define what to execute in parallel. These flows can contain a single step or several steps with a specific order. Because you can consider a split to be a step, it can have an identifier and be the target of the next attributes in steps. A split can also define a next attribute to specify what to execute after all flows in the split end. A split ends when all contained flows end.

The following listing describes how to organize the steps in our case study to read books and mobile products in parallel.

Listing 13.8   Configuring parallel steps to import products

```
<batch:job id="importProductsJob">
  <batch:step id="decompress" next="readWrite">
    <batch:tasklet ref="decompressTasklet"/>
  </batch:step>
  <batch:split id="readWrite" next="moveProcessedFiles">        ❶ Defines
    <batch:flow>                                                   step split
      <batch:step id="readWriteBookProduct"/>
    </batch:flow>                                                ❷ Defines
    <batch:flow>                                                   flows
      <batch:step id="readWriteMobileProduct"/>
    </batch:flow>
  </batch:split>
  <batch:step id="moveProcessedFiles">
    <batch:tasklet ref="moveProcessedFilesTasklet" />
  </batch:step>
</batch:job>
```

Listing 13.8 defines a job with parallel steps named importProductsJob. After receiving and decompressing product files, you process the files in parallel that correspond to products for books and mobile phones. For this task, you define a split element with the identifier readWrite ❶. This split defines two flows with a single step for each flow and for each product type ❷. Once these two steps end, you call the step moveProcessedFiles.

As mentioned previously, using parallel steps implies multithreading. By default, parallel step execution uses a SyncTaskExecutor, but you can specify your own using the task-executor attribute on the split element, as described in the following listing.

Listing 13.9 Configuring a task executor

```
<batch:job id="importProductsJob">
  (...)
  <batch:split id="readWrite"
               task-executor="taskExecutor"          ◁─┐ Sets task
               next="moveHandledFiles">                 │ executor
  (...)
  </batch:split>
</batch:job>

<bean id="taskExecutor" (...)/>
```

Our first two scaling techniques use multithreading to parallelize processing of chunks and steps where all processing executes on the same machine. For this reason, performance correlates to a machine's capabilities. In the next section, we use techniques to process jobs remotely, providing a higher level of scalability. Let's start with the remote chunking pattern, which executes chunks on several slave computers.

13.4 *Remote chunking (multiple machines)*

The previously described techniques aim to integrate concurrent and parallel processing in batch processing. This improves performance, but it may not be sufficient. A single machine will eventually hit a performance limit. Therefore, if performance still isn't suitable, you can consider using multiple machines to handle processing.

In this section, we describe remote chunking, our first Spring Batch scaling technique for batch processing on multiple machines.

13.4.1 *What is remote chunking?*

Remote chunking separates data reading and processing between a master and multiple slave machines. The master machine reads and dispatches data to slave machines. The master machine reads data in a step and delegates chunk processing to slave machines through a remote communication mechanism like JMS. Figure 13.9 provides an overview of remote chunking, the actors involved, and where processing takes place.

Because the master is responsible for reading data, remote chunking is relevant only if reading isn't a bottleneck.

As you can see in figure 13.9, Spring Batch implements remote chunking through two core interfaces respectively implemented on the master and slave machines:

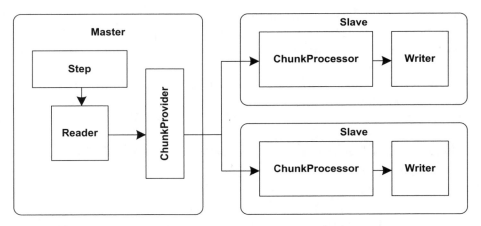

Figure 13.9   Remote chunking with a master machine reading and dispatching data to slave machines for processing

- ChunkProvider—Returns chunks from an item reader; it's used by the Chunk-OrientedTasklet.
- ChunkProcessor—Handles item writing and processing.

The ChunkProvider interface is responsible for returning chunks from an Item-Reader. Chunk processors can handle the chunks. By default, Spring Batch uses the SimpleChunkProvider implementation, which delegates to the read method of the item reader. The following snippet lists the ChunkProvider interface:

```
public interface ChunkProvider<T> {
  void postProcess(StepContribution contribution, Chunk<T> chunk);
  Chunk<T> provide(StepContribution contribution) throws Exception;
}
```

The ChunkProcessor interface receives the chunks and is responsible for processing them in its process method. By default, Spring Batch uses the SimpleChunkProcessor implementation, which handles basic item writing and processing. The following snippet lists the ChunkProcessor interface:

```
public interface ChunkProcessor<I> {
  void process(StepContribution contribution, Chunk<I> chunk)
    ➥ throws Exception;
}
```

Now that we know about the relevant mechanisms and actors used in remote chunking, it's time for a concrete example. If you look for additional remote chunking support in the Spring Batch distribution, you find nothing more. Spring Batch only provides the extensible framework to make it possible to use such a mechanism in batch processing, but it doesn't provide implementations. In addition to the remote chunking framework in the Spring Batch core, the Spring Batch Admin project provides a module called Spring Batch Integration that includes a Spring Integration–

based extension for remote chunking. This module provides facilities to implement remoting in Spring Batch and remote chunking using Spring Integration channels.

13.4.2 *Remote chunking with Spring Integration*

The major challenge in implementing remote chunking is to make the master and its slaves communicate reliably to exchange chunks for processing. Spring Batch chose Spring Integration for its communication infrastructure because Spring Integration provides a message-driven, transport-independent framework. JMS is the obvious choice for communication because it's asynchronous and provides guaranteed delivery. Nevertheless, Spring Integration wraps its use of JMS. This leaves the door open for supporting other messaging technologies, such as Advanced Message Queuing Protocol (AMQP).

> **Why does remote chunking need guaranteed delivery?**
> With remote chunking, a master node sends chunks to slave nodes for processing. You don't want to lose these chunks in case of failure! That's why reliable messaging technologies—like JMS or AMQP—are good candidates for remote chunking with Spring Batch.

The remote chunking implementation based on Spring Integration isn't in the Spring Batch distribution itself, but you can find it in the Spring Batch Admin distribution.

Chapter 11 covers the basics of Spring Integration in a real-world enterprise integration scenario. If you're in a hurry and are only interested in implementing remote chunking, you can move on directly to the next section, which describes remote chunking using channels.

REMOTE CHUNKING USING CHANNELS

A messaging channel is a communication medium between two applications using a message-oriented middleware (MOM) system, as described in *Enterprise Integration Patterns* by Gregor Hohpe and Bobby Woolf (Addison-Wesley, 2004). On one end, the application writes data on the channel, and on the other end, the application reads data from the channel. The messaging middleware is responsible for delivering the data.

A channel is a great communication medium for remote chunking. It provides the abstraction to make communication between master and slaves independent from any technology for remotely processing chunks. Moreover, channels implement reliable messaging, ensuring that no message is lost. Figure 13.10 shows which mechanisms and entities are involved when implementing remote chunking with Spring Integration and Spring Batch.

Because two types of actors—master and slave—are involved when implementing remote chunking, we successively describe the master and slave machine implementations. We focus here on how to configure these machines using Spring Integration and how to make them communicate. To keep things simple, we implement only one slave, but you can generalize this to several slaves. First, let's look at the master.

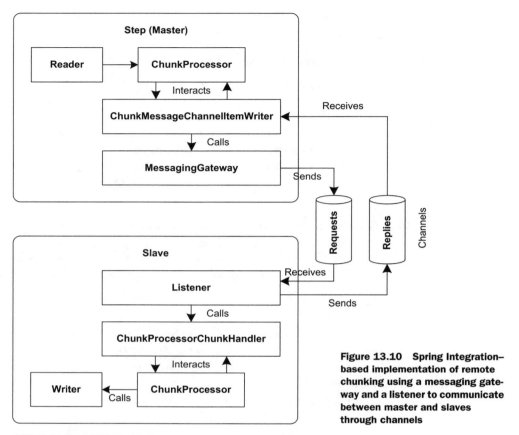

Figure 13.10   Spring Integration–based implementation of remote chunking using a messaging gateway and a listener to communicate between master and slaves through channels

IMPLEMENTING THE MASTER

In remote chunking, the master is responsible for reading input data and sending the corresponding chunks to slaves for processing. As shown in figure 13.10, you use the ChunkMessageChannelItemWriter class to exchange data using Spring Integration channels.

Because you use Spring Integration channels, you configure channels for requests, replies, and the messaging gateway. The gateway produces and consumes messages using channels. The following listing describes how to configure channels and the messaging gateway for a remote chunking master machine.

Listing 13.10   Configuring Spring Integration for a remote chunking master

```
<bean id="messagingGateway"
      class="org.springframework.integration.core.MessagingTemplate">
  <property name="defaultChannel" ref="requests" />
  <property name="receiveTimeout" value="1000" />
</bean>

<!-- Channels -->
```

Configures messaging gateway **❶**

```
<int:channel id="requests"/>                          ❷  Defines
<int:channel id="incoming"/>                              channels

<int:transformer input-channel="incoming"
        output-channel="replies" ref="headerExtractor" method="extract" />

<bean id="headerExtractor"
      class="org.springframework.batch.integration
                   ➥    .chunk.JmsRedeliveredExtractor"/>

<!-- Adapters -->
                                                      ❸  Defines channel
<int-jms:outbound-channel-adapter                         adapter for requests
          connection-factory="connectionFactory"
          channel="requests"
          destination-name="requests"/>

(...)                                                 ❹  Defines thread local
<int:channel id="replies" scope="thread">                 channel for replies
  <int:queue />
  <int:interceptors>
    <bean id="pollerInterceptor"
          class="org.springframework.batch.integration
                     ➥    .chunk.MessageSourcePollerInterceptor">
      <property name="messageSource">
        <bean class="org.springframework.integration
                         ➥    .jms.JmsDestinationPollingSource">
          <constructor-arg>
            <bean class="org.springframework.jms.core.JmsTemplate">
              <property name="connectionFactory" ref="connectionFactory"/>
              <property name="defaultDestinationName" value="replies"/>
              <property name="receiveTimeout" value="100"/>
            </bean>
          </constructor-arg>
        </bean>
      </property>
      <property name="channel" ref="incoming"/>
    </bean>
  </int:interceptors>
</int:thread-local-channel>
```

You configure the messaging gateway ❶ to send and receive messages from the messaging middleware. The gateway uses channels for requests and replies that you configure using Spring Integration XML ❷. Notice here the use of the channel adapter `outbound-channel-adapter` ❸ for the `requests` channel with a JMS outbound destination. To receive and handle messages from the reply destination, you define a `thread-local-channel` ❹.

Now that you've configured your Spring Integration XML elements, let's see how to define Spring Batch entities from the Spring Batch Integration module to implement remote chunking for the master. This configuration may seem a bit like magic. No entity mentioned in the introduction section appears in the configuration, and it's difficult to see how the `ChunkMessageChannelItemWriter` bean is involved in the processing.

In fact, the `RemoteChunkHandlerFactoryBean` class is responsible for configuring the step for remote chunking. It automatically and transparently converts an existing chunk–oriented step into a remote chunk–oriented step for the master. To achieve this, the class replaces the current chunk processor with one that writes chunks to a message channel. The following listing describes how to configure a master for remote chunking.

Listing 13.11   Configuring a master for remote chunking

```
<bean id="chunkWriter"
      class="org.springframework.batch.integration.chunk
                    .ChunkMessageChannelItemWriter" scope="step">
  <property name="messagingGateway" ref="messagingGateway"/>
</bean>

<bean id="chunkHandler"
      class="org.springframework.batch.integration.chunk
                        .RemoteChunkHandlerFactoryBean">
  <property name="chunkWriter" ref="chunkWriter"/>
  <property name="step" ref="stepChunk"/>
</bean>
```

You start by configuring a `ChunkMessageChannelItemWriter` bean using the messaging gateway. Next, you configure the factory bean for the chunk handler using the `RemoteChunkHandlerFactoryBean` class. You set the `chunkWriter` property to the chunk channel writer, and then reference the step defined with the `stepChunk` ID using the `step` property. This step corresponds to the step implementing remote chunking for the batch job.

The `RemoteChunkHandlerFactoryBean` class creates a chunk handler, which makes it possible to configure a master as a slave to process chunks. In this case, you add a service activator bean using Spring Integration. We describe this in the next section.

You've configured the master to send chunks through a channel for remote processing. Next, let's configure a slave.

IMPLEMENTING A SLAVE

In remote chunking, slaves process chunks remotely and can send data back to the master. Slaves correspond to dedicated Spring applications that are channel listeners that receive messages, process content, and use the reply channel to notify the master.

At the slave level, you use more low-level objects because you communicate through JMS destinations, the underlying mechanism for channels. The service activator is a JMS message listener that triggers processing for the chunk handler. The following listing describes JMS listener definitions and the service activator configuration. The service activator references both input and output channels.

Listing 13.12   Configuring Spring Integration for a remote chunking slave

```
<!-- JMS listener container -->
<jms:listener-container
        connection-factory="connectionFactory"
        transaction-manager="transactionManager"
        acknowledge="transacted">
```

```
<jms:listener destination="requests"
              response-destination="replies"
              ref="chunkHandler"
              method="handleChunk"/>
</jms:listener-container>
```

You use a message listener container to receive messages from a JMS message queue and drive it to a POJO defined as a listener. You set attributes on the `listener-container` element for a JMS connection factory, a transaction manager, and the acknowledgment type. The `listener` element specifies how to route messages to the chunk handler.

As shown in figure 13.10, the entry point for the listener on the slave side is a `ChunkProcessorChunkHandler`. The handler is responsible for triggering processing of the chunk processor for the received chunk. For this reason, you must configure a chunk processor in the handler. This handler knows how to distinguish between a processor that is fault tolerant, and one that is not. If the processor is fault tolerant, then exceptions can be propagated on the assumption that there will be a rollback and the request will be re-delivered.

The following listing describes how to configure a `SimpleChunkProcessor` in this context and set it on the item writer to execute.

Listing 13.13 Configuring a slave for remote chunking

```
<bean id="chunkHandler"
      class="org.springframework.batch.integration.chunk
                              ➥ .ChunkProcessorChunkHandler">
  <property name="chunkProcessor">
    <bean
     class="org.springframework.batch.core.step.item.SimpleChunkProcessor">
      <property name="itemWriter"
                ref="itemWriter"/>
      <property name="itemProcessor">
        <bean class="org.springframework.batch.item
                         ➥ .support.PassThroughItemProcessor"/>
      </property>
    </bean>
  </ property>
</bean>
```

Configuring slaves requires defining the chunk handler that the listener calls when receiving messages from the `requests` destination. In Spring Integration, the handler is a `ChunkProcessorChunkHandler` bean that specifies a chunk processor used to handle the received chunk. Here, you use the `SimpleChunkProcessor` class with the target item writer to execute (the `itemWriter` attribute) and an item processor that does nothing (the `itemProcessor` attribute).

Third-party tools like GridGain[1] provide additional implementations for remote chunking. GridGain is an innovative Java and Scala–based cloud application platform, which you can use with the Spring Batch Integration module[2] for GridGain.

---

[1] www.gridgain.com/

[2] http://aloiscochard.blogspot.com/search/label/gridgain

In summary, remote chunking uses a master to send chunks to remote slaves for processing. In the next section, we explore a flexible scaling Spring Batch technique called partitioning.

13.5   *Fine-grained scaling with partitioning*

The last technique provided by Spring Batch for scaling is partitioning. You use partitioning to implement scaling in a finer-grained manner. At this level, you can also use multithreading and remoting techniques.

> **NOTE**   Partitioning is arguably the most popular scaling strategy in Spring Batch: it's simple to configure if you stick to the defaults and local implementation; and restart still works out of the box.

Figure 13.11 shows an overview of how partitioning works in Spring Batch and how it provides scaling. The figure shows that partitioning takes place at the step level and divides processing into two main parts:

- *Data partitioning*—Creates step executions to process data. This splitting allows parallelizing and data processing. Data partitioning depends on the nature of the data: ranges of primary keys, the first letter of a product name, and so on. A batch developer would likely implement their own partitioning logic in a `Partitioner`. The Spring Batch `Partitioner` interface defines the contract for this feature.

- *Step execution handling*—Specifies how to handle different step executions. It can be local with multithreading (or not) and even remote using technologies like Spring Integration. A framework typically provides the way to handle execution, and Spring Batch provides a multithreaded implementation. The Spring Batch `PartitionHandler` interface defines the contract for this feature.

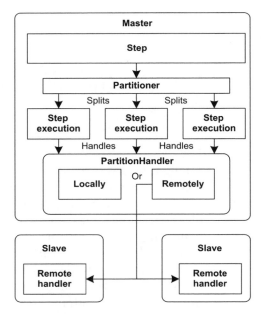

We recommended this approach when you want to parallelize processing of data partitions and when you want to control how to create and handle these partitions.

Now that we've described the general concepts behind Spring Batch partitioning, it's time to see how to implement and configure an example. This technique is configuration-centric and provides an open framework to integrate custom strategies.

Figure 13.11   Partitioning splits input data processing into several step executions processed on the master or remote slave machines.

> ### Why doesn't partitioning need guaranteed delivery?
> Contrary to remote chunking, partitioning doesn't need guaranteed delivery. With partitioning, Spring Batch handles each partition in its own step execution. On a restart after failure, Spring Batch re-creates the partitions and processes them again. Spring Batch doesn't leave data unprocessed.

13.5.1 Configuring partitioning

As described previously, to implement partitioning, you must define the splitting and processing of data. Partitioning corresponds to creating several step executions for a step. You configure this example using Spring Batch XML.

To configure partitioning, you use the `partition` element instead of the `tasklet` element in the `step` configuration. The `partition` element partitions the target step configured using the `step` attribute, which eliminates any impact on implementations of step entities like readers, processors, and writers. It's only a matter of configuration. Additional settings are also available to configure the partitioner and handler.

Listing 13.14 describes a basic partitioning configuration for the `readWriteProducts` step of our case study. The listing shows how to use the `partition` and `handler` elements and hides the configuration of additional entities like the partitioner. We focus on these later when we describe the Spring Batch partitioning Service Provider Interface (SPI) in section 13.5.2.

Listing 13.14 Configuring step partitioning

```
<batch:job id="importProducts">
  <batch:step id="readWriteProducts">
    <batch:partition step="partitionReadWriteProducts"
                     partitioner="partitioner">
      <batch:handler grid-size="2"
                     task-executor="taskExecutor"/>
    </batch:partition>
  </batch:step>
</batch:job>

<batch:step id="partitionReadWriteProducts">
  <batch:tasklet>
    <batch:chunk reader="reader" writer="writer" commit-interval="3"/>
  </batch:tasklet>
</batch:step>

<bean id="partitioner" (...)> (...) </bean>
<bean id="taskExecutor" (...)> (...) </bean>
```

The partitioning configuration is located in the step instead of in its declaration. The partition references this configuration with the `step` attribute. You set additional properties on the partition with the `partitioner` attribute and the `handler` inner element. The default value for the partition handler defined in the `handler` element is

TaskExecutorPartitionHandler. The step is now defined independently using the step that contains standard elements like tasklet and chunk. Note that using the step attribute makes sense only for *local* partitioning, because it refers to a local step bean in the current Spring application context. In the case of *remote* partitioning—when the processing happens in a different process—referring to a local step bean doesn't make sense. For remote partitioning, you usually set up the step *name* on the partition handler. The partition handler then sends the step name—a simple String—to a remote worker. The step name then refers to a step bean in another Spring application context.

The configuration schema provides the ability to use any handler implementation with the handler attribute in the partition element, as described in the following listing.

Listing 13.15 Configuring step partitioning with a partition handler

```
<batch:job id="importProducts">
  <batch:step id="readWriteProducts">
    <batch:partition step="partitionReadWriteProducts"
                     partitioner="partitioner"
                     handler="partitionHandler">       ◁┐ References
    </batch:partition>                                    │ partition handler
  </batch:step>
</batch:job>

<bean id="partitionHandler" (...)> (...) </bean>
(...)
```

Before dealing with the partitioning SPI, we emphasize an important and interesting aspect of partitioning: late binding is available with this feature. The difference here is that late binding gives access to property values present in the current step execution.

To understand this better, let's look at an example. If you split a step to handle each file in a multiresource reader separately, you can access the name of the current file using late binding, as described in the following snippet. Each partition sets the filename property for the step execution. Notice that the step is involved in a partitioned step:

```
<bean id="itemReader" scope="step"
      class="org.springframework.batch.item.file.FlatFileItemReader">
  <property name="resource" value="#{stepExecutionContext[fileName]}"/>
  (...)
</bean>
```

In this section, we described how to use partitioning in step configurations. We saw how easy implementation is and that there is no impact on the steps involved. Spring Batch provides an open framework for partitioning that allows defining and implementing advanced and custom solutions.

13.5.2 *The partitioning SPI*

It's time to look at how things work under the hood and how to extend this support. Spring Batch provides a complete SPI for this purpose, using the interfaces listed in table 13.3.

Table 13.3 Partitioning SPI

Interface	Description
PartitionHandler	Determines how to partition and handle input data. An implementation completely controls the execution of a partitioned StepExecution. It doesn't know how partitioning is implemented and doesn't manage the aggregation of results. The default implementation is the TaskExecutorPartitionHandler class.
StepExecutionSplitter	A strategy interface for generating input execution contexts for a partitioned step execution. The strategy is independent from the partition handler that executes each step. By default, this interface delegates to a Partitioner. The default implementation is the SimpleStepExecutionSplitter class.
Partitioner	Creates step executions for the partitioned step. The default implementation is the SimplePartitioner class, which creates empty step executions.

These interfaces and classes are involved when partitioning steps, as described earlier in listing 13.14. When Spring Batch executes a partitioned step, it invokes the partition handler to process the partition. The step then aggregates results and updates the step status.

The partition handler does the heavy lifting. It's responsible for triggering partitioning based on the StepExecutionSplitter that creates the step executions. A splitter implementation like the SimpleStepExecutionSplitter class uses a Partitioner to get execution contexts for each step execution: the *partitioner* performs the splitting. Once the splitting is complete, the partition handler executes each step with a defined strategy. It can be local with multithreading or remote. As a batch job developer, you would typically write (or configure) only a Partitioner implementation to partition your data.

Figure 13.12 summarizes the objects involved during partitioning.

It's now time to tackle different ways of using partition handlers and partitioners. We begin with the

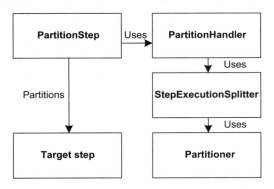

Figure 13.12 Partitioning SPI objects involved in partitioning and processing data for a partitioned step

default implementations provided by Spring Batch, describe how to use third-party implementations, and finish with custom implementations.

USING THE DEFAULT PARTITION HANDLER

The partitioning classes give you the ability to scale steps on several processing nodes and enable strategies to increase performance. Partitioning is particularly useful to distribute step processing on several computers. This isn't always necessary. In fact, the default Spring Batch `PartitionHandler` implementation uses multithreading to process steps.

Let's take our case study as an example and use multithreading to import multiple product files concurrently. Section 13.2 describes how to add multithreading for the whole step, but this approach can't control which thread processes which data. Partitioning provides this support by using dedicated threads to process all of the data for each file. Using the default `PartitionHandler` implementation, the `TaskExecutor-PartitionHandler` class, makes this possible. Figure 13.13 illustrates the multithreaded aspect of this architecture.

Configuring this strategy is simple because it's similar to the generic strategy described earlier. The difference is how to configure partitioning using XML. Spring Batch provides the `MultiResourcePartitioner` class to create a new step execution for each file to import. The following listing describes how to configure a `Multi-ResourcePartitioner` bean and how to use it on the partitioned step.

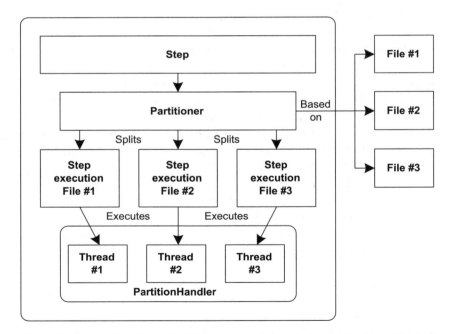

Figure 13.13   Using dedicated threads to process data when importing product files with partitioning

Listing 13.16 Configuring partitioning with a `MultiResourcePartitioner`

```
<batch:job id="importProducts">
  <batch:step id="readWriteProducts">                        Configures step  ❶
    <batch:partition step="partitionReadWriteProducts"          partitioning
                     partitioner="partitioner">
      <batch:handler grid-size="2" task-executor="taskExecutor"/>
    </batch:partition>
  </batch:step>
</batch:job>
                                                      ❷ Configures
                                                         partitioner
<bean id="partitioner"
      class="org.springframework.batch.core
                  .partition.support.MultiResourcePartitioner">
  <property name="keyName" value="fileName"/>              ❸ Specifies partitioner
  <property name="resources"                                  properties
          value="file:./resources/partition/input/*.txt"/>
</bean>

(...)

<bean id="taskExecutor"
  class="org.springframework.scheduling.concurrent.ThreadPoolTaskExecutor">
  <property name="corePoolSize" value="5"/>
  <property name="maxPoolSize" value="5"/>
</bean>
```

Configuring this strategy follows the same rules as for using the `partition` element ❶. The `step` attribute ❶ specifies the step to partition, and the `handler` child element sets the partition handler ❶. The `partitioner` attribute ❶ references a `MultiResource-Partitioner` bean ❷ that specifies a pattern for a file list in the `resources` property ❸. It also sets the `keyName` property ❸ to specify the name of the current resource to use when adding a file in the step context attributes.

The last thing you must do is specify the resource file to process in the item reader using late binding. Partitioning is most powerful when each created step execution has its own parameter values. For the `MultiResourcePartitioner` class, the `fileName` context attribute is the resource name associated with the step execution. The following snippet describes how to specify the filename at the item reader level. Remember to specify the step scope when using late binding!

```
<bean id="itemReader" scope="step"
      class="org.springframework.batch.item.file.FlatFileItemReader">
  <property name="resource" value="#{stepExecutionContext[fileName]}"/>   ◁
  (...)
</bean>                                                    Specifies resource
                                                                   to handle
```

The previous sections describe how to use the Spring Batch implementations of the partitioning SPI. It's also possible to use implementations from third-party tools like the Spring Batch Integration module or to implement custom classes.

USING CHANNEL-BASED PARTITIONS

Implementing a `PartitionHandler` remains a tricky task and, unfortunately, the Spring Batch core doesn't provide implementations other than the `TaskExecutor-PartitionHandler`. As for remote chunking, the Spring Batch Integration module

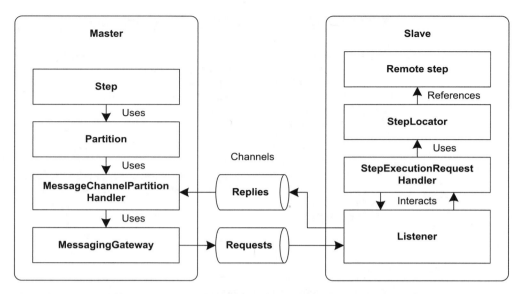

Figure 13.14 Partitioning using Spring Integration: the master and slaves communicate using channels, a messaging gateway, and a listener.

provides classes compatible with Spring Integration channels called `MessageChannel-PartitionHandler` and `StepExecutionRequestHandler`.

Figure 13.14 shows which mechanisms and types are involved when implementing remote partitioning with Spring Integration support from Spring Batch.

Master and slave machines communicate using Spring Integration channels. As with remote chunking, we apply the master-slave pattern. On the master side, we use the `MessageChannelPartitionHandler` class to send the partitioned data to slaves for processing for a particular step. We specify the step name in the configuration. The following listing describes how to configure this partition handler and set it on the partition.

Listing 13.17 Configuring a master for remote partitioning

```
<bean id="partitionHandler"                                    ⬎  ❶ Configures remote
       class="org.springframework.batch.integration                 partition handler
               ⇒ .partition.MessageChannelPartitionHandler">
  <property name="messagingOperations">
    <bean class="org.springframework.integration.core.MessagingTemplate">
      <property name="defaultChannel" ref="requests"/>
      <property name="receiveTimeout" value="10000"/>
    </bean>
  </property>
  <property name="replyChannel" ref="replies"/>
  <property name="stepName" value="importProductsStep"/>
  <property name="gridSize" value="2"/>
</bean>

(...)
```

```
<batch:job id="importProductsJob-master">
  <batch:step id="importProductsStep-master">
    <batch:partition handler="partitionHandler"
                    partitioner="partitioner" />
  </batch:step>
</batch:job>

<batch:step id="importProductsStep">
  <batch:tasklet>
    <batch:chunk commit-interval="10">
      <batch:reader> (...) </batch:reader>
    </batch:chunk>
  </batch:tasklet>
</batch:step>
```

② Sets handler in partition

You configure the remote partition handler using the `MessageChannelPartition-Handler` class **①**. This partition handler uses the `messagingOperations` property so that the Spring Integration messaging client can execute requests on channels. The `replyChannel` property is set to the channel to listen to replies. The `stepName` property is set to the step to execute on the slave. Finally, the `gridSize` property tells the underlying `StepExecutionSplitter` implementation how many `StepExecution` instances to create. In the bean that defines the job, the step `importProductsStep-master` refers to the partition handler **②**.

As for remote chunking, a listener triggers processing on the slave. The slave listener then delegates to a `StepExecutionRequestHandler` bean to process the received partition data. To determine which step to execute, you configure a step locator bean of type `BeanFactoryStepLocator`. The following listing describes how to configure a slave for remote partitioning.

Listing 13.18 Configuring a slave for remote partitioning

```
<int:service-activator
        ref="stepExecutionRequestHandler"
        input-channel="requests"
        output-channel="replies">
  <poller>
    <interval-trigger interval="10" />
  </poller>
</service-activator>

(...)

<bean id="stepExecutionRequestHandler"
      class="org.springframework.batch.integration
              .partition.StepExecutionRequestHandler"
      p:jobExplorer-ref="jobExplorer"
      p:stepLocator-ref="stepLocator"/>

<bean id="stepLocator"
      class="org.springframework.batch.integration
              .partition.BeanFactoryStepLocator"/>

<batch:step id="importProductsStep">
```

① Configures service activator

② Configures request handler

③ Configures step locator

```
  <batch:tasklet>
    <batch:chunk commit-interval="10">
      <batch:writer> (...) </batch:writer>
    </batch:chunk>
  </batch:tasklet>
</batch:step>
```

The entry point for the slave is a Spring Integration service activator ❶ that uses input and output channels to communicate with the remote partitioning step. This service activator references the request handler for processing. You configure this handler as a `StepExecutionRequestHandler` ❷ to find and execute the target step. A step locator is in charge of finding this step. You use the `BeanFactoryStepLocator` class ❸, which looks for the step in the current Spring context.

Partitioning is flexible because of the partition handler, which implements a local or remote strategy to process partitioned data. Partitioning a step also makes it possible to customize splitting data using custom implementations of the `StepExecution-Splitter` and `Partitioner` interfaces.

CUSTOMIZING DATA PARTITIONING

The two interfaces involved in custom partitioning are `StepExecutionSplitter` and `Partitioner`. A `StepExecutionSplitter` is responsible for creating input execution contexts for a partitioned step execution in its `split` method. The following snippet lists the `StepExecutionSplitter` interface:

```
public interface StepExecutionSplitter {
  String getStepName();
  Set<StepExecution> split(StepExecution stepExecution, int gridSize)
  ➡ throws JobExecutionException;
}
```

The default implementation of the `StepExecutionSplitter` interface, the `Simple-StepExecutionSplitter` class, delegates to a partitioner to generate `Execution-Context` instances. For this reason, developers don't commonly implement custom classes; instead, customizations take place at the `Partitioner` level.

Spring Batch uses a `Partitioner` at the end of the partitioning process chain. A `Partitioner` implementation provides a strategy to partition data. The partition method uses the given grid size to create a set of unique input values, such as a set of non-overlapping primary key ranges or a set of unique filenames. The following snippet lists the `Partitioner` interface:

```
public interface Partitioner {
  Map<String, ExecutionContext> partition(int gridSize);
}
```

Let's now implement a custom strategy to partition data from a database table. You first determine data ranges and then assign them to step executions. Assume here that data is distributed uniformly in the table. Figure 13.15 summarizes the use case.

You implement a custom partitioner called `ColumnRangePartitioner` that determines the minimum and maximum values for the column of a table. The partitioner

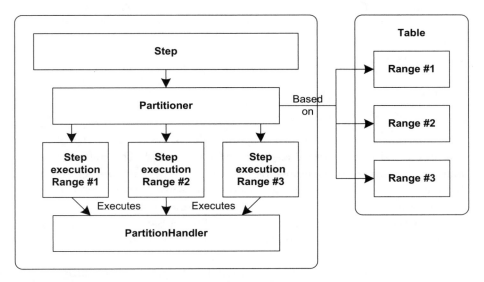

Figure 13.15 Partitioning based on database column values

uses these values to define ranges based on the grid size specified. The following listing describes the implementation of the ColumnRangePartitioner class.

Listing 13.19 Custom `ColumnRangePartitioner` class

```
public class ColumnRangePartitioner implements Partitioner {
  private SimpleJdbcTemplate jdbcTemplate;
  private String table;
  private String column;

  (...)

  public Map<String, ExecutionContext> partition(int gridSize) {
    int min = jdbcTemplate.queryForInt(
                "SELECT MIN(" + column + ") from " + table);
    int max = jdbcTemplate.queryForInt(
                "SELECT MAX(" + column + ") from " + table);
    int targetSize = (max - min) / gridSize + 1;

    Map<String, ExecutionContext> result
        = new HashMap<String, ExecutionContext>();
    int number = 0;
    int start = min;
    int end = start + targetSize - 1;

    while (start <= max) {
      ExecutionContext value = new ExecutionContext();
      result.put("partition" + number, value);

      if (end >= max) {
        end = max;
      }
```

❶ Determines range properties

❷ Creates new execution context

❸ Specifies properties for context

```
        value.putInt("minValue", start);
        value.putInt("maxValue", end);
        start += targetSize;
        end += targetSize;
        number++;
    }

    return result;
  }
}
```

❸ Specifies properties for context

The `partition` method assumes that the column is of integer type and queries the minimum and maximum values from the database ❶. The method then creates as many execution contexts as specified by the `targetSize` count ❷ and adds them to the partition Map ❸. The method also sets the `minValue` and `maxValue` properties ❸ in the context to identify the range for the current context.

We've seen throughout this chapter that Spring Batch provides several scaling patterns to improve performance. The challenge is in choosing the right pattern for a given use case. In the next section, we compare the pattern features and provide guidelines for choosing a pattern (or combination patterns) for different use cases.

13.6   *Comparing patterns*

In choosing the best pattern for a use case, you need to consider your batch jobs, overall application, and the whole information system. In this section, we provide guidelines for choosing scaling patterns.

Table 13.4 summarizes the Spring Batch approaches used to implement scaling. These patterns leverage multithreading, remoting, and partitioning to improve performance.

Table 13.4   Spring Batch scaling approaches

Pattern	Type	Description
Multithreaded step	Local	A set of threads handles a step. All resources involved must be thread-safe. Carefully consider concurrency issues.
Parallel step	Local	Execute steps in parallel using multithreading. Parallelize steps in a step flow using multithreading. Because parallel steps must be strictly independent, this approach has no concurrency issues.
Remote chunking	Remote	Execute chunks remotely. A master sends chunks to remote slaves for processing. Useful if reading on the master isn't a bottleneck.
Partitioning step	Local and remote	Define data sets for parallel processing. Control parallel data set processing. The master mustn't have a bottleneck when using remoting.

The first piece of advice we can give you about choosing a scaling techniques is, don't do it! Implement your jobs traditionally and use the techniques in this chapter only if you face performance issues. Keep it simple! Then, if your jobs take too long to execute, you can first consider using local scaling with multithreading if your hardware supports it. This is relevant if you have multicore or multiprocessor hardware. For multithreaded steps, you must be extremely cautious, think about thread-safety, and batch job state. Most of the classes involved in steps, like the built-in readers and writers, aren't thread-safe, so you shouldn't use them in a multithreaded environment. You can also parallelize processing with multithreading using parallel steps and partitioning steps. Parallel steps require organized processing in steps, which is generally a good approach. With partitioning steps, you can leverage built-in classes to select sets of data to process in parallel. For example, using one thread per file to import data is particularly convenient and efficient.

In a second round, if performance still doesn't suit you, you can consider remoting and splitting batch processing on several machines. On one hand, be aware that remote scaling introduces complexity in your batch jobs; use it only if you must. On the other hand, these techniques provide high levels of scalability.

You can use two different Spring Batch techniques in this context: remote chunking and partitioning. Remote chunking systematically sends chunks to slaves for remote processing, whereas partitioning creates data sets to send to slaves for remote processing. Table 13.5 lists the pros and cons of both patterns.

Table 13.5   Comparing Spring Batch remote scaling patterns

Approach	Pros	Cons
Remote chunking	No need to know about the input data structure Not sensitive to timeout values	Transactional middleware required to handle failures Potential bottleneck in reader for data serialization
Partitioning step	Transactional middleware not required to handle failures No bottleneck in reader for data serialization Low bandwidth and transport costs	Need to know the input data structure Can be sensitive to timeout values

For the remoting patterns, Spring Batch doesn't provide implementations in its core distribution. You can consider using the Spring Batch Integration module in Spring Batch Admin to use Spring Integration–based remoting.

As you can see, Spring Batch provides a large solution set to implement batch process scaling. The biggest challenge is in choosing the right patterns to improve performance.

13.7   Summary

Scaling in Spring Batch provides various solutions to enhance batch job performance with minimum impact on existing job implementations. Spring Batch configuration files mostly implement scaling and can involve multithreading, parallel executions, partitioning, and remoting.

Spring Batch implements nonsequential processing with multithreading. One approach is to use multithreaded steps, but you need to be cautious because this requires thread-safe code, and you must add specific state management code to keep batch jobs restartable. Spring Batch also provides the ability to execute steps in parallel. This requires proper organization of a batch process in steps. The configuration defines the execution sequence.

Spring Batch provides advanced and highly scalable patterns and frameworks. Remote chunking splits chunk processing on several computers to balance the processing load. Partitioning provides a way to split up data for remote or multithreaded processing.

Scaling can be challenging to implement and is strongly linked to batch processing and the execution environment. Spring Batch implements a set of patterns that you can use and combine to improve performance.

Chapter 14 covers an essential aspect of application development: testing. This is particularly true for batch jobs because they mainly process data without user interaction and apply complex business rules. Unit and functional testing gives us the confidence to maintain and grow applications.

Testing batch applications

In the core chapters of this book, we introduced Spring Batch concepts and you learned how to configure and run a batch job and how to read, process, and write data. Then, in the Spring Batch advanced concepts chapters, we explored exception handling, batch monitoring, and scaling. We addressed all the important aspects of creating batch jobs. The next step is to verify that an application works correctly.

Testing is a best practice in software development and is essential to batch applications. This chapter explains testing concepts and implementing unit, integration, and functional tests. We leverage the Spring Framework, Spring Batch's testing support, and the Mockito mock framework. This chapter demonstrates how to do all of this by using our case study as an example. Figure 14.1 depicts how to test our use case.

The goal of our batch application is to import products from a text file into a database. You start by validating the job's parameters: an input file and a report file. Then, you read the product flat file and convert each line into a Product object. A

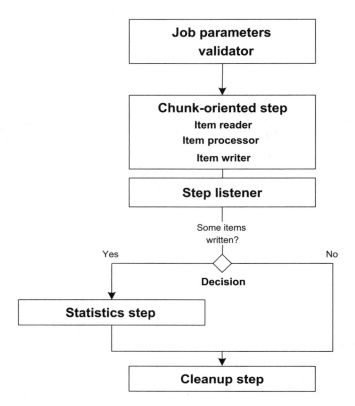

Figure 14.1   High-level view of our batch application workflow. Our testing strategy applies to all the components shown in the figure.

CompositeItemProcessor processes each Product. The CompositeItemProcessor is composed of two Validators: one for checking that a product's price isn't null and the other for checking that the price is positive. An item writer outputs products that don't match these conditions to a reject file with the help of a StepListener. You write product items with your own ProductItemWriter based on the SimpleJdbc-Template. If the job writes any product to the reject file, a statistics step generates a file that contains the average product price. The job ends with a cleanup step.

14.1   The what and why of testing

Let's talk a bit about what testing is and how testing can improve the reliability and robustness of an application. We look at different kinds of tests and then see how to implement them for our case study.

14.1.1   What is testing?

Software testing is a process used to ensure that the source code you write does what it's supposed to do. This process helps you find errors. Let's look at two main testing strategies: black-box and white-box testing.

BLACK-BOX TESTING

Black-box testing focuses on software features without relying on internal knowledge of the implementation. This kind of testing shows that the application accepts input and produces output without errors; you base tests on requirements and functionality.

WHITE-BOX TESTING

White-box testing focuses on implementation of software with internal knowledge of design, algorithms, and constraints. In white-box testing, you also focus on code coverage.

14.1.2 Different types of testing

Depending on what you want to test, you have two strategies to choose from: white-box or black-box testing. Table 14.1 lists the main types of testing.

Table 14.1 **Testing types and associated strategy**

Type	Definition	Strategy
Unit testing	Tests a single software module (a component, a service, and so on) and requires detailed knowledge of implementation internals	White box
Integration testing	Tests software modules to verify overall functionality and requires detailed knowledge of implementation internals	White box
Functional testing	Focuses on functional requirements of an application by verifying that input is accepted and expected output is produced without errors	Black box
System testing	Tests all parts of an application	Black box
Acceptance testing	Verifies that the application meets customer-specified requirements	Black box
Performance testing	Checks whether the system meets performance requirements	Black box

This chapter focuses on unit tests, integration tests, and functional tests.

A unit test should address a single point of functionality and should be fast, understandable (by a human), automatic (no human intervention), and isolated from external resources such as a database, file system, web service, and JMS broker. A unit test aims to test a public API. With integration and functional tests, you can use external systems such as a database, which can even be an in-memory database to speed up tests. All these tests must be automatic and require no human intervention.

> ### Test-driven development (TDD)
> TDD is a software development process based on short iteration cycles and unit tests. Using this process, you write an automated test first, ensure that the test fails, write the code, and then ensure that the test passes. The benefits of the TDD process are that it drives the API and design, provides good code coverage, promotes safe code refactoring, and keeps developers focused on the task.

We now know what testing is and what the different types of tests are, but you might be wondering, should I test my applications? What's the benefit?

14.1.3   Why test?

If you're reading this book, you're human and writing software. Unintentionally, at least, humans make mistakes. A defect in a production environment may cause a malfunction of a part of the software, leading to a system failure with corrupted data. For example, in an insurance company, this could result in an error to a client's refund or a salesperson may be unable to create a new contract. The later bugs are discovered, the more it costs to fix them. Software testing helps minimize bugs.

During development, we wish to add features quickly without breaking existing ones. Sometimes, developers are afraid of changing code. They don't know what the software is supposed to do or how it works. Software testing helps developers understand existing source code by reading through test source code. Software applications have grown in complexity and size, and testing in the development phase helps developers gain confidence and get feedback when a test succeeds or fails. Furthermore, automated tests save time. The benefits of testing are great: tests improve the quality, reliability, and robustness of software. Nowadays, software testing has become unavoidable.

With all the necessary pieces in place, we're ready to write some tests. For the rest of this chapter, we look at each type of test—unit, integration, and functional—and see how to create each test with Spring Batch.

14.2   Unit testing

In this section, we introduce how to write basic unit tests with JUnit, and then we look at the Mockito mock framework. Table 14.2 shows which of our sample unit tests require JUnit and a mock framework (the test class names refer to the source code from the book).

Table 14.2   JUnit and mock framework requirements for the examples

Test class name	JUnit	Mock framework
JUnitSampleTest	✔	
MockitoSampleTest	✔	✔

Figure 14.2 depicts what components we cover in our unit test examples. This figure shows that we unit test all components except for the statistics step. This is good news: Spring Batch artifacts (validator, reader, writer, and so on) are unit testable! Even if these artifacts are meant to be used in complex jobs that handle large amounts of data, they're isolated enough from their runtime environment to be unit tested. That's a direct benefit of the plain old Java object (POJO) programming model that the Spring Framework—and so Spring Batch—promotes. Table 14.3 shows our example test classes and the corresponding Spring Batch domain objects they cover.

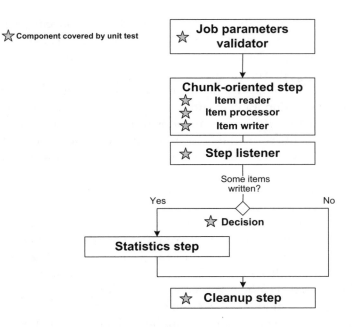

Figure 14.2 Components unit tested by our examples. We unit test all components except the statistics step.

Table 14.3 Example unit test classes and corresponding Spring Batch domain objects

Test class	Spring Batch domain object
ImportValidatorTest	JobParametersValidator
CompositeItemProcessorTest	ItemProcessor
ProductFieldSetMapperTest	ItemReader
PriceMandatoryValidatorTest	Validator in an ItemProcessor
PositivePriceValidatorTest	Validator in an ItemProcessor
ProductItemWriterMockTest	ItemWriter
ProductItemListener	StepListener
NextDeciderTest	JobExecutionDecider
CleanTaskletTest	Tasklet

14.2.1 Introducing JUnit

JUnit is an open source unit testing framework and is the de facto standard for unit testing in Java. Starting with version 4.5 (released in 2008), JUnit provides annotations and additional classes to ease the task of writing unit tests.

> **TIP** To learn everything there is to know about JUnit, read *JUnit in Action, Second Edition*, by Petar Tahchiev, Felipe Leme, Vincent Massol, and Gary Gregory (Manning Publications, 2011).

To implement a test case, you start by creating a public class; by convention, you post-fix the class name with `Test` or `TestCase`, for example, `ImportValidatorTest`. Because we use annotations, our test class no longer needs to inherit from the JUnit `TestCase` class as it did in JUnit version 3.

To create a test method, you write a public method with no return value, no arguments, and an `@Test` annotation. By convention, the method name starts with `test`.

At the start of a test run, JUnit runs methods with `@Before` annotations before each test method. Use `@Before` methods to initialize new instances of test objects stored in instance variables. These objects are available in each test method, and we call them *fixtures*.

JUnit runs methods with `@After` annotations after each test method to clean up fixtures or other resources as necessary.

Because some resources are expensive to initialize and manage, you can have JUnit call setup and tear down methods once per test run. Use the `@BeforeClass` annotation to call a method once per test run *before* JUnit has run all test methods. Use the `@After-Class` annotation to call a method once per test run *after* JUnit has run all test methods.

Methods in the `Assert` class help you compare an expected value to an actual value. You'll mostly use methods in the `Assert` class prefixed with `assert`. If an assert method contract is respected, the test continues; if not, the method throws an `Error`, and the test is stopped and marked as failed. Table 14.4 shows the main `Assert` methods.

Table 14.4   Description of the main JUnit assert methods

Method signature	Description
`assertTrue(booleanValue)`	Fails if `booleanValue` is `false`
`assertNotNull(value)`	Fails if `value` is `null`
`assertNull(value)`	Fails if `value` isn't `null`
`assertEquals(expectedValue, actualValue)`	Fails if `expectedValue` isn't equal to `actualValue`

The following listing shows a bare-bones unit test with the annotations and some of the `Assert` methods described in table 14.4.

Listing 14.1   Basic JUnit test case with annotations and assert methods

```
public class JUnitSampleTest {
  @Before
  public void setUp()
    // initialize something
  }

  @After
  public void tearDown() {
```

```
    // do something

  @Test
  public void testMethod1() {
    // do something
    assertTrue(true);
  }

  @Test
  public void testMethod2() {
    // do something
    assertNotNull("string");
  }
}
```

Listing 14.1 shows a test case without a superclass. JUnit calls the setUp method annotated with @Before before each @Test method. JUnit calls the tearDown method annotated with @After after each @Test method. These methods manage the lifecycle of fixtures. JUnit calls the @Test methods testMethod1 and testMethod2 and records which test succeeds or fails. In the method testMethod2, you use an assert method to verify that a string isn't null.

In most of the tests cases in this chapter, we use the static import coding style, so we don't need to prefix assert method calls with the Assert class name. We can now move on and test some real code.

We apply this new knowledge on simple examples first. Feel free to refer to our plan in figure 14.2 and table 14.3 to keep track of what you're doing.

TESTING A VALIDATOR

In our case study, a CompositeItemProcessor is composed of two ValidatingItemProcessors. Each one calls a custom Validator: PriceMandatoryValidator, which validates that a product's price isn't null, and a PositivePriceValidator, which validates that a product's price is positive.

For this test scenario, you instantiate a Validator, prepare a Product fixture, and verify the result. The PriceMandatoryValidator validates an input object; if this object is invalid, it throws an exception. In this case, it's easy to test a Validator, which has only one method, validate.

Listing 14.2 Testing a product validator for a non-null price

```
public class PriceMandatoryValidatorTest {
  private PriceMandatoryValidator validator;
  private Product product;

  @Before
  public void setUp() {
    validator = new PriceMandatoryValidator();
    product = new Product();
  }

  @Test
  public void testValidProduct() {
    product.setPrice(new BigDecimal("100.0"));
```

```
    validator.validate(product);
  }

  @Test(expected = ValidationException.class)
  public void testInvalidProduct() {
    validator.validate(product);
  }
}
```

In the setUp method, you create a new PriceMandatoryValidator and a new Product fixture.

In the first test method, testValidProduct, the validator checks that a product has a positive price.

In the second test method, testInvalidProduct, the test leaves the product price as null, so the validator throws a ValidationException, as expected. To tell the test you expect a ValidationException, we add the attribute expected to the @Test annotation like this: @Test(expected = ValidationException.class). If the test method doesn't throw a ValidationException, JUnit fails the test.

With the second validator, PositivePriceValidator, you have three cases: a positive, a zero, and a negative price.

Listing 14.3   Testing a product validator for a positive price

```
public class PositivePriceValidatorTest {
  private PositivePriceValidator validator;
  private Product product;

  @Before
  public void setUp() {
    validator = new PositivePriceValidator();     ❶ Creates validator
    product = new Product();                          and Product fixture
  }

  @Test
  public void testPositivePrice() {                 ❷ Asserts
    product.setPrice(new BigDecimal("100.0"));         positive price
    validator.validate(product);
  }

  @Test(expected = ValidationException.class)
  public void testZeroPrice() {
    product.setPrice(new BigDecimal("0.0"));
    validator.validate(product);
  }

  @Test(expected = ValidationException.class)       ❸ Asserts Validation-
  public void testNegativePrice() {                    Exception for negative
    product.setPrice(new BigDecimal("-800.0"));        price
    validator.validate(product);
  }
}
```

In this example, the setUp method creates a PositivePriceValidator ❶. In the method testPositivePrice ❷, you test a positive product price; this unit test validates the product, and the test method passes. In the method testNegativePrice ❸, you test a negative price; the test method throws a ValidationException, as expected, which causes JUnit to mark the test as successful.

In this section, we touched on JUnit framework basics: how to use JUnit with example test cases and how to test validators from our batch application. The next section introduces a mock framework to help you control the behavior of objects internal to our case study.

14.2.2 *Using mock objects with Mockito*

JUnit is a great tool dedicated to unit testing, but our objects aren't as simple as in the previous example. For a complex object, you only want to verify the behavior of the object, not the dependencies the object relies on. To achieve this goal, you create mock objects for dependencies. Mock objects are powerful for testing components in isolation and under total control. A mock object is a fake object, dynamically (or automatically) generated for us, that you control: you define what a method returns, when a method throws an exception, and so on. You can do all this in a few lines of code without writing new classes. After executing tests, you can verify that execution reached a mock object, what methods the test caused to call, how many times, and so forth.

For this book, we chose Mockito[1] as our mock framework, but many others are available. With Mockito, you can easily create a mock object for a class or interface and control and validate mock objects with a fluent-styled[2] API.

The following sample code, inspired by the Mockito documentation, shows how to create, manipulate, and verify a mock object:

```
// mocks an interface
List<String> mockedList = mock(List.class);
mockedList.add("one");
mockedList.clear();
verify(mockedList, times(1)).add("one");
verify(mockedList, times(1)).clear();
verifyNoMoreInteractions(mockedList);
```

This example checks that the code calls the methods add and clear only once by using the verify method and the call to times(1). The call to verifyNoMoreInteractions checks that the test caused no other method calls on the mock object. The methods prefixed with verify throw MockitoExceptions and fail a unit test when a call doesn't meet expectations.

With Mockito, you can mock a concrete class and control most of the behavior of the mock object. The following sample shows how to stub a LinkedList's get method to return the string "first":

---

[1] http://code.google.com/p/mockito
[2] http://martinfowler.com/bliki/FluentInterface.html

```
// mocks a concrete class
LinkedList<String> mockedList = mock(LinkedList.class);
when(mockedList.get(0)).thenReturn("first");
assertEquals("first", mockedList.get(0));
```

You can also create spy objects, based on real objects, and verify behavior, as shown in the following example:

```
List<String> list = new LinkedList<String>();
List<String> spy = Mockito.spy(list);
spy.add("one");
spy.add("two");
verify(spy).add("one");
verify(spy).add("two");
```

In this case, you call the add method on the List<String> object; the benefit is to confirm that the add method has been called twice, once with the parameter one and once with the parameter two. Use spying when you want to test legacy code.

Remember that, in a unit test, we want to test only a single module or component of an application and only one object if possible. In these unit tests, we use the white-box testing strategy, and we don't want to depend on other objects. Mockito helps us achieve these goals by mocking dependent objects, which we then wire into our own objects. In addition, we can control and verify how mock objects are used. The following sections explore how to test batch applications using JUnit and Mockito.

TESTING A FIELDSETMAPPER

In chapter 5, we use a FieldSetMapper to create an object from tokens with the help of a FieldSet. In our case study, a FlatFileItemReader in a product Step uses a ProductFieldSetMapper to map fields from a flat file line into a Product object. The following shows our custom ProductFieldSetMapper.

Listing 14.4   ProductFieldSetMapper implements FieldSetMapper

```
public class ProductFieldSetMapper implements FieldSetMapper<Product> {
  public static final String FIELD_ID = "ID";
  public static final String FIELD_NAME = "NAME";
  public static final String FIELD_DESCRIPTION = "DESCRIPTION";
  public static final String FIELD_PRICE = "PRICE";

  @Override
  public Product mapFieldSet(FieldSet fieldSet) throws BindException {
    Product product = new Product();
    product.setId(fieldSet.readString(FIELD_ID));
    product.setName(fieldSet.readString(FIELD_NAME));
    product.setDescription(fieldSet.readString(FIELD_DESCRIPTION));
    product.setPrice(fieldSet.readBigDecimal(FIELD_PRICE));
    return product;
  }
}
```

This FieldSetMapper implementation is simple by Spring Batch standards. The next listing tests our FieldSetMapper with and without Mockito.

Listing 14.5   Testing a `FieldSetMapper` with and without Mockito

```
import static com.manning.sbia.ch14.batch.ProductFieldSetMapper.
  ➥FIELD_DESCRIPTION;
import static com.manning.sbia.ch14.batch.ProductFieldSetMapper.
  ➥FIELD_ID;
import static com.manning.sbia.ch14.batch.ProductFieldSetMapper.
  ➥FIELD_NAME;
import static com.manning.sbia.ch14.batch.ProductFieldSetMapper.
  ➥FIELD_PRICE;
(..)
public class ProductFieldSetMapperTest {
  @Test
  public void testMapFieldMapClassic()                              ❶ Classic
        throws Exception {                                             test
    DefaultFieldSet fieldSet = new DefaultFieldSet(
        new String[] { "id", "name", "desc", "100.25" },
        new String[] { FIELD_ID, FIELD_NAME,
                       FIELD_DESCRIPTION, FIELD_PRICE });
    ProductFieldSetMapper mapper = new ProductFieldSetMapper();
    Product p = mapper.mapFieldSet(fieldSet);
    assertEquals("id", p.getId());
    assertEquals("name", p.getName());
    assertEquals("desc", p.getDescription());
    assertEquals(new BigDecimal("100.25"), p.getPrice());
  }

  @Test                                                             ❷ Mockito
  public void testMapFieldSetMock() throws Exception {  ◀──            test
    FieldSet fieldSet = mock(FieldSet.class);
    ProductFieldSetMapper mapper = new ProductFieldSetMapper();
    mapper.mapFieldSet(fieldSet);
    verify(fieldSet, times(1)).readString(FIELD_ID);
    verify(fieldSet, times(1)).readString(FIELD_NAME);
    verify(fieldSet, times(1)).readString(FIELD_DESCRIPTION);
    verify(fieldSet, times(1)).readBigDecimal(FIELD_PRICE);
    verifyNoMoreInteractions(fieldSet);
  }
}
```

The `ProductFieldSetMapperTest` class has two test methods: `testMapFieldSet-Classic` and `testMapFieldSetMock`.

The `testMapFieldSetClassic` test method ❶ creates a `DefaultFieldSet` with column names and values. Then the `assert` methods check that a product was created and correctly populated. This is the standard JUnit style; you test expected values against actual values.

The `testMapFieldSetMock` test method ❷ mocks a `FieldSet`, invokes `mapField-Set`, checks values, and also verifies that no other methods have been called on the `fieldSet`. The call to `verifyNoMoreInteractions` checks that the test didn't call other methods on the `fieldSet`. If the `ProductFieldSetMapper` calls other methods, like `readString("string")`, the test fails. Using a mock object, you can check the `mapFieldSet` behavior in detail.

TESTING AN ITEMLISTENERSUPPORT

In our next example, the `ProductItemListener` class in listing 14.6 implements a `StepListener`. Spring Batch calls a `ProductItemListener` after processing each product object in the product step. Remember that the role of our `CompositeItemProcessor` is to filter products.

Listing 14.6   A Product `ItemListener` implementation

```
public class ProductItemListener extends
            ItemListenerSupport<Product,Product> {
  private FlatFileItemWriter<Product> excludeWriter;
  @Override
  public void afterProcess(Product item, Product result) {
    if (result == null) {
      try {
        excludeWriter.write(Arrays.asList(item));
      } catch (Exception e) {
      }
    }
  }
  @Required
  public void setExcludeWriter(FlatFileItemWriter<Product> excludeWriter) {
    this.excludeWriter = excludeWriter;
  }
}
```

Note that the `@Required` annotation marks the property method `setExcludeWriter` as mandatory and causes the Spring context load to fail if it isn't called.

If the job filters out a product, the `afterProcess` method has a `null` result argument value, and you write the `Product` item to a product reject file using the `exclude-Writer`. This implementation uses a `FlatFileItemWriter` as a reject file writer to maintain less source code.

The goals of the tests in this section are to avoid using the file system and to write tests that filter and don't filter items. We also control how the `excludeWriter` is used. The following listing shows our test case for the `ProductItemListenerTest` class.

Listing 14.7   Testing an `ItemSupportListener`

```
public class ProductItemListenerTest {
  private Product p = null;
  private FlatFileItemWriter<Product> writer = null;
  private List<Product> items = null;

  @Before
  public void setUp() {
    p = new Product();
    p.setId("211");
    p.setName("BlackBerry");
    items = Arrays.asList(p);
    writer = mock(FlatFileItemWriter.class);
  }
```

```
@Test
public void testAfterProcess() throws Exception {
  ProductItemListener listener = new ProductItemListener();
  listener.setExcludeWriter(writer);
  listener.afterProcess(p, null);
  verify(writer, times(1)).write(items);
}

@Test
public void testAfterProcessResult() throws Exception {
  ProductItemListener listener = new ProductItemListener();
  listener.setExcludeWriter(writer);
  listener.afterProcess(p, p);
  verify(writer, never()).write(items);
}
}
```

In this listing, the method `setUp` populates the product `items` list fixture with one `Product` and mocks a `FlatFileItemWriter` to avoid using the file system. The `test-AfterProcess` method calls the method `afterProcess` on the `ProductItemListener` with a `Product` as the input and a `null` value as the output product. In this case, the test simulates that the `CompositeItemProcessor` filters input products for prices less than or equal to zero. The test checks that the listener invokes the `write` method on the exclude writer once.

In the `testAfterProcessResult` method, the test calls `afterProcess` with the same input product, which means that the `CompositeItemProcessor` doesn't filter this product. Finally, you ensure that this is the case.

In the next sections, we look at some of Mockito's advanced features, like controlling values returned from a method, creating elaborate tests, and spying on objects.

TESTING A JOBPARAMETERSVALIDATOR

You're ready to test a `JobParametersValidator` (listing 14.8), which the job invokes at the beginning of its processing to validate `JobParameters`. The `ImportValidator` verifies that the product input file exists and that the statistics path parameter isn't `null`. For this unit test, you don't want to depend on the file system, so you mock a `ResourceLoader`.

Listing 14.8   Testing a `JobParametersValidator` with Mockito's spy feature

```
public class ImportValidatorTest {
  String PRODUCTS_PATH =
    "classpath:com/manning/sbia/ch14/input/products.txt";
  String STATISTIC_PATH = "file:./target/statistic.txt";
  private ResourceLoader resourceLoader;
  private ImportValidator validator;

  @Before
  public void setUp() {
    resourceLoader = mock(ResourceLoader.class,
      Mockito.RETURNS_DEEP_STUBS);
    when(resourceLoader.getResource(PRODUCTS_PATH).exists())
```

```
      .thenReturn(true);
   validator = new ImportValidator();
   validator.setResourceLoader(resourceLoader);
}

@Test
public void testJobParameters() throws JobParametersInvalidException {
   JobParameters jobParameters = new JobParametersBuilder()
       .addString(PARAM_INPUT_RESOURCE, PRODUCTS_PATH)
       .addString(PARAM_REPORT_RESOURCE, STATISTIC_PATH)
       .toJobParameters();
   JobParameters spy = Mockito.spy(jobParameters);
   validator.validate(spy);
   verify(spy, times(2)).getParameters();
   verify(spy, times(1)).getString(
     PARAM_INPUT_RESOURCE);
   verifyNoMoreInteractions(spy);
}

@Test(expected = JobParametersInvalidException.class)
public void testEmptyJobParameters()
          throws JobParametersInvalidException {
   JobParameters jobParameters = new JobParametersBuilder()
     .toJobParameters();
   validator.validate(jobParameters);
}

@Test(expected = JobParametersInvalidException.class)
public void testMissingJobParameters()
          throws JobParametersInvalidException {
   JobParameters jobParameters = new JobParametersBuilder()
       .addString(PARAM_INPUT_RESOURCE, PRODUCTS_PATH)
       .toJobParameters();
   validator.validate(jobParameters);
}
}
```

❶ Spies on JobParameters

❷ Verifies mock Behavior

In the testJobParameters method, you verify the ImportValidator implementation by spying on JobParameters ❶. You use spied objects because you want to control how many times the test calls getParameter and getString ❷. This test shows that, for the given input, the ImportValidator validate method causes getParameters to be called twice (it could be with parameters.getParameters().containsKey(key), for example). The test also shows that the getString(String) method is called once with a PARAM_INPUT_RESOURCE argument value.

The testValidateEmptyJobParameters method verifies that the ImportValida-tor throws a JobParametersInvalidException when the job parameters, which are required, are empty.

The testMissingJobParameters method verifies that the ImportValidator throws a JobParametersInvalidException when the job parameters are missing a required parameter. This test checks only one case; a complete implementation would check all possible cases.

Note that Spring Batch provides a `DefaultJobParametersValidator` class in which you manually set required and optional keys. Spring Batch can also automatically discover these keys.

The next section tests an `ItemWriter`, a more complex example.

TESTING AN ITEMWRITER

Our `ProductItemWriter` writes `Product` objects to a database via a `SimpleJdbcTemplate`. The following listing shows how to do this.

> **Listing 14.9   Writing to a database with the `ProductItemWriter`**

```
public class ProductItemWriter implements ItemWriter<Product> {
  String INSERT_SQL = "INSERT INTO PRODUCT (ID, NAME, DESCRIPTION, PRICE)
      ➥VALUES (:id, :name, :description, :price)";
  String UPDATE_SQL = "UPDATE PRODUCT SET NAME=:name,
      ➥DESCRIPTION=:description, PRICE=:price WHERE ID=:id";
  ItemSqlParameterSourceProvider<Product> itemSqlParameterSourceProvider;
  SimpleJdbcTemplate simpleJdbcTemplate;

  @Required
  public void setSimpleJdbcTemplate(
     SimpleJdbcTemplate simpleJdbcTemplate) {
    this.simpleJdbcTemplate = simpleJdbcTemplate;
  }

  @Required
  public void setItemSqlParameterSourceProvider(
     ItemSqlParameterSourceProvider<Product>
     itemSqlParameterSourceProvider) {
    this.itemSqlParameterSourceProvider = itemSqlParameterSourceProvider;
  }

  @Override
  public void write(List<? extends Product> items) throws Exception {
    for (Product item : items) {
      SqlParameterSource args = itemSqlParameterSourceProvider
        .createSqlParameterSource(item);
      int updated = simpleJdbcTemplate.update(UPDATE_SQL, args);
      if (updated == 0) {
        simpleJdbcTemplate.update(INSERT_SQL, args);
      }
    }
  }
}
```

This writer uses SQL `INSERT` and `UPDATE` statements. If a product already exists in the database, the `ProductItemWriter` executes a SQL `UPDATE`. If the product isn't in the database, the `ProductItemWriter` first tries to execute an `UPDATE`, which fails, and then executes an `INSERT`, which succeeds. For each product item, the writer creates a `SqlParameterSource` to bind its values into a SQL statement's named parameters.

Let's look at the item writer test, where you unit test everything with Spring Batch, JUnit, and Mockito. The following listing shows the unit test for the item writer.

Listing 14.10   Advanced testing of an `ItemWriter`

```
public class ProductItemWriterMockTest {
  private Product p;
  private SimpleJdbcTemplate jdbcTemplate;
  private ProductItemWriter writer = new ProductItemWriter();
  private ItemSqlParameterSourceProvider<Product> ispsp;
  private List<Product> items;

  @Before
  public void setUp() {
    p = new Product();
    p.setId("211");
    p.setName("BlackBerry");
    items = Arrays.asList(p);
    writer = new ProductItemWriter();
    ispsp = new BeanPropertyItemSqlParameterSourceProvider<Product>();
    writer.setItemSqlParameterSourceProvider(ispsp);
    jdbcTemplate = mock(SimpleJdbcTemplate.class);              ◄──── ❶ Mocks
    writer.setSimpleJdbcTemplate(jdbcTemplate);                      SimpleJdbcTemplate
    writer.setItemSqlParameterSourceProvider(ispsp);
  }

  @Test
  public void testUpdateProduct() throws Exception {
    when(jdbcTemplate.update(eq(UPDATE_SQL),                   ❷ Mocks
      any(SqlParameterSource.class)))                              return value
        .thenReturn(1);
    writer.write(items);
    verify(jdbcTemplate, times(1))
      .update(eq(UPDATE_SQL),                                  ❸ Verifies
        any(SqlParameterSource.class));                            invocations
    verify(jdbcTemplate, times(0))
      .update(eq(INSERT_SQL),
        any(SqlParameterSource.class));
    verifyNoMoreInteractions(jdbcTemplate);
  }

  @Test
  public void testInsertProduct() throws Exception {
    when(jdbcTemplate.update(eq(UPDATE_SQL),
      any(SqlParameterSource.class)))
      .thenReturn(0);
    writer.write(items);
    verify(jdbcTemplate, times(1))
      .update(eq(UPDATE_SQL),
        any(SqlParameterSource.class));
    verify(jdbcTemplate, times(1))
      .update(eq(INSERT_SQL);
        any(SqlParameterSource.class));
    verifyNoMoreInteractions(jdbcTemplate);
  }
}
```

First, you set up your fixture objects in the `setUp` method where you also set up a mock object for a `SimpleJdbcTemplate` ❶ and initialize it with its required dependencies.

The first test, `testUpdateProduct`, simulates at ❷ that the `UPDATE` statement returns only one affected row, which means that the product already exists. Using the `eq` and `any` methods, Mockito allows you to control method arguments for any instance of `SqlParameterSource`. After that, you count how many times the test called each SQL statement ❸; you expected one `UPDATE` and zero `INSERT`s.

In the second test, `testInsertProduct`, if the `UPDATE` statement affects zero rows, the `SimpleJdbcTemplate` executes a SQL `INSERT`. You expected one call to `UPDATE` and one call to `INSERT`.

You have now successfully tested a `FieldSetMapper`, an item listener, and an item writer, which are all key components of Spring Batch. The ability to test these core components gives you the confidence to proceed with changing and growing the application.

In the previous sections, we introduced JUnit, a powerful unit testing framework, and the Mockito mocking framework. We can't use unit testing for most of our case study yet, but it won't be long before we can. Next, we look at techniques that allow you to test Spring Batch applications at all levels.

14.2.3 Mocking Spring Batch domain objects

Spring batch manages beans during a batch application's lifecycle. Some of these objects are too complex to create outside the Spring Batch infrastructure, like a unit test. That's why Spring Batch provides the *Spring Batch Test* module. This module includes classes like `MetaDataInstanceFactory`, whose goal is to create test instances of `JobExecution`, `JobInstance`, and `StepExecution`. The following example creates a test `StepExecution` and `JobExecution` using the `MetaDataInstanceFactory` class:

```
StepExecution stepExecution = MetaDataInstanceFactory
  .createStepExecution();
JobExecution jobExecution = MetaDataInstanceFactory.createJobExecution();
```

The `Test` module opens up Spring Batch domain objects to be tested. Classes like `JobExecutionDecider` and `Tasklet`, for example, have APIs that require the types of objects supplied by `MetaDataInstanceFactory`.

TESTING A JOBEXECUTIONDECIDER

Remember that, in figure 14.2, the `JobExecutionDecider` manages the batch flow. You use the `MetaDataInstanceFactory` to create a `JobExecution` and `StepExecution`. The `NextDecider` sits between `CleanStep` and `StatisticStep`. It returns `NEXT` if the job writes any products, based on the number of written items for this execution, and `COMPLETED` otherwise. It's important to test `JobExecutionDecider` because it's responsible for the batch workflow. The following listing shows the `NextDeciderTest` class.

Listing 14.11 Testing batch workflow with `JobExecutionDecider`

```
public class NextDeciderTest {
  StepExecution stepExecution = null;
  JobExecution jobExecution = null;
  NextDecider decider = null;
```

```
  @Before
  public void setUp() {
    stepExecution = MetaDataInstanceFactory
      .createStepExecution();
    jobExecution = MetaDataInstanceFactory
      .createJobExecution();
    decider = new NextDecider();
  }

  @Test
  public void testNextStatus() {
     stepExecution.setWriteCount(5);
    FlowExecutionStatus status = decider.decide(
      jobExecution, stepExecution);
    assertEquals(status.getName(), "NEXT");
  }

  @Test
  public void testCompletedStatus() {
    stepExecution.setWriteCount(0);
    FlowExecutionStatus status = decider
      .decide(jobExecution, stepExecution);
    assertEquals(status,
      FlowExecutionStatus.COMPLETED);
  }
}
```

This test case creates a StepExecution and a JobExecution with the Spring Batch Test
class MetaDataInstanceFactory. You set the write count value to a positive value, call
the decide method, and check that the result is NEXT.

In the next test method, you set the write count to zero and check that the result is
COMPLETED.

Let's continue to explore the MetaDataInstanceFactory class by testing a Tasklet.

TESTING A TASKLET

You can also manipulate complex Spring Batch domain objects like a ChunkContext
(a requirement of the Tasklet API) with the MetaDataInstanceFactory class. The following listing demonstrates testing such a tasklet.

Listing 14.12 Testing a simple tasklet with Spring Batch domain mocks

```
public class CleanTaskletTest {
  @Test
  public void clean() throws Exception {
    StepExecution stepExecution =
      MetaDataInstanceFactory.createStepExecution();
    StepContribution contrib = new StepContribution(stepExecution);
    ChunkContext context = new ChunkContext(
      new StepContext(stepExecution));                                    ◁─── ❶ Creates chunk
    CleanTasklet clean = new CleanTasklet();                                      context
    RepeatStatus status = clean.execute(contrib, context);
    assertEquals(RepeatStatus.FINISHED, status);
  }
}
```

In the `CleanTaskletTest` class, you create a `ChunkContext` ❶ to test the `Tasklet`, which doesn't require any dependencies. The implementation of the `CleanTasklet` class always returns `RepeatStatus.FINISHED`.

This unit test ends this section. We created unit tests for our case study with JUnit, Mockito, and Spring Batch mock domain objects. These examples show you how to improve the reliability and robustness of batch applications. The next section covers creating integration tests.

14.3 *Integration testing*

In this section, we address another aspect of testing where we test software modules in realistic production conditions to validate overall functionality. As a white-box strategy, integration testing is aware of internal implementation details. This time, we use a real database, Spring, and Spring Batch application contexts, including batch job definitions.

Table 14.5 shows test class names and corresponding Spring Batch domain classes.

Table 14.5   Integration testing plan with Spring Batch domain classes

Test class	Spring Batch domain class
`ReaderWithListenerTest`	`ItemReader`
`ReaderWithStepScopeTestUtilsTest`	`ItemReader`
`CompositeItemProcessorTest`	`ItemProcessor`

Figure 14.3 depicts what components we cover in our integration test examples.

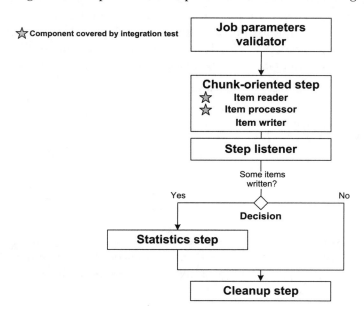

Figure 14.3   Components covered by integration tests

To go on with integration testing of our case study, we introduce the Spring TestContext Framework and the Spring Batch `StepScopeTestExecutionListener` class. To track what you're testing, please refer to figure 14.3. We focus next on testing instances of `Step`, `ItemReader`, and `ItemProcessor`.

14.3.1   *Introducing the Spring TestContext Framework*

The Spring Framework provides support for integration testing with the Spring Test-Context Framework, which lets you write tests for a framework like JUnit. In JUnit, the `@RunWith` annotation sets a `Runner` class, which is responsible for launching tests, triggering events, and marking tests as successful or failed.

> **SPRING TESTCONTEXT REQUIREMENTS**   To use the Spring TestContext framework, you need Java 5 or greater and JUnit version 4.5 or greater. Annotate your test class with the `@RunWith` annotation and the value `SpringJUnit4Class-Runner.class`.

For integration testing, we use the following Spring TestContext Framework features:

- The `@ContextConfiguration` annotation is used to load a Spring context from an XML file, for example, `@ContextConfiguration("/path/context.xml")`. By convention, if an application context path isn't set, the path is set to `[Test-ClassName]-context.xml`.
- Spring TestContext caches the application context for better performance. This saves time on each test startup.
- The `@DirtiesContext` annotation indicates that the application context for a test is dirty and that TestContext should close it after each test.
- Spring TestContext defines a listener API for tests to interact with objects with the `@TestExecutionListeners` annotation. For example, the `DependencyInject-TestExecutionListener` class provides support for dependency injection and initialization of test instances. Spring TestContext adds this listener by default and injects field by type, annotated with `@Autowired` or by name with `@Resource`.

The following simple example uses these features:

```
@RunWith(SpringJUnit4ClassRunner.class)
@ContextConfiguration("/path/to/context.xml")
public class SampleIntegrationTest {
  @Autowired
  private AnObject anObject;

  @Test
  public void test() {
  }
}
```

For integration tests, you hit a real database: the H2 Database,[3] which is a fast Java SQL database. You configure it as an in-memory database to avoid file system access. The following snippet shows the Spring configuration of the `DataSource` bean:

---

[3]   www.h2database.com

```
<bean id="dataSource"
    class="org.springframework.jdbc.datasource.SingleConnectionDataSource">
  <property name="driverClassName" value="${datasource.driver}" />
  <property name="url" value="${datasource.url}" />
  <property name="username" value="${datasource.username}" />
  <property name="password" value="${datasource.password}" />
</bean>

<context:property-placeholder location="/path/to/batch-h2.properties" />
```

In this configuration, you import the H2 configuration properties from the batch-h2.properties file. The following snippet shows the content of this file:

```
datasource.driver=org.h2.Driver
datasource.url=jdbc:h2:mem:products;DB_CLOSE_DELAY=-1
datasource.username=sa
datasource.password=
```

The keyword mem indicates that H2 should work only in memory. For database initialization, you add jdbc:initialize-database to the application context, which refers to the Datasource used to execute a list of SQL scripts:

```
<jdbc:initialize-database data-source="dataSource">
  <jdbc:script
    location="classpath:com/manning/sbia/ch14/sql/create-tables.sql" />
</jdbc:initialize-database>
```

You now have the basic elements in place to begin integration testing of our batch job. You load a Spring application context and set up an in-memory database based on SQL scripts. The next step is to deal with Spring Batch components using a special scope.

14.3.2 *Using the Spring Batch StepScopeTestExecutionListener*

In Spring Batch, you can configure components at runtime with a special scope named *step* and a late binding SpEL (Spring Expression Language) expression based on a step or a job execution:

```
<bean id="reader"
    class="org.springframework.batch.item.file.FlatFileItemReader"
    scope="step">
  <property name="resource" value="#{jobParameters['inputResource']}" />
  (...)
</bean>
```

To help test these components, the Spring Batch Test module includes a special listener called StepScopeTestExecutionListener that implements the Spring Test TestExecutionListener interface. By default, this listener creates an empty Step-Execution. If a getStepExecution method exists, StepScopeTestExecutionListener invokes it to create a StepExecution.

The following example illustrates this usage:

```
@RunWith(SpringJUnit4ClassRunner.class)
@ContextConfiguration
@TestExecutionListeners(StepScopeTestExecutionListener.class })
public class SampleIntegrationTest {
```

```
public StepExecution getStepExecution() {
  JobParameters jobParameters = new JobParametersBuilder()
    .addString("author", "Olivier B.").toJobParameters();
  return MetaDataInstanceFactory.createStepExecution(jobParameters);
}
(...)
}
```

It's time to begin integration testing based on our case study and practice what we've learned.

TESTING AN ITEMPROCESSOR

In our case study, you use an `ItemProcessor` in the `Product` step. Specifically, you use a `CompositeItemProcessor` composed of two `ValidatingItemProcessors`, which use `PositivePriceValidator` and `PriceMandatoryValidator`. Remember that you already tested each `Validator` separately in unit tests (see the previous section on unit testing). For an integration test, you test the real processor chain, which the Spring context defines. The following listing shows the `CompositeItemProcessorTest` class.

Listing 14.13   Testing an `ItemProcessor` with the Spring TestContext Framework

```
@ContextConfiguration
@TestExecutionListeners({ DependencyInjectionTestExecutionListener.class,
    StepScopeTestExecutionListener.class })                    ◁──┐  Adds
@RunWith(SpringJUnit4ClassRunner.class)                        ❶  StepScopeTestExecutionListener
public class CompositeItemProcessorTest {
  @Autowired                                                      ❷  Injects
  private ItemProcessor<Product, Product> processor;           ◁──┘  processor

  public StepExecution getStepExecution() {                    ◁──┐  Creates custom
    JobParameters jobParameters = new JobParametersBuilder()   ❸  step execution
        .addDouble("maxPrice", "200.0")
        .toJobParameters();
    StepExecution execution = createStepExecution(jobParameters);
    return execution;
  }

  @Test
  @DirtiesContext
  public void testProcessor() throws Exception {               ◁──┐
    Product p1 = new Product();
    p1.setPrice(new BigDecimal("100.0"));
    Product p2 = processor.process(p1);
    assertNotNull(p2);                                            ❹  Tests different
  }                                                                  use cases

  @Test
  @DirtiesContext
  public void testNegativePriceFailure()
        throws Exception {
    Product p1 = new Product();
    p1.setPrice(new BigDecimal("-800.0"));
    Product p2 = processor.process(p1);
    assertNull(p2);
```

```
   }

   @Test
   @DirtiesContext
   public void testZeroPriceFailure()
         throws Exception {
     Product p1 = new Product();
     p1.setPrice(new BigDecimal("0.0"));
     Product p2 = processor.process(p1);
     assertNull(p2);
   }

   @Test
   @DirtiesContext
   public void testEmptyProductFailure()
         throws Exception {
     Product p1 = new Product();
     Product p2 = processor.process(p1);
     assertNull(p2);
   }
}
```

❹ Tests different use cases

You start by adding a StepScopeTestExecutionListener ❶ to create a custom Step-Execution ❸ with a mandatory parameter in the step scope. You take advantage of the Spring TestContext Framework to autowire the real ItemProcessor ❷.

You can now validate your test scenarios based on various product price values ❹. If a product price is positive, the ItemProcessor returns the same product object; otherwise it returns null. The test testNegativePriceFailure tests a negative price, and testZeroPriceFailure tests a price product equal to zero. The last test, testEmpty-ProductFailure, tests an empty Product object.

Note that the ValidatingItemProcesors for this job are configured with filter = true, which means they don't throw exceptions.

This integration test validates that the CompositeItemProcessor has no bugs in its Validator order. If you had the PositivePriceValidator in the first position, these tests would fail with a NullPointerException because the validator assumes that the price product isn't null.

Let's continue with a more complex example: testing an ItemReader.

TESTING AN ITEMREADER

In this section, we describe two ways to test an ItemReader. First, we see an example using the same technique as previously shown. Then we use the Spring Batch Test class StepScopeTestUtils.

In the test in the following listing, you read data from a real file in the file system (but you could mock it). The test checks the content of the first line of data and how many lines the file includes.

Listing 14.14 Testing an `ItemReader` with the Spring Batch Test module

```
import static com.manning.sbia.ch14.batch.ImportValidator.
   ➥ PARAM_INPUT_RESOURCE;
(..)
```

```
@ContextConfiguration
@TestExecutionListeners({
DependencyInjectionTestExecutionListener.class,
  StepScopeTestExecutionListener.class })
@RunWith(SpringJUnit4ClassRunner.class)
public class ReaderWithListenerTest {
  String PRODUCTS_PATH =
    "classpath:com/manning/sbia/ch14/input/products.txt";

  @Autowired
  private ItemReader<Product> reader;

  public StepExecution getStepExecution() {
    JobParameters jobParameters = new JobParametersBuilder()
        .addString(PARAM_INPUT_RESOURCE, PRODUCTS_PATH)
        .toJobParameters();
    StepExecution execution = createStepExecution(
      jobParameters);
    return execution;
  }

  @Before
  public void setUp() {                                            ❶ Creates new
    ((ItemStream) reader).open(new ExecutionContext());              execution context
  }

  @Test
  @DirtiesContext
  public void testReader() throws Exception {                      ❷ Reads from
    Product p = reader.read();                                       item reader
    assertNotNull(p);
    assertEquals("211", p.getId());                                ❸ Checks
    assertNotNull(reader.read());                                    first item
    assertNotNull(reader.read());
    assertNotNull(reader.read());
    assertNotNull(reader.read());
    assertNotNull(reader.read());
    assertNotNull(reader.read());
    assertNotNull(reader.read());                                  ❹ Checks reading
    assertNull(reader.read());                                       is done
  }
}
  @After                                                           ❺ Closes
  public void tearDown() {                                           reader
    ((ItemStream) reader).close();
  }
}
```

We start each test with the @Before setUp method ❶ to open the stream with a new
ExecutionContext. We read a first line ❷ and compare the expected ID value ❸. The
product file contains eight lines, which we verify by calling read eight times and
checking that each call returns data. Then, we expect the ninth call to read to return
null ❹, indicating that we've reached the end of the file. After each @Test method,
we close the stream in the @After tearDown method ❺.

   The Spring Batch Test StepScopeTestUtils method doInStepScope is the other
way to test a Spring Batch component in a step scope for the ItemReader in our case

study. We must create an implementation of the java.util.concurrent.Callable interface that returns an object, in this case, the count of lines read. Listing 14.15 shows our ReaderWithStepScopeTestUtilsTest class.

Listing 14.15   Testing an ItemReader with StepScopeTestUtils' doInStepScope

```
import static com.manning.sbia.ch14.batch.ImportValidator.
    PARAM_INPUT_RESOURCE;
(..)
@ContextConfiguration
@RunWith(SpringJUnit4ClassRunner.class)
public class ReaderWithStepScopeTestUtilsTest {
  String PRODUCTS_PATH =
    "classpath:com/manning/sbia/ch14/input/products.txt";
  @Autowired
  private ItemReader<Product> reader;

  public StepExecution getStepExecution() {
    JobParameters jobParameters = new JobParametersBuilder()
      .addString(PARAM_INPUT_RESOURCE, PRODUCTS_PATH)
      .toJobParameters();
    StepExecution execution = createStepExecution(jobParameters);
    return execution;
  }

  @Test
  @DirtiesContext
  public void testReader() throws Exception {
    int count = StepScopeTestUtils.doInStepScope(getStepExecution(),
      new Callable<Integer>() {                          ❶ Creates step-
        @Override                                          scoped behavior
        public Integer call() throws Exception {
          int count = 0;
          try {
            ((ItemStream) reader).open(new ExecutionContext());
            while (reader.read() != null) {
              count++;                                   ❷ Reads
            }                                              all items
            return count;
          } finally {
            ((ItemStream) reader).close();
          }
        }
      });                                    ❸ Checks read
    assertEquals(8, count);                     items count
  }
}
```

You start the test by creating an anonymous implementation of the Callable interface ❶. Then you open a stream with a new ExecutionContext, and while the reader reads items in a loop, you count lines as you read them ❷. Finally, you close the stream. Again, you ensure that you have read eight lines ❸.

We don't see a best approach here. Using a listener is simpler than using `Step-ScopeTestUtils`, but the latter is more flexible and may be more effective for a complex `ItemReader`.

Now we move on to functional testing.

14.4   *Functional testing*

Table 14.6 shows functional test classes and corresponding Spring Batch domain objects.

Test class	Spring Batch domain object
ProductStepTest	Step
StatisticStepTest	Step
WholeBatchTest	Job

Table 14.6   Functional testing plan and Spring Batch domain objects

Figure 14.4 shows what components we cover in our functional test examples.

Here, we focus on the functional requirements of an application, and remember that we use the black-box testing strategy. Considering the job's overall functionality, we provide input values and verify output values without concern for any implementation details. This kind of testing gives you confidence in the correctness of a whole batch job.

Because this is a section on testing `Step` and `Job` objects, we validate the product and statistics step and the batch overall (see the test plan in figure 14.4).

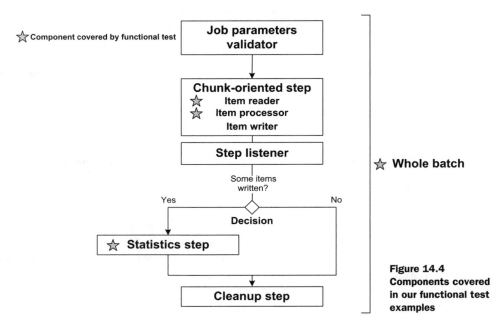

Figure 14.4 Components covered in our functional test examples

14.4.1 Introducing JobLauncherTestUtils

The `JobLauncherTestUtils` class is another class from the Spring Batch Test module to help you test a single `Step` or `Job`. The `JobLauncherTestUtils` class automatically injects a job by type from the application context; this implies that there's only one batch job in your test application context. This is a best practice. With `JobLauncher-TestUtils`, you can launch a single step of a job by specifying the step name. You can also specify job parameters. The following snippet shows how to launch only one step:

```
JobExecution jobExecution = jobLauncherTestUtils.launchStep(
  stepName,jobParameters
);
```

You can also launch a whole job with job parameters, as shown in the following snippet:

```
JobExecution jobExecution = jobLauncherTestUtils.launchJob(jobParameters);
```

The `AssertFile` class from the Spring Batch Test module includes `assert` methods to compare `File` and `Resource` contents. You use the `AssertFile` class to compare the content of the expected reference file with an actual exclude or statistics file. Recall that JUnit uses the terms `expected` and `actual` in its APIs consistently, where the expected value comes first and the actual value second:

```
// Assert that two files are the same
assertFileEquals(File expected, File actual);
assertFileEquals(Resource expected, Resource actual);
// Assert that file expectedLineCount lines
assertLineCount(int expectedLineCount, File file);
assertLineCount(int expectedLineCount, Resource resource);
```

Using these new testing classes, we can now work on the `Step` test.

14.4.2 Testing a step

Steps define the sequence of actions in a job. A step is a critical part of a job, so it's important to test it in isolation. It's easy to write such a test with the `JobLauncherTest-Utils` class. Our test scenario in the following listing provides input data, launches the `productsStep`, ensures that the batch status is `COMPLETED`, counts how many lines the job has filtered and written, and finally compares the rejected products file with a reference file.

Listing 14.16 Functional testing of the product step

```
@RunWith(SpringJUnit4ClassRunner.class)
@ContextConfiguration
public class ProductStepTest {
  String PRODUCTS_PATH =
    "classpath:com/manning/sbia/ch14/input/products.txt";
  String EXCLUDES_REF_PATH = "com/manning/sbia/ch14/output/excludes.txt";
  String EXCLUDES_PATH = "./target/excludes.txt";
  @Autowired
```

```
        private JobLauncherTestUtils jobLauncherTestUtils;          ◀──┐      Injects testing
        @Autowired                                                     ❶      utilities
        private SimpleJdbcTemplate jdbcTemplate;             ◀──┐     Injects
                                                                ❷    SimpleJdbcTemplate
        @Test
        @DirtiesContext
        public void testIntegration() throws Exception {
          JobParameters jobParameters = new JobParametersBuilder()
              .addString(PARAM_INPUT_RESOURCE, PRODUCTS_PATH)
              .toJobParameters();

          JobExecution exec = jobLauncherTestUtils                      ❸   Launch
            .launchStep("productsStep",jobParameters);                      step
          assertEquals(
            BatchStatus.COMPLETED, exec.getStatus());
          StepExecution setpExec = exec.getStepExecutions()
            .iterator().next();
          assertEquals(2, setpExec.getFilterCount());
          assertEquals(6, setpExec.getWriteCount());              ❹   Checks
          assertEquals(6, jdbcTemplate.queryForInt(                   expectations
            "SELECT COUNT(*) from PRODUCT"));
          assertFileEquals(
              new ClassPathResource(EXCLUDES_REF_PATH),
              new FileSystemResource(EXCLUDES_PATH));
        }
      }
```

In this test, you start by declaring instance variables for `JobLauncherTestUtils` ❶ and `SimpleJdbcTemplate` ❷, and use Spring TestContext dependency injection to initialize them. In the `testIntegration` method, you set up `JobParameters` and use `JobLauncherTestUtils` to launch the `productsStep` ❸. At ❹, you start checking expectations. You expect the `COMPLETED` batch status for the job execution. Then you retrieve the first step in the `StepExecution`, count filtered items, and count written items. Finally, you count the products in the database and compare file contents from the exclude product file and the reference file.

The statistics step calculates the average price of products; there's no code, only Spring Batch configuration, as shown in the following listing.

Listing 14.17 Compute and write the product average into a file from a step

```xml
<step id="statisticStep" next="cleanStep">
  <tasklet>
    <chunk reader="statisticReader" writer="statisticWriter"
           commit-interval="100" />
  </tasklet>
</step>

<bean id="statisticReader"
      class="org.springframework.batch.item.database.JdbcCursorItemReader">
  <property name="dataSource" ref="dataSource" />
  <property name="rowMapper">
    <bean class="org.springframework.jdbc.core.SingleColumnRowMapper">
      <constructor-arg value="java.math.BigDecimal" />
    </bean>
```

```
      </property>
      <property name="sql">
        <value>SELECT AVG(PRICE) FROM PRODUCT</value>
      </property>
  </bean>

  <bean id="statisticWriter"
        class="org.springframework.batch.item.file.FlatFileItemWriter"
        scope="step">
      <property name="resource" value="#{jobParameters['reportResource']}" />
      <property name="lineAggregator">
        <bean class="org.springframework.batch.item.file.transform.
➥ PassThroughLineAggregator" />
      </property>
  </bean>
```

This step uses a reader based on a `JdbcCursorItemReader` that computes the average price for all products using the AVG SQL function. The step has a simple writer to get the result, via a `PassThroughLineAggregator`, and write it with a `FlatFileItemWriter`.

The following listing shows you another example by testing the step `statistic-Step` and setting up data in a database.

Listing 14.18 Functional testing of a step with a database

```
@RunWith(SpringJUnit4ClassRunner.class)
@ContextConfiguration
public class StatisticStepTest {
  String STATISTIC_REF_PATH =
    "com/manning/sbia/ch14/output/statistic-summary.txt";
  String STATISTIC_PATH = "./target/statistic-summary.txt";
  @Autowired
  private JobLauncherTestUtils jobLauncherTestUtils;
  @Autowired
  private SimpleJdbcTemplate jdbcTemplate;
  ItemSqlParameterSourceProvider<Product> ispsp;

  @Before
  public void setup() {
    ispsp = new BeanPropertyItemSqlParameterSourceProvider<Product>();

    Product product = new Product();
    product.setId("1");
    product.setDescription("");
    product.setPrice(new BigDecimal(10.0f));

    SqlParameterSource args = ispsp.createSqlParameterSource(product);
    jdbcTemplate.update(INSERT_SQL, args);

    product = new Product();
    product.setId("2");
    product.setDescription("");
    product.setPrice(new BigDecimal(30.0f));
    args = ispsp.createSqlParameterSource(product);
    jdbcTemplate.update(INSERT_SQL, args);
  }
```

```
@Test
@DirtiesContext
public void integration() throws Exception {
  JobParameters jobParameters = new JobParametersBuilder()
      .addString("reportResource", "file:" + STATISTIC_PATH)
      .toJobParameters();

  JobExecution exec = jobLauncherTestUtils.launchStep("statisticStep",
      jobParameters);
  assertEquals(BatchStatus.COMPLETED, exec.getStatus());
  StepExecution setpExec = exec.getStepExecutions().iterator().next();
  assertEquals(1, setpExec.getWriteCount());

  assertFileEquals(
      new ClassPathResource(STATISTIC_REF_PATH),
      new FileSystemResource(STATISTIC_PATH));
  }
}
```

This test is similar to the product step test except that you set up data in a database. You launch the step statisticStep and check that the file content is equal to the content of the reference file.

These examples show that it's easy to test with Spring and Spring Batch. What a difference from using a bash shell! With Spring Batch, applications are easy to write and test. Stay with us: the final section tests a whole job.

14.4.3   Testing a job

We finish this chapter with The Big One: testing an entire job—an easy task with all that we've learned. With the help of the Spring TestContext framework and the Job-LauncherTestUtils class, it takes only a few lines of code to do the job, as demonstrated in the following listing.

> **Listing 14.19   Testing a whole job**

```
@RunWith(SpringJUnit4ClassRunner.class)
@ContextConfiguration
public class WholeBatchTest {
  String PRODUCTS_PATH =
    "classpath:com/manning/sbia/ch14/input/products.txt";
  String STATISTIC_PATH = "file:./target/statistic.txt";
  @Autowired                                                      ❶ Injects test
  private JobLauncherTestUtils jobLauncherTestUtils;                 utilities
  @Autowired
  private SimpleJdbcTemplate jdbcTemplate;

  @Test
  @DirtiesContext
  public void integration() throws Exception {
    JobParameters jobParameters = new JobParametersBuilder()
        .addString(PARAM_INPUT_RESOURCE, PRODUCTS_PATH)
        .addString(PARAM_REPORT_RESOURCE, STATISTIC_PATH)
        .toJobParameters();
```

```
    JobExecution exec = jobLauncherTestUtils
      .launchJob(jobParameters);
    assertEquals(BatchStatus.COMPLETED,
      exec.getStatus());
    assertEquals(6, jdbcTemplate.queryForInt(
      "SELECT COUNT(*) from PRODUCT"));
  }
}
```

 Launches job

You start with Spring injecting a `JobLauncherTestUtils` ❶, then call `launchJob` ❷, and check the batch status. Finally, you count product table rows, and that's all! You have successfully tested a whole batch job!

It's now time to conclude our journey in the land of batch application testing.

14.5 Summary

In this chapter, you learned how to implement unit, integration, and functional tests for batch applications. You looked at test concepts and why writing tests improves the reliability and robustness of applications. We introduced the notion of test strategies like white-box and black-box testing. You also learned how to write unit tests with JUnit and the Mockito mock framework, where you learned how to test your application's behavior. Then, you looked at the Spring TestContext Framework and the Spring Batch Test module, which helped a lot. Finally, you created `Step` and `Job` tests to check overall functionality. Based on our case study, you created many test cases to show that all aspects of a batch job can be tested. Indeed, it has never been easier to create tests for batch jobs.

This is the final chapter; we hope you enjoyed this book. Now, go out and practice on your own. The appendixes that follow show you how to configure your favorite IDEs and Maven for use with Spring Batch and how to set up Spring Batch Admin, the web administration console for Spring Batch.

appendix A
Setting up the
development environment

This appendix shows you how to set up your development environment. We begin with Apache Maven 3: installing Maven and using basic commands. We then create a new Maven project from scratch and add the necessary dependencies for Spring Batch. We also explore Spring Batch features from the SpringSource Tool Suite for Eclipse and learn how to set up a Spring Batch project quickly from a blank Maven project and use the Spring Batch development tools.

A.1   Apache Maven 3

Apache Maven provides build tools, documentation, dependency management, and reporting for your projects. One of the benefits of Maven is to promote standards and conventions that accelerate the development cycle. At the heart of all Maven projects is the POM—the Project Object Model—represented in a pom.xml file. The POM contains general project information like name, version, dependencies, and plug-in descriptions.

First, we install Maven and learn some basic commands. We then create a new Maven project from scratch and configure it to use Spring Batch.

NOTE   For more information about Maven, visit http://maven.apache.org.

A.1.1   Installation

Maven is a Java program, so you need Java on your computer to be able to run it. To check that your computer has the Java SDK (software development kit) installed and available, run the command java -version; you should see this output:

```
% java -version
java version "1.6.0_26"
Java(TM) SE Runtime Environment (build 1.6.0_26-b03)
Java HotSpot(TM) 64-Bit Server VM (build 20.1-b02, mixed mode)
```

439

The `java -version` command shows you the Java version in detail. At the time of this writing, the latest version of Apache Maven is 3.0.3.

NOTE Maven 3 requires a Java 5 SDK installed (a JRE isn't sufficient).

You can download Maven 3 from its official website: http://maven.apache.org. It comes as an archive file that creates an apache-maven-3.0.3 directory where it's extracted. You then need to create an `M2_HOME` environment variable that contains the directory where you installed Maven 3. To make the `mvn` command available in your shell, add `M2_HOME/bin` to your `PATH` environment variable: use `$M2_HOME/bin` if you're using a UNIX/Linux-based OS; use `%M2_HOME%\bin` for Windows.

You can check that you installed Maven properly by running the `mvn -version` command, which outputs information about your system:

```
% mvn -version
Apache Maven 3.0.3 (r1075438; 2011-02-28 18:31:09+0100)
Maven home: /home/acogoluegnes/bin/apache-maven-3.0.3
Java version: 1.6.0_26, vendor: Sun Microsystems Inc.
Java home: /home/acogoluegnes/bin/jdk1.6.0_26/jre
Default locale: en_US, platform encoding: UTF-8
OS name: "linux", version: "2.6.38-8-generic", arch: "amd64",
  ➥ family: "unix"
```

The output you get will differ, but it ensures that Maven is correctly installed on your computer. Now that you've installed Maven, let's use it! But before we look at the Maven command line, let's go over some concepts.

A.1.2   *Understanding Maven*

Maven uses the concept of a build lifecycle, where the three built-in build lifecycles are default, clean, and site.

- *Default*—Handles project deployment
- *Clean*—Handles project cleaning
- *Site*—Handles the creation of site documentation

Each build lifecycle consists of an ordered list of build *phases*. For example, the default lifecycle has the following phases, in this order: `validate`, `compile`, `test`, `package`, `integration-test`, `verify`, `install`, and `deploy`. When you run a given phase, all prior phases run before it in sequence. For example, if you run `install`, phases from `validate` to `verify` run first. A build phase consists of *goals*, where a goal represents a task smaller than a build phase. For example, the Maven Clean plug-in contributes to the *clean* phase with a goal named *clean*. Also, note that Maven uses two phases by default: *clean* and *site*.

To get some basic help, run the following command:

```
% mvn --help
usage: mvn [options] [<goal(s)>] [<phase(s)>]
```

Table A.1 lists some common and useful Maven commands.

Table A.1 Common Maven commands

Maven command	Description
mvn clean	Deletes all build output, usually the target directory
mvn test	Compiles main and test source trees and runs unit tests
mvn clean package	Cleans, compiles, tests, and packages the project
mvn clean install	Cleans, compiles, tests, and produces an artifact like a JAR file or a WAR file, and installs it in the local repository
mvn clean install -P bootstrap	As above but using a bootstrap profile

Thanks to its build lifecycles, phases, and goals, Maven commands are the same whatever the project. Developers are no longer lost.

Next, we look at the steps necessary to create a blank Maven project from scratch. We'll then add the necessary dependencies before importing the project in the SpringSource Tool Suite.

A.1.3 Creating a blank project

In this section, we create a blank Maven project, a necessary step before making the project Spring Batch–powered. Maven includes features to generate projects using an archetype. An archetype is a project template that contains model files like pom.xml and a standard directory tree.

On UNIX/Linux-based systems:

```
% mvn archetype:generate \
   -DarchetypeArtifactId=maven-archetype-quickstart \
   -DarchetypeVersion=1.1 \
   -DgroupId=com.manning.sbia \
   -DartifactId=appA \
   -Dversion=1.0-SNAPSHOT \
   -Dpackage=com.manning.sbia.appA
```

On Windows:

```
mvn archetype:generate ^
   -DarchetypeArtifactId=maven-archetype-quickstart ^
   -DarchetypeVersion=1.1 ^
   -DgroupId=com.manning.sbia ^
   -DartifactId=appA ^
   -Dversion=1.0-SNAPSHOT ^
   -Dpackage=com.manning.sbia.appA
```

To create a new project, you use the maven archetype plug-in. This command generates an empty project based on the Maven file and directory layout. Maven creates the project in the appA directory (the name of the project). The project contains a couple of Java classes; you can delete them and create directories to make your project look like the following:

```
appA/
  pom.xml
  src/
    main/
      java/
      resources/
    test/
      java/
      resources/
```

The previous snippet shows Maven's standard project structure. If you follow this structure, Maven will know automatically where to find Java classes, test classes, and so on. Hurrah for convention over configuration!

You have your Maven project—this is great, but it's empty. If you were to develop some Spring Batch inside the project, Maven wouldn't be able to compile your code. This is because you need to add Spring Batch dependencies, so let's see how to add them.

A.1.4   Adding Spring Batch dependencies to the Maven project

There's nothing related to Spring Batch in your blank Maven project, so you need to add these dependencies inside the pom.xml file. Maven downloads all dependencies from internet repositories, so you don't have to worry about hunting the JAR files from multiple websites. The following listing shows the content of the pom.xml file once you add the Spring Batch dependencies.

Listing A.1   The pom.xml file Spring Batch dependencies

```
<project xmlns="http://maven.apache.org/POM/4.0.0"
         xmlns:xsi="http://www.w3.org/2001/XMLSchema-instance"
         xsi:schemaLocation="http://maven.apache.org/POM/4.0.0
           http://maven.apache.org/xsd/maven-4.0.0.xsd">
  <modelVersion>4.0.0</modelVersion>
  <groupId>com.manning.sbia</groupId>
  <artifactId>appA</artifactId>
  <version>1.0-SNAPSHOT</version>
  <packaging>jar</packaging>
  <name>appA</name>

  <properties>
    <project.build.sourceEncoding>UTF-8</project.build.sourceEncoding>
    <spring.batch.version>
      2.1.8.RELEASE                                          ❶ Defines property
    </spring.batch.version>                                      for Spring Batch
    <maven.compiler.source>1.6</maven.compiler.source>          version
    <maven.compiler.target>1.6</maven.compiler.target>
  </properties>

  <dependencies>

    <dependency>                                             ❷ Declares Spring
      <groupId>org.springframework.batch</groupId>               Batch dependencies
      <artifactId>spring-batch-core</artifactId>
```

```
      <version>${spring.batch.version}</version>
      <exclusions>
        <exclusion>
          <groupId>commons-logging</groupId>
          <artifactId>commons-logging</artifactId>
        </exclusion>
      </exclusions>
    </dependency>

    <dependency>
      <groupId>org.springframework.batch</groupId>
      <artifactId>
        spring-batch-infrastructure
      </artifactId>
      <version>${spring.batch.version}</version>
    </dependency>

    <dependency>
      <groupId>org.springframework.batch</groupId>
      <artifactId>spring-batch-test</artifactId>
      <version>${spring.batch.version}</version>
      <scope>test</scope>
    </dependency>

  </dependencies>
</project>
```

❷ Declares Spring Batch dependencies

❸ Declares Spring Batch test dependency

You define a `spring.batch.version` property ❶ because you'll need the Spring Batch version in several places. It's more convenient to define a property once and then refer to it. You also set up `maven.compiler` properties the for the Java compiler. You then add Spring Batch dependencies ❷. Note the use of the version property and the exclusion of the Apache Commons Logging dependency. As soon as you refer to a dependency—Spring Batch, in our case—Maven downloads all transitive dependencies. Commons Logging would come as a transitive dependency of the Spring Framework, and you don't want it: that's why you exclude it with the `exclusion` element (more on logging later). At ❸ you add the Spring Batch test module. Chapter 14 introduces you to this test module, but you can still test your Spring Batch jobs without it (import the dependency only if you need it). You use the `scope` element for the test dependency. With the `scope` element set to `test`, Maven adds the corresponding dependency only for compiling and running tests.

You now have the bare minimum to use Spring Batch, but you need to add some other dependencies to make the case study from chapter 1 work.

ADDING SPRING DEPENDENCIES

Spring Batch 2.1 is compatible with both Spring 2.5 and Spring 3.0, but it pulls Spring 2.5 dependencies by default. We use Spring 3.0 in this book, so you should add the dependencies listed in table A.2 to your pom.xml.

By using Spring 3.0, you'll benefit from the latest bug fixes and from features like the `jdbc` namespace to easily create an in-memory database—handy for testing—or Representational State Transfer (REST) support. Let's now see about the logging dependencies.

Table A.2   Spring dependencies to add to the pom.xml file

Group ID	Artifact ID	Version
org.springframework	spring-beans	3.0.5.RELEASE
org.springframework	spring-context	3.0.5.RELEASE
org.springframework	spring-core	3.0.5.RELEASE
org.springframework	spring-jdbc	3.0.5.RELEASE
org.springframework	spring-tx	3.0.5.RELEASE

ADDING LOGGING DEPENDENCIES

Logging to the console or a file is useful: it can help with debugging. You can add your own logging statements in your code, but all the frameworks—including Spring Batch—produce their own logging messages. Logging can be complicated to set up in Java. For the full story, look at the sidebar about logging; for the short story, add the dependencies listed in table A.3.

Table A.3   Logging dependencies to add to the pom.xml file

Group ID	Artifact ID	Version
org.slf4j	slf4j-api	1.6.1
org.slf4j	jcl-over-slf4j	1.6.1
ch.qos.logback	logback-classic	0.9.29

Logging in Spring Batch

Let's face it: logging in Java is a mess. There are standards, de facto standards, and several logging façades. How can a beginner sort this out? Covering logging and logging configuration best practices is beyond the scope of this book. To make it short, we use SLF4J as a façade, the implementation of Apache Commons Logging over SLF4, and Logback as the SLF4J implementation. For a thorough explanation of the logging configuration in Spring Batch—and in Spring in general—take a look at this blog entry: http://blog.springsource.com/2009/12/04/logging-dependencies-in-spring/.

As you can see from table A.3, we're using Logback as the logging implementation. It needs a configuration file: logback-test.xml, which you can create in src/test/resources. The following listing shows the content of the logback-test.xml file.

Listing A.2   Configuring Logback in logback-test.xml

```
<configuration>
  <appender name="STDOUT" class="ch.qos.logback.core.ConsoleAppender">
    <encoder>
```

```
      <pattern>
        %d{HH:mm:ss.SSS} [%thread] %-5level %logger{36} - %msg%n
      </pattern>
    </encoder>
  </appender>

<logger name="org.springframework.batch" level="warn" />

  <root level="error">
    <appender-ref ref="STDOUT" />
  </root>
</configuration>
```

The logback-test.xml file is okay for a test configuration, but you should have a look at the Logback documentation for a more production-oriented configuration.

We're done with logging dependencies; let's now configure dependencies that the case study uses.

ADDING DEPENDENCIES FOR THE CASE STUDY

Chapter 1 introduces the case study: the batch job for the online store application. The batch job uses Apache Commons IO to deal with decompressing the input ZIP archive and H2, the Java database. Table A.4 lists the dependencies that the study uses.

Table A.4   Case study dependencies to add to the pom.xml file

Group ID	Artifact ID	Version
commons-io	commons-io	2.0.1
com.h2database	h2	1.3.156

We're getting close to the end of the dependencies: next, we test dependencies!

ADDING TEST DEPENDENCIES

We use JUnit and the Spring TestContext Framework to write an integration test for our case study batch job. Table A.5 lists the corresponding dependencies.

Table A.5   Test dependencies to add to the pom.xml file

Group ID	Artifact ID	Version
junit	junit	4.8.2
org.springframework	spring-test	3.0.5.RELEASE

Don't forget to use the test scope for these dependencies! We're done with the dependencies: your Maven project is ready to compile and launch Spring Batch jobs. But are you going to use a text editor to write these jobs? Surely not. Now that your Maven project is all set up, you can start using a full-blown IDE—with some Spring and Spring Batch support—to write your jobs: the SpringSource Tool Suite for Eclipse.

A.2   *The SpringSource Tool Suite for Eclipse*

The SpringSource Tool Suite (STS) is an Eclipse-based IDE. The focus of STS is to provide tools to help Spring developers create and manage Spring-based applications. STS offers tools to edit XML Spring contexts using a completion editor and wizards to facilitate project creation. STS also includes Groovy, Grails, and OSGi tools. You can download STS from www.springsource.com/products/springsource-tool-suite-download.

> **NOTE** You don't need a specific IDE to work on a Spring Batch project. STS is free and provides some nice tooling for Spring and Spring Batch. That's why we use it, but you could use NetBeans or IntelliJ IDEA on a Spring Batch project as well. It's also worth mentioning that you can install STS's tooling on top of an existing Eclipse installation (instead of downloading STS as a bundle) because it's a set of plug-ins.

This section covers how to import a Maven project into STS and use the tooling to create a Spring Batch job.

A.2.1   *Importing the Spring Batch project*

STS has built-in support for Maven, so you can easily import the Maven project you created in section A.1 with STS. You'll end up with a ready-to-edit project, with configuration managed by the STS-Maven integration plug-in.

To import the Maven-based Spring Batch project in STS, choose File > Import > Maven and Existing Maven Projects. You can then browse to the project directory and click on Finish, as figure A.1 shows.

Once created, the project shows up in the Eclipse workspace with a Maven layout, as figure A.2 illustrates.

The project is now in the STS workspace. Let's see how to create and edit a Spring configuration file.

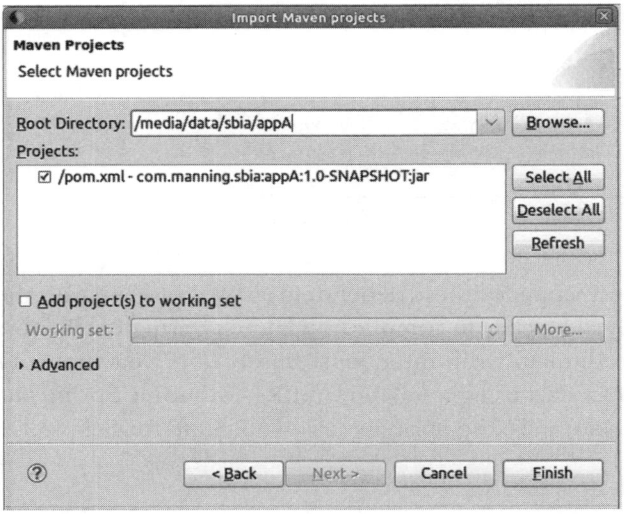

Figure A.1 STS can import a Maven project. STS then configures the project by using the project POM.

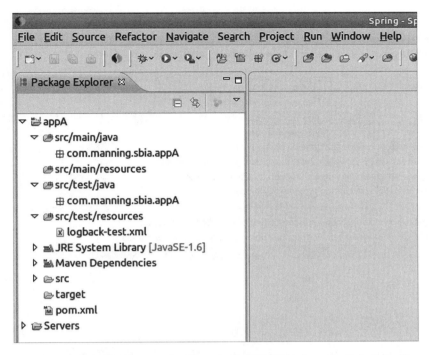

Figure A.2 The blank Maven project imported in STS. STS automatically includes the dependencies specified in the POM.

A.2.2 *Creating and editing a Spring configuration file*

Spring Batch configuration relies on Spring configuration. STS has first-class support to manage Spring configuration files. This support includes a wizard to create a Spring file, namespace management, code completion (Ctrl-Space works in Spring XML files!), and much more. STS also provides a nice visualization tool for Spring Batch jobs. Let's explore all of this now.

You start by using a wizard to create a Spring configuration file. From the package explorer, right-click the src/main/resources source directory and select New > Spring Bean Configuration File. Use the file import-products-job-context.xml and click Next. You can then choose the namespaces you want to include. Include the batch namespace, as figure A.3 shows, and then click Finish.

Once the Spring configuration file is created, you can select and edit it, as shown in figure A.4. The editor validates the syntax and provides code completion.

You're now ready to create a Spring Batch job: use the batch namespace to declare the job, steps, your item reader and writer, and so on. You can then visualize the Spring Batch job by choosing the Batch-Graph tab in the editor. Figure A.5 shows the Spring Batch graphical editor.

STS speeds up Spring Batch development by offering useful tools, particularly the Spring Batch visual development tool.

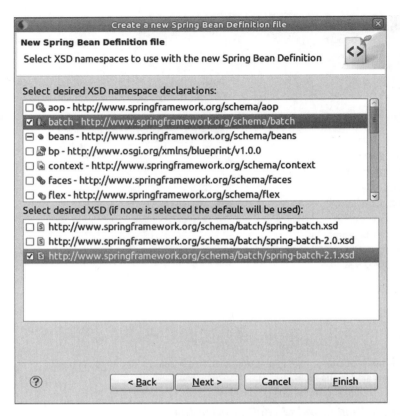

Figure A.3 When creating a Spring configuration file with the wizard, STS lets you choose which XML namespaces you want to include in the file declaration. You can also change the namespaces once the wizard creates the file, on the Namespaces tab.

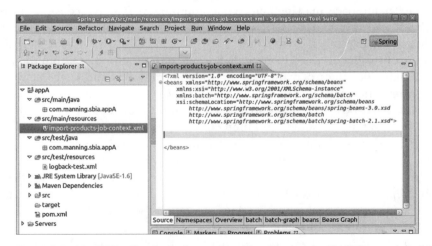

Figure A.4 The XML editor for Spring configuration files is arguably STS's most useful tool for the Spring developer. It provides validation, code completion, and graphical visualization for Spring Batch.

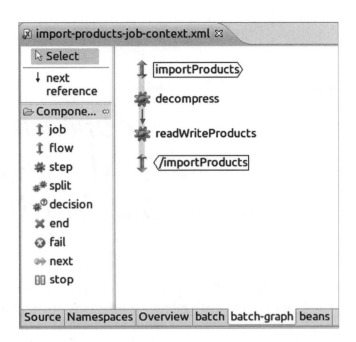

Figure A.5 Visualizing a Spring Batch job inside STS, thanks to the Batch-Graph tab. You can also edit the job definition by dragging components from the left to the main editor area. You can edit each component by double-clicking it.

A.3 Summary

In this appendix, we set up Maven and Eclipse development environments for Spring Batch applications. We introduced Maven, installed it, and learned its basic commands. Using a simple Maven archetype, we created a blank project and added the necessary dependencies for Spring Batch development.

Finally, we saw how the STS for Eclipse facilitates Spring Batch application development. We used STS to import the Maven project and to create and edit a Spring configuration file for a Spring Batch project.

Appendix B shows how to install Spring Batch Admin, the web-based administration console for Spring Batch.

appendix B
Managing
Spring Batch Admin

Spring Batch Admin is a web-based administration console for Spring Batch. With it, you can monitor the execution of batch jobs and start and stop executions. You can make Spring Batch Admin the only entry point in your batch infrastructure, because it provides all the features to manage and monitor the behavior of your jobs. In addition, if you find a missing feature, you can implement it and contribute it back to the project, because Spring Batch Admin is an open source project.

Spring Batch Admin builds on top of Spring technologies like the Spring Framework, Spring MVC, and Spring Integration. Spring Batch Admin is a full-blown web application, but it remains easy to configure and deploy. This appendix shows you how to deploy a Spring Batch Admin instance in a couple of minutes. Even if your Spring Batch Admin instance runs on top of an embedded database, it will be helpful for you to discover the web console. You'll also see how to deploy Spring Batch Admin in its own web application and how to make it cohabit with other applications inside the same web application.

Spring Batch Admin uses Spring for its configuration, and you'll see how to set it up to connect to your batch metadata. If you're already running a Spring Batch infrastructure, you'll be able to browse a web view of it in a matter of minutes. This appendix also covers more advanced configuration scenarios, like deploying job definitions and overriding infrastructure Spring beans in Spring Batch Admin.

B.1 Downloading Spring Batch Admin

Table B.1 lists the relevant web pages about Spring Batch Admin and includes the download page.

NOTE We're using Spring Batch Admin 1.2.0.RELEASE in this appendix.

Table B.1   Web pages related to the Spring Batch Admin project

URL	Description
http://static.springsource.org/spring-batch-admin/index.html	Home page
http://static.springsource.org/spring-batch-admin/reference/reference.xhtml	User guide
http://www.springsource.com/download/community	Download page

If you download the Spring Batch Admin distribution from the download page, you'll see the package is small. Spring Batch Admin is a web frontend, so it runs inside a web application, but you can easily embed it in any web application. You can also choose to let it run alone in a dedicated web application. You have multiple deployment options, and we'll start with the latter, as the distribution contains a sample project to build a web application with Spring Batch Admin in it. This is the quickest way to have a Spring Batch Admin instance running. We'll then study the second deployment option before covering how to configure Spring Batch Admin in more detail.

B.2   *Building Spring Batch Admin from the distribution sample*

We're going to build a web archive with Spring Batch Admin in it. We use the sample provided in the distribution, which uses Maven as the build tool. You'll need Maven 2 or greater installed on your computer

Unzip the Spring Batch Admin distribution and open an OS command shell in the corresponding directory. Then, type the following commands:

```
cd sample/
cd spring-batch-admin-parent/
mvn install
cd..
cd spring-batch-admin-sample/
mvn install
```

The first set of commands installs a parent POM inside your local Maven repository. The sample uses this POM. The second set of commands builds the web archive. Once the last command has finished, you should find a WAR file in the directory spring-batch-admin-sample/target. You can deploy this WAR file in any web container (like Jetty or Tomcat) or any application server (like Glassfish or JBoss).

Once Maven has deployed the archive, go the following URL to check the installation: http://localhost:8080/spring-batch-admin-sample-1.2.0.RELEASE/

The home page of your Spring Batch Admin instance is shown in figure B.1. From this home page, you can navigate through the application and discover its interface.

The Spring Batch Admin sample uses an embedded database and has some default jobs installed. This is useful for a quick tryout of Spring Batch Admin and its main features. You can also use the sample as a starting point for your own Spring Batch Admin installation and customize its Spring configuration files and web.xml file. We'll see more about the configuration of Spring Batch Admin in section B.4.

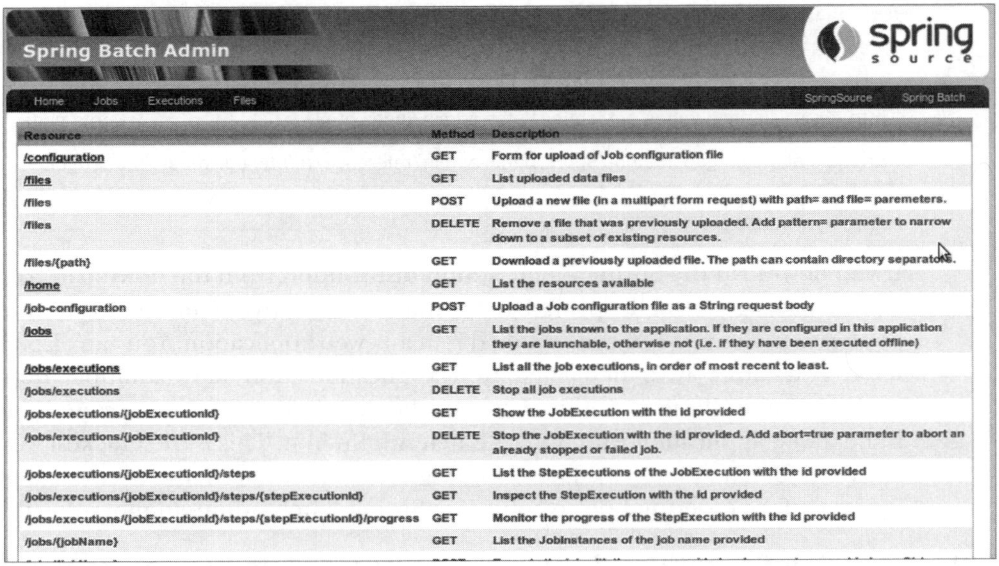

Figure B.1 The home page of a Spring Batch Admin instance lists the services the application provides.

Perhaps you already have a web application running and you would like to run Spring Batch Admin in this same application, next to your business application. The next section shows how to embed Spring Batch Admin in an existing web application.

B.3   *Embedding Spring Batch Admin in a web application*

Spring Batch Admin is a lightweight application: it consists of only two JAR files containing web controllers, Spring configuration files, images, and views. Embedding Spring Batch Admin in a web application is as easy as including these two JARs and their dependencies and configuring the web.xml file. Let's see how to add Spring Batch Admin dependencies in a Maven project.

B.3.1   *Adding Spring Batch Admin dependencies*

The following listing shows a Maven POM file that contains Spring Batch Admin dependencies. Spring Batch Admin has its own dependencies (Spring Batch, the Spring Framework, and so forth), but Maven pulls them in automatically.

Listing B.1   Maven dependencies for Spring Batch Admin

```
<?xml version="1.0"?>
<project (...)>
  <modelVersion>4.0.0</modelVersion>
  <groupId>com.manning.sbia</groupId>
  <artifactId>appB</artifactId>
  <version>1.0.0</version>
  <name>appB</name>
```

```
<packaging>war</packaging>
<dependencies>

  <dependency>
    <groupId>org.springframework.batch</groupId>
    <artifactId>spring-batch-admin-resources</artifactId>
    <version>1.2.0.RELEASE</version>
  </dependency>

  <dependency>
    <groupId>org.springframework.batch</groupId>
    <artifactId>spring-batch-admin-manager</artifactId>
    <version>1.2.0.RELEASE</version>
  </dependency>

</dependencies>

<properties>
  <project.build.sourceEncoding>UTF-8</project.build.sourceEncoding>
</properties>

</project>
```

When adding Spring Batch Admin dependencies to an existing project, be careful of conflicts between dependencies. Your project can have its own dependencies, so you may need more configuration than what listing B.1 provides. This extra configuration can exclude transitive dependencies from Spring Batch Admin, or from your own project.

B.3.2 *Declaring Spring Batch Admin in web.xml*

The easiest way to configure Spring Batch Admin in the web.xml of your web application is to use the sample's web.xml file as inspiration. Spring Batch Admin needs the following elements in web.xml:

- *A servlet listener to bootstrap the root application context*—If your web application uses Spring, this listener is already there, so just add an entry for the Spring Batch Admin Spring configuration file.
- *Servlet filters to deal with HTTP headers in requests and responses*—They're useful mainly because Spring Batch Admin uses some RESTful-styled communication between the client and the server.
- *A Spring MVC `DispatcherServlet`*—Spring Batch Admin uses Spring MVC as its web layer.
- *A `ResourceServlet`*—To serve static resources from JAR files.

Be careful to avoid conflicts with your own application when configuring the URL mapping of Spring Batch Admin. The sample uses /* which handles all inbound URLs.

Once you have completed this configuration, you can package your web application with Maven and deploy it in a web container. You'll get the same result as in the previous section, but now Spring Batch Admin will be bundled inside your own application!

The next section covers how to configure Spring Batch Admin to plug in your own environment.

B.4   *Configuring Spring Batch Admin*

Spring Batch Admin uses Spring for its configuration, and it's straightforward to set up for your own environment. We'll see first how to plug Spring Batch Admin into the batch metadata. You'll be able to monitor the execution of your batch jobs, even if they don't run in the same process as Spring Batch Admin. Then, we'll see how to add job configurations to Spring Batch Admin. You'll be able to monitor job executions and start and stop jobs from Spring Batch Admin. We'll finish with advanced settings used to integrate Spring Batch Admin more deeply with an existing application.

B.4.1   *Plugging into your batch metadata*

Spring Batch Admin needs only one thing to plug into batch metadata: how to connect to the database that hosts these metadata. In Java terms, this means configuring a data source. You don't have to bother with Spring configuration; you can just specify the connection parameters in a batch-default.properties file located at the root of the classpath. The following listing shows an example of such a properties file to connect to an H2 database.

Listing B.2   Configuring the database connection in batch-default.properties

```
batch.jdbc.driver=org.h2.Driver
batch.jdbc.url=jdbc:h2:tcp://localhost/sbia_appB          Database connection
batch.jdbc.user=sa                                        settings
batch.jdbc.password=
batch.database.incrementer.class=org.springframework.jdbc
   .support.incrementer.H2SequenceMaxValueIncrementer

batch.data.source.init=false
batch.business.schema.script=
batch.schema.script=
batch.drop.script=
batch.remote.base.url=
```

The batch-default.properties file must be located at the root of the classpath. In a Maven project, the file can be in the src/main/resources directory. The file must contain the four usual database connection settings: driver class, URL, username, and password. You can also specify the implementation of a value incrementer for Spring Batch to generate primary keys. Look at implementations of the DataFieldMaxValueIncre-menter interface in the Spring Framework and pick the one matching your database.

> **NOTE**   Don't forget to put the JDBC database driver JAR file on the classpath of the web application.

The configuration in listing B.2 tells Spring Batch not to run any SQL scripts on the target database. This assumes the database contains all the batch metadata tables (remember, the scripts to create these tables are in the Spring Batch core JAR file).

Once you complete the database settings, you can package the application and deploy it. The application will connect to the batch metadata, and you'll be able to monitor the execution of your jobs. By configuring just the connection to the batch metadata, you can't really use Spring Batch Admin as the only entry point to your batch infrastructure. To be able to launch executions directly from Spring Batch Admin, add all your job resources—Java classes, Spring Batch configuration—to the web application.

B.4.2 *Deploying your own job files*

Spring Batch Admin scans a specific location to find Spring configuration files that define jobs. This specific location is the META-INF/spring/batch/jobs directory on the classpath (any JAR file is eligible as a root for scanning, as is the WEB-INF/classes directory in the web application).

Each configuration file must be self-contained: it must define a job and all the Spring beans the job depends on, except for infrastructure beans like the job repository, the data source, and the transaction manager. Every bean defined in the root application context of the web application is visible to a job in a Spring configuration file. That's why job configurations can depend on such common beans and don't need to define them.

A typical job configuration file inside the META-INF/spring/batch/jobs directory will then contain the job definition—using the batch namespace—and Spring beans like item readers and item writers for the job.

Such a deployment is powerful: you can write your Spring Batch jobs in standalone projects and deploy them inside a Spring Batch Admin instance. As long you locate the configuration files in the META-INF/spring/batch/jobs directory, Spring Batch Admin will pick them up and make them available in the user interface.

> **NOTE** The sample from the Spring Batch Admin distribution defines some dummy jobs in its META-INF/spring/batch/jobs directory. Delete these jobs if you don't want them to appear in your Spring Batch Admin instance.

The Spring Batch Admin UI isn't the only way to trigger a job execution: you can embed a Java scheduler like Quartz or Spring Scheduler inside the application and let jobs be kicked off periodically. Look at chapter 4 for the various ways to use a Java scheduler with Spring Batch.

Once Spring Batch Admin connects to your batch metadata and can accept your new jobs, it gives you a great view of your batch infrastructure. You can even go further through the configuration and change some Spring Batch Admin internals. This is especially useful when Spring Batch Admin must cohabit with an existing business application in the same web application.

B.4.3 *Overriding the Spring Batch Admin configuration*

Spring Batch Admin includes configuration for Spring beans like the data source, the transaction manager, and the job repository. Spring Batch Admin lets you configure parts of these beans, as we saw in section B.4.1 when we used a properties file for the connection to the database. Spring Batch Admin also lets you *override* part of its configuration. This means you can define Spring beans that Spring Batch Admin will use in place of the default beans. Imagine that your data source comes from an application server as a Java Naming and Directory Interface (JNDI) resource. In this case, the database connection settings don't make sense because you only need to perform a JNDI lookup. You can define a data source bean and use Spring's JNDI support for the lookup.

There are two conditions for overriding to work:

1 The bean must have the same ID as the bean defined in the Spring Batch Admin configuration.
2 The bean definition must be loaded after Spring Batch Admin bean definitions.

To meet the first condition, you need to know the names of beans in the Spring Batch Admin configuration. Table B.2 lists some of the beans that are likely to be overridden. If you want to know all the beans you can override, the best source is…the source code! The Spring configuration files are located in the META-INF/spring/batch/bootstrap directory of the Spring Batch Admin manager module. The Spring Batch Admin reference guide also provides the list of the beans you can override.

Table B.2 Some beans to override in Spring Batch Admin

Bean name	Interface	Default
dataSource	DataSource	Commons database connection pool
transactionManager	PlatformTransaction-Manager	DataSourceTransaction-Manager
jobLauncher	JobLauncher	SimpleJobLauncher
jobLauncherTaskExecutor	TaskExecutor	Asynchronous, with Java 5 thread pool
jobRepository	JobRepository	Persistent job repository

You now know about overriding infrastructure beans, which is the first condition to meet to change the configuration of Spring Batch Admin. The second condition is to ensure that the definitions of the new beans are loaded after the Spring Batch Admin configuration. This doesn't mean you need an extra application context; it means you need to be careful about the order in which Spring configuration files are loaded. Bean definitions override previous definitions with the same ID, so the order in which configuration files are loaded matters. This a rule Spring enforces in its application context implementations. To be sure your properly named beans override the default beans, you have two options (you can use one or the other or both):

1 *Declare your beans in files located in the /META-INF/spring/batch/override/ directory*— Spring Batch Admin ensures such files are loaded *after* the default files.

2 *Declare your configuration files after the Spring Batch Admin files*—In the `context-ConfigLocation` parameter that specifies the files for the root application context in the web.xml file, declare the Spring Batch Admin configuration file in the first position, followed by your own application files.

Once both conditions are met (names for the beans and correct locations for the files), you're ready to configure some the Spring Batch Admin infrastructure. The following listing shows how to override the data source and the task executor to launch jobs.

Listing B.3 Overriding infrastructure beans

```
<?xml version="1.0" encoding="UTF-8"?>
<beans (...)>

    <jee:jndi-lookup id="dataSource"                      Looks up data
        jndi-name="java:comp/env/jdbc/SpringBatchAdmin"/>   source from JNDI

    <task:executor id="jobLauncherTaskExecutor"           Defines thread pool
                   pool-size="10"                          to launch jobs
                   rejection-policy="ABORT"/>

</beans>
```

By default, the `task:executor` element uses the Java 5 thread pool. Being able to override some of the key components of Spring Batch Admin is powerful. Spring Batch Admin can share any resource you use in your business application. You can plug in a server-provided data source, as we did in listing B.3, where Spring looks up the data source through JNDI. In listing B.3, we also defined our own thread-pooled task executor for the job launcher to use. Note that you can also plug in a server-provided thread pool like the JCA WorkManager or CommonJ (depending on what's available in your application server). Spring provides a bridge with a `TaskExecutor` implementation for CommonJ. Spring Batch Admin can then use resources from the application server.

B.5 Summary

Spring Batch Admin includes all the features needed to monitor accurately your Spring Batch–powered infrastructure. You have multiple deployment options with Spring Batch Admin: you can deploy it in its own web application or let it cohabit with other applications in the same web application. The former is well suited to headless batch jobs if they're not part of any web frontend. The latter works nicely when you embed Spring Batch in a web application and run it as a business application frontend.

The first setup step is to plug Spring Batch Admin into your batch metadata to monitor the execution of your jobs. You can then go further and use Spring Batch Admin to start and stop job executions. You can also override the Spring Batch Admin infrastructure to plug in existing infrastructure components, like a data source or a thread pool provided by your server.

index

Q

restarting, on error *(continued)*
  in middle of chunk-oriented step 247–250
  limiting number of restarts 246
  no restart option 244–245
RestTemplate class 329, 331
result sets, reading with 140–144
ResultSet 140–142, 144, 146, 381
retrieval, of data 144–148, 150–151
retry feature
  combining with skip feature 236
  in action with skip and restart features 226–227
retry policies, controlling retrying on error
    with 236–238
retry-limit attribute 64–65, 234–237, 239
retry-listeners element 66, 239
retry-policy attribute 64
retry-policy element 66
retryable-exception-classes 67, 234–237, 239
retrying, on error 234–242
  configuring retryable exceptions 234–236
  controlling with retry policy 236–238
  listening to retries 238–239
  RetryTemplate implementation 239–242
RetryListener interface 238
RetryListenerSupport 238
RetryOperations interface 239
RetryOperations property 240
RetryOperationsInterceptor 240–241
RetryPolicy interface 64, 237, 240
RetryTemplate implementation
  retrying in application code with 239–240
  retrying transparently with AOP and 240–242
RMI (Remote Method Invocation) 312, 369
RmiRegistryFactoryBean class 369
robustness, Spring Batch 5
rollback convention 71
rolling back, choosing whether to 258–259
root-database-context.xml file 39
rootElementAttributes property 174
rootTagName property 174–175, 177
router classifier 190
routerDelegate 191–192
RowMapper 139, 141–142, 146, 206–207
run method 36, 88–89, 92
Runnable interface 377
Runner class 426
RuntimeException class 71

S

samples, building Spring Batch Admin console
    from 451–452
SampleTask class 377
SamsungStatementSetter 142–143
saveOrUpdate 182–183

saveState property 161, 174, 383–384
sbia-servlet.xml file 108
scale out approach 374
scale up approach 374
scaling 373–406
  comparing patterns 404–406
  enhancing performance by 374–375
  local and remote 376–377
  model of 375–378
    local and remote scaling 376–377
    task executor abstraction 377–378
  multithreaded steps 378–385
    configuring 379–381
    issues with 381–385
  parallelizing processing, configuring parallel
    steps 385–387
  remote chunking 387–394
    description of 387–389
    with Spring Integration framework 389–394
scaling strategies 7–8
scaling, fine-grained 394–404
schedulers 6
scheduling jobs 115
scheduling.xml file 105
schema-.sql 348
schema-[database].sql naming convention, SQL
    scripts 38
schema-drop-.sql 349
scope attribute 76
SCP (Secure Copy) 20, 137
Secure Shell. *See* SSH
SELECT statement 140–143, 147–148, 434–435
SERIALIZABLE level 71, 75, 255
server connector, JMX 369
service activator 317
Service Provider Interface. *See* SPI
service-activator 319
service-interface attribute 328
service=batch,bean=jobOperator 368–369
services, as input 151–154
serviceUrl 369
servlet filters 453
servlet listener 453
[servlet-name]-servlet.xml file 108
SessionFactory interface 99, 149–150, 182
sessionTransacted 264–265, 271
setExcludeWriter 418–419
setResource 162
Shared database 309
shared resource transaction pattern 262–263
Short Message Service. *See* SMS
shoudDeleteIfExists property 162
shouldDeleteIfEmpty property 162
SimpleAsyncTaskExecutor implementation 378
SimpleChunkProcessor class 388, 393

RELATED MANNING TITLES

Spring Dynamic Modules in Action
by Arnaud Cogoluegnes, Thierry Templier,
  and Andy Piper

> ISBN: 978-1-935182-30-6
> 548 pages, $59.99
> September 2010

Spring in Action, Third Edition
by Craig Walls

> ISBN: 978-1-935182-35-1
> 424 pages, $49.99
> June 2011

Spring Integration in Action
by Mark Fisher, Jonas Partner,
  Marius Bogoevici, and Iwein Fuld

> ISBN: 978-1-935182-43-6
> 400 pages, $49.99
> November 2011

DSLs in Action
by Debasish Ghosh

> ISBN: 978-1-935182-45-0
> 376 pages, $44.99
> December 2010

For ordering information go to www.manning.com